The Environmental Politics of Sacrifice

D0729818

The Environmental Politics of Sacrifice

Edited by Michael Maniates and John M. Meyer

The MIT Press
Cambridge, Massachusetts
London, England

For information about special quantity discounts, please email special_sales@ mitpress.mit.edu.

This book was set in 10/14 pt Sabon by Toppan Best-set Premedia Limited. Printed and bound in the United States of America.

Library of Congress Cataloging-in-Publication Data

The environmental politics of sacrifice / edited by Michael Maniates and John M. Meyer.
    p.   cm.
Includes bibliographical references and index.
ISBN 978-0-262-01436-6 (hardcover : alk. paper) — ISBN 978-0-262-51436-1 (pbk. : alk. paper) 1. Environmental policy. 2. Sacrifice. I. Maniates, Michael. II. Meyer, John M.
GE170.E5774 2010
363.7'0561—dc22

2009045912

10 9 8 7 6 5 4 3 2 1

Contents

Acknowledgments

This book has been a long time coming. While, as editors, we are primarily responsible for the drawn-out timeline, we could never have finished without the support, hard work, and encouragement of a great many people. Foremost among these, of course, are the contributors themselves. Far more than mere chapter authors; they were also crucial to the definition and contours of the book itself. This was especially the case for those who participated in a workshop we facilitated on "The Politics of Sacrifice," held at Allegheny College in September 2007: Peter F. Cannavò, Cheryl Hall, Karen Litfin, Simon Nicholson, Anna Peterson, Thomas Princen, Paul Wapner, and Justin Williams. Hans Bruyninckx was also a participant, and although he did not ultimately contribute a chapter, he shaped our conversations in important ways. Shane Gunster and Sudhir Chella Rajan joined the project at later points (in Shane's case, *much* later!) and have immeasurably enriched the volume. Clay Morgan of the MIT Press attended the first panel discussion on these themes at the annual meetings of the International Studies Association in San Diego in 2006 and has been an enthusiastic and patient supporter ever since. Three anonymous reviewers for the press also provided very valuable suggestions to us and to many of the chapter authors.

One thing we have learned to count on is that every public presentation of the themes in this book—at professional conferences and on numerous university campuses—has led to passionate, thoughtful, and provocative questions from, and discussion with, audience members. This was especially true of the public forum held at Allegheny as part of our workshop. While we cannot individually thank each of our interlocutors, they have deeply influenced our thinking. As editors, we have returned, time and again, to questions raised in these venues while crafting elements of the book. Such vibrant and insightful discussion gives us hope for the sort of public confrontation with sacrifice called for in these pages.

In addition to those listed previously, Michael writes: I wish to thank David Orr and Adam Joseph Lewis for making possible a teaching leave during a critical point in this project. The rich collaboration and wide-ranging conversation around sacrifice, environmental politics, and climate change fostered by the work on this book would not be happening without the foresight of these two individuals. Thanks are also due to my friends at Allegheny College for their encouragement and support, especially Terry Bensel, Richard Cook, Linda DeMeritt, Scott Friedhoff, David Miller, Kathy Roos, Josh Searle-White, Shannan Mattiace, Barry Shapiro, Dan Shea, Ben Slote, Bruce Smith, Barb Steadman, Howard Tamashiro, and Sharon Wesoky. For the opportunity to field test the evolving arguments of this project on their students and colleagues, I thank Beth Conklin and Michael Vandenbergh (Vanderbilt University), Monty Hempel (University of Redlands), John Petersen (Oberlin College), Anna Peterson (University of Florida), Rocky Rohwedder and Sascha von Meier (Sonoma State University), David Swerdlow (Westminter College), Richard Wallace (Ursinus College), Michael Williams (St. Bonaventure University), and Richard Cameron and Jennifer Everett (DePauw University). They were more helpful to my thinking than they could ever know. Of course, none of this would have gotten off the ground without the initial, unceasing prodding of Tom Princen, who saw the potential of this project well before I appreciated its true power.

John writes: I thank my Humboldt colleagues in the Department of Politics and in the Environment and Community Program for their continued support and fellowship. Invitations to present ideas from the book in public talks at Ohio University and at Humboldt proved invaluable; thanks to Wendy Parker at Ohio and Mark Baker and Arne Jacobson at Humboldt for these opportunities. Thanks also to Kirsten Jerch and Jonas Siegel of the *Bulletin of Atomic Scientists*, whose invitation to write for their magazine, and pointed and insightful queries, forced me to think more carefully about how these arguments can be heard outside the academy. On a personal note, I thank Carolyn Benson, without whom none of this work would be possible. Nothing I write here could be sufficient to express my abiding gratitude and love. Finally, I thank our children, Jake and Emelia, for their patience (at times) and their insistence that I stop working and get off the computer (at others).

1

Must We Sacrifice?: Confronting the Politics of Sacrifice in an Ecologically Full World

John M. Meyer and Michael Maniates

Addressing climate change will require citizens of wealthy consumer societies to sacrifice. But that's never going to happen.

While this statement is imagined, the sentiment it conveys is not. Discussion about how to avoid the worst risks of climate change—through radical reductions of the carbon emissions of the world's wealthy—often leads to easy pronouncements and conclusions about the unavoidable centrality yet political impossibility of "sacrifice." And it's not just climate change. Similar sentiments bubble up, in academic literature and kitchen-table talk, around any number of environmental challenges: peak oil, species extinction, and pressures on planetary resources from growing consumerism in China and India, to name but a few. Together, these challenges suggest a new set of political and ethical demands in an ecologically full world, where the capacity of key environmental and resource systems to deliver more wealth or absorb additional abuse has been fully taxed. Wealthy consumer societies must soon change their patterns and perceptions of consumption, perhaps radically, and likely soon, to create ecological room for the three billion or so poor eager to improve their standard of living. But, it is said, the well off won't sacrifice their level of consumption, and policy makers aren't foolish enough to insist that they do. If we accept this perspective, then it seems that the only remaining possibilities are a catastrophic event that would shock people into action or the rise of informed experts capable of imposing sacrifice on us before it's too late.

Neither of these scenarios (waiting for massive ecological damage or for eco-guardians to flex their muscle) is particularly heartwarming. Other options, though, are harder to see. This is the basis for what we have come to refer to as the political *stickiness* of sacrifice-talk. The existing rhetoric of "sacrifice" solidifies an antipathy to popular participation and fosters an unsubstantiated faith that catastrophe will prompt reasoned and effective policy responses. It weakens our ability to imagine bold, far-reaching action for change. Most alarmingly, perhaps, this rhetoric of sacrifice understates the range of politically viable options on the table by blinding us to the important ways in which sacrifice figures into everyday life. Sometimes individuals and societies respond with foresight and grace to challenges that demand hardship now for benefits later. Asking when and why they do so (rather than assuming that they do not) is vital to an ambitious and imaginative environmental politics, one up to the challenge of global crises.

Of course, one way around the argument that the global wealthy will never willingly sacrifice to protect the environment is to insist that we won't have to. Enthusiasts for this position have argued that new technology, fostered and ushered in by the wisdom of the competitive marketplace, can resolve environmental challenges independent of any hard choices. The key to such a view is not simply that technological innovation can save the day, but that the market will recognize the economic value of such innovation and painlessly implement it on the scale necessary. One of the editors of this volume (Meyer) recalls a lunchtime discussion at his university with a renowned advocate of this view. This proponent was talking with graduate students in a practically oriented environmental program about their projects. As the students proceeded to describe their work—promoting sustainable agriculture, fair access to water, and ecological restoration, among others—this prominent expert asked how they could frame their projects as leading to a product that could compete successfully in the marketplace or as an innovation that could enhance the profitability of existing products or services. In other words, he prodded each student to develop what he referred to as the "business case" for their proposals. Toward the end of the hour, Meyer asked him, "How far do you think the business case for sustainability will take us?" Without hesitation, he replied, "Much farther than we'll ever need to go."

Readers who are comforted by this assertion will find little of value in this book. For if all we need is to make the business case, then the only volume worth reading would be one that teaches us how to be better businesspeople—how to better read market trends, identify and promote effective innovators, and market and distribute green products that accommodate growing consumption at reduced environmental cost. If, though, one has doubts about whether this approach will prove sufficient, then closer inspection of the conceptual and political baggage that attends the casual use of *sacrifice* in contemporary environmental debates seems unavoidable.

This focused inspection proves harder than it would seem. Despite the centrality of this idea of sacrifice, the concept remains curiously unexamined in both activist and academic conversations about environmental politics. In particular, the ways in which talk of sacrifice narrows the range of acceptable environmental policies and funnels us down a few unpromising paths is vastly underexplored. This became increasingly apparent to the editors and contributors as this project evolved. Several of us initially explored this theme as participants in a roundtable on "The Politics of Sacrifice" at the 2006 annual meetings of the International Studies Association. There was electric interest among many at the roundtable—panelists and audience members alike—in asking how an especially onerous narrative of sacrifice had insinuated itself into contemporary conversation about an environmental politics of transformation and hope. The fecundity of the topic led us to envision a larger project. In September 2007, we convened a workshop at Allegheny College in Meadville, Pennsylvania, with an expanded group of participants, including most of the contributors to this volume. Several days of writing and debate led us to a more nuanced assessment of sacrifice, together with a greater understanding of how the term can both enable and undermine an environmental politics of change. We didn't arrive at any easy or certain answers at this workshop, but the importance of asking the question, boldly and from multiple vantage points, became even clearer.

The result is the volume you now hold in your hands. U.S. readers will find much that is familiar as most authors focus their attention on the United States. To some readers, this focus may seem parochial, especially given the global character of contemporary environmental challenges. Yet we find it to be valuable for at least two reasons. First, the United States appears to be ground zero for a particularly debilitating treatment of sacrifice in environmental politics. Although non-U.S. readers will likely recognize elements of this treatment in their countries or communities, we expect that they'll also be struck by revealing differences. Perhaps this volume can encourage a fruitful new conversation on the comparative environmental politics of sacrifice. Second, given the United States' material and political influence over global environmental concerns, a dissection of the interplay between sacrifice and environmental politics in this country seems critical for all to understand.

Dimensions of Sacrifice in Environmental Politics

Much of this, however, begs the question of how we parse this sticky notion of sacrifice. The short answer is that it depends – on the elements of environmental politics each chapter explores and on the disciplinary and methodological approaches of the volume's contributors. We knit together this diversity in brief preludes to each part and also in the volume's conclusion.

The longer answer is that our contributors are in productive tension along at least two dimensions. One dimension highlights the tension between an approach that views individuals as unconstrained free agents and one that views social and political structures as determining individual actions. Some authors focus their attention on the opportunities for individuals to make choices. They explore the values, engrained behaviors, and psychology of change that may foster or deter an expanded individual appreciation for the complexity of sacrifice in environmental debates. Other writers emphasize the ways in which structures shape what seem to count as a sacrifice. They describe how political debate, and culture more generally, frame some forms of hardship as sacrificial and other forms as natural or unavoidable, to our shared detriment. Some also worry that *calls* to sacrifice, by political leaders, may foster a sense of victimization among citizens, who perceive such calls as oppressive.

In spite of these differences in emphasis, all our authors recognize a role for individual action while drawing out the structural elements that shape everyday life choices. Each notes how contemporary pundits who insist simplistically that "people won't sacrifice" miss the bigger picture. Claiming, for example, that people won't give up their car because they refuse to "sacrifice" on behalf of the environment fails to ask if other meaningful transportation choices exist. Nor does it grapple with why these same drivers appear to choose, with little hesitation, to assume the formidable risk of death or injury from an autocentric transportation system.

A second dimension goes to the very notion of choice. For some contributors, the question is, will we sacrifice? But for others, the option of *not* sacrificing is an illusion—one reinforced by cultural forces that take economic growth and ever escalating consumption to be value neutral. From this perspective, whatever choices individuals make entail giving up something of value. This directs our gaze to the important question of why some sacrifices are brightly illuminated, whereas others are cloistered in the shadows. What do we make of instances in which, for example, it is assumed that Americans won't ride their bikes a mile to pick up milk for dinner, yet exercising on a stationary bike at the gym is viewed by many as virtuous and anything but a sacrifice? From this second perspective, issues of power, convention, language, and framing matter, much more so than any innate preferences on the part of individuals about the importance of environmental issues.

Wherever our authors locate themselves on these two dimensions, they do so within the seemingly contradictory language of sacrifice itself. Our own experience has been that once we began to listen for the word in everyday conversation, we found it used in strikingly diverse contexts. Glancing through the chapters of this book will confirm this impression. People often talk of foregoing immediate advantage or pleasure, in favor of long-term benefit, as a sacrifice. Here, sacrifice appears to be some sort of self-interested calculation. At the same time, sacrifice is also familiar as an important part of religion, mythology, and ritual. While it is tempting to think of this as a radically different understanding of the term, our contributors make it plain that these differing ways of talking about sacrifice actually share much in common and shape contemporary environmental debate to a degree that may surprise readers.

Shared Convictions about Sacrifice

Despite these tensions in focus and emphasis, the chapters to follow share at least four overarching convictions about sacrifice, environmental politics, and prospects for an environmentally sustainable future. The first is that, by boxing us into a narrow set of alternatives for resolving environmental threats, talk of sacrifice poses a challenge that must be addressed. As we see it, this is not a term—or a political terrain—that we have chosen to *embrace*, but rather, one we must *confront and engage*. Activists, students, policy makers, and academics all have a role to play here. Their capacities to envision, assess, and act are constrained by the unexamined assumptions about human nature and social change embedded in casual reference to sacrifice.

Second, a clear-eyed confrontation with the emotional and rhetorical power of the language of sacrifice requires us to do something more than simply change the subject. In early presentations of this volume's themes, some commentators suggested that we set aside the politically charged language of sacrifice and substitute a conversation about "stewardship" or reframe this as a question about "the good life." Yet as work on this volume progressed, we became convinced that there is something especially salient and powerful about the theme of sacrifice that can't readily be captured by seemingly more palatable alternatives. We're happy to report that in our experience, exploring the implications of sacrifice in environmental politics can be surprisingly disarming. It has the power to open up conversation at precisely the point at which initial claims about the need to sacrifice threaten to shut it down.

A third point of agreement is that any interrogation of sacrifice must *uncover* some of the many and varied forms of sacrifice that already exist in society. The assumption that citizens are unwilling to forego current prosperity for future gain rests on the rather implausible belief that most of us are wholly content with our lives and the society within which we live now. Only in this circumstance would we experience any change in our consumption or our behavior on behalf of the environment as a net and intolerable loss. But when environmental debate illuminates the many sacrifices that permeate daily life—sacrifice imposed as well as chosen; sacrifice defined not just as a response to environmental issues, but driven by livelihood, family, opportunity, and social expectations—a politics can emerge to temper or redress existing patterns of sacrifice. Environmental action previously dismissed as unrealistic because it imposes sacrifice can then be seen in the new light of trading one kind of sacrifice for another, with beneficial results. This approach also carves out space to explore notions of environmental action that promote a richer sense of human flourishing and communal possibility, while reducing our ecological footprint.

A fourth conviction tying the volume together is that a critical investigation of sacrifice becomes a vehicle for discerning the structural in the everyday. Our lives are our own, and with them, we daily make choices that matter. We act, though, within a set of social rules, norms, and relationships that, like a curtain, selectively obscure and reveal the paths before us; they paint for us what is possible or impossible, realistic and utopian. Grappling honestly with the promise, dangers, and, ultimately, the power of sacrifice allows us, in small ways, to pull aside the curtain and see a broader range of possibilities before us.

Understand that contributors to this volume do not dismiss the importance of technological innovation to problems like climate change. We do reject the presumption that technological fixes can be developed and successfully scaled up through autonomous market processes. Whether the alternative is massive public investment schemes, higher taxes on energy, deeper regulation to promote new technologies, or reduced consumption, difficult social and political choices await us. With these choices comes the unavoidable need to distill the reality from the rhetoric of sacrifice in environmental politics.

Plan of the Book

The chapters that follow pursue these themes at different levels of analysis. Some consciously connect prevailing notions of sacrifice to contemporary environmental politics. Others seek ways in which sacrifice in both theory and practice can more creatively inform current environmental practice. Many draw on concrete examples of public and private practices in daily life to illuminate the power that conventional notions of sacrifice hold over our sense of the possibilities for, and limitations of, a more ambitious politics of environmental sustainability.

We have organized the chapters into three parts. Authors in part I ("Asking the Right Questions") each challenge some aspect of what appears to be conventional wisdom about the role of sacrifice in environmental politics. By opening up the conceptual terrain in new and provocative ways, they set the stage for the parts that follow. Part II ("Seeing Sacrifice in Everyday Life") explores the familiar terrain of the family, religious community, and economic marketplace. Chapter authors highlight the often provocative ways in which cultural expectations, widely recognized myths, and public philosophies shape connections between sacrifice and human fulfillment. In doing so, they draw out new possibilities that enrich our environmental imaginary. Finally, part III ("Obstacles and Opportunities") takes a more fine-grained look at particular practices and policies that shape environmental problems and our understanding of them. Authors in this part are concerned with both ideas and structures: with the ways in which environmental campaigns are framed and the ways in which the built environment and other structural constraints shape the physical terrain of sacrifice.

We introduce each of these parts with a brief essay that provides an overview of key themes within the chapters and connections between them. These offer readers something of a road map to the approaches and arguments of chapter authors. That said, we have written these "preludes" with a particular eye to our student readers and others who may be less familiar with the ideas that swirl around contemporary environmental concerns and debates. We hope they will provide readers with an inviting point of entry to the chapters that follow.

I

Asking the Right Questions

Critical environmental systems are faltering under the strain of expanding human consumption. Cheap oil, and other previously abundant resources, are thought to be "peaking." China, India, and other large, poor countries are climbing aboard the consumer bandwagon. Appropriately alarmed, many argue that now is the time to persuade (or even force) people to sacrifice—that is, to give up what they want (and perhaps deserve) in the name of "environmental sustainability." Others scoff at such notions. They emphasize the political impossibility of asking the rich or the poor to do with less, and instead vest faith in new technologies that will facilitate growing human consumption with minimal environmental pain. On what foundation should an individual and collective politics of the environment best rest? On the need for austerity and self-deprecation in a world of environmental limits? Or on the necessity of technology-driven abundance that expands the boundaries of the possible?

Despite the raft of books and reports devoted to these questions, they are not the ones now worth asking. That's the central message of part I, in which our authors (John M. Meyer, Paul Wapner, and Cheryl Hall) invite us to think hard about sacrifice and, more generally, about the common juxtaposition of austerity versus affluence as the foundation for contemporary environmental politics. For them, this juxtaposition is debilitating, both politically and morally. Not only does it make us insufficiently critical of technological approaches to environmental ills by suggesting that no-cost, no-pain environmental technologies are just waiting to be developed, but it also dampens our curiosity about the kinds and conditions of sacrifice that might be rewarding and affirming, rather than (as this juxtaposition so often implies) painful, diminishing, and base. In doing so, it robs the environmental movement of its power to inspire necessarily bold changes in production and consumption.

In his opening chapter ("A Democratic Politics of Sacrifice?"), John M. Meyer reminds us that we ought to be skeptical of anyone who'd ask us to sacrifice. Who does the asking, however, and why, may prove to be just as important as what's being asked. Rather than fixating on an environmental politics that contemplates imposed sacrifice from above (by elites, in the name of "environmental sustainability"), how might more democratic processes for determining sacrifice prove to be hopeful, without relying on the dream that new technologies—on their own—can solve our problems?

This question has never been more pertinent to environmental politics than now, for, as Paul Wapner argues (in "Sacrifice in an Age of Comfort"), a promethean technological faith is again ascendant. From this perspective, austerity, prudence, and sufficiency are yesterday's old ideas—strategically naive, hopelessly romantic, ecologically unnecessary. Wapner thinks it important to interrogate these promethean ideas, but for him, the more important questions—intellectual *and* strategic—run deeper. They're questions about the moral center of social movements, environmentalism included, and the ambiguous relationship between material prosperity and happiness. For both, sacrifice is pivotal.

Still, if sacrifice in contemporary environmental politics can be a source of hope and power (Meyer), and if it could emerge as the animating moral core of a revitalized environmentalism (Wapner), why does the notion seem to fare so poorly in an everyday politics of the environment? Why aren't people lining up to sacrifice some portion of their consumption on behalf of the sustainability of ecosystems? Cheryl Hall ("Freedom, Values, and Sacrifice") suggests that the reason lies less with peoples' values than with the political and economic systems within which they live. These systems lead individuals to make unintended, hidden, and false sacrifices. For Hall, the question isn't whether our environmental politics should favor technological abundance over sacrificial austerity. This frame obscures the reality that people *are already sacrificing* in ways hidden from them and often at odds with their values.

Instead, the important questions focus on the depth and breadth of these ongoing sacrifices, on the values of those doing the sacrificing, and on the ensuing openings for a new kind of environmental politics.

Together, Meyer, Wapner, and Hall add complexity to important questions about sacrifice and environmental politics. They do so not to make the questions themselves more complicated, but rather, to make them more interesting, more hopeful, and, above all, more honest.

2

A Democratic Politics of Sacrifice?

John M. Meyer

Must citizens of wealthy consumer societies sacrifice to avert the worst consequences of climate change and achieve environmental sustainability? Many environmentalists suppose that considerable sacrifice is necessary but that it is unlikely to be achieved because these citizens are too self-satisfied, apathetic, or ignorant to change willingly. By contrast, other environmentalists reject the notion that sacrifices are necessary, asserting that new technologies can enable us to achieve a sustainable society painlessly. It might appear that these opposing positions represent the full range of possible answers to the question. In fact, these positions share commonplace—yet misguided—assumptions about self-interest and citizenship, justice and efficacy. By drawing these assumptions out of the shadows and subjecting them to the light of critical scrutiny, the limitations of the original question become evident, and new possibilities emerge. We can then see that while calls *for* sacrifice tend to reinforce paternalistic strains among environmentalists and therefore will be more likely to alienate than motivate, calling *out* sacrifice—recognizing, for example, that climate change is *already* leading to tremendous human and economic sacrifices—can help us identify obstacles to effective environmental action.[1] In this way, sacrifice can reflect a democratic hope that citizen action might cultivate a better future. This stands in stark contrast to both the despair that leads some to contend that leaders must "get" people to sacrifice *and* the optimism that leads others to believe that an invisible hand will carry us into a clean and green society.

Superficially, at least, the character of environmentalist calls for sacrifice—like the frequent and despairing invocation of "limits to growth" a generation ago—seems to foster a survivalist and so authoritarian tendency.[2] After all, in a wide variety of contexts (the "war on terror" comes to mind) appealing to "expert" knowledge and warning of catastrophe in the absence of change has been a reliable basis for top-down, coercive political action. Yet this is not the only political role that talk of sacrifice might play. A democratic conception of sacrifice is possible and can promote connections between familiar environmentalist concerns and many people's everyday lives, values, and experiences. Doing so cultivates sensitivity to the plurality of contexts and audiences in which sacrifice is invoked. It also enables us to recognize sacrifice in places where we otherwise might not. Only then can we begin to differentiate sacrifice by willing citizens, acting on behalf of higher concerns, from sacrifice imposed on unwilling victims, in violation of their interests. This provides a richer appreciation for the conditions of human flourishing, from which we can develop more salient criticisms of existing practices and stimulate effective action for change.

In her recent meditation on race and American citizenship, *Talking to Strangers*, political theorist Danielle Allen offers one of the few substantive and constructive discussions of the politics of sacrifice in a democratic context.[3] Allen builds much of her analysis through an interpretation of work by novelist and social critic Ralph Ellison. Although nothing in her book explicitly addresses environmental challenges, her discussion of sacrifice offers insight in this context. In the pages that follow, I draw liberally on her analysis to develop both the importance and possibilities for a democratic politics of sacrifice.

Sacrifice and "Self-Interest"

Sacrifice, *n.* 4.a. *The destruction or surrender of something valued or desired for the sake of something having, or regarded as having, a higher or more pressing claim.*
—*Oxford English Dictionary*

There is no such single thing, self-interest.
—Danielle Allen, *Talking to Strangers*[4]

Sacrifice, in contemporary discourse, is often regarded as the negation or denial of self-interest—performed by heroes or saints, but not willingly by ordinary people. Sacrifice, in this sense, is often equated with altruism.[5] To rethink contemporary characterizations of personal sacrifice, we will first need to reexamine the notion of self-interest that lies at its core.

While the equation of sacrifice with altruism is seen in arguments advocating sacrifice, it is even more readily found among those who reject sacrifice. To judge by a cursory search of the Web, among the most likely to associate both altruism and sacrifice with environmentalism are advocates of Ayn Rand's libertarian philosophy of objectivism. Objectivists engage in antienvironmentalist diatribes premised on a dichotomy between egoism (good) and altruism (bad), which informs claims such as the following:

Environmentalism is altruism unadulterated and uncamouflaged. . . . We are being urged to sacrifice the human to the non-human. And if it *is* evil to live for your own sake, how can you resist such a demand? If self-abnegation is noble, what could be more praiseworthy than to subordinate your existence to that of bugs, weeds and dirt?[6]

The guiding principle of environmentalism is self-sacrifice: the sacrifice of longer lives, healthier lives, more prosperous lives, more enjoyable lives, i.e., the sacrifice of human lives. But an individual is not born in servitude. He has a moral right to live his own life for his own sake. He has no duty to sacrifice it to the needs of others and certainly not to the "needs" of the non-human.[7]

While the Randians might be viewed as extreme or eccentric, this dichotomy between self-interest and (altruistic) sacrifice is rooted in a conception of individual self-interest that is relatively commonplace, particularly among economists, rational choice theorists, and many other liberal theorists.[8] The Randians embrace it as "egoism"; Charles Taylor critiques it as "atomism"; C. B. Macpherson calls it "possessive individualism."[9] Danielle Allen characterizes this as a "rivalrous" conception of self-interest, which she—like other critics—attributes largely to our culture's patrimony from Hobbes.[10] When self-interest is tightly circumscribed like this, there is less room for envisioning sacrifice as anything other than self-abnegation—a giving up "to the needs of others," as in the Randian quotation earlier, whether human or nonhuman. The narrow construction of self-interest can be contrasted, then, to a more expansive and relational understanding—one that Alexis de Tocqueville describes as the doctrine of "self-interest properly understood."[11] Allen refers to this as an "equitable" form of self-interest, one necessary to "sustain the political bond, or any form of social bond."[12]

Closer attention to the meaning of sacrifice makes it clear that a complementary relationship with this more expansive sense of self-interest is well established. The most prominent context for speaking of sacrifice has long been religious, where the *Oxford English Dictionary* (*OED*) defines it as "an offering to God or a deity."[13] A seminal work describes sacrifice as "*communication between sacred and profane worlds, through the mediation of a victim, that is, of a thing that in the course of the ceremony is destroyed.*"[14] This communication with the sacred, then, is the goal of the sacrifice. We, the profane, elevate ourselves to something holy—at least enough to be able to communicate with the sacred. This elevation is a consequence of our sacrifice. There is an offering, but also a return. "Thus sacrifice shows itself in a dual light; it is a useful act and it is an obligation. *Disinterestedness is mingled with self-interest.*"[15] The victim is understood to be in the possession of the sacrificer, yet the roles of the agent and the victim of sacrifice are distinct, in this description, even in those cases where their identity is the same (as in "self-sacrifice").

When the term is used in a secular context, there can be a similar mingling with self-interest. The *OED* definition, quoted at the opening of this section, is "the destruction or surrender of something valued or desired for the sake of something having, or regarded as having, a higher or more pressing claim."[16] Rather than the negation of interest, it is "regarded as" the pursuit of a higher interest, albeit at a recognizable cost. It is in this sense, for example, that we often speak of parents making a "sacrifice" to create opportunities for their children. Yet some, if not many, proud parents—gaining satisfaction from the flourishing of their children—deny that they have sacrificed at all. Of course, the sacrifice that such parents deny is one conceptualized as the negation of their self-interest. It would seem, instead, to be an act rooted in a relational, rather than autonomous, sense of self. A consequence of this sense is to view their hopes and aspirations for their children, and hence for the future, as in their own interest. When sacrifice is viewed as consistent with this definition, such parents would be less likely to deny having made a sacrifice while simultaneously more likely to be comfortable describing their children's flourishing as a manifestation of their own interest (see chapters 5 and 8 for further exploration of this theme).

Just as a dichotomous view of the relationship between sacrifice and self-interest could lead parents to deny that they have properly sacrificed for their children, so does it lead many environmental thinkers to reject sacrifice because they regard it as synonymous with self-abnegation. The argument is strategic as well as principled: "As long as environmentalism seems to require only denial and sacrifice, its political effectiveness will be limited. Emphasis needs to be placed on the fact that changes sought are intended to increase quality of life."[17] In the words of Thomas Princen, the aim is to convince potential supporters that environmentally sound choices do not involve "abstinence" or "hardship"; are "not second best, not a concession, not a sacrifice."[18] "The problem," as Ted Nordhaus and Michael Shellenberger describe it, "is that none of us, whether we are wealthy environmental leaders or average Americans, are willing to significantly sacrifice our standard of living."[19] Notice, of course, that such arguments reject an association between environmentalism and self-abnegation, yet retain the identification of self-abnegation with sacrifice.

I concur with the preceding authors that environmentally sound policies and choices can—in many contexts and for many people—improve quality of life and hence facilitate changes consistent with one's self-interest. Where these authors assert that such changes make sacrifice unnecessary, however, I wish to argue the opposite: sacrifice is, in fact, enabled by a more expansive sense of self-interest. As Tocqueville puts it, this understanding of self-interest "does not inspire great sacrifices, but every day it prompts some small ones."[20] Correspondingly, but more forcefully, Allen characterizes friendship as a model for citizenship based on "equitable self-interest." While "one wishes a friend well for one's own sake," she concludes that "sacrifice is friendship's fundamental act."[21] Thus sacrifice and human flourishing need not be mutually exclusive and *can* be mutually reinforcing. And yet a reader has good reason to remain wary of, if not resistant to, the possibilities for an environmental politics of sacrifice at this point. Even if we are persuaded that sacrifice *can* be consistent with self-interest, after all, this is not sufficient to give us confidence that any sacrifice we are called on to make actually *will* promote human flourishing.

Sacrifice as Ubiquitous

We ought to maintain a healthy skepticism of leaders or governments who call on citizens to sacrifice. They seem to impose a moral obligation or a legal command on us in a way that can cast citizens as victims *to be* sacrificed. I explicate this distinction between agents and victims in the next section. There is, however, another problem with such a call: it seems to presume that we rarely sacrifice now. Rather than valorizing such a problematic call for sacrifice, we can *call out*—and highlight the significance of—the often invisible, unrecognized, yet everyday character of sacrifice.[22]

When we characterize sacrifice as self-abnegation, or the denial of self-interest, such acts appear extraordinary and unexpected. When self-interest is understood to be always already a part of acts of sacrifice, these acts begin to appear much more common. Jane Mansbridge argues that the intermingling of self-interest in what she describes as altruism is, in fact, commonplace, but that we often fail to recognize such acts precisely because we set the bar so high and describe an act as altruistic—or, I would argue, sacrificial—only in those rare instances in which we can conclude that self-interest was decisively absent: "We seriously underestimate the frequency of altruism when, having designed our lives to make self-interest and altruism coincide, we interpret such coincidences as demonstrating the pervasiveness of self-interest rather than altruism. And because thinking that another has acted unselfishly often leads people to behave unselfishly themselves, underestimating the frequency of altruism can itself undermine unselfish behavior."[23] Similarly, by highlighting, rather than marginalizing, sacrifice, we become more likely to recognize ourselves in a relational web that weakens an atomistic sense of self and self-interest. This is not merely a conceptual point, but rather, as Mansbridge makes clear, it can have important consequences for action.

Even extreme acts of sacrifice may appear less exceptional to the actors at the time. An individual who rushes into a burning building to save a child is often celebrated as a hero, yet her own interpretation of the act often appears far more ordinary: "I heard the cries and ran inside; what else could I do?" In war, the willingness to sacrifice for one's fellow soldiers also appears extraordinary, yet as J. Glenn Gray explains in *The Warriors* that while "such sacrifice seems hard and heroic to those who have never felt communal ecstasy . . . in fact, it is not nearly so difficult as many less absolute acts in peacetime and civilian life. . . . It is hardly surprising that men are capable of self-sacrifice in wartime."[24] The "communal ecstasy" that Gray finds so central to the explanation of extreme sacrifice certainly does suggest that the privileging of the public good of the community—whether in the more limited and concrete sense of one's immediate comrades or in the expansive and imagined sense of the nation—above the private safety of the individual is key. Yet the ecstasy that he identifies also makes clear that this common good is not necessarily experienced as self-abnegation, but can be a deeply, perhaps uniquely, fulfilling personal experience. Even here, where the possibility of the "ultimate sacrifice" is so palpable, the notion that it is experienced as the denial of self-interest seems to miss the mark.

Allen describes sacrifice as "a democratic fact" and draws on the experiences of families during the 1957 civil rights battle to integrate Little Rock's Central High School to support her argument. At the forefront of this battle, quite visible in front of the cameras facing angry white mobs, were high school students. Yet she offers an account of African American parents who struggled not with the need to sacrifice for their children's education, but to allow their children to sacrifice, both for their own future opportunities and for those of the broader African American community. She quotes an account of one father temporarily balking at the sacrifice his daughter would make to integrate the school: "I won't let Gloria go. She's faced two mobs and that's enough."[25] Speaking in reference to the parents of another student, Allen concludes that "the result was psychological terror for them and for their daughter, which was endured in the hope of future benefit. This constitutes sacrifice."[26] More generally, Allen concludes,

Of all the rituals relevant to democracy, sacrifice is preeminent. No democratic citizen, adult or child, escapes the necessity of losing out at some point in a public decision. "It is our fate as human beings," Ellison writes, "always to give up some good things for other good things, to throw off certain bad circumstances only to create others." . . . Only vigorous forms of citizenship can give a polity the resources to deal with the inevitable problem of sacrifice.[27]

To see sacrifice as commensurate with self-interest is to provide a basis for recognizing it in a broad variety of acts. While such acts are sometimes extraordinary, they might also be much more familiar and ordinary ones. Here, individuals appear in relation to others, and sacrifice is understood in a way that navigates between the poles of egoism and altruism, ultimately denying conceptual power to both extremes.

Understood in this way, society itself—to say nothing of environmental commitment—could not be sustained in the absence of acts of sacrifice, both great and small. Whether to sacrifice is not at issue. Instead, the vital question becomes, on behalf of what—or whom—do we sacrifice? The preceding examples appear as the acts of willing and engaged citizens. To appreciate the ubiquity of sacrifice, however, we must also recognize the many ways in which it is structured by social and political institutions.

Take, for example, private cars. Given that automobile usage accounts for a sizeable percentage of fossil fuel consumption and greenhouse gas emissions, no serious effort to curb climate change can ignore it. Yet simply raising the issue is easily characterized as a call to sacrifice personal mobility. It must be understood, however, within the social and political system that has been termed *automobility*—facilitated by the tax code, massive investment of public infrastructure, and mitigation of public safety and health effects.[28] In this context, we can recognize that driving is not always a choice, but often a structural necessity due to the geographic distribution of residential and commercial spaces, the absence of convenient public transportation, and growing impediments to walking and bicycling as auto traffic increases. For many—the young, elderly, poor, and disabled—access and mobility are therefore already sacrificed. One recent study, for example, found that elderly nondrivers become increasingly isolated, making 15 percent fewer trips to the doctor and 65 percent fewer trips for social, family, and religious activities than those who drive.[29]

As for those of us who do drive (and own a vehicle), recent studies correlate living in more car-dependent communities with poorer health and greater weight gain. Moreover, when we are stuck in rush-hour traffic, when we have to take time off work to transport an elderly parent to the doctor, when we shuttle our children to and from school, friends, and sports, it should become clear that while we may make such everyday sacrifices willingly, they are sacrifices nonetheless. Where political choices lead to a different communal structure—one that makes it convenient to walk, bike, and use public transportation—then these sacrifices can become both more visible and less necessary (see chapters 10 and 11 for further development of this point).

An environmentalist appeal is comprehensible only in this broader context of sacrifice; to call for reduced auto usage without simultaneously addressing this context is to be aloof from the lived experience of those whose driving one hopes to reduce. To *call* for sacrifice suggests a belief that sacrifice is only now being introduced—that in the absence of such a call, most would regard this as a world in which their interests are being realized and in which change would be regarded as a loss. But we do not live in the best of all possible worlds; sacrifice exists all around us. A failure to recognize sacrifice thus becomes a basis for misrecognizing the obstacles to reduced auto use. By clearly recognizing the sacrifices people already make, we can open a discussion about social and political change that might lessen or redistribute its burden, thereby enabling more effective environmental action.

It is when involuntary sacrifice is recognized that it also becomes possible to imagine it treated in a more democratic manner. Yet what does Allen mean when describing sacrifice as a "democratic" fact? On one hand, she is challenging the Rousseauian dream that truly democratic decision making could preclude the need for sacrifice at all (because such decisions would be true expressions of a general will). Allen, via Ellison, argues persuasively that it is a fact inescapable *even in* democracies. Sacrifice is not precluded by the existence of democracy, though a liberal society that cultivates a possessive individualism may find that it becomes less willingly embraced. Here, it is not the need that has been precluded, but rather, the conviction that public action matters has been impoverished.[30] Allen's account of the struggles in Little Rock make it clear that the hope that gave both African American parents and children the courage to sacrifice was nonetheless deeply imbued with an awareness of the tragic and potentially deadly character of their acts.

On the other hand, of course, sacrifices that African Americans made in Little Rock and elsewhere during the civil rights movement were aimed at overturning a racist and exclusionary system whose policies toward them could hardly be described as democratic. Sacrifice may well be ubiquitous in a democracy, but clearly the lack of democratic norms doesn't result in the absence of sacrifice. What Allen seems to be gesturing toward, here, is a distinction that she only develops later in her book: between "legitimate"—that is, democratic—sacrifice initiated "voluntarily and knowingly" by citizens such as the Little Rock activists and illegitimate sacrifice, which is imposed on an unwilling or unknowing public.[31] It is to this vital distinction that I turn now.

Willing Agents and Unwilling Victims

Any use of the term "sacrifice" in political discourse introduces problems of agency: the word can mean either the giving or the taking of sacrifices.
—Danielle Allen, *Talking to Strangers*[32]

Sacrifice, *n.* 4.b. *A victim; one sacrificed to the will of another.*
—*Oxford English Dictionary*

Recognizing sacrifice in the context of environmental politics can be a basis for opening a broader conversation about the choices and challenges we all face. Yet to do so, we must distinguish forcefully between the *act* of sacrifice and *being* sacrificed. This key distinction is often elided.

William Connolly has argued that one reason white, male, blue-collar workers in the United States have tended to resist the appeal of environmentalism since its emergence in the 1960s is because of a perception that "environmental programs sacrifice luxuries of consumption most available to the working class, so . . . they threaten one of the compensatory outlets available to it."[33] Yet for these men, resistance to environmentalism was not rooted in resistance to sacrifice per se. In fact, Connolly argues that an "ideology of sacrifice" was central to their identity:

Their dignity was primarily defined by their role as "head of household," their freedom by a willingness to sacrifice personal pleasures now to insulate their spouses from the rigors of the workplace and to improve future prospects for their children. Their masculine, working-class identity doubtless contained considerable self-delusion and self-aggrandizement within it, and the opportunities provided for others were ambiguous. . . . Nonetheless, sacrifice through work was pivotal to the identity of this constituency and to the political loyalties it cultivated."[34]

While sacrifice is integral to their identity, they resist it when introduced by others. It is the perceived uncoerced quality of the former that lends sacrifice its dignity and allows it to become so deeply entwined with aspirations for a better future. Note the shifting grammar of *sacrifice* itself between these accounts. Using *sacrifice* as a verb, I can actively and willingly sacrifice; as a noun, I can also be sacrificed. In the first case, I am an agent; in the second case, I am a victim. Under such circumstances, Connolly rightly notes that the "relations between dignity, sacrifice, and freedom" are jeopardized.[35]

Among the sources of authority external to oneself that might be seen as imposing sacrifice (or victimizing), God, Nature, and political rulers are among the most familiar possibilities. To this list, Peter Berger—in *Pyramids of Sacrifice*—adds those who offer comprehensive theories or models that "are based on the willingness to sacrifice at least one generation for the putative goals" of the theory.[36]

The analysis gets trickier when we try to identify the source of an ideology of sacrifice that comes from within. Again, it seems, we could point to inspiration from God or religion; Nature or the nature of things; inspirational leaders, political or otherwise; and theories or ideas. Of course, some would also point to our genes to try to explain behavior that appeared sacrificial as ultimately "selfish,"[37] or alternately, to an autonomous will as the basis for acts of sacrifice.

The fact that so many of the sources appear the same, however, is worthy of closer attention. How might we distinguish between someone who makes a willing sacrifice because she believes that a just God commanded it and one who feels victimized by the directive of religious authorities? Does a soldier sacrifice life and limb willingly in battle—out of loyalty to nation and comrades—or does he feel like cannon fodder, beholden to the ambitions of a tyrannical ruler? Does a mother sacrifice her time and opportunities willingly for her children, or is she constrained by unjust gender roles? Do we joyfully affirm our embeddedness in ecological relationships, or do we feel compelled by "environmentalists" to give up comforts that are meaningful to us?

From the perspective of one claiming a position of authority, the interpretation in the latter half of each of these pairings may be characterized as merely "false consciousness." Authority asserts itself as informed, farsighted, and public spirited, acting in the true interest of subjects who are uninformed, shortsighted, or self-interested. This, as Berger argues, is the perspective of the missionary.[38]

From the subject's point of view, such missionary authority appears arrogant and paternalistic. Sacrifice, under such circumstances, is resisted not on principle, but because in this context, it would represent compliance with a view whose premises are not accepted. Coercion may achieve compliance, but not the conversion that is sought. Individuals become the unwilling victims of sacrifice, in this context, rather than the agents sacrificing for the sake of something having a higher or more pressing claim.

The distinction between sacrificing agent and sacrificed victim is thus vital. And yet the difference is neither straightforward nor open to objective definition. Instead, it depends on the judgments of the actors themselves, which are formed through their perceptions of the justice and efficacy of sacrifice.[39]

Justice and Efficacy

Calling attention to perceptions of justice and efficacy highlights the multidimensional character of sacrifice. Posing one-dimensional questions, such as whether sacrifice is necessary to advance environmental sustainability, or how to get people to sacrifice, is fatally flawed. Building on an awareness of the ubiquity—yet frequent invisibility—of sacrifice, we must begin by recognizing its presence.

It has become increasingly common for political theorists to move beyond a distributive framework for thinking about justice, viewing *recognition* as a vital concern of justice—and injustice—claims.[40] This appears especially crucial to the politics of sacrifice. As Connolly's distinction suggests, an environmentalist appeal that is perceived as requiring sacrifice will be resisted by some because their own, ongoing sacrifice is not recognized or reciprocated by those making the appeal. Allen draws the relevant political conclusion when she states that "democratic citizens are obligated to recognize that even the subjective experience of loss is politically significant, for it establishes the extent of any given citizen's consent to a polity's policy."[41]

By recognizing and honoring the ubiquity of sacrifice, we acknowledge that something of value is lost. When environmentalists do so, they can avoid the paternalistic claim that what may be threatened—cheap gasoline, spacious homes, rural resource jobs, or simply familiar ways of doing things—wouldn't *really* be a loss or would readily be compensated. Moreover, they can better recognize established patterns of sacrifice, where certain groups and communities regularly lose and are rarely compensated. Sacrifice thus is not merely an individual phenomenon, but also a consequence of political decision making and institutional structure.

Understood in this way, recognition is enmeshed with concern for equity or distributive justice. Where responsibilities and burdens are perceived to be shared widely, then they are also more likely to be embraced as one's own. Where the distribution of such burdens appears to fall disproportionately on the poor or disadvantaged, then they will carry the added weight of this hypocrisy and maldistribution. We see this when Western leaders urge the reduction of climate change emissions in the third world, while promoting more modest changes (or none at all) at home. Yet in the third world, these emissions often represent survival strategies and always represent a dramatically lower per capita rate than in the states of Europe, Australasia, and North America.[42]

Judgments about the background conditions of justice or injustice are not the only ones that shape the likelihood of willingly engaging in sacrificial acts. Considerations of the efficacy of action are also key. This is at the heart of so-called collective action problems. Sacrifice must accomplish something; the thing "for the sake of" which I sacrifice must appear closer for my act to seem something other than self-abnegation.

Garrett Hardin and others have identified "mutual coercion"—typically through governmental action—as an avenue for overcoming this obstacle to collective action.[43] Yet the question of efficacy is not resolved simply by noting that a government policy exists and will be enforced. First, even if the policy is adequately implemented, the success of the policy in actually correcting the original problem remains open to question.[44] Second, even where they are resolved nationally, globalization of both economic relations and ecological footprints replicates collective action problems on an international level.

While justice is widely viewed as a normative concern, efficacy is more typically taken to be a matter for empirical assessment. Yet *perceptions* of efficacy will be vital to one's willingness to make sacrifices. The role of both ought to be front and center in discussions of when and how people might be willing to act on behalf of environmental concerns.

Again, we don't "get people to sacrifice." Yet we might work to ensure that citizens' sacrifice is recognized and equitable and then help enable them to see certain sorts of actions that might involve loss as being collectively efficacious. In this way, such actions *become* sacrifice, in the sense that it becomes reasonable to imagine them as advancing a "higher or a more pressing claim." "People who offer up sacrifices do not do it for nothing; they always aim to engage equitable reciprocity, and at the very least . . . implicitly expect to earn honor, gratitude, and respect."[45]

In sum, to sacrifice in this manner is aspirational; it is an expression of the hope that our actions matter and that we have the ability to act in a way that will bring us closer to something that we value more than what we are giving up. It is hope that can inspire us to live in a way that is consistent with our aspirations, based on the belief that it matters.[46]

If sacrifice is understood to be rooted in hope, then it can be understood as situated between despair, on one side, and optimism, on the other. If we despair for the future, then sacrifice will lose its apparent efficacy—the "higher interest" will not be achieved, so whatever is given up will be wasted. Optimists reject sacrifice for opposite reasons—adherents to a vision of inevitable human progress, they can adopt a more passive approach, rooted in a confidence that everything will work out well in the end. Why sacrifice now if we can be confident that the future will be better regardless of our actions? It would seem that one must believe that sacrifice itself can make a difference if one is to do it.

Democratic Sacrifice as an Expression of Hope

It is hope, not despair, which makes successful revolutions.
—Petr Kropotkin[47]

To embrace the possibilities for a democratic conception of sacrifice is to reject two familiar yet contrasting views of the relationship between environmental concern and sacrifice. The first is what I have been referring to as an environmentalist call to sacrifice. It reflects a conviction that we, the aware and altruistic, *know* what must be done and that they, the unaware and egoistic, must sacrifice. This conviction can, as Berger describes, manifest itself as the arrogant zeal of the missionary. Such a position can be challenged not just for its paternalistic attitude, but also for its blindness to the lived experience of sacrifice central to the lives of many. The vital distinction between sacrificing and being sacrificed is not clearly delineated and thus participation and democratic legitimacy are displaced by claims to authoritative expertise.

A democratic politics of sacrifice also stands in contrast to the all-too-easy optimism of those offering a technocratic way out of our ecological challenges. Often discussed under the rubric of "ecological moderniza-tion" in Europe, this view is even better captured in U.S. works, including Paul Hawken, Amory Lovins, and Hunter Lovins's *Natural Capitalism* and William McDonough and Michael Braungart's *Cradle to Cradle*.[48] According to this view, the same technological changes needed to avert crisis will also, happily, make all our lives more comfortable and enjoy-able. The opening pages of *Natural Capitalism* make this point vividly:

Imagine . . . a world where cities have become peaceful and serene because cars and buses are whisper quiet, vehicles exhaust only water vapor, and parks and greenways have replaced unneeded urban freeways. . . . Living standards for all people have dramatically improved, particularly for the poor and those in devel-oping countries. . . . Industrialized countries have reduced resource use by 80 percent while improving the quality of life. Among these technological changes, there are important social changes. The frayed social nets of Western countries have been repaired. . . . In communities and towns, churches, corporations, and labor groups promote a new living-wage social contract as the least expensive way to ensure the growth and preservation of valuable social capital. Is this the vision of a utopia? *In fact, the changes described here could come about in the decades to come as the result of economic and technological trends already in place.*[49]

While the quotation does exhibit the authors' sensitivity to social change, it is striking that such change is characterized as entirely dependent on "economic and technological trends." It is because they are convinced that the "trends [are] already in place" that they assert that this imagined world is neither naive nor utopian, but likely. Where do citizens fit into this vision of progress? The answer is somewhat elusive, yet beguiling. It seems to go like this: read their book; embrace the bright future; hop on board before the natural capitalism train leaves the station. Their view of economy and technology as autonomous displaces both the need for and the value of a more vigorous conception of citizenship or demo-cratic legitimacy because the task at hand is avowedly instrumental.[50] Sacrifice—loss of any kind—is uncalled for; their vision is presented as merely an improved means of achieving already established and desirable ends.[51]

A democratic politics must, then, recognize the deep inadequacies of a dichotomy between self-interest narrowly construed as egoism versus altruism understood as selflessness. Rather than the action of a virtuous few or of the many only under extraordinary circumstances, sacrifice is commonplace—yet typically mingled with self-interest. It must also place emphasis on the distinction between sacrificial agency and victimhood, privileging the participatory, voluntary character of the former. Deeming action voluntary is a tricky business, of course, especially while emphasizing a relational conception of self-interest. Fortunately, our goal is not to demonstrate free will in a philosophically rigorous manner, but rather, to account for the judgments of citizens engaged in such actions.

Reconceptualized in this manner, democratic sacrifice can be understood—in the manner described earlier—as an expression of hope. Hope is the basis for action in a world that is evidently not the best of all possible ones. Environmental justice activists, for example, are far too familiar with racism and injustice to be optimists. Yet despite the evidence that history and daily experience may offer for despair, their action itself is a manifestation of hope. Such action often comes at great cost, which must be acknowledged, yet this cost is not adequately understood when characterized as the denial of self-interest.

Ayn Rand's followers criticize environmentalism on the grounds that it promotes sacrifice and hence threatens egoism. They do so consistently, albeit not convincingly, only because they actually believe that a purely egoistic world would be the best of all possible ones. When we come to see sacrifice motivated by our aspirations and hope, however, then we can recognize that in a variety of ways—great and small—we all make everyday choices and decisions that reflect nonegoistic, and noncommodified, values. Society could hardly exist otherwise.

Surprisingly, then, sacrifice—*democratic* sacrifice—offers resources for a constructive and expansive environmental politics. Environmentalists would do well to enable such sacrifice. But unlike the top-down version of sacrifice imposed on the many, this form can only be approached indirectly. A way to facilitate or enable democratic sacrifice, then, is to focus on the obstacles to the perceived justice and efficacy of sacrificial actions. This can positively influence individual and collective judgments, making us more likely to regard ourselves as agents willing to make sacrifices. Where people are convinced that they can, indeed, "make a difference," and be fairly recognized for such action, their willingness to act will be bolstered.

Acknowledgments

Earlier (and very different) versions of this chapter were presented at the annual meetings of the International Studies Association (2006), the Western Political Science Association (2006), and the American Political Science Association (2007). Thank you to David Schlosberg and Bill Chaloupka for their thought-provoking comments and to attendees and fellow panelists for their vigorous engagement at each of these venues. Justin Williams, Jason Lambacher, and Michael Nordquist each read the chapter with care and offered insightful suggestions. A special thanks to the participants in our Allegheny College workshop and to my coeditor, Mike Maniates, for his insightful comments, attention to language, and persistent coaxing to write with diverse audiences in mind.

Notes

1. Global Humanitarian Forum, "Human Impact Report: The Anatomy of a Silent Crisis," Global Humanitarian Forum, http://www.ghfgeneva.org/Portals/0/pdfs/human_impact_report.pdf

2. On the antidemocratic invocation of environmental limits, see Garrett Hardin, "The Tragedy of the Commons," *Science* 162 (1968): 1243–1248; Robert Heilbroner, *An Inquiry into the Human Prospect: Updated and Reconsidered for the 1980s* (New York: W. W. Norton, 1980); and William Ophuls, *Ecology and the Politics of Scarcity: Prologue to a Political Theory of the Steady State* (San Francisco: W. H. Freeman, 1977).

3. Danielle Allen, *Talking to Strangers: Anxieties of Citizenship after Brown v. Board of Education* (Chicago: University of Chicago Press, 2004).

4. Ibid., 137.

5. Tim Hayward, *Political Theory and Ecological Values* (New York: St. Martin's Press, 1998), critically examines the concept of altruism in relation to environmentalism, arguing that for altruism to be a virtue, it must not preclude self-interest (72). He contrasts this favorably with what he takes to be a more conventional view of "altruism as self-sacrifice," in which "the agent is prepared to act in ways which promote others' interests at the expense of her own" (70).

Thus he challenges the received view of "altruism" but accepts the connotation of "sacrifice." My aim here is to challenge the latter. Both of us end up in roughly similar positions in the end.

6. Peter Schwartz, "In Moral Defense of Forestry," Ayn Rand Institute, http://www.aynrand.org/site/News2?JServSessionIdr006=kx059qcm34.app7a&page=NewsArticle&id=6160&news_iv_ctrl=1225.

7. Michael S. Berliner, "Against Environmentalism," Ayn Rand Institute, http://www.aynrand.org/site/PageServer?pagename=objectivism_environmentalism.

8. On rational choice, in particular, see Michael Taylor, *Rationality and the Ideology of Disconnection* (Cambridge: Cambridge University Press, 2006).

9. Charles Taylor, "Atomism," in *Communitarianism and Individualism*, ed. Shlomo Avineri and Avner de-Shalit (New York: Oxford University Press, 1992), 29–50; C. B. MacPherson, *The Political Theory of Possessive Individualism: Hobbes to Locke* (Oxford: Oxford University Press, 1962).

10. Allen, *Talking to Strangers*, 137–138.

11. Alexis de Tocqueville, *Democracy in America*, trans. George Lawrence, ed. J. P. Mayer (Garden City, NY: Anchor Books, 1969), 525.

12. Allen, *Talking to Strangers*, 138.

13. *Oxford English Dictionary* (*OED*), definition 1.a.

14. Henri Hubert and Marcel Mauss, *Sacrifice: Its Nature and Function* (Chicago: University of Chicago Press, 1964), 97–98; cf. M. F. C. Bourdillon and Meyer Fortes, eds., *Sacrifice* (London: Academic Press, 1980), 10–12.

15. Hubert and Mauss, *Sacrifice*, 100; emphasis added.

16. *OED*, definition 4.a.

17. Andrew McLaughlin, *Regarding Nature: Industrialism and Deep Ecology* (Albany: State University of New York Press, 1993), 184.

18. Thomas Princen, *The Logic of Sufficiency* (Cambridge, MA: MIT Press, 2005), 2.

19. Ted Nordhaus and Michael Shellenberger, *Break Through: From the Death of Environmentalism to the Politics of Possibility* (Boston: Houghton Mifflin, 2007), 125.

20. Tocqueville, *Democracy in America*, 527.

21. Allen, *Talking to Strangers*, 133–134.

22. Allen, ibid., 200n1, makes a similar distinction: "My argument . . . is not that we should introduce sacrifice as an ethical term, but rather that we must recognized how much of a role it is already playing and has always played, in democratic politics."

23. Jane J. Mansbridge, "The Relation of Altruism and Self-Interest," in *Beyond Self-Interest*, ed. Jane J. Mansbridge (Chicago: University of Chicago Press, 1990), 141. Cf. Val Plumwood, "Nature, Self, and Gender: Feminism, Environmental Philosophy, and the Critique of Rationalism," *Hypatia* 6, no. 1 (1991): 3–27, who critiques the egoism/altruism dichotomy in favor of a relational self.

24. J. Glenn Gray, *The Warriors: Reflections on Men in Battle* (New York: Harcourt, Brace, 1959), 47; Jean Bethke Elshtain discusses this quote in "Sovereignty, Identity, Sacrifice," *Social Research* 58, no. 3 (1991): 551.

25. Allen, *Talking to Strangers*, 34.

26. Ibid.

27. Ibid., 28–29.

28. Matthew Paterson, *Automobile Politics: Ecology and Cultural Political Economy* (Cambridge: Cambridge University Press, 2007); Sudhir Chella Rajan, *The Enigma of Automobility: Democratic Politics and Pollution Control* (Pittsburgh, PA: University of Pittsburgh Press, 1996); John Urry, "The 'System' of Automobility," *Theory, Culture, and Society* 21, no. 4/5 (2004): 25–39.

29. Matt Palmquist, "Old without Wheels," *Miller-McCune*, August 2008, 18.

30. Cf. Elshtain, "Sovereignty, Identity, Sacrifice," 562–563, for a discussion of moral impoverishment in an individualistic world without sacrifice.

31. Allen, *Talking to Strangers*, 110.

32. Ibid., 109.

33. William Connolly, *The Ethos of Pluralization* (Minneapolis: University of Minnesota Press, 1995), 112–113. Connolly's characterization is not limited to environmentalism, but rather, extends to all those "social movements, political rhetoric, public programs, and changing job markets," including civil rights, feminism, defeat in Vietnam, and the rise of a service economy.

34. Ibid., 111–112.

35. Ibid., 112.

36. Peter L. Berger, *Pyramids of Sacrifice: Political Ethics and Social Change* (New York: Basic Books, 1974), xiii; also 13–16.

37. Richard Dawkins, *The Selfish Gene* (New York: Oxford University Press, 1989).

38. Berger, *Pyramids of Sacrifice*, 118.

39. Allen outlines four questions, the answers to which might allow us to draw this distinction: "Who sacrifices for whom? Are sacrifices voluntary? Are they honored? And are they reciprocated?" (118). These criteria are illuminating. All but the second question can be usefully related to justice and efficacy, as I discuss later. Yet, as I hope to have shown here, the question about the voluntarism of sacrifice is of a different sort than the others because the answer is guided by our judgments about questions such as the other three.

40. For an excellent overview, see Patchen Markell, "Recognition and Redistribution," in *The Oxford Handbook of Political Theory*, ed. John S. Dryzek, Bonnie Honig, and Anne Phillips (Oxford: Oxford University Press, 2006), 450–469.

41. Allen, *Talking to Strangers*, 151.

42. Cf. Anil Agarwal and Sunita Narain, "Global Warming in an Unequal World: A Case of Environmental Colonialism," in *Green Planet Blues*, 2nd ed.,

,ed. Ken Conca and Geoffrey D. Dabelko (Boulder, CO: Westview Press, 1998), 157–161.

43. Hardin, "Tragedy of the Commons."

44. Deborah Stone, *Policy Paradox: The Art of Political Decision Making* (New York: W. W. Norton, 1997).

45. Allen, *Talking to Strangers*, 155.

46. Christopher Lasch, *The True and Only Heaven: Progress and Its Critics* (New York: W. W. Norton, 1991), 80–81, 390–392.

47. Petr Alekseevich Kropotkin, *Memoirs of a Revolutionist* (New York: Houghton, Mifflin, 1899), 418.

48. Paul Hawken, Amory Lovins, and Hunter Lovins, *Natural Capitalism: Creating the Next Industrial Revolution* (Boston: Little, Brown, 1999); William McDonough and Michael Braungart, *Cradle to Cradle: Remaking the Way We Make Things* (New York: North Point Press, 2002).

49. Hawken et al., *Natural Capitalism*, 1–2; emphasis added.

50. The classic source for a discussion of "autonomous" technological development as the displacement of politics is Langdon Winner, *Autonomous Technology: Technics-out-of-Control as a Theme in Political Thought* (Cambridge, MA: MIT Press, 1977).

51. "It is neither conservative nor liberal in its ideology . . . since it is a means, and not an end." Hawken et al., *Natural Capitalism*, 20.

3

Sacrifice in an Age of Comfort

Paul Wapner

The modern dogma is comfort at any cost.
—Aldo Leopold

Give me convenience, or give me death.
—Dead Kennedys

Environmentalism has long preached sacrifice. Since its inception, it has counseled a type of restraint that requires foregoing certain immediate pleasures for the higher goal of ecological well-being. Environmentalism tells us, for instance, to reduce our ecological footprint, restrict the depth of our interventions into the natural world, and generally hold ourselves back from living out all our materialist desires in the interest of environmental protection. Environmentalism advocates such sacrifice for both individuals and collectivities. Individually, we can do our part by minimizing the amount of resources we use and waste we produce; collectively, we can implement policies that privilege environmental concerns over other specialized interests. In both cases, doing so is not a matter of course, but rather, requires making choices about our lives—choices that call for giving up certain practices, forms of production, technological trajectories, monetary gains, or comforts in the interest of ecological protection.

These days, a growing wing of the environmental movement is rejecting a politics of sacrifice. Emerging out of the developed world, this wing is arguing that though sacrifice may have made sense in the past, it is increasingly anachronistic. The route to ecological well-being is no longer through austerity in the form of a preservationist or conservationist ethic, but rather, through abundance. Economic growth, technological innovation, and material prosperity in general, far from being the cause of environmental harm, are its solutions. Indeed, the route to environmental well-being is through embracing, rather than sacrificing, our material desires. Furthermore, environmental protection need not involve policy trade-offs. Environmental policies can create jobs, promote justice, enhance security, and be part of a comprehensive approach to social well-being.

Advocates advance a postsacrifice orientation for at least two reasons. First, they point out that a message of sacrifice goes against the grain of our consumerist culture and thus, as more people throughout the world join the middle class and begin to taste the fruits of affluence, its resonance will increasingly diminish. Many of us are the beneficiaries of the post–World War II economic boom. Economic growth has become a staple of our individual and collective experience. To the degree that sacrifice calls for rejecting material prosperity, it is out of sync with the momentum of contemporary society and its values. Sacrifice is a hard sell in prosperous consumer societies. Second, sacrifice is inappropriate these days for the sensibility it conveys. Sacrifice is part of the old-time "doom and gloom" environmentalism that seeks to motivate people through fear, rather than hope. It suggests that people must restrict, stop, prevent, constrain, or otherwise limit their impact on the earth, *or else*. Critics of sacrifice see such warnings as paralyzing people, rather than inspiring them toward effective environmental action. Sacrifice sounds like a desperate, misanthropic strategy that will win few subscribers. As such, it represents an unlikely route to genuine environmental protection.

The new breed of environmentalists suggest that we can best address environmental challenges not by forfeiting our material desires and engaging in collective trade-offs, but rather, by satisfying such yearnings and engaging the political process in more intelligent ways. The new environmentalists call for unleashing humanity's innovative spirit and looking at environmental problems as technological, economic, or policy challenges that require simply better design, engineering, market adjustment, or reformist public policy. Environmentalism, in other words, is not a matter of cutting back; rather, with some adjustment, it is simply another route to having it all. If done right, we can continue to consume resources, produce waste, and procreate as much as we would like; we simply have to be smarter about doing so—an approach that calls for, among other things, using resources more efficiently. Indeed, those voicing this orientation are making clear that environmentalism should not be about giving things up in the face of danger, but rather, about embracing new and more expansive ways of living in the face of untold opportunity. The new environmentalism is a movement of promise: a promise of greater freedom, economic growth, and the continual expression of humanity.

In this chapter, I criticize the new environmentalism. I do so with some hesitation. Those forging a positive, have-it-all environmentalism offer much hope and insight that can genuinely move us into ecologically safer waters. In fact, I believe that any effective environmentalism for the twenty-first century must include a strong dose of such an orientation. We are in deep, as it were, and thus all ways up the ecological mountain are welcome. Nonetheless, this new breed of environmentalism must be practiced in the context of a broader movement. It has its place in environmentalism but will be ultimately most effective when checked by principles that direct it in certain directions rather than others. At the heart of these principles is the idea of sacrifice.

As I will suggest, sacrifice is fundamentally a matter of morality. It has to do with caring for others, especially a kind of care that entails limiting oneself so that others can have the ecological space to live out their lives. In words attributed to Gandhi, sacrifice is a call to "live simply so others can simply live." This sensibility is central to environmentalism. The new breed of have-it-all environmentalism often neglects the moral dimension of the movement. It suggests that our environmental woes are fundamentally technical in nature—a matter of technological, economic, or political adjustment, rather than greater moral expression. There are, of course, many technical elements to environmental protection, and we should listen carefully to and adopt many of the prescriptions emerging out of the new environmentalism. But, in doing so, we must guard against the technical vision bleaching out the moral one. Without moral insight, environmentalism loses its compass. Its goals get defined in mere functional terms, and it ceases to be a movement animated by concern for others and able to be practiced by all who hear its call. The new environmentalism threatens to transform the movement into a specialized endeavor undertaken primarily by the technologists, economists, and policy-wonks among us. The idea of sacrifice serves to resist this.

The notion of sacrifice can play this role to the degree that it retains its core conventional meaning and, concomitantly, is translated to make sense in today's "societies of comfort." One of the reasons the new environmentalism is so attractive is that it promises greater comfort. It tells us that we will not have to alter our lifestyles to create and live in a green world, but rather, that we can continue on our current trajectory with only minor, technical adjustments—adjustments that will, we are told, enhance, rather than diminish, the quality of our lives. To be persuasive, contemporary notions of sacrifice have to speak to this promise. In other words, to be able to hold in check a have-it-all environmentalism, sacrifice needs to speak to the urge toward "comfort at any cost." Fortunately, voices are emerging in the environmental movement that are rethinking the idea of sacrifice in just this way. Alongside the new environmentalism, a set of thinkers is working to reframe the rhetoric of sacrifice and make it palatable and attractive in an age of comfort. At the heart of these expressions is the notion that we must learn to see sacrifice not as a "politics of less," but one of "more." We must begin to see sacrifice as holding out its own promises toward better and more fulfilling living. Sacrifice—newly appreciated in an ecologically fragile but, for many in the West, comfortable world—offers not simply a promising route to ecological well-being, but also a potential avenue toward richer meanings to life itself. In the following pages, I sketch out such a promise.

Before doing so, let me clarify two things—one substantive, the other stylistic. What I have been calling, and will continue to call, the "new environmentalism" is not new in the sense of being completely novel. The idea of enlisting technology and design to engineer our way out of environmental dilemmas shares much with ecological modernization theory, and readers familiar with the scientific management orientation associated with Progressive Era politics will recognize it as a long-standing dimension of environmentalism and social policy more generally. What is new is the increasing appeal of this orientation and its ability to generate activist, corporate, and governmental action. There has always been a battle for the heart and soul of the environmental movement. For most of the movement's history, the conservationist and preservationist voices have held sway. They have argued that humanity's ecological footprint is too large, and they have advocated individual and collective sacrifice as the most significant kind of response. This voice is currently being overtaken by one that calls not for reducing our impact on the earth, but enlisting our innovative, technological, and design spirit in the service of a have-it-all environmentalism: one that says we can consume as much as we like, as long as we properly address resource and sink issues. This latter voice, while long-standing in the history of the environmental movement, is new in its prominence and articulation. The following worries about the newfound strength of this voice within environmentalism.

In terms of style, throughout the chapter, I use the word *we* as if I share much with the reader. I use the word in two ways. Most often, I refer to those who live in the developed world and enjoy a degree of affluence. I see myself as part of the world's rich and assume that many readers of this volume share such a station with me. This assumption may well be false. I also employ the word *we*, at certain times, to mean members of our species, *Homo sapiens*. When I do so, I try to make this expanded meaning clear.

The New Promethean Environmentalism

In the ancient Greek myth, Prometheus steals fire from Zeus and bestows it on humanity. Armed with fire, which provides heat, light, and energy, humans are able to do all kinds of things that were previously off limits. The end result is that humans are able to become like gods. They can use fire to light up darkness, cook food, power machines, and all the other wonders that combustion brings. Fire, as such, represents human ingenuity. The Prometheus myth provides a metaphorical account of how humanity came to possess and practice its many intellectual and practical powers. In contrast to other beings, we can use our minds to think ourselves out of predicaments and create new avenues for meaningful living. This ingenuity has brought us technological powers that continually develop the human experience. The Prometheus myth reminds us of these powers. It highlights humanity's ability to innovate and its resourcefulness.

The new environmentalism is, at base, Promethean. It believes that our environmental challenges are no different than other collective trials. Our best bet is simply to put our heads together and think ourselves through environmental dangers. This can be done by a combination of design and policy making. We can surmount environmental problems not by turning off our innovative, technological spirit or otherwise shrinking our presence on earth, but rather, by embracing our presence and expressing it in environmentally beneficial ways.

Among the most eloquent and insightful thinkers of this breed are William McDonough and Michael Braungart. McDonough and Braungart, an architect and chemist, respectively, claim that our ecological woes are fundamentally design failures. Environmental degradation, in other words, is not a structural or cultural defect in society; it is simply the result of bad design. Design, for them, is the first signal of human intention. Addressing environmental challenges involves setting the right intention. They point out, for instance, that there was nothing evil about the Industrial Revolution per se; it simply had a design flaw in it. It prized the idea of using brute force against nature, a design plan that implicitly involves the widespread use of toxic materials, generation of enormous amounts of waste, creation of prosperity through extracting and disposing of natural resources, erosion of biological diversity, and extensive regulation to protect ourselves from being poisoned too quickly.[1] For McDonough and Braungart, such a design plan has brought us the challenges of climate change, ozone depletion, loss of biological diversity, freshwater scarcity, and so forth. McDonough and Braungart argue for a different design plan. They suggest that we can continue our lifestyles as we wish; we need only design our material systems for sustainable and safe use. We can do this by designing products that can be infinitely reused. This can happen once we embrace the notion that waste equals food: what we take to be garbage can be used directly to feed other ecological or technical systems. McDonough and Braungart refer to this orientation as "cradle to cradle," underlining the idea that we need to design our material world in a way that considers the full life cycle of products. If we do so, we can use as many resources as we wish and produce as much "waste" as we wish. A cradle-to-cradle orientation dismisses the notion of sacrifice. In McDonough and Braungart's world, we need not cut back or otherwise restrict our material desires; rather, we can have it all. We need simply to design better our materialist system.[2]

Another duo promoting a Promethean type of environmentalism is Ted Nordhaus and Michael Shellenberger. These two thinkers penned the now famous essay titled "The Death of Environmentalism,"[3] which they later expanded into a book, *Break Through: From the Death of Environmentalism and the Politics of Possibility*.[4] Nordhaus and Shellenberger share the view that sacrifice is unnecessary to create a greener, more just and sustainable world. For them, environmentalism has long peddled in the politics of fear. Doom and gloom have been providing the leitmotif for the movement premised on the idea that unless human beings change their lives dramatically—especially by giving up material comforts and economic abundance—they will suffer severe ecological consequences. Nordhaus and Shellenberger suggest that this kind of environmentalism must die. In its place, we need a positive, proactive orientation that celebrates economic growth, human ingenuity, and humanity's presence more generally. The "politics of possibility," for them, entails rejecting the notion of ecological limits and embracing humanity's ability to burst through all kinds of constraints. They call for a new kind of economic development that sparks innovation in alternative fuels, materials production, carbon sequestration, and other strategies for addressing global environmental challenges. Such development need not involve giving up or otherwise altering our lifestyles; rather, it calls for huge investments in research and development into new products and processes that will allow us to continue living our high-resource and wasteful lives but have industrial systems that will support them in ecologically sound ways.

McDonough, Braungart, Nordhaus, and Shellenberger are far from alone in their embrace of a Promethean environmentalism devoid of sacrifice. Different only by degrees, thinkers such as Paul Hawken, Amory Lovins, Jay Inslee, Bracken Hendricks, Dan Esty, Andrew Winston, Diane MacEachern, Ellis Jones, and scores of others promote an environmentalism that is compatible with contemporary economic and political practices, premised on the notion that we need not alter our lives dramatically to address environmental challenges. To them, the route to environmental well-being is not through denying ourselves certain goods or familiar practices, but rather, through designing and investing in smarter ways of provisioning ourselves. MacEachern and Jones, for instance, demonstrate how we can buy our way out of ecological challenges;[5] Hawken and Lovins show how we can reengineer buildings, automobiles, and industrial processes to usher in a greener world;[6] Inslee and Hendricks talk about how a green energy economy can produce jobs, boost profits, and enhance national security, all while combating climate change,[7] a view long shared and powerfully expressed by Thomas Friedman;[8] Esty and Winston express a Promethean orientation in a different way, by showing that our contemporary industrial system is not only compatible with, but can actually enhance, environmental protection.[9] They, like others, explain how companies can profit by becoming more efficient and investing in clean energy systems.[10]

Behind all these voices is the notion that there is nothing fundamentally wrong with the way we do things—our appetites, patterns of procreation, technological fascinations, and the like are all fine—and thus we need not, individually or collectively, sacrifice to address environmental issues; rather, we need only alter our production practices or realize the profit potential of greening our businesses or capitalizing on new engineering feats, or similar suggestions. These voices envision an environmentalism that calls not for sacrifice, but for embracing opportunity. They do so out of a combination of, what they take to be, realistic prospects for change and the potential of emerging technologies and economic trajectories. They are skeptical that people will welcome a message of sacrifice and, given this, seek to support the positive dimensions of responsible environmental action. As Inslee and Hendricks put it, "we can try to scold people into embracing sacrifice and change nothing . . . or offer choices that are cheaper and better."[11] Characterizing a part of the approach they recommend, they further write, "This is not about sacrifice; it is about economic growth, productivity, and investment."[12] One could also say that it is about "comfort."

Prometheus among the Affluent

It is no coincidence that Promethean environmentalism is emerging in the affluent, developed world. It is completely compatible with the values and structures of "societies of comfort." While there is still much physical pain and emotional distress in our lives, many of us are living at the pinnacle of material comfort. Those of us with money can live in comfortable housing, wear a variety of clothes, eat high on the food chain, drive our own cars, and populate our lives with untold gadgets that meet our every need and satisfy our many desires. While such lifestyles involve lots of implicit sacrifice in terms of time, money, and relationships associated with career, family, and recreational goals (see chapter 7), the message of conscious material sacrifice has trouble gaining a hearing in such a world. It rubs against the grain of greater economic growth, material expansion, and technological innovation—all processes that created and provide our current standard of living. Furthermore, pampered on all sides, our privilege has rendered us inexperienced with the practice of sacrifice and tone-deaf to the need to undertake it. Our antisacrificial sensibility and practical disengagement come from various corners.

One source is pragmatic. Garrett Hardin, Mancur Olson, and others who have wrestled with the challenge of collective action problems have long pointed out that people are fearful of sacrificing for the general good when they are unsure that others will do the same.[13] Sacrifice, in this sense, is a collective endeavor. It has to do with sharing the burden of communal well-being. If I know that others will not join me when I forfeit something meaningful in the service of a greater collective good, I become skeptical about the practical consequences of my actions. Why should I sacrifice if I know that, without others joining me, my efforts will come to naught? The logic, of course, goes in the other direction, as well: if I know that others will take action and that this might actually address the collective problem, I may feel that I need not do so. This is the classic "free rider" problem, a challenge fundamental to public goods in general and transboundary environmental dilemmas in particular.[14] We have seen collective action problems work against sacrifice in international environmental affairs in the form of the United States pulling its signature from the Kyoto Protocol. One of the reasons former president Bush rejected Kyoto is that the accord, according to Bush, lets developing countries off the hook. It allows them to continue emitting CO_2 and other greenhouse gases, while constraining the United States. Without developing world participation, Bush was unwilling to commit the United States to the multilateral treaty. Collective action problems can often undermine one's urge to sacrifice (whether in the developed or developing world).

Along with the problem of others joining our sacrificial actions is the challenge of being able to trace the effects of our efforts. We live in a globalizing world. This means that time and space horizons are increasingly shrinking, as we trade goods, communicate, and otherwise interact across geographical boundaries. Ironically, while globalization has compressed time and space, it has also generated lengthy commodity chains. We can no longer easily trace, or even really know, the sources and routes of our manufactured world.[15] We draw resources from across the globe, process and assemble products in multiple facilities, package and transport goods across national boundaries, and discard our waste through numerous media and across various geographical regions. The feedbacks in such a system are hard to chart, and this makes it difficult to trace the effects of our environmental actions. A globalizing world makes it difficult to have confidence that what I do in my corner will actually have its intended effect in another part of the earth.

We see this in even our most genuine attempts to shrink our ecological footprint. For instance, climate change now towers over all other environmental challenges, and addressing it surely involves reducing the carbon footprint of the most affluent. However, as various analyses point out, reducing this footprint is far from straightforward. Many recommend, for example, eating locally as a small contribution to reducing one's carbon impact because this would reduce the amount of fuel needed to transport food across great distances. But is eating locally always a good idea from a carbon reduction perspective? There are reasons for doubt. It turns out that food's carbon footprint involves not simply the amount of petroleum needed for transportation, but also the sum of sunlight, soil fertility, pesticide use, water utilization, and human labor hours devoted to crop production, distribution, sales, and consumption. According to Michael Specter, ironically, it may make more sense for people living in England to purchase lamb raised and shipped from New Zealand, rather than Yorkshire, because New Zealand agricultural lands receive more sunlight and its farmers use less pesticides, fertilizers, and so forth.[16] Sacrifice becomes difficult to undertake in the midst of such complexities. Globalization often conceals the ecological impacts of even our most genuine actions through both long commodity chains and the complexities resting at the interface between the social action and biophysical consequences.

A third source that problematizes sacrifice among today's affluent is the absence of a strong sense of community. Many scholars have noted the increasing individualist tendencies among Western societies, an individualism that runs deep through our ideological past.[17] Centuries ago,

Tocqueville noted that Americans love to join civic groups out of a sense of public interest and the joy of participatory action. As Putnam documents, this spirit has been flagging in the United States, and, as others have noted, an individualist sensibility seems to be increasingly prevalent in other parts of the world. The United States was founded on, and has always maintained, both a communitarian and liberal spirit, but lately, the latter has been overshadowing the former. This is partly a consequence of globalization, in the sense that many of us live in multiple and virtual communities, without feeling particularly deep roots in any single community. It is also connected to the commodification of life to the degree that we treat other people more like means to fulfilling our own desires, rather than as ends in themselves.[18] Whatever its roots, the result is that many of us feel a diminution of community itself. Dazzled by globalized networks of interaction, few of us feel a sense of solidarity to a specific group of people, an experience mimicked by people's decreasing sense of loyalty to a particular place.[19] This undermines proclivities toward sacrifice because, without a strong sense of community, people are that much more reluctant to deny themselves things in the service of what they take to be an abstract public good.

Thin solidarity is particularly problematic in the context of environmental dilemmas. The ultimate scope of environmental concern is the planet itself. Yes, we need to take stewardship responsibility for our own geographical locale and bring environmental mindfulness to our globalized interdependencies, but the ultimate frame of reference is the earth, complete with its panoply of people, other species, and nonliving entities. To be sure, the ideal of cosmopolitanism has been around since at least the Stoics, and there has always been a strong voice for conceiving of ourselves as global citizens.[20] Moreover, in a globalizing world, one would think cosmopolitanism would be having a field day. Nonetheless, this seems to be more theoretical than empirical. Nationalism, ethnic solidarities, and the like still demand much allegiance, and even more important, increasing numbers of people feel that they have no meaningful community at all. Global citizenry, while normatively attractive, is still elusive for all but a few. The lack of global solidarity or a strong sense of an earth community makes sacrifice that much more challenging. To the degree that people have sacrificed throughout their lives, it has most often been for the benefit of their families, friends, community members, or fellow citizens, not the world as a whole. Without a meaningful sense of global sociality, environmental sacrifice becomes significantly demanding.

It becomes even more so as we realize our tenuous connection to the nonhuman world. As critics of anthropocentrism have long argued, humans practice a type of speciesism in which we reserve moral consideration only for human beings[21] (and as the ethical history of our species makes clear, mostly only for *certain* human beings).[22] Aldo Leopold argued forcefully that we must conceptualize ourselves as part of the "land community," in which we are not lords over the plants and other animals, but fellow citizens. When we recognize how distant such an ideal is, it becomes clear how challenging sacrifice is. For if we feel only weak moral ties to our fellow human beings, how much shakier are our ethical commitments to the more-than-human world? A lack of community—both among humans and the other-than-humans—raises significant challenges for any practice of environmental sacrifice.

The weight against environmental sacrifice is quite powerful among anthropocentric individualists living in a globalizing world. There is an additional element at work, however, and this is perhaps one of the most damning. It has to do with the character of modern environmentalism as a movement and its inherent challenge of speaking persuasively about sacrifice. The modern environmental movement arose in the West in the 1960s and 1970s amid significant material prosperity.[23] The post–World War II economic boom lifted many out of poverty and enabled them to stop focusing on meeting their immediate material needs and start caring about the quality of their lives. To use social scientific language, economic prosperity of the 1960s and 1970s enabled Western publics to become "postmaterialists."[24] Having secured their basic economic needs, many living in the West were able to move up Maslow's hierarchy of needs and pursue less materialist desires. These included environmental well-being. Indeed, environmentalism is often considered a "new social movement" to the degree that it is concerned with quality-of-life issues, rather than the provision of basic needs.[25] To the degree that affluence accounts for the rise of the environmental movement, political strategies that emphasize sacrifice, austerity, and decreasing materiality sound off-key. You cannot preach environmental asceticism to publics raised on economic abundance. This is why Promethean environmentalism dismisses the whole idea of sacrifice. In its stead, Prometheans prescribe the very juice that jump-started the environmental movement in the first place, namely, economic plenty. As Prometheans see it, greater wealth is not, as many environmentalists claim, the cause of environmental harm so much as the solution to it.[26]

The point of all this is that, on some level, Promethean environmentalism is spot-on compatible with the kind of consumerist, affluent societies in which more and more of us live. Our age is one of, as Leopold puts it, "comfort at any cost." It is no surprise, then, that Promethean environmentalism is increasingly being voiced these days. Few of us want to hear a message of restriction, limit, constraint, and so forth. We have come to prize our economic freedom and resent calls to harness or otherwise rein it in. Much more palatable is the message of unleashing humanity's innovative spirit to remake the world so that we can continue living high-consumptive lifestyles. As Nordhaus and Shellenberger make clear, "the problem is that none of us, whether we are wealthy environmental leaders or average Americans, are willing to significantly sacrifice our standard of living."[27] We have become accustomed to comfort, and few of us are willing to give it up.

Prometheus Rebound: The Necessity of Sacrifice

The Promethean myth does not stop with Prometheus bestowing fire on humanity. Eventually, Zeus catches wind of Prometheus's trickery and, appreciating its consequences, punishes Prometheus for his deed. Prometheus is tied to rock on a mountain in the Caucasus and each day an eagle descends on him and eats out his liver. During the evening, his liver grows back, only to be visited the next morning by the eagle.

Technological optimists or those enthralled with human ingenuity rarely tell this second part of the Promethean story. They prefer focusing attention on the promise of humanity's ability to use its intellectual and practical resources to address various problems and scale new heights of human endeavor. Nonetheless, Prometheus's punishment offers a cautionary tale that warns against humanity's hubristic tendencies. It reminds us that there may, in fact, be limits to what humans can achieve.

My critique of the new environmentalism draws insight from Prometheus's punishment. It questions the reach of humanity's knowledge, technical ability, and policy adeptness. As I will explain, this critique is less about human pridefulness so much as a sober look at ecological realities and the requirements of forging effective policy. It does not eschew human ingenuity and the like, but sees that, in and of itself, this will never usher in a green world. There must be some element of self-limitation involved in crafting environmentally sound practices, some dimension in which we identify limits within ourselves and in the context of our relationship with the more-than-human world. Put differently, ecological wisdom consists of knowing that though we have the ability to burst through a seemingly infinite number of constraints, we choose not to for the well-being of ecological health and biological abundance.

One of the marks of maturity is knowledge about one's mortality. As kids, many of us lived as though we would never die. We had a sense of invincibility and infinite possibility. When asked about our future professional lives, many of us offered multiple professions as though we could concomitantly be ballerinas, brain surgeons, veterinarians, rock stars, global humanitarians, and mountain climbers. As we grew, we realized that the options narrow: there is only so much time in the day, only so much talent that can be directed toward our endeavors, only so many resources that can be devoted toward professional development. We learn, in other words, about limits. What distinguishes maturity from immaturity is the understanding that such limitation is not a tragic condition of human life, but actually an avenue into a deeper engagement with our lives and the world. We learn to fold the various pleasures of our many ambitions into our day-to-day lived experience. Put differently, we see the narrowing of our lives not as a constriction on our freedom, but rather, as an invitation to season our lives with greater enrichment.

Environmental maturity entails recognizing that there are biophysical limits to life and finding ways to flourish within them. The earth provides many ecosystem services. It supplies food and water, cleanses the air and soil, and otherwise affords the conditions to support life. Its ability to do so can be pressed only so far. When humans overharvest natural resources or overload sinks, for instance, we compromise the earth's regenerative and absorptive capacities. Our actions transgress ecosystem thresholds and therewith undermine the earth's ability to support life.

These days, we live in a full world. Our species has extended its reach into every ecosystem on the planet, and our numbers and the appetites of many have grown so much that we are testing, like never before, the earth's resourcefulness. For example, we are clearly depleting ocean fisheries, petroleum deposits, and the earth's biological diversity; we are also overwhelming the earth's terrestrial, marine, and atmospheric sinks, as evidenced by the buildup of toxic poisons, ocean garbage, and carbon dioxide.[28] If we wish to sustain the natural world in a manner that supports humans and a diverse set of other species, we cannot seemingly continue the path we are on. We cannot simply keep populating the earth and seeking to satisfy our every desire. Sooner or later—and certainly sooner, for the most vulnerable among us—the earth will say, as David Brower once put it, "I'm sorry, but your credit's no good. You can't borrow any more from me."[29]

The Promethean dream is that we can avoid catastrophe through technological, economic, and policy adjustment and that such adjustment can be made without sacrifice. It suggests that we can continue eating, drinking, manufacturing, driving, and otherwise interacting with the natural world as much as we want, without having to make hard choices about consumption. The absence of hard choices, however, represents, in my mind, a type of ecological immaturity. It does not want to admit that there are genuine biophysical limits that, no matter how much we want to ignore or surmount them, are fundamental to earth's ecology. Yes, we can and have tweaked natural constraints at the margins, and it is true that there is no single, identifiable, hard-and-fast threshold across which we know we should not go. But this doesn't mean that the earth is biophysically forever pliable. The earth *is* finite. It provides only so many resources and can absorb only so much waste over time and still be able to support a panoply of life. Thriving, or even simply surviving, within those constraints thus requires some type of self-limitation. It calls on us to make choices. With finite resources, we can only have so many people on earth with a certain level of material appetite. We can, and do, skew things so that the rich among us tend to garner a larger proportion of the earth's ecosystem services and the poor's hardship underlines ecological finitude. This is simply the sociopolitical expression of the more generalized condition of ecological limits; that is, the rich secure a disproportionate amount of resources and displace environmental problems precisely because there *are* ecological limits.[30]

Limits play a similar role when it comes to collective choices. The Prometheans pretend that environmental action serves everyone's interest. They rightly note the indispensability of ecosystem services for everyone on earth—everybody needs fresh air, clean water, safe food, and so forth—and therewith claim that promoting ecological well-being will lift all boats, as it were. While attractive, this orientation is rather naive. Yes, it is true that building a clean-energy economy in the United States, for instance, will create jobs, spur investment, enhance national security, and provide a communal goal that may build citizen solidarity.[31] But that is in the abstract. On the ground, building such an economy will clearly privilege some interests over others and lead to, at a minimum, short-term economic, social, and cultural dislocations. For example, creating a clean-energy economy, at this point in time, requires investment in wind, solar, hydroelectric, and sea wave power. Such investment concomitantly involves reducing, if not eliminating, subsidies that have been going to the oil and gas industry. While we can rationalize such action by claiming that, in the long run, a clean-energy economy will enhance overall economic, national, social, and environmental security, undertaking such action will certainly adversely affect particular industries and entire sectors of society. To pretend otherwise is to ignore sociopolitical limits.

Interdependence is both an ecological and social phenomenon. Policies will directly and indirectly impact certain interests. Everything is not possible, neither in the social nor the ecological world, and the sooner we recognize this, the more mature we can be about addressing environmental challenges, and the more we can open to the rewards environmental sacrifice offers.

Prometheus Unbound: Toward a Sacrificial Politics of More

When Prometheans or others warn against sacrifice, what are they worried about? Why do they take such a strong stance against forfeiting certain goods, pleasures, practices, and so forth? They constantly make it sound as though our lifestyles are so sacrosanct that any alteration in them is, by definition, a compromise. By why is this? As I see it, it is about comfort. They do not want to sacrifice the ease of our lives. But what is it about comfort that makes its absence seem so dreadful?

On one level, it is pretty straightforward. It has to do with something economists call *loss aversion*. This means that once we possess something, we have a hard time giving it up. In fact, we dislike forfeiting much more than gaining something we previously did not have.[32] Who in her right mind would surrender the pleasures of high consumption in favor of the vague goal of environmental protection, especially when, as noted earlier, there is no guarantee that one's sacrifices, either as a nation or individual, will have a marked environmental impact? Who would voluntarily give up routines, favored products, convenience, economic gain, policies, and appetites for the uncertain promise of environmental well-being? Why would one want to sacrifice if it means individual or collective privation?

These are the kinds of questions against which Promethean environmentalism poses itself. The new environmentalism is always harping on the losses we each, as individuals and particular collectivities, will suffer if we follow conventional environmentalism. It consistently states, in fact, that sacrifice is so far from desirable that it isn't even an option. To substantiate this, they claim that sacrifice is not even necessary. We can get through our environmental woes without altering our lifestyles or otherwise compromising our comfort. We can have it all: economic growth, technological advance, seemingly infinite resource availability, greater security, and more ease in the process of pursuing ecological health. Such a promise is quite attractive. But, before we get carried away with it, we should scrutinize the problem the promise is trying to solve, for the questions against which Prometheanism offers promise are, as I hope to show, ill formulated and misleading. They assume a certain view of human life with implicit answers to age-old inquiries about happiness and what constitutes "more" versus "less" in our lives. Critically assessing these assumptions is essential for contextualizing Promethean environmentalism within the broader environmental movement and introducing a revised understanding of sacrifice for the contemporary age.

As most of us understand it, the notion of sacrifice has to do with a "politics of less." Environmental sacrifice, after all, calls on us to reduce our impact on the earth. It requires that we give up certain practices, cherished products, particular foods, economic gain, and so forth out of a commitment to environmental well-being. The critics of sacrifice arguably understand this best when they complain that environmentalism is all about saying no. It involves restricting, limiting, regulating, reducing, constraining, and otherwise holding back our ecological impact on the earth.[33] They rightly point out how unattractive such a politics is. It *is* hard to get excited about trying to shrink oneself or, ideally, having zero ecological impact.

It is the sensibility of less that renders the notion of sacrifice problematic. Given the choice between "more" or "less," most of us would choose the former. But this need not—nor, as I will argue, should it—be the end of the story. We need to ask ourselves about the meaning of "more" in an environmental context.

Today, a set of voices within the environmental movement is coming to the defense of sacrifice and is doing so in a way that gets to the heart of "more" versus "less." People like Wendell Berry, Bill McKibben, David Suzuki, Gary Snyder, Leslie Thiele, and others are suggesting that environmental sacrifice is not a matter of reduction, but rather, enlargement. They explain the many ways in which giving up some practice, product, habit, economic reward, or even attitude buys one not less liberty and more hardship, but actually greater freedom and deeper experience. Sacrifice, for these authors, involves gaining more: more ecological health, greater spiritual enrichment, enhanced appreciation for others, deeper relationships, and more fun. It does so through an appreciation of environmental maturity, an appreciation that is, at bottom, a moral insight.

If we scrape away the many dimensions of environmentalism, we find that, at its core, it involves concern for the "Other." Environmentalism's fundamental insight is that we are not the center of the universe, but rather, we share our lives with other people, creatures, and entities.[34] Moreover, we don't just live alongside others; rather, we depend on them. None of us could have made it as infants without parents or caregivers who were willing to sacrifice individualist yearnings for our well-being, and none of us could continue to exist without the assistance of other people and the material and other benefits we enjoy from the more-than-human world.

Environmentalism, in other words, should acknowledge and celebrate this interdependence.

Environmentalism has long advanced interdependence through its decentering orientation. In various ways and across diverse traditions, environmentalist sensibilities tell us that we, as individuals, family members, ethnic groups, citizens of particular countries, and even *Homo sapiens* are part of the larger fabric of the earth; that is, there is more to the world than our individual affiliations, desires, associations, and loves. Likewise, there is more to the world than the concerns and pre-occupations of our immediate social group or even our challenges and virtues as a species. Environmentalism is about realizing this reality and translating it into individual and collective action. It does so by trying to knock off the privileged status we often assume for ourselves and our affiliations and cultivate a sense of care for Others.

Leslie Thiele explains such action by cataloguing and analyzing the way environmentalists extend moral concern. For Thiele, environmentalists extend moral consideration across three dimensions: space, time, and species.[35] In terms of space, environmentalists care about their fellow human beings and thus worry and take action to prevent those who live "downstream" or are otherwise vulnerable to environmental degradation from experiencing unnecessary harm.[36] In terms of time, environmentalists feel the obligation to leave the world the same or in better condition to future human beings. Taking space and time together, environmentalists embrace the call for sustainable development, an endeavor that seeks to "meet the needs and aspirations of the present without compromising the ability to meet those of the future."[37] In terms of species, environmentalists translate interdependence into a practice of extending care to other living entities and even to inanimate aspects of the earth. When we recognize how much we are a part of the broader earth community, or what Leopold called the "Land Community," many of us experience a type of spontaneous kindness toward Others.[38] We see them not simply for what they can provide us, but also as having some right to exist simply because they are also a part of the earth. In its strongest form, this moral sensitivity involves a biocentric or ecocentric orientation. At a less ideological level, it implies merely a sense of appreciation and care for the more-than-human world. Extending moral consideration across space, time, and species is the result of decentering because it removes us as individuals, social groups, and a species from the center of ultimate concern and privilege. Decentering, as such, inculcates a "land ethic," which, as Leopold explains, "changes the role of *Homo sapiens* from conqueror of the land community to plain member and citizen of it."[39]

For many of us, becoming a member of the land community may sound like an exercise in diminution. We lose our privileged ontological status and must stand alongside the apes, weeds, and poor of the world. It may further sound like an attenuation of our lives to the degree that it implicates us in helping others. It says that we can't simply do whatever we want—the motto of our consumerist, individualist culture—but rather, we must actively consider the well-being of Others. And this certainly rings of a kind of obligation that hems us in. If I have to extend concern to other human beings with whom I now share the planet, to those who will come after me, and to the panoply of life that presently exists and will exist in the future, and even to the inanimate domains of the earth, my freedom is certainly going to be curtailed. Moral concern, as such, sounds like a burden. However, this understanding—prevalent among many these days, including the new Promethean environmentalists—misconstrues or simply fails to appreciate the notion of environmental maturity.

A number of years ago, Bill McKibben published a book arguing that would-be parents in the developed world should consider having less children.[40] He pointed out how individuals in the global North use a disproportionate amount of resources and produce more than their fair share of waste and thus explained how smaller family size could contribute to global environmental well-being. (He specifically counseled having single-child families.) At the heart of McKibben's book, *Maybe One*, is an acknowledgment of limits and a call for sacrifice. Instead of having as many kids as we may want, McKibben encouraged us to think of Others: the poor who occupy the forefront of and most intensely experience ecological degradation, other-than-human species that are being driven to extinction because of our growing numbers and insatiable appetites, and the nonliving aspects of the earth that support life by providing ecosystem services and that simply constitute the earth itself.

McKibben recognized that his message would fall on resistant ears to the degree that it advances a politics of less and to the degree that it speaks of privation, rather than wealth. He counters by explaining how self-limitation—in this case, in terms of numbers of children we might each want to have—gets us more, not less. It gets us more in terms of time to be devoted to things other than child rearing and thus available for humanitarian or communal efforts; more in terms of resources we would not otherwise commit to raising kids; more in terms of additional opportunity to get to know more intimately our child. McKibben importantly adds that it also gives us more to the degree that it enhances our maturity. McKibben defines maturity as "the understanding that you're not at the center of creation, the most important thing in the world."[41] He defines it, in other words, as the prerequisite to a practice of extending moral consideration across space, time, and species. All of us know that maturity, which we gain only in pieces and often through hardship, is priceless. It is a kind of wisdom that enlarges and enriches our lives. Taking Others into consideration by realizing that we are not the center of the universe, then, is not a politics of less, but one of inestimable more. McKibben has spent much of his writing career explaining the many virtues and advantages of living our lives by making room for Others.

McKibben is only one voice among many explaining the benefits of self-limitation in the service of environmental, moral appreciation. Wendell Berry details how taking care of our own lives through self and land stewardship enhances our sense of connection to others and therewith amplifies our groundedness in the world.[42] David Suzuki speaks eloquently of how we can gain deep insight into the world and a fuller sense of well-being by contemplating biophysical interdependence and adopting a life that expresses consequent appreciation.[43] E. O. Wilson similarly calls on us to celebrate how braided we are into the earth's ecosystems and other species and sees such appreciation as central to our happiness. He talks about this through his concept of biophilia as well as his many explanations for how much more we gain by actively working to preserve species and ecosystems, rather than destroying them.[44] Indeed, a chorus exists among many environmentalists singing the praises of environmental sacrifice. Sacrifice, for these people, is not a deprivation, but a provision—it involves feeding our moral selves.

These voices promote sacrifice not simply as a moral exercise, but also as a route to more environmental health, personal safety, right livelihood, spiritual engagement, and sheer pleasure. This latter aspect is important. One of the ironies of life in the affluent world is that, for all its material abundance, people report only modest levels of happiness. Surveys demonstrate that in the United States, for instance, people have grown increasingly less happy, even though, over the decades, the economy and their spending power have grown. Surveys show that Americans were happiest in the 1950s, and despite significant economic growth (until very recently), their happiness level has decreased steadily since then.[45] This is counterintuitive as many of us see greater financial wealth as the route to more security, choice, and capacity to experience more of life. Studies have consistently explained this pattern as they have documented how personal happiness and economic capacity are—once one fulfills one's basic needs (at a level of approximately ten thousand dollars per year)—unrelated. For example, between 1958 and 1986, Japan experienced a fivefold increase in per capita income but saw no change in people's satisfaction with their lives. Likewise, the United Kingdom saw a 66 percent increase in per capita gross domestic product between 1973 and 2001, yet people's satisfaction with their lives remained unchanged.[46] Astonishingly, the relationship between economic abundance and happiness appears especially tenuous among the superrich. *Forbes* magazine's richest Americans report happiness scores indistinguishable from those of the Pennsylvania Amish and only a tiny bit higher than those of the Swedes and Masai tribesmen.[47] The point is that the lifestyle that the Prometheans are so scared of altering has not really brought increasing happiness. While financial wealth does not necessarily make one less happy, it is clear that it offers no guarantee to happiness.

It is in this light that some environmentalists promote environmental sacrifice as an actual route to greater happiness. "Less stuff, more fun" is a slogan of the Center for a New American Dream, an organization that deliberately tries to get people to change their lifestyles. The center argues that an overabundance of stuff in our lives compromises our ability to pursue deeper levels of happiness. We need to spend greater amounts of time making money so that we can afford more things, larger homes to store all our stuff, and insurance plans and so forth to ensure that our things are protected. The irony is that many of us end up getting on a spinning wheel in constant pursuit of greater economic might, while forfeiting many of the pleasures—time with our friends and families, relaxation, and so forth—that such efforts aim to provide. (As Thomas Princen makes clear in chapter 7, such a lifestyle is a huge sacrifice; we simply do not recognize it as such.)

A similar point is made by people like Barbara Kingsolver and Michael Pollan, who speak of the pleasures of giving up exotic food transported into our lives over great distances in favor of purchasing locally grown food and growing food ourselves. Eating locally may seem like the epitome of privation. One's menu choices are certainly limited. But, as Kingsolver and Pollan point out, such limitation can actually enhance one's sense of culinary pleasure. Knowing where one's food comes from; interacting with producers through community-supported agriculture efforts; rejecting fast, institutional food; and even taking one's hand at cultivating crops provide their own joys. They do not offer the ease that comes along with less mindful eating, but in its stead, one gains a sense of knowledge, control, and appreciation for one's meals.[48]

In short, moral action in the form of environmental sacrifice is not only altruistic behavior practiced with a sense of austerity; it can also provide a different kind of richness to our experience. For people like McKibben, Pollan, and so forth, sacrifice is a politics of more, not less. It enhances, rather than compromises, the quality of our lives.

Conclusion

Environmentalism, like all social movements, is constantly trying to remake itself to be relevant to contemporary sociohistorical conditions. Recently, a new breed of environmentalists has emerged, whose spokespersons are saying that we no longer need the sacrificial message of earlier environmentalism. People these days, especially the affluent, do not want to be told that they need to cut back on their consumption or generation of waste; moreover, technological advances promise to deliver ways for us to disregard the whole notion of restricting our lifestyles or asserting policies that are at odds with other specialized interests.

In this chapter, I have critically assessed this wing of the environmental movement. While Promethean environmentalism is compatible with contemporary social, economic, and political trends and promises much in our collective efforts to usher in a greener world, it ignores the idea of limits and thus deserves criticism. Without self-limitation of any sort,

Promethean environmentalism offers a technical answer to our environmental woes, and yet our environmental dilemmas involve much more
than mechanistic or directly practical engagement. Environmentalism is,
at bottom, a moral movement. It seeks to extend moral consideration to
our fellow humans, to those who will come after us, and to the wider
more-than-human world of which we are a part and which deserves
support independent of its contributions to our lives. Environmentalism,
to put it differently, acknowledges and forges practices that respect and
celebrate interdependence. This involves cultivating a sense of kindness
toward Others and holding oneself back so that everyone and everything
can have the opportunity of living or simply existing on earth with sufficient ecological space and services.

Holding oneself back is a matter of sacrifice. It involves restricting
one's desires in the service of something larger. In this chapter, I tried
to explain that environmental sacrifice represents not a politics of less,
but of more. It provides more environmental health, more personal and
collective security, deeper communal connection, and greater pleasure.
Many thinkers have been detailing these rewards, but the effort must
continue. We live in an age of comfort. For sacrifice to resonate at all
these days, it must respond meaningfully to the deep desire for ease. It
can do so when we realize that sacrifice is not about giving up things,
attitudes, practices, and so forth, but rather, about gaining a deeper
appreciation for our lives and engagements. It includes braiding ourselves
more intimately into the lives of the earth's species and our fellow human
beings and the entire panoply of the biophysical world. Detailing these
rewards must become an even stronger element of the environmental
movement.

Prometheanism is about mastery. It involves mastering nature—both
our own and the nonhuman world's. For centuries, we have prized such
mastery, and the sensibility has provided wonderful possibilities and
gifts. In criticizing the new environmentalism, I do not mean to dismiss
the urge in all of us toward mastery and its accompanying appreciation
for human ingenuity and resourcefulness. I mean only to place such an
urge into its appropriate environmentalist context. As I see it, our challenge in an age populated with various environmental dangers is not to
repress mastery, but ironically, to master it. We need to be aware of our
ability to control and outsmart human and nonhuman nature. But then,

we also need to express that ability by choosing to respect certain limits. Limits can make us free.

Notes

1. William McDonough and Michael Braungart, *Cradle to Cradle* (New York: North Point Press, 2002), 18.

2. Ibid.

3. Michael Shellenberger and Ted Nordhaus, "The Death of Environmentalism," Environmental Grantmakers, 2004, http://www.thebreakthrough.org/images/ Death_of_Environmentalism.pdf.

4. Ted Nordhaus and Michael Shellenberger, *Break Through: From the Death of Environmentalism to the Politics of Possibility* (New York: Houghton Mifflin, 2007).

5. Diane MacEachern, *Big Green Purse* (New York: Avery, 2008); Ellis Jones, *The Better World Shopping Guide: Every Dollar Makes a Difference* (Boston: New Society, 2008).

6. Paul Hawken, Amory Lovins, and L. Hunter Lovins, *Natural Capitalism: Creating the Next Industrial Revolution* (New York: Back Bay Books, 2000).

7. Jay Inslee and Bracken Hendricks, *Apollo's Fire: Igniting America's Clean Energy Economy* (Washington, DC: Island Press, 2007).

8. Thomas Friedman, *Hot, Flat, and Crowded: Why We Need a Green Revolution, and How It Can Renew America* (New York: Farrar, Straus, and Giroux, 2008).

9. Daniel Esty and Andrew Winston, *Green to Gold: How Smart Companies Use Environmental Strategy to Innovate, Create Value, and Build Competitive Advantage* (New Haven, CT: Yale University Press, 2006).

10. See, e.g., Stuart Hart, *Capitalism at the Crossroads: Aligning Business, Earth, and Humanity* (Upper Saddle River, NJ: Wharton School, 2007).

11. Inslee and Hendricks, *Apollo's Fire*, 11.

12. Ibid., 18.

13. Garrett Hardin, "The Tragedy of the Commons," *Science* 162 (1968): 1243–1248; Mancur Olson, *The Logic of Collective Action: Public Goods and the Theory of Groups* (Cambridge, MA: Harvard University Press, 1971).

14. Olson, *Logic of Collective Action*.

15. Thomas Princen, Michael Maniates, and Ken Conca, eds., *Confronting Consumption* (Cambridge, MA: MIT Press, 2002).

16. Michael Specter, "Big Foot: In Measuring Carbon Emissions, It Is Easy to Confuse Morality and Science," *The New Yorker*, February 25, 2008, http:// www.newyorker.com/reporting/2008/02/25/080225fa_fact_specter.

17. Robert Putnam, *Bowling Alone: The Collapse and Revival of American Community* (New York: Simon and Schuster, 2001); Crawford Macpherson,

The Political Theory of Possessive Individualism: Hobbes to Locke (Oxford: Oxford University Press, 1964).

18. Michael Lerner, *Left Hand of God: The Healing of America's Political and Spiritual Crisis* (New York: HarperOne, 2007).

19. Wendell Berry, *The Way of Ignorance and Other Essays* (Emeryville, CA: Shoemaker and Hoard, 2006).

20. Kwame Appiah, *Cosmopolitanism: Ethics in a World of Strangers* (New York: W. W. Norton, 2007).

21. Peter Singer, *Animal Liberation: A New Ethics for Our Treatment of Animals* (New York: Random House, 1975); Robyn Eckersley, *Environmentalism and Political Theory: Toward an Ecocentric Approach* (Albany: State University of New York Press, 1992).

22. Jonathan Glover, *Humanity: The Moral History of the Twentieth Century* (New York: Pimlico, 2001).

23. Nordhaus and Shellenberger, *Break Through*.

24. Ronald Inglehart, *The Silent Revolution: Changing Values and Political Styles among Western Publics* (Princeton, NJ: Princeton University Press, 1977).

25. As environmental degradation becomes more acute, I think we can dispense with the title of "new social movement" because it is increasingly a matter of basic needs and survival.

26. Nordhaus and Shellenberger, *Break Through*, 37.

27. Ibid., 125.

28. Lester R. Brown, *Plan B 2.0: Rescuing a Planet under Stress and a Civilization in Trouble*, 1st ed. (New York: W. W. Norton, 2006).

29. Jeff Greenwald, "The Future of Adventure," *Sierra*, January/February 2000: 37.

30. Paul Wapner, "The Moral Architecture of Global Environmental Governance," in *UNEO: Toward a United Nations Environmental Organization*, ed. Andreas Rechkremmer (Baden-Baden, Germany: Nomos, 2005), 63–75.

31. Inslee and Hendricks, *Apollo's Fire*; Friedman, *Hot, Flat, and Crowded*.

32. Richard H. Thaler and Cass R. Sunstein, *Nudge: Improving Decisions about Health, Wealth, and Happiness* (New Haven, CT: Yale University Press, 2008).

33. McDonough and Braungart, *Cradle to Cradle*; Nordhaus and Shellenberger, *Break Through*.

34. Bill McKibben, *Maybe One: A Personal and Environmental Argument for Single-Child Families* (New York: Simon and Schuster, 1998).

35. Leslie Thiele, *Environmentalism for a New Millennium* (New York: Oxford University Press, 1999).

36. Paul Wapner, "Environmental Ethics and Global Governance: Engaging the International Liberal Tradition," *Global Governance* 3, no. 2 (1997): 213–231.

37. World Commission on Environment and Development, *Our Common Future* (Oxford: Oxford University Press, 1987).

38. Norman Fischer, *Taking Our Places: The Buddhist Path to Truly Growing Up*, 1st ed. (San Francisco: HarperSanFrancisco, 2003).

39. Aldo Leopold, *A Sand County Almanac and Sketches Here and There* (New York: Oxford University Press, 1989).

40. McKibben, *Maybe One*.

41. Ibid., 161.

42. Wendell Berry and Norman Wirzba, *The Art of the Commonplace: The Agrarian Essays of Wendell Berry* (Washington, DC: Shoemaker and Hoard, 2002).

43. David T. Suzuki, Amanda McConnell, and Adrienne Mason, *The Sacred Balance: Rediscovering Our Place in Nature*, updated and exp. ed. (Crows Nest, NSW, Australia: Allen and Unwin, 2008).

44. Edward O. Wilson, *The Creation: An Appeal to Save Life on Earth* (New York: W. W. Norton, 2006).

45. Bill McKibben, *Deep Economy: The Wealth of Communities and the Durable Future*, 1st ed. (New York: Times Books, 2007), 36.

46. Ibid., 36.

47. Ibid., 42.

48. Michael Pollan, *In Defense of Food: An Eater's Manifesto* (New York: Penguin Press, 2008); Barbara Kingsolver, Steven L. Hopp, and Camille Kingsolver, *Animal, Vegetable, Miracle: A Year of Food Life*, 1st ed. (New York: HarperCollins, 2007).

4

Freedom, Values, and Sacrifice: Overcoming Obstacles to Environmentally Sustainable Behavior

Cheryl Hall

Absent some tremendous technological fix, it seems clear that achieving global environmental sustainability will require significant reductions in current levels of material throughput, particularly by citizens in advanced industrialized states. Yet calling on people to sacrifice consumption seems doomed to fail: people don't like to sacrifice, and they won't do it willingly. And if this is the case, then it seems there will eventually be only two alternatives: either environmental devastation or authoritarian control.[1] But not all is as it seems. In this chapter, I contend that while sacrifice is, by definition, never easy, in fact people only ever do it willingly. This means that a freely chosen, democratic transition to sustainability is possible. Making that transition a reality, however, requires figuring out what motivates people to sacrifice and what makes it easier or harder for them to do so.

The purpose of this chapter is to identify the complex relationship between sacrifice and freedom or agency. I begin by examining the nature of sacrifice, tracing the fundamental place of values in both the need for and the act of sacrifice. This discussion is the foundation for my argument that people only sacrifice willingly, even within a context of limited freedom. While it is helpful to see the role of agency in sacrifice, though, it doesn't yet explain why people who care about environmental sustainability might still choose to consume in unsustainable ways. To understand this phenomenon, I explore what I call *unidentified*, *false*, and *hard* sacrifices. I focus in particular on the difficulties involved in choosing to forego immediate material gratification for the sake of longer-term, bigger-picture values. I then discuss what it might take to overcome these obstacles. I conclude by showing how a new focus on the core element of freedom in sacrifice can itself further the goal of achieving environmental sustainability.

The Nature and Necessity of Sacrifice

What does it mean to sacrifice? In its origins, the word means to make sacred. This original sense clearly underlies the notion of sacrifice as an offering to the gods. While others have explored the implications of this sense of sacrifice for environmentalism, in this chapter I focus on a more secular sense of the word.[2] I also highlight the internal dispositions and deliberations involved when people choose whether and how to sacrifice, paying less attention to the web of relationships that both calls forth and is significantly constituted by sacrifice.[3] In spite of this different emphasis, though, I see my exploration of sacrifice as essentially compatible with those explorations that emphasize its sacred-making and/or gift-giving nature.

On the other hand, my argument that sacrifice as such must be willing is not compatible with the commonly held notion (evident in most other chapters in this volume) that sacrifice may be imposed or forced as well as chosen. I do not dispute the legitimacy of this usage or the fact that drawing a distinction between voluntary and involuntary sacrifices may be helpful in some respects. But I believe that, in its essence, the concept of sacrifice requires some meaningful kernel of agency, and, furthermore, that there is significant benefit to keeping to this sense of the word. The distinction between voluntary and involuntary sacrifice is, in my view, even better cast as a distinction between sacrifice and involuntary denial or deprivation.[4] Although this point may seem a mere semantic quibble, language is important. Insofar as the core element of freedom in sacrifice is clear, considerations of whether and when sacrifice is possible or even likely begin to take on a different hue.

While I emphasize the agency involved in sacrifice, though, this emphasis does not require that sacrifice be viewed only in individual terms. Individuals and groups alike may make choices; thus individuals and groups alike may choose to sacrifice. To include both possibilities, in this chapter I will speak in terms of the sacrifices "we" make, by which I will usually mean both individuals and communities in general. (Toward the latter part of the chapter, I will shift to a more specific emphasis on "we" who live in advanced industrialized countries.) Nevertheless, it is crucial to note that even democratically run groups are rarely unanimous in their decisions. Following my understanding of sacrifice as necessarily voluntary, this means that individuals within communities who do not share the priorities underlying the community's choice to sacrifice will experience the loss of whatever is being given up as deprivation, rather than sacrifice. Thus sacrifice does require at least a final component of individual ownership.

With these points in mind, let us turn to a closer look at the concept of sacrifice. The *New Shorter Oxford English Dictionary* defines *sacrifice* as "the surrender of something valued or desired, especially one's life, for the sake of something regarded as more important or worthy, or in order to avoid a greater loss, reduce expenditure, etc." As this definition suggests, acts of sacrifice are expressions of value; indeed, they are expressions of the relationships between values. Clearly to sacrifice means to forego or give up something we care about. It is literally no sacrifice to give up something we don't care about anyway.[5] But to sacrifice also means to forego or give up something we care about *for the sake of* something else we care about even more. Otherwise, the act of giving up this valued thing is simply deprivation or loss, an experience that is wholly, or at least on balance, negative. Unlike deprivation, the notion of sacrifice implies that there is something beneficial or even "redeeming" (whether religious or secular) entailed in the experience of relinquishing something we value. Giving it up is ultimately "worth it" for the sake of our own greater goals.[6] Thus sacrifice is not synonymous with deprivation. Nor is it synonymous with altruism, self-denial, or self-abnegation.[7] On the contrary, insofar as our values and priorities are our "selves," sacrifice is actually a form of self-expression and self-fulfillment.

Of course, most people would prefer not to give up any of the things they value. Their self-expression and fulfillment would arguably be even greater if they could do or have everything they care about. But circumstances are rarely ideal. People commonly find that at least some of their values are competing, making it impossible to act in accordance with all of them. There are at least two possible sources for such competition. First, values can be inherently inconsistent. A commitment to one principle or activity (say, a religious faith requiring observance of a sabbath) can itself require rejection or at least subordination of a commitment to another principle or activity (say, a profession requiring work on the weekends). In situations such as these, there is no way to avoid sacrificing one value for the sake of the other, so long as one continues to value both things. In the second case, though, values that are not inherently incompatible may nevertheless be put into tension by the limits of some external resource (such as time, space, energy, or money) necessary to achieve them. Thus, for example, people often end up sacrificing sleep to take care of babies not because the activity of caring for an infant in itself requires sleeplessness, but because there are only so many hours in the day and, at least in nuclear family structures, only so many people available to help. Here, because there is no inherent contradiction, it may be possible to avoid sacrificing one value for the sake of another insofar as it is possible to overcome the limits on the relevant resources. In either case, though, it is necessary to sacrifice only when—and precisely because—values are in tension, whether through inherent incompatibility or through external limits on satisfying them all.

The connection to values should help make it clear that a sacrifice is not just an act in itself. It is, more precisely, an act that has a specific meaning, an act that is interpreted in a specific way. As noted previously, giving something up only counts as a true "sacrifice" if we both value the thing we are giving up and are giving it up for something we value even more. Other people or groups may give up the very same thing without any sacrifice being involved, either because they don't value the thing to begin with or because their surrender of it is not motivated by commitment to a greater value or cause. The key point here is that the interpretation of an act as an act of sacrifice must ultimately come from those engaged in the act.[8] People need not actually use the word *sacrifice* to describe what they are doing for an action to be a sacrifice; they do, however, need to see what they are doing as surrendering something they value in the service of a greater value.

Sacrifice and Freedom

If sacrifice is an expression of our own values, then, in an important sense, we only sacrifice willingly. Other people cannot force us to give up one thing we value for the sake of something else we value even more—or at least not without our participation in holding these particular values in the first place. There may, of course, be rules, penalties, or rewards that are meant to induce, encourage, or even require us to do without certain things. But unless we share the values embodied in those rules (that is, unless we, too, see the sacrificed thing as less valuable than the thing for which it is sacrificed), such "sacrifices" turn out to be enforced restrictions instead. In other words, deprivation can be imposed; sacrifice cannot. The concept of sacrifice necessarily implies personal commitment to the value system underlying the act of doing without something for the sake of something else "regarded as more important or worthy."

But this formulation is still too simple: it does not pay enough attention to context. Recall that what makes sacrifice necessary is a situation in which values are competing, either through inherent incompatibility or through external limits on satisfying them all. The important point is that individuals, and even communities, do not create this situation on their own. Incompatibilities in both values and external limits are endemic to life itself as well as prevalent in ongoing human institutions and systems. It is life itself, then, or human institutions, or (perhaps most often) a combination of the two that makes sacrifice necessary. For example, some potentially valuable elements of life are at odds with other elements by their very nature. The benefits of solitude and companionship may be balanced in a life, but they can never be had at the very same time, so anyone who values both always faces the potential need to sacrifice one for the other. On the other hand, the example of religious values conflicting with professional values mentioned earlier is a specific incompatibility created by complex human institutions—institutions that, in spite of their complexity, are neither inevitable nor unchangeable. Turning to external limits, as with incompatibility in values, some come from the very nature of life. Time is finite, bodies are finite, natural resources are finite, the whole world is finite. Given this reality, some sacrifices will always be necessary. But human beings also create external limits through the social, political, economic, and cultural institutions they establish.[9] More often than not, these institutions distribute resources unequally, as, for instance, a competitive capitalist economy produces significant inequalities in wealth. In a capitalist society, where many of the things that people value can or must be purchased (think education, health care, and child care), the obvious consequence is that those with fewer financial resources will be faced with the need to sacrifice one of their values for the sake of another far more often than those whose resources are not so limited.

So some sacrifices are prompted by conflicts and limits that are inherent in life, some by conflicts and limits that are socially produced, and most, probably, by a combination of the two. Moreover, due both to chance and human institutions, some people face the need to sacrifice more than other people do. Together, these observations begin to cast doubt on the argument that sacrifice is a voluntary act. Since sacrifices are made necessary by a situation that we have not created or chosen ourselves, or at least not entirely so, it appears that circumstances and/or other people force us to (have to) sacrifice. How, then, can our sacrifice be willing?

To explore this question, consider the example of the sacrifice entailed in caring for people who cannot care for themselves, whether due to youth, old age, illness, or disability. One could argue that we willingly accept the possibility of such sacrifice when we "choose" to have such people in our lives—except that, as the awkwardness of this formulation already indicates, human relationships are rarely a matter of simple choice. We do not choose our parents, our siblings, our extended family, the people in our community, and possibly even our children. While we may (in some cultures) choose our friends and partners, we rarely do so with full knowledge of the kind of care they may someday need. Moreover, as noted previously, for the most part, we do not choose the circumstances that cause the need for care or the fact that others may be unwilling or unable to help provide it.[10] If caring for someone requires that we give up something we value (time, energy, money, education, opportunities, etc.), then it may seem that this act of sacrifice is effectively an imposed obligation, dictated to us by life, our society, and/or other individuals. Nevertheless, it is not. It is true that life, our society, and/or other individuals are creating a situation in which our options are limited, but having limited options is not the same thing as having no options. If sacrifice is about surrendering something we value for the sake of something else we regard as more worthy, then it implies some level of choice, or at least concurrence, in the determination of what is more worthy. There are many people who refuse to forego something they value to care for someone who needs help. It *is* possible to reject calls for help, whether occasionally or entirely. It may (or may not) be morally wrong to do so, but even if it is wrong, that doesn't make it impossible. If we do *not* refuse to forego something we value to care for someone in need, we take that course of action because we hold an overall set of values in which caring for that person is more important than whatever we will need to give up to do so. We probably do see the issue in moral terms (as well as in terms of love), and while we may not have constructed those terms ourselves, we *accept* the moral hold on us of the "obligation" to care. So we sacrifice both in service of the person's value and meaning to us (as expressed in our love for them) and in service of our beliefs about how we ought to act in the world (our sense of morality). As an expression of our own values, then, our sacrifice is a willing one.

Of course, we may be required by law or threatened by other sanctions to care for someone, especially a child. Some acts of abandonment are not only immoral, but illegal. But if these threats are the *only* reason we are providing care, we are not sacrificing for the person; we are simply enduring enforced deprivation to stay out of jail. Alternatively, we may be giving up something we value to provide care because we fear social disapproval if we do not or because we have been socialized to believe that we must (as women, in particular, often are).[11] The first case, that of fearing social disapproval, is either just an indirect form of enforced deprivation or else a sacrifice of a different character, for here what we seem to value most—and are thereby sacrificing for—is not so much the person we are taking care of as the social approval we are seeking. The case of socialization, however, is more challenging because it cuts to the heart of the argument. It highlights that there is agency in sacrifice only if there is agency in values. A full theory of agency is clearly beyond the scope of this chapter, but I can make two key points here. First, it is crucial to counter the ideology of autonomous individuality: no one arrives at her or his values independently. Second, in my view, this reality still does not preclude the possibility of some important level of individual agency in values. Human beings are capable of thinking and feeling about the values they find themselves holding, and through this process, of accepting, rejecting, and modifying them. Though this process itself does not happen in a vacuum, neither is it entirely controlled by external forces. So, for example, while we may find ourselves valuing people we did not consciously choose to value, at some point we may well need to evaluate more deliberately what this or that person means to us. Indeed, this point is quite likely to come precisely when we are faced with the question of how much to sacrifice for her or him. Insofar as we decide to put our commitment to a person ahead of other things we care about, we make the value our own. In this way, the very moment of sacrifice becomes the moment of agency.[12]

None of this is to deny the power structures shaping the circumstances, or the injustice they frequently produce through distributing external limits unequally. People can and perhaps usually will be forced into the situations in which they have to sacrifice, and in most societies, some people are forced into such situations much more often than other people. Nevertheless, the sacrifices themselves cannot be forced without losing their character *as* sacrifices. That is to say, the choice of what to forsake for what must be made relatively freely, or sacrifice loses its sense as a meaningful surrender in the service of a higher value. On one hand, then, the need to sacrifice may point to limitations of human freedom that are humanly constructed and (depending on the circumstance) perhaps illegitimate. Though it may be difficult to do, humanly created constraints can be changed, thus altering or reducing the need to sacrifice altogether and increasing freedom (and justice). On the other hand, the need to sacrifice may also point to the inherent finitude or incompatibilities of life, which cannot be changed. While the finitude of life sets boundaries on human freedom, it does not eliminate it. One might argue here that our freedom is precisely our ability to make choices within the context of life's limitations. To make conscious choices to prioritize what we value most—to sacrifice things we care about, but care about less, for the sake of things we care about more—is to be free because it is to live in accordance with our own values. And in fact, this element of freedom exists even within humanly constructed limitations. Sacrifice is thus a product of, and mediates between, freedom and constraint, for to sacrifice is to choose freely how best to live within limits that circumscribe freedom.

Unidentified Sacrifices, False Sacrifices, and Hard Sacrifices

Let us turn now to look more closely at the context of the need to sacrifice in the environmental case. Recall one more time that what makes sacrifice necessary is a situation in which values are competing, either through inherent incompatibility or through external limits on satisfying them all. While inherently inconsistent values with regard to the environment set the stage for any number of sacrifices, my focus in this chapter is on the specific goal of environmental sustainability, which is precisely about living within limits to preserve a healthy environment for the future.[13] For this reason, for the rest of the chapter I focus on sacrifice as prompted by external limits. These limits are both natural and humanly created. Again, the earth itself is finite, and while it may not be clear just where its limits lie or how they may affect us, it is clear that life on earth does not afford human beings with endless options. At the same time, human beings in the industrialized North, in particular, have exacerbated the earth's limits through our forms of production and consumption, our residential patterns and modes of transportation, and our sources and uses of energy. The combination of these circumstances has created ecological footprints that exceed the earth's capacity, putting northern citizens in the position of needing to sacrifice either our current patterns of consumption or a healthy environment in which we and the rest of life on earth can flourish over the long term.[14]

Notice the phrasing here. The choice is not *whether* to sacrifice; rather, the choice is *which* value to sacrifice for the sake of which. For in a situation of competing values, *any* choice requires sacrifice. Now, clearly this formulation presupposes that people in northern states actually do value a healthy environment. There is evidence to suggest that we do.[15] In any case, given the concept of sacrifice elaborated earlier, talking about sacrifice only makes sense if people do value both things. If people do not value environmental sustainability at all, then reduced consumption can only come about through imposed restrictions, not "sacrifice." For the remainder of this chapter, then, I will work with the presumption that environmental sustainability is at least of some value to a reasonable percentage of northern citizens.

The obvious question, then, is, if northern citizens do value sustainability, why aren't we choosing, individually or collectively, to forego the consumption patterns that threaten it? Why are we sacrificing sustainability for the sake of consumption, instead of consumption for the sake of sustainability? The most obvious answer is that we simply value sustainability *less* than we value the cheap material goods, comforts, and conveniences to which many of us currently have access. No doubt this is true to some extent and/or for some people, but I think that, for many of us, the explanation is considerably more complicated. To understand why we are sacrificing sustainability, rather than consumption, we need to consider several additional factors. First, the sacrifice of sustainability is, to some extent, an unidentified sacrifice. Second, the sacrifice of sustainability may well be what I am going to call a false sacrifice. And finally, for these reasons and more, it is in many ways simply easier to sacrifice sustainability than it is to sacrifice consumption.

Let us begin with the unidentified sacrifice of sustainability. An unidentified sacrifice is an act that only becomes apparent as a sacrifice in retrospect. As employed here, the term refers to those choices that we don't realize at the time will entail the loss of something else we care about. The loss is thus unintentional and, at least initially, unrecognized.[16] Unidentified sacrifices are produced by one of two things: either a lack of knowledge about the external limits of the situation, and thus of the unavoidable consequences that pursuing one value has for the viability of another value, or a lack of awareness of one's own values (or possibly a change in one's values, which may feel similar to a lack of initial awareness); that is, what is unidentified is either external (the limits and consequences) or internal (our real or ultimate values). In the first case, we don't name what we are doing as a sacrifice because we don't even realize that we are in a situation that requires sacrifice. We are not aware that the resources to have both values are not available, and so we pursue one without realizing the consequences for the other. The result is that we end up giving up the other value without having intended to. In the second case, we don't name what we are doing as a sacrifice because, even though we know that we cannot have both things in question, we are not clear on how much we actually value each thing, especially in relation to the other. Probably because we have not given it much thought and feeling, we underestimate how much we value what we are giving up or overestimate how much we value what we are giving it up for. So our choice to give up the one thing seems to be no real sacrifice, at least under the circumstances, when it fact it is in the end. To repeat, then, unidentified sacrifices are actually about unidentified limits and consequences or else about unidentified values.

Now, the notion of an unidentified sacrifice is rather counterintuitive, for in the original sense of the word, a sacrifice is clearly recognized as such at the time. When we offer a sacrifice to God, we are obviously aware that we are doing so. But it is too limiting to say that sacrifices can only be identified proactively. People not uncommonly look back at their choices and feel that they have sacrificed something, even if they didn't consider themselves to be doing so at the time. So in the contemporary use of the term, sacrifices can be identified retroactively. A more difficult question, though, is whether a previously unidentified sacrifice can still be considered a willing sacrifice. The key to this puzzle lies in understanding that a sacrifice is not so much the act itself as the interpretation of the act. Unidentified sacrifices only come to be experienced and interpreted as sacrifices, and thus in effect to *be* sacrifices, in retrospect. With an unidentified sacrifice, we do not experience either the pain of losing the thing we are giving up or the fulfillment involved in doing so for a higher cause at the time of our action. It is only later, after learning about the consequences of our action and/or clarifying or revising our values, that we experience this pain and fulfillment (unless it is also a false sacrifice, as discussed later, in which case, we will feel only pain). In essence, we only feel the sacrifice now, which is why we only name it as such now. And it is the agency involved in naming it as a sacrifice now that makes it a willing sacrifice. Indeed, whenever an act is interpreted as a sacrifice, whether it is proactively or retroactively, what makes it willing, what makes it ours, is that it is a reflection of our own values. In (now) defining our act as a sacrifice, we (now) will it to be a sacrifice.

There is no doubt that the sacrifice of sustainability is, for many people, an unidentified sacrifice. Partly this is the result of unidentified values, for to the extent that we still have a relatively healthy environment, it is easy to take it for granted, not thinking about how much it matters to us. Indeed, people often don't fully realize how much things matter to them until they are gone. But the unidentified nature of the sacrifice is also clearly the result of unidentified limits and consequences, for while most northern citizens probably have a general sense that we are doing things to damage the global environment, many of us have little concrete information about how much we are actually consuming and how fast various resources and waste sinks are being used up as a result.[17] Chances are, the notion that those of us in the industrial North need to reduce our ecological footprint by up to 80 percent would be shocking to large numbers of people. Moreover, a large part of the reason why the consequences of our choices are unidentified is because they affect things that are not in our ordinary range of vision: people we don't know and never will, future generations not yet living, elements of ecosystems that we don't see or interact with in our daily lives, and occurrences that are embedded in the ways our society is set up and therefore appear as mere accidents or "just the way things are," rather than as consequences of our societal choices (e.g., the enormous number of traffic injuries and fatalities that attend automobile-based transportation systems).[18] The invisibility of these effects makes it harder to see what we are sacrificing when we consume and therefore harder to see that we are sacrificing anything at all.

But the possibility of unidentified sacrifices is only one part of the picture. Another part of the picture stems from the possibility that we are making a false sacrifice. A false sacrifice is a sacrifice of the wrong thing, given our values. It is giving up something we value *more* for the sake of something we value *less*.[19] A false sacrifice is a sacrifice that we will later regret. Unlike an unidentified sacrifice, which may stem from an initial lack of awareness of our own values and priorities, a false sacrifice stems from ignoring or disregarding values and priorities of which we *are* aware. We make false sacrifices when we procrastinate until it is too late to do something that is important to us, or when we lack the willpower or commitment or integrity to align our actions with our values. Aligning our actions with our values is often fairly difficult, particularly when doing so requires giving up something that we also value. It is not unusual for people to believe in all sincerity that they can and should and indeed want to act in a certain way, while nevertheless failing to act in that way. The Greeks called this phenomenon *akrasia*. *Akrasia* is usually translated as weakness of will or lack of self-control, but a more literal and helpful translation is "powerlessness." When we fail to act the way we ourselves want to act, we are in effect powerless to carry out our own agenda. This kind of powerlessness easily leads to sacrificing the wrong thing.

As with unidentified sacrifices, there is no doubt that the sacrifice of sustainability is, for many people, a false sacrifice. Many of us consciously value sustainability more than we value consumption, and yet we continue to consume more than is sustainable. Much of the reason why this is the case stems from the fact that, as I will discuss in a moment, at least for now, it is easier to sacrifice sustainability than it is to sacrifice consumption. But there is at least one other feature of environmental sustainability that, as Chrisoula Andreou argues, makes it especially likely that we will procrastinate in taking action to reduce our consumption. As Andreou explains, with any pleasurable or gratifying action whose effects are "individually negligible" but nevertheless "cumulatively devastating," it is extremely difficult to avoid the temptation to enjoy doing the thing (as we tell ourselves) "just one more time"—over and over again.[20] For at every point in time, *one* more action will give us more pleasure without *in itself* causing significant harm. Of course, the problem is that all the points in time add up, ultimately leading to a situation that we clearly do not prefer. But it is still difficult to draw the line and start cutting back at any particular point. Andreou uses Michael Glantz's category of "creeping environmental problems" to apply this to the case of global climate change: "Although the effects of increasingly intense global warming can be disastrous, the individual instances of greenhouse gas emissions that contribute to it are typically negligible. Global warming is thus a monumental but creeping environmental problem. Because a timely response is essential, the problem is pressing; but because putting off responding to the problem for a little longer is negligible in terms of making things worse, it is easy not to feel pressed."[21] To make matters even worse, Andreou notes that we are even more likely to procrastinate in situations such as this one, in which the stakes are high but there are no "simple and obvious solutions" because "we are prone to defer difficult decisions."[22] In this way, we may erroneously sacrifice a healthy environment in spite of actually valuing it more highly than any given act of consumption.

The last part of the explanation for why most of us in northern states are sacrificing sustainability, rather than consumption, has to do with the relative difficulty of the two sacrifices. Of course, all sacrifices are hard, by definition. If it is truly easy to give something up, chances are that it is not something we valued much anyway. But in some cases, people seem especially willing, if not exactly eager, to sacrifice. To return to perhaps the most obvious example, parents and other caretakers regularly make considerable sacrifices for children. They give up sleep, they relinquish their privacy, they forego activities they enjoy (at least some of the time), they spend money on the children instead of themselves, they devote massive amounts of time and energy to the children that they might have devoted to other things they care about, and so on. No one finds it easy to do all this, and yet, for many people, it is also not so *very* hard to do. Why not? For one thing, parents and other caretakers usually care very deeply about the welfare of the children in their lives. Moreover, much of the time, it is easy to see the need to sacrifice in a specific way and to feel personally responsible for meeting that need. Finally, it is also usually easy to see or experience the good that the sacrifice will bring. There is often an immediate sense of joy and reward in doing things for children, and even when there isn't, many people strongly believe that the sacrifice will be worth it in the not-too-distant future.[23] So the value of what one is sacrificing for is high, the need is obvious, the sense of responsibility is high, and the good is manifest. As a result, the motivation to sacrifice is strong, which makes it easier to do. Needless to say, hard sacrifices are when these circumstances don't apply: the value of what one is sacrificing for is not so high, or the need not so obvious, or the responsibility not so clear, or the good that will come from the sacrifice not so apparent or close at hand (or all of the above). Consequently, there is less motivation to sacrifice, which makes it harder to do.

If sacrificing consumption and comfort and convenience for the sake of sustainability fit into the category of a (relatively) easy sacrifice, we would already be doing it. Clearly it is harder to sacrifice consumption than it is to sacrifice sustainability, at least for now. Temporarily setting aside the question of which thing we value more, the need to sacrifice consumption (instead of sustainability) is indeed not so obvious: as I've already suggested, it is even unidentified to us insofar as we don't realize the true limits of the situation and don't see the consequences of our actions. Put another way, what we lose when we sacrifice sustainability is in many ways unidentified and/or distant in time and space and person, while the losses involved in sacrificing consumption are patently obvious and close to home. Meanwhile, we experience the benefits of consumption immediately, tangibly, and personally, whereas the full benefits of sustainability are in many ways, again, distant to us in time and space, affecting people and animals and entities beyond ourselves, and/or aspects of life we can't literally see (such as our emotional or spiritual well-being), and/or our future lives more than our present ones.

In addition, the enormous scale of the problem makes it difficult to feel personally responsible. Finally, our society and its institutions are set up to support and value, and even subsidize, consumption. We are socialized to care about material goods and to believe in economic "growth," we are bombarded throughout our lives by advertising and exhortations to consume, our infrastructure steers our consumption (promoting the use of personal automobiles, consumption of food grown by agribusinesses, etc.), and sustainable alternatives are not readily available. These social and structural elements make it logistically and psychologically and financially hard to reduce consumption. So to summarize: the sacrifice of sustainability is a relatively easy sacrifice to make because it is often unidentified, many of the losses involved are distant, the benefits of sacrificing it (when we recognize we are doing so) are obvious, and our society encourages us to sacrifice it. In turn, the sacrifice of consumption is a hard sacrifice to make because it is clearly identified in advance, the costs of the sacrifice are right in front of us, the benefits are distant, the responsibility to make this sacrifice is diffuse, and our society discourages doing it.

It seems that it is all too easy to sacrifice sustainability, at least for many of us. The problem, unfortunately, is that the hard part is just going to come later. If we are to avoid that consequence, we need to figure out how to address the obstacles involved in sacrificing consumption. As others have pointed out, the question is not "how can we 'get' people to sacrifice?"[24] Since sacrifice cannot be compelled or manipulated, a better question might be "how and why do any of us come to choose to make sacrifices in our lives? How do we make conscious decisions to willingly forego something we care about?" On the basis of the preceding discussion, though, let me suggest an even more specific question: "What does it take for us to consciously choose to limit ourselves here and now for the sake of more distant, big-picture values? What does it take for us to forego obvious, personal, material gratifications for the sake of the longer-term well-being of everyone?"

Overcoming the Obstacles

In the previous section, I argued that the sacrifice of sustainability is often not identified as a sacrifice until later. Even when we are aware of it, it is, for many of us, a false sacrifice, but it is also the easier sacrifice to make compared to the sacrifice of consumption. These realities constitute the main obstacles preventing people from choosing to sacrifice consumption, rather than sustainability. Understanding what contributes to unidentified, false, and hard sacrifices can help us (activists, theorists, and citizens alike) to overcome these obstacles, though, because it can help us to devise solutions that are tailored to the specific nature of the problem. Even familiar solutions to environmental problems gain strategic clarity once they are understood in terms of the specific obstacles they address. In light of the factors that produce unidentified, false, and hard sacrifices, then, I argue that the following elements are key to helping people consciously choose immediate limits on consumption for the sake of the more distant, big-picture value of sustainability.

First, insofar as the sacrifice of sustainability is an unidentified sacrifice, the possibilities of choosing to sacrifice consumption instead are obstructed by both ignorance of the limits in the situation and a lack of clarity about values. Enabling the sacrifice of consumption thus requires both education and values clarification. With regard to education, northern and southern citizens alike need better knowledge of the reality of external limits and the consequences of our actions so that we can begin to identify what our true choices are. While our knowledge of the earth's extremely complex systems and processes can never be complete, it can be far more developed than it currently is. Northern citizens, in particular, have to realize that we cannot have everything we want: a healthy, life-sustaining environment; a peaceful, equitable global society; and our current modes and levels of production, consumption, and energy usage. We have to understand that there are some unalterable external limits. (I address the humanly created limits, which can be changed, later.) We have to understand that *because* there are external limits, we will bump up against limits one way or another—that there are costs associated with *any* of our choices. We have to be able to see the consequences of our actions: both the potential costs of choosing the "easy" route and the potential benefits of choosing the "hard" route. Moreover, we have to not only understand, but really *feel*, the impact of our choices on ourselves and other people and ecosystems across the globe and into the future. Better knowledge is emotional as well as cognitive; it is not just theoretical knowledge, but deep understanding. Such knowledge and understanding will require continuing education in the facts (which our societies can help with, as I discuss later) as well as, most likely, some level of attention, community engagement, and introspection by each of us.

Turning to values clarification, it is not difficult to see that any choice to limit oneself here and now for the sake of a distant, long-term good depends enormously on how clear one is about the greater value of that long-term good. Enabling the sacrifice of consumption thus necessitates developing a strong sense that sustainability is more important and beneficial than consumption. Up to this point, I have presumed that northern citizens value sustainability at least to some extent, though I have also suggested that we probably do not realize just how much we value it. But I do not wish to deny the other possibility either: that we do not value it enough. Overcoming this obstacle to sacrificing consumption for the sake of the bigger-picture good thus requires, at least, inquiry into our own values and priorities and, quite likely, a greater focus on the benefits of that bigger-picture good, as well. The latter, in turn, cannot occur without extending our sense of what personally benefits us to include nonmaterial and nonindividual goods.[25] I have elided this issue to some extent so far by generally speaking in terms of "we" and "us," without much differentiation or acknowledgment of inequities between members of that group. We the human race will unavoidably bump up against the limits of the planet (indeed, in some areas, we already have). But at this point, numerous individuals *are* able to escape at least some of the more material consequences. That number will likely decrease in the future, but for now, it is still a large number, and it may never get to zero. As I result, I think there is no getting around the fact that at least some of us whose lives remain less materially affected by the consequences of our consumption need to care more about the lives of those who will be more affected by our choices (even, and perhaps especially, those who don't exist yet) to believe that it is important to sacrifice now.[26]

But knowing the consequences of one's actions and being clear on one's values is not sufficient: values and knowledge have to translate into action. Here we move from the challenge posed by unidentified sacrifices to the challenge posed by false sacrifices. Insofar as the sacrifice of sustainability is a false sacrifice, the problem is *akrasia*, and the solution is to develop integrity, that is, the integration of conflicting elements in the psyche. While *akrasia* is a particularly difficult problem to understand, let alone resolve, Philip Pettit's analysis of the phenomenon may be of some use here. Drawing on an analogy to group dynamics, Pettit suggests that *akrasia* in individuals is not necessarily about a breakdown in hierarchy ("the failure of a higher self to subdue a lower self, or the failure of the superior faculty of reason to suppress the base passions"); rather, it may be about a failure of "coordination" or "collaboration" between the various parts of ourselves.[27] Working through *akrasia* is thus not so much a matter of one part of the self more effectively controlling another, but rather, of all parts finding a way to "get their act together" to agree on a course of action they can all support.[28] If Pettit is right, then caring about environmental sustainability while failing to act on that concern is not so much a problem of weakness of will as a problem of improving communication between diverse internal voices. To avoid false sacrifices, then, we need to "get our acts together," to harmonize the voices inside ourselves. Andreou also suggests that political strategies such as binding deadlines and laws requiring timely if imperfect "implementation intentions" may be necessary to help us all overcome our procrastination about taking action for the sake of environmental preservation.[29]

The third and final obstacle is the challenge posed by hard sacrifices. Insofar as the sacrifice of sustainability is a relatively easy sacrifice to make, while the sacrifice of consumption is particularly hard by comparison, several of the strategies discussed earlier—identifying the unrecognized costs in the sacrifice of sustainability and the unrecognized benefits in the sacrifice of consumption as well as developing a stronger sense of the value of sustainability—will certainly help to overcome this obstacle. But it is also important to address the issues of personal responsibility, collective action, and community support. With regard to personal responsibility and collective action, when responsibility for making a sacrifice is diffuse, the impact of individual actions seems minuscule, and/or the expected burdens of sacrifice are (or even just seem to be) distributed inequitably, people will understandably find it extremely difficult to sacrifice. To overcome these obstacles, we need good reasons to believe in the importance, power, and justice of our sacrifice.[30] Motivation to forego a more immediate benefit for the sake of a longer-term good requires the belief that the choice truly makes a difference: both that sacrificing the immediate benefit will genuinely help the cause *and* that refusing to sacrifice it will genuinely harm the cause. Especially if it involves giving up something that is not trivial in our own lives, a sacrifice whose effect appears trivial or a mere drop in the bucket will be a particularly hard sacrifice to make. And it will be even harder to give up that thing if it appears that we are alone in doing so. On the other hand, insofar as we have the sense that we are all "in it together," this sense in itself is likely to boost the motivation to sacrifice. Ultimately, then, overcoming this obstacle to sacrifice requires developing a sense of personal responsibility, organizing with others to multiply the effects of our actions, and addressing the inequities that enable some people to avoid making sacrifices that others cannot.

Finally, the issue of community support is also key in effectively addressing the elements that make the sacrifice of consumption particularly hard. At minimum, the institutions and structures and social norms that discourage the sacrifice of consumption need to be eliminated. But ultimately, we need structures and resources that will actively encourage and support sacrificing for the sake of the longer-term good of sustainability. There are a number of ways in which political communities can provide such structures and resources. To begin with, they can facilitate the production and dissemination of knowledge so that individual citizens don't have to do all the work of discovering unidentified limits and consequences themselves. Mandating environmental education in the public school curriculum and requiring companies to eco-label their products are but two examples of how political communities can facilitate knowledge. They can also require full-cost accounting of goods and services to bring to light the usually unidentified externalization of production costs (onto the environment, workers, people living downstream, and future generations) that results in cheap products we are then tempted to buy. In addition to or instead of full-cost accounting, they can choose, through democratic procedures, to assign penalties or taxes or surcharges to represent, in monetary terms, the higher costs of activities that are environmentally unsustainable, and/or they can provide subsidies or incentives to encourage activities that are sustainable. They can even legislate prohibitions on activities that are particularly harmful to the environment so we don't have to use our own willpower to resist doing them. Although this last measure moves out of the realm of freely chosen individual sacrifice, insofar as it is done through democratic procedures, it represents the community's decision to impose limits on itself as a group. Finally, political communities can provide the infrastructure and public resources, such as good public transportation systems, bike lanes, renewable energy-powered utility plants, curbside recycling, and so on, that make it much easier for individual citizens to live in a sustainable way.

At this point, one might question whether we are still talking about sacrifice. For the more our communities help us in these ways, the less we have to sacrifice in the first place. It might also seem as though individual agency has dropped out to some extent. In response to the first point, it is certainly true that getting rid of communal obstructions to sustainable practices would reduce the level of sacrifice required, precisely because it would eliminate some humanly created external limits (such as the current limits people face in trying to live without a personal automobile). But significant unalterable limits remain, so the need to sacrifice is not eliminated, only made more feasible. On the second point, even if we are not sacrificing entirely on our own, even if we have "help," individual agency remains important. In most cases, we still have to make the choice to refrain from engaging in unsustainable practices, and in all cases, our abstention has to resonate with our own values or it is not sacrifice, just deprivation.

Conclusion: Empowering Sacrifice for Sustainability

Overcoming the obstacles to sacrificing an immediate benefit (such as consumption) for the sake of a longer-term good (such as sustainability) thus requires good knowledge of the reality of external limits, clear appreciation for the greater value of the longer-term good, the psychic integrity to stay focused on the big picture and align actions with values, good reasons to believe in the importance and power and justice of the sacrifice, and concrete communal support. The possibilities for a democratic transition to sustainability, avoiding both environmental devastation and authoritarian control, rely in great part on the possibilities of citizens and communities developing these resources, skills, values, perspectives, and institutions.

Beyond these specific tools, though, probably the most fundamental element in facilitating the sacrifice of consumption for the sake of sustainability is a clear understanding of the essential role of agency in sacrifice. In contemporary Western culture, and perhaps especially in American culture, sacrifice tends to be perceived in largely negative terms. While there is occasional valorization of the heroic sacrifices of soldiers, firefighters, and other supposedly selfless individuals, there is also widespread rejection of the idea that ordinary people can be expected to sacrifice willingly. This rejection is based not only on pessimism about human nature, but also on a conception of sacrifice as synonymous with obligation, loss, and deprivation. Precisely because of this exclusive focus on loss, sacrifice is perceived as something people have to do (and will therefore resist whenever possible), rather than something they choose to do. But as I have argued in this chapter, this conception misunderstands the nature of sacrifice. It fails to appreciate the key characteristic of sacrifice: that it is about surrendering something valued *for the sake of* something else regarded as more important or worthy. In other words, it fails to recognize that sacrifice is an expression of people's own values. Understanding this crucial aspect of sacrifice opens up the possibility for a different attitude and approach to it. If people can focus on the fact that the loss involved in their sacrifice is for the sake of something they themselves regard as more important, they can take more control and ownership over the choice to sacrifice. That is to say, seeing sacrifice as a matter of their own agency can enable people to take up that agency more actively. The motivation to sacrifice will be stronger because it will be understood as coming from within.

Understanding the essential role of agency in sacrifice also makes it clear where theorists, activists, and political leaders who care about a sustainable environment should and should not direct their focus. There is little to be gained from trying to find solutions that do not require any sacrifice (at least as an exclusive approach because this ignores the context of sacrifice), from attempting to force people to sacrifice or even just "getting" them to do so, or from bemoaning the presumed inability or unwillingness of people to sacrifice. Because sacrifice is a matter of people's own agency, it is not something that can be controlled by governments, nongovernmental institutions, or anyone else. But that does not mean that nothing can be done to encourage and facilitate certain kinds of sacrifice. The more productive approach, then, is to focus on identifying and creating the conditions that will empower people to sacrifice for the sake of sustainability. Instead of telling people what they "must" give up, theorists, activists, and leaders need to ask people what they care about, help them clarify their values, help them see the consequences of their actions, encourage them to keep the longer-term goal in the forefront of their minds, and provide them with support to make different choices.[31] Doing this would not deny people agency or impose deprivation on them. Rather, it would empower them to sacrifice consumption freely, that is, to consciously acknowledge the need to choose and then to make the choice that prioritizes what they themselves value most.

Acknowledgments

This chapter is inspired by and indebted throughout to a set of papers originally presented at the annual conference of the International Studies Association in San Diego in March 2006 and a corresponding workshop on "The Politics of Sacrifice" at Allegheny College in September 2007. I am grateful to Hans Bruyninckx, Peter Cannavò, Karen Litfin, Michael Maniates, John Meyer, Simon Nicholson, Anna Peterson, Thomas Princen, Stefan Renckens, Paul Wapner, and Justin Williams for much thought-provoking dialog and writing on the concept of sacrifice. Many thanks as well to Kennan Ferguson, Teena Gabrielson, Steve Johnston, Mike Maniates, John Meyer, Casey Rentmeester, Denise Roemer, Steve Vanderheiden, and an anonymous reviewer for comments and suggestions on earlier drafts and to the University of South Florida Humanities Institute for supporting this work through a summer grant.

Notes

1. These are the alternatives offered by, among others, Garrett Hardin, "The Tragedy of the Commons," *Science* 162 (1968): 1242–1248; Robert L. Heilbroner, *An Inquiry into the Human Prospect* (New York: W. W. Norton, 1975); William Ophuls, "The Scarcity Society," *Harper's Magazine*, April 1974, 47–52; and William Ophuls and Stephen A. Boyan Jr., *Ecology and the Politics of Scarcity Revisited* (San Francisco: W. H. Freeman, 1992). I do not share these authors' conclusion that no other alternatives are possible primarily because I do not share their Hobbesian assumptions about human nature.

2. See chapters 5 and 6.

3. This web is addressed in different ways in chapters 2, 3, 5, and 6.

4. It should be noted that there is one case some people may intend to include in the category of "involuntary sacrifice" that might not be fully captured by my terminology of denial or deprivation or loss: the case in which there is *something* a person values that is being advanced, some cause the person believes in that is being served, even if, for that person, that thing or cause does *not* outweigh the value of whatever she or he was forced to give up for it (which is why the person had to be forced to do it). If *deprivation* implies no positive outcome at all, then the term leaves this case out. But I do not think that *deprivation* need imply no positive outcome at all. Thus I would argue that forcing someone to give up what she or he values *most*, even for the sake of something she or he does value to some (lesser) extent, is still better described as deprivation than as sacrifice.

5. An important question follows from this observation. If it is no sacrifice to give up something one does not value anyway, this begins to cast doubt on the notion that a person (or perhaps even any living being) can be an object of sacrifice. For it might well be argued that treating human beings (and possibly all beings) as objects, rather than as subjects or agents, inherently belies the idea that one values them. If this is so, one cannot sacrifice other human beings to one's own end; one can only use or exploit them. For example, a government's *sacrifice* of its nation's young women and men in combat, *absent their willingness to serve*, is more properly termed *exploitation*, even if the war is just. While it is important to acknowledge and analyze the long-standing history of using the term *sacrifice* to refer to unwilling victims, I argue against continuing this usage. Here, I depart from arguments by several of the authors in this collection, including Meyer, Litfin, Peterson, Princen, and Rajan.

6. Note that our own greater goals may not be "selfish" ones.

7. See chapters 1 and 6.

8. As will be discussed later, individuals and groups may well not recognize their own values. In this case, someone else may be the one to suggest the sacrificial nature of a particular act to them. Still, because sacrifice is defined in terms of people's own values and interpretation of their actions, final authority rests with those actually involved. This point is closely linked to my argument that sacrifice cannot be imposed. The key factor here is the issue of whether there are objective standards of value. Those who believe there are—for example, those who believe that their god is indisputably the Supreme Being—will consider giving something up for this god's sake to be a sacrifice even if it is forced because for them, the hierarchy of values is a matter of objective reality. Those who do not believe value systems can be matters of "fact," as I do not, must depend on people's own assessments of what matters to them in understanding what qualifies as sacrifice.

9. See chapter 2.

10. Although she likely would not agree with my conclusion that one only sac-rifices willingly, my argument in this section is indebted to Nancy Hirschmann's feminist analysis of obligation. See Nancy Hirschmann, "Rethinking Obligation for Feminism," in *Revisioning the Political: Feminist Reconstructions of Traditional Concepts in Western Political Theory*, ed. Nancy J. Hirschmann and Christine Di Stefano (Boulder, CO: Westview Press, 1996), 157–180.

11. I use the term *socialization* here as shorthand for any of the ways in which a person's subjectivity may be influenced, shaped, or constructed by other human beings or human institutions.

12. Because we are human and life is complex, sometimes—indeed probably often—we will be ambivalent about foregoing things, even for the sake of some-thing we regard as more worthy. We may be only partly committed to doing so. We may be committed to doing so but also somewhat resentful about it and/or fearful of judgment or punishment if we don't. We may also be angry at other people for not doing their part or for actually creating the situation in which we are faced with the need to sacrifice. All of this is to say that our willingness to give something up may be less than wholehearted. In this case, however, it is not that our sacrifice is only partly willing; rather, it is that our act of surrender is only partly a sacrifice.

13. The fact that incompatible values exist, and would continue to exist even in the absence of external limits, is one of the main reasons why environmental approaches that seek only to resolve the problems of external limits (for example, by developing clean and renewable energy sources) are not sufficient to eliminate all sacrifices. For even presuming success in this project, the sacrifices entailed in, for example, choosing either an anthropocentric or an ecocentric relationship to the rest of nature would remain.

14. Not to mention a more just, equitable distribution of environmental benefits and harms across the globe, which would also help to create the conditions for peace.

15. See R. E. Dunlap, "Trends in Public Opinion toward Environmental Issues: 1965–1990," *Society and Natural Resources* 4 (1991): 285–312; R. E. Dunlap, G. Gallup, and A. Gallup, "Global Environmental Concern: Results from an International Public Survey," *Environment* 35 (1993): 7–39; and Willett Kempton, J. Boster, and Jennifer Hartley, *Environmental Values in American Culture* (Cambridge, MA: MIT Press, 1999).

16. This language of an unidentified sacrifice echoes Litfin's language of "under-ground" or "unconscious" sacrifices, Meyer's language of "invisible, unrecog-nized" yet "ubiquitous" sacrifices, and Princen's language of "covert" sacrifices. My argument is probably closest to Litfin's: her references to distancing implicitly point to a lack of awareness of external limits, while her argument that people are unaware of what "gods" they are sacrificing to explicitly speaks of a lack of awareness of values. At the same time, in her concept of underground sacrifices, Litfin employs the idea that people can turn other people or beings into invol-untary objects of sacrifice or scapegoats, which, in my argument, is exploitation, rather than sacrifice (see n. 6). Meyer has two categories of "invisible, unrec-

ognized" sacrifices: those that are invisible because the concept of sacrifice has falsely excluded anything other than self-abnegation, and those that are invisible because social and political institutions are structured in such a way as to make life difficult for various groups, though this difficulty is not acknowledged when calls for sacrifice are made. The former category is different from my sense of an unidentified sacrifice because in this case, people *are* aware that they are giving up something they value, even if they don't use the word *sacrifice*; the latter category is different insofar as, in this case, the sacrifice is essentially involuntary, which, in my argument, is deprivation, rather than sacrifice. Princen's argument about "covert" sacrifices blends the point that people are unaware of the values for which they are sacrificing (as Litfin argues), with the point that sacrifice is built into public institutions (as Meyer argues). The same similarities and differences thus apply.

17. See the discussions of "distancing" in Thomas Princen, Michael Maniates, and Ken Conca, eds., *Confronting Consumption* (Cambridge, MA: MIT Press, 2002).

18. Chapter 7 and Peter Dauvergne, "Dying of Consumption: Accidents or Sacrifices of Global Morality?" *Global Environmental Politics* 5, no. 3 (2005): 35–47.

19. One might question whether a false sacrifice should even be called a sacrifice at all. If *sacrifice* means giving up something valued "for the sake of something regarded as more important or worthy," then technically, the reverse does not belong in the category. But that restriction is indeed too technical. One of the key elements of sacrifice, I have argued, is that it involves making a choice between competing values when one cannot have both. Given that circumstance, it not only makes sense, but is useful, to say that either choice will entail sacrifice. However, there is still the crucial question of whether one will make the *right* sacrifice, based on what one values *most*. My terminology of a false sacrifice is meant to name those situations in which one does not make the right sacrifice.

20. Chrisoula Andreou, "Environmental Preservation and Second-Order Procrastination," *Philosophy & Public Affairs* 35, no. 3 (2007): 240. See also Chrisoula Andreou, "Environmental Damage and the Puzzle of the Self-Torturer," *Philosophy & Public Affairs* 34, no. 1 (2006): 95–108.

21. Andreou, "Environmental Preservation," 243.

22. Ibid., 244.

23. In chapter 5, Litfin discusses a notion of joyous sacrifice.

24. Chapter 2.

25. This is precisely what Meyer and especially Litfin and Wapner argue for in various ways; see chapters 2, 3, and 6.

26. Considering the tremendous inequities between those who have been and continue to be responsible for causing most existing environmental degradation and those who suffer or will suffer the consequences of that degradation, one might well argue that the language of sacrifice is precisely the wrong language to use. According to this argument, when we talk about "giving up" something, we

reveal an underlying belief that we are actually entitled to have it. Put another way, we have to think a thing is ours to begin with to think that we are sacrificing not to have it. Indeed, even the act of doing without the valued thing reinforces the idea that it was ours to give up. Following this argument, citizens of advanced industrialized countries should not think in terms of sacrificing their current consumption of environmental resources; rather, they should think in terms of consuming only as much as is globally and intergenerationally just. The appropriate language to use is the language of justice, not sacrifice. This is an important objection to the project of focusing on sacrifice and one that is worthy of a much more extensive response than I can provide here. Nevertheless, I would suggest two initial points in reply: first, the concept of sacrifice is inherently linked to values, but it is not inherently linked to rights. We may well value, and thus desire or appreciate, things that we are neither entitled to nor believe we are entitled to. Second, if this is the case, then we need to talk about both what we value and what we are entitled to—that is, about both sacrifice and justice. (I thank Teena Gabrielson and Steve Vanderheiden for bringing this objection to my attention.).

27. Philip Pettit, "Akrasia: Collective and Individual," in *Weakness of Will and Practical Irrationality*, ed. S. Stroud and C. Tappolet (Oxford: Oxford University Press, 2003), 89, 90.

28. Ibid., 90.

29. Andreou, "Environmental Preservation," 242–248.

30. Chapter 2.

31. This argument shares important points with Stephen Kaplan's conclusion in "Human Nature and Environmentally Responsible Behavior," *Journal of Social Issues* 56, no. 3 (2000): 491–508. Although Kaplan unfortunately defines *sacrifice* as synonymous with *altruism*, and thus argues against appeals to sacrifice, his primary thesis is compatible with mine and nicely emphasizes the importance of democratic participation: "Rather than telling people what they must do or do without . . . [provide] people with an opportunity to figure out for themselves how various broadly defined goals can be met" (499).

II

Seeing Sacrifice in Everyday Life

At some point, moving forward on a complicated task means seeing the bigger picture. Commanders of armies methodically assess multiple arenas of conflict before redeploying their forces. Perceptive entrepreneurs gauge market conditions and the capabilities of their competitors before making new investments. Successful professors and students recall the broad goals of the course they're sharing before setting to work devising or completing a pivotal classroom assignment. Addressing problems in effective, imaginative ways demands a panoramic view capable of seeing into the shadows. It's true, as part I argues, that asking the right questions is important. But it isn't enough. Seeing completely the field of play—with its serendipitous opportunities, perilous traps, and unexpected allies—is equally essential.

In complementary ways, the following four chapters suggest that if students and practitioners of environmental politics were to cultivate a broader vision of sacrifice, they'd see political opportunities and policy openings currently hidden in the shadows. Sacrifice could shift from the sand in the gears of a politics of sustainability to an unexpectedly powerful lubricant, one rooted in everyday experience and common perception. From there, bold politics of social transformation could follow.

In the first chapter of this part ("Ordinary and Extraordinary Sacrifices"), religious studies scholar Anna Peterson lays the foundation for this broader, politically enabling vision. She begins by drawing our attention to the varieties and logic of sacrifice in everyday life. Her special focus on religious practice reveals important distinctions between extraordinary and everyday sacrifice, and on the sacrifices we choose to accept versus those we're conditioned to shoulder. These distinctions lead to an intriguing question: if so much of daily life already involves sacrifice of one sort or another, couldn't important elements of sacrifice likewise become normalized as part of a transition to a sustainable society? For Peterson, clues to how this politics might unfold are evident throughout everyday life.

The next two contributions build on Peterson's call to find ways of weaving sacrifice into environmental practice. Karen Litfin's rich chapter ("The Sacred and the Profane in the Ecological Politics of Sacrifice") argues that even if painful and difficult, sacrifice has long been a central component of human culture and psychology. Doing the difficult and doing without are essential elements of what ties us to one another, and to the nonhuman world. Modernity didn't end these patterns of sacrifice, says Litfin; instead, it drove them underground. Making visible these continuing, often profound, and sometimes coerced practices of sacrifice opens up the political space for debating which sacrifices we want and need. It also offers the opportunity to highlight what she calls an affirmative politics of sacrifice, in which assuming burden or bearing pain becomes sacrificial in the best sense of the word. In this context, says Litfin, the current environmental debate of sacrifice versus no sacrifice is a hollow caricature of reality and of our human needs.

Thomas Princen (in "Consumer Sovereignty, Heroic Sacrifice") echoes these themes from a different vantage point. Like Litfin, he notes that we live in a world where profound, often onerous sacrifice unfolds on a daily basis. For Princen, such sacrifice—degraded ecosystems, deepening poverty, a decline in community life—is the consequence of an inherently unsustainable, endlessly expanding economy. Seeing these sacrifices for what they are, and challenging them in ways that question popular conceptions of the good life, is vital to an effective politics of sustainability. But two rhetorical and political forces manufacture and reinforce an inability to see and act on these sacrifices: the notion of consumer sovereignty and the selective, always negative deployment of *sacrifice* in political conversation. Seeing consumer sovereignty and negative sacrifice for what they are—distractions and distortions that serve the powerful—moves us toward an environmental politics capable of rising to Peterson's challenge.

In the final chapter of part II ("Parental Sacrifice as Atonement for Future Climate Change"), Sudhir Chella Rajan reflects on ideas of parental love and self-sacrifice. He wonders what these familiar notions might tell us about our capacity and willingness to act on deeper interpretations of sacrifice in the political realm. Through the exploration of myth and practice around family life, Rajan argues that humans—in diverse cultural contexts, including India and the United States—are more than ready to assume the kinds of sacrifice demanded by climate change. His exploration of traditions of parental sacrifice around the world, and how these traditions could extend to the environment, offers another avenue toward a politics of making sacrifice on behalf of the environment something normal and affirming.

Sacrifice presents many faces. Seeing them, and understanding the forces that make this seeing so difficult, holds potential for shifting environmental politics in new directions. Some of these directions unfold in the chapters of part II, while others become apparent in part III.

5

Ordinary and Extraordinary Sacrifices: Religion, Everyday Life, and Environmental Practice

Anna Peterson

The Varieties and the Logic of Sacrifice

Especially in relation to environmental problems, many people view sacrifice as an extreme demand that bears little connection to everyday experience. In some significant aspects of our lives, however, sacrifice is frequent, mundane, and even taken for granted. The disjuncture stems from the fact that sacrifices take many forms, which vary by context, content, and intention. However, a similar logic undergirds both ordinary and extraordinary sacrifices, insofar as in both cases, people relinquish something valuable for other things considered to be more valuable still. In extraordinary sacrifices, the value of what is being given and what is being gained is made explicit. People reflect on their options and decide consciously to make a particular sacrifice. In everyday sacrifices, however, the sacrificial logic very often lies buried. We give up things (not just objects, but also experiences and relationships) of value without reflecting clearly on the motivations, reasons, and consequences of our actions. I argue that one of the reasons sacrifice is so problematic for environmental politics is that we have largely failed to understand both the differences between ordinary and extraordinary sacrifices and the common logic that undergirds them both. Making these distinctions and commonalities clearer can help illuminate both the sacrifices we are already making, with largely dismal ecological results, and the ones we might need to make to achieve a more sustainable society.

Perhaps the best place to begin is with religion, where sacrifice is often expected and accepted. In fact, a faith that does not demand some disciplined forswearing of private satisfactions for larger goods strikes many believers as shallow and unappealing. An important part of what renders religion meaningful is precisely the "making sacred" that constitutes sacrifice. The logic of sacrifice, which demands that we give up something valued to receive something even more precious, lies at the heart of religious ethics and ritual life. Religious sacrifices take many forms, from the minor to the dramatic. A fuller picture of the different meanings and functions of different kinds of religious sacrifice can help us make better sense of the politics of environmental sacrifice.

While religion is probably the most obvious place to look for both everyday and extraordinary sacrifices, there are plenty of examples in secular experience, as well, and especially in domestic life. People readily and repeatedly give up personal comfort, convenience, time, and other benefits for the good of loved ones, especially children. These sacrifices are so ordinary as to go largely unnoticed, by the practitioners, their beneficiaries, and the larger society. It is part of the definition of parenting, and perhaps of family life more broadly, to give up or postpone individual desires for the sake of others. Thus it is part of the identity of parents, as it is of religious believers, to make certain sacrifices on behalf of the larger good that helps make their lives meaningful. A parent (or a true believer) who gives up nothing is probably not a real parent (or believer) at all.

Thus in two important dimensions of human life, familiar even to those without religious affiliation or family commitments, sacrifice is accepted, taken for granted, and often highly valued as part of what makes such experiences meaningful. The kinds of sacrifice expected, and their meaning and impact, vary widely across cultures. Historical and cultural changes, for example, shape the ways that people think about the sacrifices associated with parenting or faith. What some people might reasonably be required to give up, and what is expected in exchange, varies over time. When we think about environmentally motivated sacrifice, it is important to keep in mind the fact that not only are people always giving up some goods for other goods, but that these exchanges vary over time, and it is indeed possible for groups, even entire societies, to accept new forms of sacrifice that seem necessary and worthwhile. This is obviously true in times of crisis, such as a depression or war, but it is also evident in relation to more subtle historical changes, for example, in women's access to education and professional work or in religion's role in cultural identity and cohesion.

The normalcy of sacrifice in some aspects of our lives is not paralleled by acceptance of sacrifice in environmental discourse and practice. Even though the logic of sacrifice is woven into major aspects of most people's lives, in other words, environmentally motivated sacrifices—such as changing eating or driving habits—seem to many an impossible barrier. This paradox is explained, in part, by the fact that some ongoing sacrifices are not acknowledged. We are constantly giving up some goods without having consciously decided to do so, and the lack of explicit acceptance obscures the sacrifices involved. No rational person would willingly give up drinkable water or breathable air, but we do so every day. To talk about the politics of environmental sacrifice, we need to be clearer about sacrifice, in at least two senses: clearer about the different varieties of sacrifice and clearer about the logic of sacrifice embedded in our everyday lives. A better understanding of the nature and role of sacrifice in other contexts, especially in religion and family life, can help reframe, in more acceptable and meaningful terms, the sacrifices necessary for a more effective environmental politics. This will help us reflect on the kinds of sacrifice we are already making and their real costs and benefits. The question for environmental politics, then, becomes not so much whether sacrifice is demanded, but rather, what kinds of sacrifice we are making and should make, and to what end.

Religious Sacrifice

Scholarly discussions often note that the definition of sacrifice is "to make sacred," suggesting a place at the heart of religion itself. Sacrifice is part and parcel of both ordinary and extraordinary experience for participants in a wide range of religions. It takes many forms, some of which are familiar and acceptable to a contemporary Western audience, while others seem strange, offensive, or cruel. More moderate and familiar types of religious sacrifice encompass individual disciplinary practices, such as fasting, pilgrimage, tithing, and penances, in which relatively trivial goods, such as temporary convenience or pleasure, are relinquished in exchange for religious merit. Similar sorts of sacrifice are enacted in some kinds of social action such as charitable works or participation in a sacred crusade or movement. In some rituals, such as the Christian Eucharist (Lord's Supper) or *via crucis* (Way of the Cross), a sacrifice is not so much experienced as represented and reenacted. More extreme forms of religious sacrifice include the infliction of pain, usually on oneself, for example, through severe fasting or self-flagellation, and the killing of nonhuman animals. Here something more significant is being given up, either because the good desired is greater or because the cultural or personal context generates a greater demand. All these varieties of sacrifice were common in many traditions in the past and continue today in some contemporary religions. The most extreme form is human sacrifice, evident in a wide range of cultures, from the biblical story of Abraham and Isaac to precolonial Aztec society, the most extensive collective practitioner of human sacrifice known in human history.

Religious sacrifice thus ranges from ordinary and rather trivial offerings to extraordinary practices that involve great effort and even bloodshed. What unites these sacrificial acts, from the most mundane to the most extreme, is the logic on which they rest: they all gain meaning from the relinquishment of one good for another. This sacrifice is made explicitly religious when it is done for, or in the name of, a divine power. In monotheistic religions, offerings may be understood as thanksgiving, praise, or penance owed to an all-powerful god. In polytheistic traditions, including many indigenous and African-based religions in the Americas, sacrifice is an integral aspect of the reciprocal relationships between humans and the divine, according to which humans give up something precious in return for sacred gifts that make continued life possible.

The ubiquity of sacrifice in diverse religious traditions has generated a great deal of scholarly analysis. One of the most influential theorists of sacrifice is René Girard, whose book *Violence and the Sacred* proposes that violence is the "heart and secret soul" of religion.[1] For Girard, the purpose of sacrificial ritual, and of religion in general, is to contain the universal human inclination to violence. Even more provocatively, Girard asserts that in all sacrifices, "a mob murder is being reenacted, although the scenes will vary in details."[2] This "mob murder" takes as its victim a surrogate, whose suffering enables the ritual participants to suppress or expel the truth about the violence inherent to human nature. This violence must be shifted to a scapegoat, Girard argues, to make possible civilized social life.[3] This view of sacrifice leads Girard to contend that its absence, or at least the absence of dramatic ritual killings, in most contemporary societies is risky because violence that is not displaced in sacrifice might seek expression in other, less controllable aspects of social life.[4] Sacrificial rituals thus perform a valuable and even vital function by displacing and suppressing wilder forms of violence. However, sacrifice also may blind people to their own intrinsic violence so that they are unable to come to terms with it and thus contain it.[5] (Here Girard's debt to Freudian psychology is evident.)

For Girard, religious sacrifice differs in only arbitrary ways from other forms of human violence.[6] Sacrifice is a ritualized, formalized, and contained way of acting on our bloodthirsty instincts. Sacrifice has a definite underlying logic, in Girard's analysis, but one that differs from the version I have described. For Girard, the logic of sacrifice is not the relinquishment of one good to gain something of more value, but rather, the controlled release of violent impulses to prevent more widespread violence. Girard's theory of sacrifice has been widely discussed, approvingly by scholars who believe that religion is inextricably linked to violence of one sort or another, less positively by those who do not find this connection so inevitable. I mention Girard's work because it invariably arises in discussions of religious sacrifice and also because it highlights the significance of sacrifice as a theological, ethical, and practical category within diverse religious traditions. Even if we disagree with Girard, as I mostly do, he provides a starting point for placing sacrifice at the heart of religious and human experience.

Other scholars have acknowledged the centrality of sacrifice but have proceeded less polemically than Girard. For some, religious rituals, including sacrifice, provide a controlled setting in which people can explore and sometimes resolve larger philosophical, moral, and practical issues—not necessarily the barely contained brutality that Girard describes, but perhaps the moral, epistemological, and emotional dilemmas posed by both ordinary and extraordinary events of human life. As Emile Durkheim and many other scholars have asserted, rituals, including sacrifice, can also cement and affirm collective identity, without understanding this identity as requiring the "mob murder" of innocent surrogates.[7] Sacrifice, in this perspective, serves as a specific kind of religious ritual, sharing the more general qualities and purposes of other rites. If ritual is "consecrated behavior," as anthropologist Clifford

Geertz puts it, then sacrificial rituals are those that consecrate particular actions, objects, or beings.[8] They do so by forfeiting certain goods in the name, or for the benefit, of a higher good. In the process, they consecrate the human act of offering, the object offered, and the greater good for which the sacrifice is made.

The most dramatic religious sacrifice is the ritual killing of human beings. Human sacrifice has been significant in a number of cultures, but "the most thorough record of real, historical human sacrifice," as Davíd Carrasco notes, comes from the precolonial Aztec (Mexica) culture, for which regular human sacrifices were a central part of religious life. Curiously, Carrasco adds, most major theories of ritual sacrifice, including Girard's, have ignored Aztec history in favor of examples from Western literary and scriptural sources.[9] While many theorists have avoided Aztec sacrifice, it has received attention from other scholars, whose interpretations have ranged from simplistic condemnations of the Aztecs as brutal heathens to more complex discussions of the ways in which human sacrifice was thought to sustain both the deities and the natural cycles on which human life depended. For historian of religion Kay Almere Read, Aztec sacrifices constitute a kind of "cosmic meal," and acts of sacrifice, while violent, "are also part of biological life, even in the present. No organism can exist without eating, none will exist forever, and when an organism dies, its remains rot and change into that which nourishes other organisms. Destruction does indeed create, even now."[10]

Read's analysis of Aztec rituals underlines the fact that sacrifice simultaneously "makes sacred" and gives up something valued for something even more valuable. In human sacrifice and other sacrificial rituals, Aztecs offered individual lives to the gods to sustain the larger community and even the cosmos itself. This, as Read and others point out, is the sacrificial logic at the heart of the Aztecs' social and moral community. It expresses the fact that we are always giving up some things for other things, consciously or not. It is important to understand this logic not only in relation to religious rituals, but also with regard to the demands of environmental politics. Environmentalists would be well served, I argue, by making explicit the sacrificial logic of everyday life in American culture and by posing explicitly the question of what we are willing to give up, and why.

Sacrifices are made not only in the course of formal rituals, but also in a variety of other contexts, spontaneously or with forethought. In the Christian West, narratives of Jesus' passion, crucifixion, and resurrection communicate a distinctive sacrificial logic that lies at the heart of Christian theology, ethics, and community life. Jesus' martyrdom is not the start of a sacrificial tradition, but rather, the continuation and transformation of long-standing Jewish understandings. In particular, Jewish scriptures express a belief that God may deliver the chosen people because of the sacrifices of martyrs such as the heroes of the Maccabean revolt (c. 176–63 BCE). The sacrifice of select individuals may atone for the collective sins of Israel, a concept that undergirds the Christian understanding of Jesus' sacrifice as a "ransom for many." The sacrifices of the Maccabean martyrs, of Jesus, and of others are commemorated in diverse religious rituals, from the lighting of Hanukkah candles to the via crucis that marks Jesus' path to crucifixion. From the perspective of believers, at least, such rituals do not reenact mob murder, but rather, celebrate particular acts in which individual lives were given up for a greater good. They thereby connect human and sacred histories. They provide models of moral conduct as well as a reminder of what makes their faith, and lives, most meaningful.

Jesus' crucifixion is especially significant for many Christians as a supersacrifice that promises eternal salvation. However, it also marks the start of a tradition of sacrifice that presents martyrdom as a model response to persecution. In this sense, it grounds a model of ethical practice that emphasizes the imitation of Christ (*imitatio Christi*) and especially of his sacrifice. Being a true Christian, in this perspective, entails not simply "worshiping" Jesus, but above all, following his example, which may—probably will—involve risks, dangers, and sacrifices.

Both Jesus' crucifixion and the more general understanding of sacrifice that it evokes are celebrated in Christian rituals such as the Eucharist and via crucis. Such events inculcate a sacrificial logic that encourages people to give up goods of their own. Dramatic, public, religiously celebrated sacrifices, such as those of the Maccabees, of Jesus, or of the Aztec *teotl ixipitlas* (deity impersonators), can give meaning to other sorts of sacrifice, enacted in ordinary or extraordinary circumstances. A powerful example emerged in many parts of Latin America during the political persecution of progressive Christians by military regimes during the 1970s and 1980s. Especially in Central America, activists found parallels between their experiences and stories of Jesus' passion, and also of the martyrdom of early Christians in the Roman Empire. The story of Jesus' life, death, and resurrection provided a culturally familiar and religiously sanctioned lens through which people could make some sense of the difficult times through which they were living. In light of Jesus' passion, the violent deaths of loved ones and their own risks and sacrifices acquired a redemptive meaning.

This was true for many Roman Catholics with whom I spoke during El Salvador's civil war (1981–1992). They often pointed out strong parallels between their experiences and the persecution of Christians in the Roman Empire, who were attacked and often killed for practicing their faith. The early "church of the catacombs" embodies the sacrificial logic of Christianity, in which true believers are willing to give up comfort, safety, and even their lives to follow the true God. Many Salvadorans went further in their analysis of contemporary sacrifice, asserting a similarity between the deaths of Christian activists and Jesus' crucifixion. Well-known victims of political violence, most notably Oscar Romero, the archbishop of San Salvador assassinated in 1980, do not only follow Jesus, but in fact, reenact his passion in their own deaths. This understanding of Christianity as *imitatio Christi* was prominent in early Christianity, when persecution forced believers to be deliberate about what defined their faith and what they were willing to risk in its name. After the persecution of Christians ended in the fourth century CE, faith was understood more often as following or witnessing to, rather than imitating, Christ. The revival of *imitatio Christi*, with its explicitly sacrificial logic, is a notable feature of the progressive Roman Catholicism that developed in Latin America starting in the late 1960s.

These Roman Catholic understandings of political violence were articulated and communicated in specific rituals but also diffused much more broadly throughout the religious community. The logic of sacrifice thus gave meaning to a host of experiences, some with little apparent religious significance. In Central America, tens of thousands of Christian activists acted in politically effective ways because they believed that "unless a grain of wheat falls into the earth and dies, it remains alone; but if it dies, it bears much fruit" (John 12:24). In other words, the suffering and deaths of Christians are required to bring forth the fruit promised by Jesus' incarnation and resurrection.[11] Some members of the community must die to achieve an end that will benefit all—a conclusion perhaps not far removed from the Aztec conviction that divine purposes required the sacrifice of individual human bodies so that the larger community could continue to thrive.

These ancient and contemporary religious examples reveal the connection between religious sacrifice and a more generalized sacrificial logic. Religious rituals, along with scriptures, myths, and moral guidelines, can communicate the message that sacrifice is a necessary part of life, or at least necessary to achieve certain highly valued goods and benefits. This conception, when widely diffused throughout a culture, shapes behavior in areas of life that seem distant from formal religious rituals and institutions such as family life or apparently secular social movements. In such contexts, sacrifice may be experienced as difficult and painful, but still accepted, sometimes even taken for granted. This brings us back to the distinction between ordinary and extraordinary sacrifice, both of which have a place in religious thought and practice. The ubiquity and diversity of sacrifice in religion reveal the distinction as a continuum. Mundane, taken-for-granted religious practices, such as confession, penance, tithing, fasting, and other dietary restrictions, can help inculcate a sacrificial logic that is magnified in extreme and dramatic cases such as Aztec human sacrifices or Central American revolutions.

This logic of sacrifice assumes a basic reciprocity in human social action, including, but not necessarily limited to, interactions with the divine. It teaches people to accept sacrifices of pleasure, comfort, time, or profit not only as meaningful signs of devotion to a divine power, but also as an unavoidable cost of membership in a larger community, which may not be limited to humans, but also includes natural forces, places, and nonhuman animals. Participation in this larger community provides personal identity, peer support, and meaning as well as the basic necessities of life. Sacrifice, perhaps paradoxically, often strengthens social capital, the connections and trust among participants that hold groups together and make them valuable to members. As a result, the associated sacrifices seem worthwhile to most group members. Understanding the logic of sacrifice implicit in religious rituals thus reinforces a crucial point for environmental politics: just as shared sacrifice can reinforce social bonds, so meaningful, worthwhile, and voluntary sacrifice requires participation in community.

Ultimately, the distinction between ordinary and extraordinary sacrifice turns out to be a continuum. The same thing happens to the distinction between seemingly voluntary and imposed kinds of sacrifice. Some sacrifices seem clearly voluntary, such as individual choices to give up something for Lent. Other sacrifices seem to fall well on the opposite end of the spectrum, such as the intended sacrifice of Isaac by Abraham or the actual sacrifice of civilians as a necessary cost of victory in many wars. Some sacrifices are ambiguous in this respect, and others entail both voluntary and involuntary dimensions. Scholars of Aztec culture, for example, debate whether, and which, people went willingly to their fates. Similar debates surround the contemporary phenomenon of suicide bombing, especially when the bomber is a very young person. In all these cases, sacrifice takes on different meanings for the person being sacrificed and for the community as a whole.

Furthermore, the practicalities and the meaning of religious sacrifices vary over time and across cultures, even within the same or closely related religious traditions. Christians living in the Roman Empire during the first few centuries CE must have been willing to sacrifice their lives, at least potentially, simply by practicing their faith. After the conversion of Constantine in the early fourth century, Christianity no longer carried this cost. Roman Catholic priests must forswear sexual activity and parenting, but Protestant pastors need not give up either. Members of Old Order Amish communities do without higher education, motorized vehicles, and utility lines, while their Anabaptist relatives, the Mennonites, embrace all these conveniences. The association of religious commitment with sacrifice, in other words, must be given specificity because not all sacrifices are created equal. Both what must be given up and what is to be gained vary widely.

Religiously mandated sacrifices, further, face varying receptions. Probably not all Aztecs viewed human sacrifice with complete acceptance, just as not all early Christians were willing to sacrifice their lives for their faith. Nor are all Roman Catholics with a vocation to the priesthood willing to sacrifice celibacy, as evidenced by the large number of seminarians and priests who ultimately leave the clergy to marry. Cultural and social trends also affect the ways in which people view religious sacrifice. For example, the ritual killing of nonhuman animals has become less acceptable over time in many traditions, and contemporary religions that practice animal sacrifice, such as Santería, face public opposition from nonpractitioners. Specific practices such as fasting, tithing, and other religious sacrifices have also declined in many religions, even while the symbolic import of sacrifice lingers. In the United States today, according to some observers, religious identity is often defined more by individual expression and satisfaction than by participation in a community that sets standards and makes demands—including demands for sacrifice.[12] Cultural changes, including the privatization and individualization of religious identity, can weaken believers' willingness to make serious sacrifices. A new generation may reject sacrifices that were once taken for granted, especially if they do not acknowledge the sacrifices they *are* making.

Changes in religious life, and the nature and meaning of religious sacrifice, can bring to the surface elements of sacrifice that are relevant for environmental politics. The deliberate, explicit, and even dramatized character of sacrifice in many religious settings can help us identify and analyze the sacrificial logic that lurks less obviously, though not necessarily less powerfully, in other aspects of our lives. It becomes easier to recognize and reflect on sacrifice if we understand that it takes various forms, some less evident than others. Just as Spanish colonizers condemned Aztec sacrifice without questioning the killings sanctioned by their own faith, contemporary Americans may reject the sacrifice of certain goods, such as individual car transport, cheap meat, or expansive single-family homes, without relating these to the loss of other goods, such as clean air, potable water, or endangered species.

Sacrifice in Everyday Life

Religion gives rise to many of the most familiar and resonant examples of ordinary sacrifice. However, in many nonreligious practices, people accept, and often expect, sacrifices both large and small as inextricable dimensions of participation in something larger that is worth the cost. People give up things they value all the time, often with little hesitation or reflection. Many of these everyday sacrifices are not recognized as such, however, because they are not deliberate, voluntary offerings to gain larger, recognized goods. For example, people in the United States daily, little by little, give up things they most value, such as clean water and air, for things that few prize or even want, such as corporate profits.[13] These undesired yet accepted, and even taken for granted, sacrifices are worth attention especially in relation to environmental politics because reframing the debate on sacrifice requires bringing ongoing, often covert sacrifices into the open.

It is helpful to look at some everyday practices that parallel religious sacrifice in being both voluntary and perceived as contributions to a higher good. Most notable, or at least most common, are the sacrifices that accompany everyday domestic commitments, and especially parenting. For the benefit of their children, parents expect, and are expected, to give up or postpone a host of personal goods—freedom, money, flexibility, and above all, time. Time, as sociologist Lillian Rubin points out, has become many parents' "most precious commodity—time to attend to the necessary tasks of family life; time to nurture the relationships between wife and husband, between parents and children; time for oneself, time for others; time for solitude, time for a social life."[14] Working mothers, in particular, give up sleep and leisure activities, including hobbies and time with friends, to get the work done at the job and at home. They sacrifice vacations, they forego time with their spouses and children, and when they are at home, their time is filled not with pleasant activities, but rather, with household maintenance.[15]

Most parents resent these sacrifices at least some of the time. However, most also accept them as part of the cost of raising children. As Sara Ruddick notes, mothering does not "come naturally," but rather requires hard work, discipline, humility, and compromise.[16] The larger good that emerges from such work and sacrifice lies in the present satisfactions of a loving, mutually pleasing relationship between parents and children and also in the future expectation of healthy and happy adults. Parents, especially mothers, who are reluctant to make the necessary sacrifices for their children's well-being are widely perceived as both selfish and unrealistic. The definition of necessary sacrifice varies widely, of course, from those who believe mothers should stay home full-time to those who argue that working mothers can "have it all." Even the most optimistic in the latter category acknowledge that to have both careers and children, parents must give up other goods such as free time, sleep, and discretionary spending.

My point is not to itemize the personal costs of parenting, but rather, to underline that the logic of sacrifice is deeply embedded and widely accepted in family life. People who raise children, in other words, almost invariably realize that their decision will require them to give up important goods over a long period of time. Nonetheless, a high proportion of adults still choose to become parents. They do so because they perceive the inevitable sacrifices as well worth the larger good of rearing children. This is perhaps the clearest and largest-scale example of sacrifice in our society, and probably in any society, apart from the demands of a generalized crisis such as war or devastating natural disaster.

The sacrifices required by parenthood are ordinary, insofar as they are mundane, taken for granted, and generally of a low level, although extreme situations clearly can and do arise. It is important to note that the ordinariness of such sacrifices does not mean that they are natural or inevitable. Some of the burdens of parenting are generated by unjust gender relationships, by legal and political institutions that do not support families, and by economic systems that make it hard for parents to make a living without giving up benefits such as leisure time. In other words, the fact that a certain kind of sacrifice—domestic or religious— is familiar, widespread, and generally accepted does not mean that it cannot be questioned, challenged, and perhaps transformed. This point is important as we move to a discussion of environmental sacrifice.

Ordinary Sacrifices and the Common Good

The ordinary, daily sacrifices of parenting relate to religious sacrifice in several important ways, which can help illuminate both kinds—and ultimately, perhaps, shed light on some of the problems associated with environmentally motivated sacrifice, as well.

First, both religious and parental sacrifices are seen, by those who undertake them and by outsiders, as meaningful and even necessary components of commitment to a larger good. That good may be a god, a child's future, society, or even the cosmos as a whole, but in all cases, it is valuable enough to outweigh the goods that it postpones or eliminates. If the good for which the sacrifice is performed is not of great value, we say the sacrifice is "in vain." And if the goods sacrificed are not truly valued, giving them up is meaningless. This is implicit in the story of Abraham's willingness to kill his only son, Isaac, on God's demand (Genesis 22:1–13): only because the act is so difficult and painful does it seem, to some readers, as religiously meaningful. If it were easy, it would not count in the same way. A sacrifice is not a sacrifice if it does not entail giving up something that the sacrificer values deeply.

Second, when the logic of sacrifice is made explicit, sacrifice does not appear surprising or unreasonable. To the contrary, people who question the demand for sacrifice are the unrealistic ones. New mothers cannot reasonably expect to sleep through the night, Roman Catholic priests should not complain about the demand for celibacy, and soldiers must not (as just war theory insists) shy away from physical danger. These risks, and the actual or potential sacrifices they entail, are part of the identity of a mother, a priest, or a soldier. They are, arguably, part of what makes these roles special and meaningful, even morally elevated. Not just everyone can take on these responsibilities; those who do so must accept sacrifice, loss, and even danger, but in turn, they gain greater goods such as a healthy child, a flourishing church, or a safer nation. If such undertakings were easy and demanded no real sacrifice, more people might sign up, but the meaning and value attached to their roles would diminish considerably.

Third, explicit sacrifices in any sphere are meaningful and acceptable only when they contribute to a good that is greater than the goods being forgone. Sacrifices demanded for lesser goals meet with cynicism and often rejection. This is evident in the maternal activism of antiwar activist Cindy Sheehan, whose soldier son Casey was killed in Iraq in 2004. Sheehan attributes her activism to her maternal role, a combination of regret for her inability to protect her son, anger at the men she holds responsible for his death, and a desire to prevent similar tragedies from shattering other families. In an April 2006 interview, she explained, "I buried my son, and I don't want anyone else burying their son for lies."[17] She is angry not simply because her son died, but because his sacrifice, and hers, was in vain. Sacrifice is part of parenting, as it is part of soldiering, but the sacrifice must be for a good that transcends the goods it swallows.

It is worth noting how exceptional Sheehan is, insofar as she has called into question the normalized sacrifice of young men in war. By challenging the rightness of the Iraq War, she makes explicit a sacrifice—of soldiers' lives—which, while hardly invisible, is sometimes taken for granted. This raises an important point: people routinely make major sacrifices for things that they do not value because these sacrifices are not made explicit and thus are not subject to question. We take for granted the fact that we "have to" sacrifice excellent health care or public education, or clean air and water, or safe highways, or a number of other public (and private) goods, not because we do not value them, and not even because we value the goods for which they are sacrificed (usually lower taxes or corporate profits). We take these sacrifices for granted because they are not called sacrifices; they are simply part of "the way things are." An environmentalist politics of sacrifice must challenge this assumption about how things are and must be.

Fourth, the ordinary, taken for granted, perhaps barely noticed sacrifices demanded by religious or parental commitment are rarely seen as connected to sacrifices required for other goods. The values of the private sphere, including religion and the family, include un-self-interested goods such as loyalty, mutual care, and self-sacrifice. However, these values rarely extend to larger communities, at least in part because the logic of sacrifice is not extended from our personal lives to the public sphere. Many Americans understand their commitments and their sacrifices in religion and family life as discrete, private, and limited, rather than as part of a larger web of commitments to public goods. Religious values and disciplines, for example, are largely contained within a narrow, well-defined sphere, rather than understood as part of a broad commitment to enact religiously grounded values in all aspects of one's life. When the logic of sacrifice is not understood in a broader context, the willingness to make sacrifices for religious or parental commitments is less likely to be transferred to public goods such as environmental sustainability.

Sacrifice and Sustainability

Although the connections between personal life and the public sphere may be weaker than in the past, people still sacrifice for their families and children as well as for their religious institutions. They make sacrifices, as well, through military service, employment, and volunteer activities, at a scale sufficient to suggest that not all sacrifices have become untenable in contemporary culture. However, environmentally motivated sacrifices seem especially difficult to achieve, at least voluntarily. I think that environmental sacrifices are seen as extremely difficult in part because they are categorized as extraordinary practices. Extraordinary sacrifices are those taken for a limited time frame as a result of a major social crisis such as war, natural disaster, or economic collapse. As long as changes in consumption patterns and other environmentally motivated changes are seen as extraordinary sacrifices, they cannot become integrated into major institutions or everyday practices. We would think differently about the politics of environmental sacrifices, I argue, if sustainable patterns in our institutions and behavior could be connected to the logic of sacrifice that is taken for granted in other parts of our lives. This will happen, however, only under conditions that make voluntary sacrifice acceptable on a wide scale.

The first condition is that sacrifice must be for a good that is truly valued. Americans do value the environment, as study after study confirms. However, studies also show that this value only rarely translates into effective action. While approximately 80 percent of the U.S. population express strong concern for the environment, only about 20 percent act on this concern in even small ways.[18] The widespread and well-documented consensus that the natural world is valuable and deserves care does not motivate Americans to put their ecological concern into practice. As the authors of a major study on environmental values in American culture point out, "for environmentally beneficial actions, environmental beliefs and values are necessary but often are not sufficient, given the multiple existing barriers to action."[19] These barriers to action are in many ways barriers to the sacrifices that are perceived as part and parcel of meaningful ecological practice.

One of the barriers is that "the environment" remains fairly abstract, seemingly lacking in immediate benefit. In this respect, environmental sacrifices differ from those that parents make for children, or even those extraordinary sacrifices made during times of crisis. As ecological problems, such as global warming, appear more urgent, they may seem less abstract in the near future. Another barrier is, in some cases, a lack of accurate information. This entails not just inadequate scientific information about the nature of environmental problems, but also, perhaps more often, uncertainty about what sort of action can be effective. People need to understand not simply that we have environmental problems that demand solutions, but precisely what these problems demand in the way of effective actions. We need to know what sacrifices a more sustainable society reasonably requires and what results can reasonably be expected from our individual and collective efforts. This goes hand in hand with making explicit the environmental sacrifices in which we are already engaged, often unconsciously.

Acceptance of environmental sacrifices also requires social networks and support. As noted earlier, social trust and networks are important for acceptance of religious sacrifice, while mutually accepted sacrifices can also reinforce collective ties and group identity. In the case of environmental politics, similarly, social capital can increase community involvement in local sustainability initiatives.[20] A number of social scientists have documented declines in social networks and increases in social isolation in American culture in recent years, although others argue that social networks have not diminished, but rather, merely changed shape.[21] The role of the Internet and other electronic media in democratic politics remains controversial, for instance, on the issue of whether such media reinforce or replace other social ties. There is evidence on both sides of this argument. What is clear is that environmentalists need to understand social capital much better because people who are socially isolated are less likely to act on their values, and people who are socially connected in new ways may well act on their values in similarly innovative forms.

Social capital is especially important if living out ecological values requires sacrifices of time, money, comfort, or other goods. Sacrifices of this sort require shared values and norms as well as social networks of peer support and reinforcement, which make informal punishments and rewards more effective. (In such settings, formal punishments are rarely needed, as is evident in the lives of close-knit religious groups.[22]) Members of such groups accept as normal sacrifices that might seem extraordinary to outsiders. This is due not only to high levels of social capital, but also to structural and institutional arrangements, such as the Old Order Amish rejection of public utilities or private automobiles, that are much less difficult than they would be for outsiders. The

Amish community is organized, socially and technologically, to make life possible, and indeed pleasant, without cars, electricity lines, and other modern conveniences. Even more important, many Amish people would readily point to the ways that mainstream Americans sacrifice, apparently without much resistance or even awareness, goods that the Amish take for granted: the presence of extended family members, mutual aid among neighbors, significant leisure time, and so forth. For example, fifty or more hours of work away from the family every week, which seems ordinary to many Americans, would be unacceptable in an Amish community.

Another important factor in people's willingness (or reluctance) to sacrifice for the common good is political leadership. This is especially evident in regard to environmentally motivated sacrifice. As is often noted, after the attacks of September 11, 2001, President George W. Bush asked Americans to "go shopping." Numerous commentators have contrasted this with President Roosevelt's response to the Pearl Harbor attacks, among other occasions when leaders asked for—and received— significant voluntary sacrifices. Bush again called for shopping as a response to danger in summer 2007, when an economic recession began to appear likely. When national leaders assert that increased consumption is an appropriate and adequate civic response to such challenges, it becomes much more difficult for environmentalists to propose other responses such as reduced consumption.[23]

Reducing consumption for environmental reasons seems subject to particular attack,[24] perhaps because the changes required seem especially burdensome or especially challenging to deeply ingrained habits and values. As presidential spokesperson Ari Fleischer noted in May 2001, "the President also believes that the American people's use of energy is a reflection of the strength of our economy, of the way of life that the American people have come to enjoy. And he wants to make certain that a national energy policy is comprehensive, that includes conservation, includes a way of allowing the American people to continue to enjoy the way of life that has made the United States such a leading nation in the world."[25] Statements such as these suggest that energy consumption is tied up with larger, and largely untouchable, goods such as "the strength of our economy" and "our way of life." Reducing our present use of fossil fuels thus appears to many as an overwhelming burden and an unreasonable sacrifice. Such sacrifices appear so difficult not only because of such political discourse, it is important to note, but also because our society is organized around high levels of individual and collective consumption. In this context, even relatively simple acts as walking or taking the bus, eating less meat, or hanging laundry on a clothesline feel difficult.

Once again, environmentalists need to point out that the American way of life already requires numerous sacrifices. Many of our taken-for-granted practices and institutions, including foreign policy, labor practices, and consumerism, force us to give up things that most Americans value greatly: time with families, open spaces, clean air and water, and security for future generations. For a variety of reasons, many Americans have come to accept these sacrifices and even to believe that they are necessary and inevitable. In this respect, our culture is not so different, perhaps, from that of the Aztecs, who believed that the sun would not continue to shine nor the rain continue to fall if they did not perform human sacrifices. Many Aztecs may have disliked the practice, if they thought about it at all, at the same time as they accepted its necessity. Human sacrifices in the Aztec world were daily, or at least weekly occurrences, widely accepted because they were woven into widespread assumptions about what kept the cosmos intact. Similarly, though less dramatically, contemporary U.S. culture accepts many sacrifices as a result of assumptions about "the way life is" and "the cost of doing business" (or of being a parent, or being Roman Catholic, or working in a particular industry). Seeing parallels such as these may help us understand that every culture accepts certain sacrifices, and certain forms of violence, as so-called normal, our own no less than the Aztecs. Kay Read proposes an important lesson from the study of Aztec sacrifice: "Our initial horror at the practice of human sacrifice may even help if understanding its normality in the Mexica world causes us to question the violence in our own and to ponder how that violence came to be either condoned or considered a normal and familiar part of experience."[26]

The routine acceptance of certain sacrifices, paradoxically, can make it harder for people to accept other sorts of sacrifices. People who take for granted the sacrifice of their health and security as a necessary cost of corporate profits, for example, reject out of hand the possible sacrifice of private automobile travel. Environmentalists need to challenge these assumptions and to ask what is being sacrificed, for example, when green spaces diminish, when air pollution causes widespread health problems, or when species diversity drops. What are we giving up, and for what? Making explicit the implicit sacrifices we make every day is a necessary part of reconceptualizing the environmental politics of sacrifice.

In addition to challenging some presently accepted sacrifices, we need to make certain presently unaccepted sacrifices acceptable. Here we need not only social capital, correct knowledge, and good leadership, but also shifts in cultural perspectives and values, including a reconception of both pleasure and necessity. It is undeniable, at least to all but the most Pollyannaish technological optimists, that to reduce their ecological impact, Americans will have to give up certain pleasures and conveniences. Most people view these sacrifices as unalloyed losses: I won't be able to drive, I won't be able to eat fast food, I'll have to spend more time on the bus, and so forth. Some groups, however, have argued that pleasure and overall quality of life can, in fact, increase when certain kinds of consumption are reduced. The Center for a New American Dream (CNAD), for example, takes as its slogan "More fun, less stuff!" CNAD and other advocates of "voluntary simplicity" emphasize what people gain from reducing consumption, rather than what they give up. Another example is the "Compact" in San Francisco, a group of professionals who decided to give up new purchases for an entire year. While the project began with an image of environmental activism as "penitential fasting,"[27] the reality for the participants seems to have been quite different. The group's dependence on social networking has greatly enriched their sense of community and their quality of life. Rather than feeling deprived, they report feeling happier, freer, and more energized. Having developed a taste for their new lifestyle, some members of the Compact are carrying on for another year. Such projects suggest that the reconceptualization of pleasure along more sustainable lines is, in fact, possible, and they indicate some possible paths toward the larger cultural, political, and economic transformations that will be necessary.

Reconceiving pleasure so that it encompasses environmentally responsible behavior is a vital part of the struggle to create a more just and sustainable society. Sometimes the change will entail not the substitution of pleasures for pleasure, but rather, the sacrifice of pleasure and convenience for a less comfortable but more sustainable alternative. The pleasures and the sacrifices will vary, as different people have different options available to them. Structural and material factors, such as the availability of alternative transportation, local food, and responsive local (and larger) governments, will shape the possibilities open to people in any particular place, just as their personal circumstances will help determine what changes they can make. In almost every case, however, it is possible to begin some kind of transformation, to help people develop the "taste," as philosopher Nathaniel Barrett puts it, for environmental action, even sacrifices.[28]

I started with religion as one of the most important realms of human action in which sacrifice is acceptable, meaningful, and even desirable. Religion not only serves as a model in this way but also holds the potential to inspire and sustain specifically environmental sacrifices in contemporary American culture. Religion undergirds environmental values for many Americans, as the authors of *Environmental Values in American Culture* note. Even nonreligious people, they found, refer to "divine creation" in relation to the value of nature. "Regardless of whether one actually believes in biblical Creation," they explain, "it is the best vehicle we have to express this value."[29] While the expression of value does not lead to practical action, religion has proved an effective motivator of moral action in many other circumstances. Religious institutions and communities might serve as powerful allies, then, in efforts to make environmentally motivated sacrifices acceptable, meaningful, and even normalized throughout American culture.

Environmentalists, including those contributing to this book, disagree about whether sustainability requires sacrifice. Some argue that it will certainly require changes in individual lifestyles but that these shifts need not be seen or felt as sacrifices. It is true that the sacrifices of individuals can be reduced by technological innovations and by public policies that support more sustainable regional planning, energy and food production, and so forth. I am not convinced, however, that all sacrifice can be avoided. We—especially the affluent Western we—will have to give up some things that we rightly value. The transition to a more environmentally sustainable society will entail major changes not only in institutions, infrastructure, and technology but also in most people's everyday practices. Many people will view at least some of these changes—eating differently, driving less, living in different kinds of houses, perhaps in different settings—as sacrifices of goods they value, including flexibility, comfort, convenience, and money. Widespread adoption of these practices will thus require willingness to sacrifice such goods, which in turn will require at least some of the factors discussed earlier: leadership, social support, and new definitions of pleasure, among others.

Individual behavioral changes, of course, will not be adequate to resolve environmental problems. We also need major political and economic shifts, but these cannot be enacted without political will and, thus, a certain degree of ideological consensus. This consensus must go beyond the already existing sense that "nonhuman nature is important and needs protecting" to decisions to protect it in concrete ways. Such political agreements will emerge not only from different electoral decisions, but also from significant institutional shifts, for example, in the regulatory roles of local, state, and national governments. All these changes can emerge, at least in a democratic society, only as a result of a widespread political consensus, which requires leadership, organizing, and ultimately, personal commitments not just to a movement, but to the kind of identity and actions it demands. This means, again, that people will have to accept certain apparent sacrifices as part of a larger political vision. We will have to be willing, for example, to take the bus, to live in smaller houses, to lower the thermostat, to eat differently, and to pay higher taxes.

We can help to make these and other environmentally motivated sacrifices more acceptable by connecting them to the sacrificial logic of everyday life. Most of us give up things we value, large and small, all the time, for our children, our faith, and our careers. These sacrifices are not only accepted, but often are essential to making our lives meaningful and pleasurable. They are, furthermore, bound up with participation in such an undertaking, part of the identity of a parent or a believer. As a student at Allegheny College noted during a discussion of sacrifice, such sacrifice becomes "ingrained in who you are and doesn't feel like a sacrifice."[30] Presently, the identity of a person who "cares about the environment" does not carry with it any concomitant practical demands. This needs to change so that environmentally responsible behavior becomes part of environmental identity, not an exceptional or heroic undertaking that cannot be expected of ordinary people. Only with such normalizing of environmental sacrifice can we create a more sustainable society.

Acknowledgments

I am grateful to John Meyer for his very helpful comments on an earlier version of this chapter, and also to John, Michael Maniates, and the participants in the September 2007 meeting at Allegheny College for their insights and inspiration. I am indebted to Kay Read for the notion of a logic of sacrifice as well as for her work on Aztec sacrifice and ethics.

Notes

1. René Girard, *Violence and the Sacred* (Baltimore: Johns Hopkins University Press, 1977), 30.

2. Ibid., 199–200.

3. Ibid., 83.

4. Ibid., 188.

5. Ibid., 82.

6. Ibid., 40.

7. Emile Durkheim, *The Elementary Forms of the Religious Life* (New York: Free Press, 1965), 475–476.

8. Clifford Geertz, "Religion as a Cultural System," in *The Interpretation of Cultures* (New York: Basic Books, 1973), 112.

9. Davíd Carrasco, *City of Sacrifice: The Aztec Empire and the Role of Violence in Civilizations* (Boston: Beacon, 1999), 7–8.

10. Kay Almere Read, *Time and Sacrifice in the Aztec Cosmos* (Bloomington: Indiana University Press, 1998), 59.

11. Anna L. Peterson, "Religious Narratives and Political Protest," *Journal of the American Academy of Religion* 64, no. 1 (1996): 27–44. See also Anna L. Peterson, *Martyrdom and the Politics of Religion: Progressive Catholicism in El Salvador's Civil War* (Albany: State University of New York Press, 1997), and Anna L. Peterson and Brandt G. Peterson, "Martyrdom, Sacrifice, and Political Memory in Central America," *Social Research* 75 (2008): 511–542.

12. Bellah, Robert, Richard Madsen, William M. Sullivan, Ann Swidler, and Steven M. Tipton, *Habits of the Heart: Individualism and Commitment in American Life* (Berkeley: University of California Press, 1985), 232.

13. Michael Maniates points out that alternative energy and other sustainable businesses often show higher profits than polluting and exploitative industries, despite government policies and subsidies favoring the latter.

14. Lillian Rubin, *Families on the Fault Line: America's Working Class Speaks about the Family, the Economy, Race, and Ethnicity* (New York: Harper and Row, 1994), 244–245.

15. Arlie Russell Hochschild with Anne Machung, *The Second Shift* (New York: Penguin Books, 2003), 10.

16. Sara Ruddick, *Maternal Thinking: Toward a Politics of Peace* (Boston: Beacon Press, 1995), and Sara Ruddick, "Maternal Thinking," *Feminist Studies* 6, no. 2 (1980): 342–367.

17. Sam Kornell, "Maternal Instincts" [interview with Cindy Sheehan], *The Santa Barbara Independent*, April 20, 2006, http://www.independent.com/news/2006/apr/20/maternal-instincts/.

18. Duke University, "Survey: Why Pro-Environmental Views Don't Always Translate into Votes," Duke University, October 2005, http://www.dukenews.duke.edu/2005/09/nicholaspoll.html.

19. Willett Kempton, James S. Boster, and Jennifer A. Hartley, *Environmental Values in American Culture* (Cambridge, MA: MIT Press, 1995), 220.

20. Paul Selman, "Social Capital, Sustainability and Environmental Planning," *Planning Theory and Practice* 2, no. 1 (2001): 13–30.

21. Robert D. Putnam, *Bowling Alone: The Collapse and Revival of American Community* (New York: Simon and Schuster, 2000). See also Bellah et al., *Habits of the Heart*.

22. Anna L. Peterson, *Seeds of the Kingdom: Utopian Communities in the Americas* (New York: Oxford University Press, 2005).

23. Leaders must not only ask for sacrifices, but must also possess the moral authority to make this call seem legitimate. In August 2007, Democratic presidential candidate John Edwards told a labor group in Florida that he would ask Americans to make a big sacrifice: their sport utility vehicles. "I think Americans are actually willing to sacrifice," Edwards said during a forum held by the International Association of Machinists and Aerospace Workers. "One of the things they should be asked to do is drive more fuel efficient vehicles." The former North Carolina senator was asked specifically if he would tell them to give up their SUVs. He said yes. Perhaps predictably, Edwards received massive and often vicious criticisms for his comments. (His wife, Elizabeth Edwards, was attacked just as harshly for suggesting, around the same time, that she would give up eating nonlocal foods, such as tangerines, for environmental reasons.) One reason for the attacks on Edwards was his perceived "hypocrisy"—here is a wealthy man who has several expensive cars (perhaps an SUV) and a big house, calling on ordinary Americans to give up something he had not already sacrificed. Edwards didn't appear to be walking his talk, which opened him to criticism. Similar attacks have faced other ecologically motivated calls for sacrifice and behavioral change, as Al Gore, among others, can attest. However, most public figures walk their talk imperfectly, at best. A gap between expressed values and actual behavior is common, if not practically mandatory, in politics. Quite often, the gap is ignored or accepted as a necessary "part of doing business" or politics. On John and Elizabeth Edwards, see "Do 'Do as I Say,' Not as I Doo-Doo," Grinning Planet, http://www.grinningplanet.com/2007/03-13/environmental-hypocrites.htm, and "John Edwards: Americans Should 'Sacrifice'

SUVs for Environment," Fox News.com, August 27, 2007 http://www.foxnews .com/story/0,2933,294974,00.html.

24. E.g., Adam Stein, "Paging Nordhaus and Shellenberger: Please, Can We Lay Off the Calls for Sacrifice in the Face of Climate Change?" Grist, http://grist-mill.grist.org/story/2008/1/2/144732/4299, responding to the *New York Times* editorial "The One Environmental Issue," January 1, 2008, http://www.nytimes .com/2008/01/01/opinion/01tue1.html?_r=1&oref=slogin.

25. "Press Briefing by Ari Fleisher," Whitehouse.gov, May 7, 2001, http:// georgewbush-whitehouse.archives.gov/news/briefings/20010507.html.

26. Read, *Time and Sacrifice*, 32. See also Kay Read, "Three Spaces Marking Child Sacrifice," in *Suffer the Little Children: Urban Violence and Sacred Space*, ed. Kay Almere Read and Isabel Wollaston (New York: Continuum, 2001), 121–142.

27. Nathaniel Barrett, unpublished statement prepared for a conference on "Values and Practices," Gainesville, FL, April 2007.

28. Ibid.

29. Kempton et al., *Environmental Values*, 92.

30. Student member of the audience, panel discussion on "The Politics of Sacrifice," Allegheny College, Meadville, PA, September 18, 2008.

6

The Sacred and the Profane in the Ecological Politics of Sacrifice

Karen Litfin

A Crisis of Meaning

If progress is synonymous with increased consumption of goods, does ecological sustainability entail the end of progress? "We'll all have to make personal sacrifices," we often hear, which, given the equation of progress with material accumulation, can only be heard as a gloomy prognosis. But what if our culture's concept of sacrifice is upside down? What if, rather than being a painful exercise in self-abnegation, sacrifice is actually "a celebration of consumption and being consumed?"[1] What if, rather than being either a superstitious act of futility or a heroic act of altruism, sacrifice is understood as a fundamental law of the cosmos to which humans can align themselves joyously? This chapter articulates a life-affirming perspective on the politics of sacrifice, a perspective that is rooted in a cosmology of interdependence that understands people as an integral part of a participatory universe. This reading of sacrifice helps to address the crisis of meaning implicit in concerns about "the end of progress."

The "environmental crisis"—really a creeping megacrisis, in which the exponential expansion of human populations is coupled with even greater increases in consumption—is generally understood as a material phenomenon. This many tentacled crisis includes the mass extinction of species, unprecedented climate change, unsustainable resource depletion, and myriad pollution dangers. While the widespread formula for quantifying environmental degradation, $I = PAT$,[2] is a useful thumbnail sketch of the *material* dimensions of the crisis, it is silent about the deeper *ideational* forces at work. If human behavior is rooted in systems of meaning, as I believe it is, then the environmental crisis must be understood as a crisis of meaning. Human action, relationships, and their material effects are a reflection of human consciousness.[3]

The prevailing materialist framing of the crisis inevitably sends a bleak and moralistic message to the mainstream public in high-consumption societies, or at least one that is received as such. The common perception is that sustainable consumption will entail sacrifice, which in turn implies unwanted limitations on personal freedom and comfort. Ironically, this perception of sacrifice as negative and limiting is shared not only by those who oppose policies aimed toward sustainable consumption, but even by many environmentalists themselves. The primary difference is that the former see such sacrifice as morally and politically offensive, while the latter view it as necessary. This places environmentalists in the awkward position of appearing to dictate through policy what, in the minds of many, should be personal lifestyle choices—thus the embittered accusation of "eco-fascism." Less strident global consumers, on the other hand, may simply succumb to paralyzing guilt. As Mitchell Thomashow notes, the blame-guilt circuit involves "feeling victimized and exploited by a situation that is out of one's control, that was unexpected, or for which someone else was initially responsible. This casts a disquieting shadow, becomes a place of perpetual suffering, in which people shift from blame to guilt to denial, powerless to take action, and plagued by doubt. Rather than being moved to action, they are immobilized by guilt."[4]

Yet across the spectrum from green to antigreen, and including the immobilized guilt-ridden, there is broad agreement that sustainable consumption will require personal sacrifice and varying degrees of self-denial. At first glance, this consensus might seem surprising. Yet, as I will argue, it is symptomatic of a deeper cultural ontology to which both sides subscribe. In cultures premised on individualism and a notion of progress as consumptive accumulation, sacrifice will inevitably be understood as fundamentally constraining, painful, and self-abnegating. From this perspective, such a "reflexive focus on sacrifice funnels scholars, activists and policymakers alike into a dismal, depressing, and anti-democratic politics of change."[5]

There is, however, a far more uplifting perspective, one that recognizes the need for major reductions in consumption by global overconsumers, yet frames that recognition in light of an affirmative view of sacrifice. One point of entry to that perspective is through the root meaning of sacrifice, derived from *sacre* (sacred) and *facere* (to make).[6] Rather than engendering a sense of limitation and constraint, true sacrifice is a gift that enlarges the giver by linking him or her to forces and wider circles of identification beyond his or her ordinary sense of self. Outside our own modern cultural context, sacrifice is a nearly universal practice whose effects have been generally understood as positive. Though the forms it takes vary greatly from one culture to the next, anthropologists affirm that sacrifice typically promotes both social cohesion and a sense of deep relationship with the cosmos and transcendental forces. Naturally, we may find specific forms of sacrifice, especially the most gory rituals of human sacrifice, morally abhorrent, and given our own cultural context, we may even find the whole idea of sacrifice economically dangerous or politically irrelevant. Nonetheless, if sacrifice is in its essence a nearly universal social practice with beneficial effects, then a deeper understanding of its inner meaning and contemporary relevance could cut across the lines that divide greens and antigreens, and perhaps also inspire the guilt-ridden and the immobilized. Yet, as I will suggest, sacrifice in a postindividualistic world will entail significant differences from earlier forms in terms of how it functions both in material and ideational terms.

To the secular mind, introducing any notion of the sacred into the politics of sacrifice can only mean trouble. From this perspective, the superstitious, dangerous, and wasteful sacrificial practices of the past have been supplanted by reason, individual rights, and market exchange. I hope to show, however, that sacrifice has not disappeared in rationalized societies; it has merely gone underground. Far from being an invalid or nonexistent form of human activity, sacrifice in modernity is ubiquitous but largely unconscious. The point, then, is to uncover its dynamics and its manifestations. If sacrifice is, in fact, a nearly universal cultural practice, then there are two crucial questions to ask with respect to an ecological politics of sacrifice. First, what is and has been sacrificed in the name of the modern pursuit of progress? Second, how might we articulate an affirmative vision of sacrifice that is politically relevant in an ecologically full world?

I will first frame sacrifice in terms of a holistic ontology rooted in cyclical processes and the reciprocity of gift exchange, and then consider some possibilities for a scientific grounding of an affirmative perspective on sacrifice, including earth systems science, the universe story, and the positive psychology movement. Drawing from history, the social sciences, and theology, I then suggest that sacrifice, far from being rare, is actually ubiquitous and serves many of the same crucial functions across cultures. If this is the case, then we should expect to find sacrifice showing up in some surprising places in societies that place a high value on rational choice and individual rights. Ironically, as I will argue, consumptive individualism, rejecting either the existence of sacrifice or its validity (or both), has spawned a global sacrificial economy.

The challenge, then, is to uncover who and what are being sacrificed and in the name of what "gods." Finally, I cite some concrete contemporary examples of an affirmative sacrificial ontology and relate these to a general outline of a celebratory politics of sacrifice, one that offers a promising proxy to "the end of progress" in an ecologically full world. As Thomas Princen argues in chapter 7, the "sovereign consumer" must be dethroned. While he rightly highlights the possibilities for an affirmative politics of sacrifice implicit in alternative sources of individual identity, such as citizenship, I highlight also the possibilities implicit in ontological sources of meaning making. To revive, in our present context, the ancient meaning of sacrifice as "to make sacred by offering" would be to rejoin the larger community of life that extends to other people and creatures living now and in the future. Under such a cosmology of radical interdependence, the emphasis shifts from consumer society's preoccupation with *belongings* to a more deeply satisfying focus on *belonging*.

An Alternative Ontology and Its Transhistorical Expression

As we see the world, so shall we act on it. If we fundamentally believe that the world consists of separate, disconnected entities and that the security of the individual depends on his or her ability to protect himself or herself from the vicissitudes of external forces, whether natural or human, then we will construct the social and technological means to gain that protection. The pursuit of consumptive accumulation seems to be an inevitable consequence of such an ontology. This is not necessarily a good or a bad thing. As I will suggest later, individualism has served a noble purpose in constituting the person as a self-aware bearer of rights and responsibilities. Yet its usefulness is wearing thin in an ecologically full world—most acutely so among the global overconsumers. From the vantage point of an individualistic ontology, sacrifice is generally associated with loss. The dictionary definition[7] begins with the traditional idea of an offering to a deity in propitiation or homage, at most a marginal practice in secular societies, and then turns to the commercial context of sacrifice as "selling at a loss." In those cases in which it is seen as surrendering a desired good for the sake of "a higher or more pressing claim," sacrifice takes on the hue of bargaining by a rational actor. Yet, from what we can glean of traditional cultures and what we can infer from a holistic ontology, the emphasis on loss or bargaining misses the point.

A cosmology of interdependence and wholeness offers a very different perspective. Here, the root impulse behind sacrifice is a devotional movement, a "celebration of consumption and being consumed," a recognition of cosmic or transcendental forces beyond the individual to which one is indebted for one's very existence and to which one responds with spontaneous gratitude. To sacrifice, then, is to celebrate these forces and to link oneself intimately with them by returning the gift. The psychology of loss or bargaining associated with sacrifice in the secular mind is quite foreign to the more reverential attitude that we find in a holistic ontology. While the forms that sacrifice has taken traditionally vary greatly, as do the forces and deities to which sacrifice is offered, the deeper psychological and social meaning of sacrifice as participation in a cosmos rooted in gift exchange seems to be universal.

An eloquent expression of a holistic ontology, one that does not revert to what might be perceived by the modern mind as an archaic outlook, is offered by Sri Aurobindo. Because it stands in such contrast to the individualistic worldview, I quote from it extensively:

The law of sacrifice is the common divine action that was thrown out into the world in its beginning as a symbol of the solidarity of the universe. . . . The acceptance of the law of sacrifice is a practical recognition by the ego that it is neither alone in the world nor chief in the world. . . . Each existence is continually giving out perforce from its stock; out of its mental receipts from Nature or its vital and physical assets and acquisitions and belongings a stream goes to all that is around it. And always again it receives something from its environment in return for its voluntary or involuntary tribute. For it is only by this giving and receiving that it can effect its own growth while at the same time it helps the sum of things. At length, though at first slowly and partially, we learn to make the conscious sacrifice; even, in the end, we take joy to give ourselves and what we envisage as belonging to us in a spirit of love and devotion to That which appears for the moment other than ourselves and is certainly other than our limited personalities. . . . The true essence of sacrifice is not self-immolation, it is self-giving; its object is not self-effacement, but self-fulfillment; its method not self-mortification, but a greater life.[8]

We find in this passage a profound intermingling of the transcendent and the ordinary. Though Sri Aurobindo's words hearken back to the mystical formulation of the Upanishads, "the eater eating is eaten," they also resonate in very practical terms with the essence of social life. In community and family life, one receives in proportion to what one gives. Similarly, in sports and education, one grows in aptitude to the extent that one gives oneself to the process. We become what we give ourselves to. The scholar becomes a scholar by giving himself or herself to studies; the musical becomes a musician by giving himself or herself to music. Even the secular mind, with its reflexive aversion to the transcendental and cosmic dimensions of sacrifice, is compelled to acknowledge its social and psychological function, although the subsequent instinct is to reduce apparent self-giving to self-interested bargaining. Still, this recognition represents perhaps a small crack in the armor.

Given the modern aversion to sacrifice, one may be surprised to learn of its ubiquity across human culture. While its forms vary widely, ranging from the concrete offerings of human, animal, and plant life to the spiritual sacrifice of self, sacrifice has historically served a range of social, psychological, and religious functions. From a religious perspective, sacrifice is "a gift to a god that establishes a flow between the giver and the god."[9] It may serve as a vehicle for redemption, expiation, or transcendence. Many traditions, including those of Judaism, Christianity, and Islam, posit in their conceptions of sacrifice a direct connection between divine generosity and human generosity. Yet the social and religious aspects of sacrifice are not distinct; sacrifice is foundational to communal living and, in many cultures, confers on the offerer the qualities of a deity.[10] At a minimum, in the minds of its practitioners, sacrifice establishes a crucial relationship and flow of communication between oneself and forces or beings beyond oneself.

From a social perspective, sacrifice and its close relative, gift giving, are rooted in the perception of interdependence and reciprocity in a holistic cosmos. In such a cosmos, the notions of psychological and social independence that are so foundational to modern life are foreign; every level of existence, from the family, to the community, to the larger sphere of nonhuman nature, is constituted by relationship and reciprocity. M. F. C. Bourdillon finds as a common feature of all forms of sacrifice the ability to bring peace and contribute to social order.[11] More generally, gift giving is considered by anthropologists as "a fundamental bedrock of human civilization," which, although "marginalized in the modern context of utilitarian economic exchange," displays an impressive continuity through widely disparate historical periods and cultures.[12]

The social, psychological, and religious dimensions of sacrifice, while conceptually distinct, are in practice intimately interwoven. According to Marcel Mauss, perhaps the most eminent social scientist on the subject, sacrifice simultaneously serves religious, juridical, economic, social, and psychological functions. It is a "total social phenomenon, . . . a paradigmatic engagement of the material, the organic and bodily, the psychological and political in a wider choreography of social form which itself had a lasting historical character."[13] Because sacrifice serves as an integrative bridge within a holistic cosmos, there are no categorical oppositions between psyche and body, the individual and society, the sacred and the profane. Likewise, sacrifice is a means of both integration and differentiation. Sacrifice is a primary means by which people are brought together and constituted as a community; conversely, sacrifice is believed to separate and protect them from defilement and disease. In this sense, the functions of communion and expiation are interdependent. Communion, a form of integration, and expiation, a mode of differentiating, work together; integration is not possible without differentiation. The community that forges communal bonds, for instance, through participation in a sacrificial meal, simultaneously distinguishes itself from other social groups and perhaps also expiates itself from sin or some negativity.[14] The Christian Eucharist is perhaps the most prominent premodern sacrificial ritual that has persisted alongside secular society.

While the history of sacrifice points to a common underlying ontology of interdependence and reciprocity, that history is not static, but rather, suggests a developmental trajectory. Most anthropological and theological studies concur with Mauss's finding that the earliest forms of sacrifice emphasized physical offerings made according to highly ritualized practices, whereas later modes of sacrifice emphasize consciousness and "attitudes of soul."[15] In many traditions, most obviously Vedic culture, a given sacrificial ritual could be understood literally and practiced mechanically by the masses, while having an altogether esoteric meaning for spiritual initiates. Within the Judeo-Christian tradition, there was a movement away from earlier pagan "cultic sacrifices" toward a focus on morality and obedience to God's law. In the Psalms, for instance, God demands a total sacrifice of self, rather than any burned offering.[16] With the sacrifice of Jesus and the spread of Christianity, human sacrifice became increasingly rare.[17] Thus the New Testament calls on its readers to be "like living stones built into a spiritual house, to be a holy priesthood, to offer spiritual sacrifices acceptable to God."[18] One might wonder if there is any relationship between, on one hand, the dematerialization of sacrifice over time and, on the other, its relative invisibility in modern societies. As I will suggest in the next section, sacrifice did not disappear with modernity, but only went underground.

The developmental trajectory of sacrifice is also associated with widening circles of identification and the enlargement of self. At various points in human history, the family, then the tribe, then the nation became so dear that people were willing to sacrifice themselves for "the greater good." The consequences of consumption in today's economy seem to call us beyond the family, community, and nation to a planetary circle of identification.

Contrary to modernity's embrace of "possessive individualism,"[19] self-giving seems to be built into the human condition and correlated with psychological maturity. Parenting, which for many species is a short-term commitment, is an eighteen-year project, at a minimum, and a lifelong labor of devotion for humans. Developmental psychologists believe that, while the adolescent's task is to establish a clear sense of individual identity, the adult's developmental task is one of "generativity," cultivating and propagating one's creative energies to return the gifts one has received.[20] Yet this propensity toward generosity does not only emerge with adulthood. As recent findings in experimental evolutionary anthropology indicate (and any observant mother will affirm), the human impulse toward self-giving shows itself as early as eighteen months in the spontaneous helpfulness of toddlers.[21] This suggests that the sacrificial ontology of interdependence and reciprocity is not just a relic of primitive cultures, but is endemic to human social and psychological life.

Because there is a close relationship between sacrifice, gift giving, and gratitude, our understanding of an ontology of interdependence would not be complete without some discussion of the nature of gifts and the psychology of gratitude. This discussion will also return us to the seemingly forgotten question of environmental politics. In his wide-ranging investigation into "the gift," Lewis Hyde contrasts gifts, which create and enhance the sense of relationship, with commodities, which are acquired through transactions and tend to erase the perception of bonds. "Gifts," he observes, "do not earn profit, they give increase."[22] The potlatch, for instance, was a sometimes extravagant gift-giving ceremony that celebrated the abundance of nature. The tribes of the Pacific Northwest, for instance, believed that salmon took on human form while they lived in the ocean and returned to the rivers as fish to feed their brothers on land. The potlatch not only fostered a sense of social solidarity, but also honored the sacrificial gift of the salmon in a spirit of deference and gratitude.[23] Their relationship to the salmon was a natural consequence of an underlying ontology of interdependence, in which human existence is embedded in a world of gift exchange. Such examples of naturalistic practices of gift giving among native peoples abound and were part of a worldview that generated relatively sustainable consumption in those cultures.

The nature of the gift, unlike goods that can be bought and sold, is that it must be kept in motion. The recipient of a gift may be said to suffer a debt of gratitude until he or she somehow returns the favor or sets the gift back into motion. The logic of gifts, like a river, is one of flow, whereas in a market system, wealth is disengaged from the flow and becomes concentrated in pools. Scarcity appears when wealth cannot flow. Like a river, if the gift flow is dammed up, it will stagnate, and the dam (the one who hoards) will metaphorically burst.[24] A similar logic holds for one's personal talents; if we do not offer our inner gifts to something beyond ourselves, then we stagnate with them. Contrary to the logic of possessive individualism, we do not own our gifts, but rather serve only as a channel for their movement. As an example, on a Roman birthday, a person was expected to give a gift that came from his or her *genius*, or his or her endowment at birth. If the gift of one's own talents was not set free during the course of one's life, one's *genius* was thought to be in bondage when one died.[25]

As I will suggest in the following section, this perspective did not disappear with the rise of secular modernity; it only became marginalized. From the vantage point of radical interdependence, gift flow, which lies at the crux of sacrifice, can never disappear; it can only be occluded or misunderstood. On closer inspection, we see that the market economy actually rests on the foundation of a multilayered gift economy of symbiotic biological and social relationships. Modern societies, like all societies, are built on the accumulated wealth of previous ages. Family, friendship, mutual assistance, and solidarity are the very fabric of society; in the absence of what has been called the unpaid "care economy," market economies could not function. Indeed, the care economy often repairs some of the social, psychological, and ecological damage done by the commercial and public economy in the name of development.[26]

The dawning environmental megacrisis, we might say, reveals the hidden existence of natural gift flows on which the global economy depends. The relatively new scientific fields of ecology and earth system science, for instance, encompass the study of the basic cycles of give and take that make human existence possible.[27] Under an ontology of interdependence, "natural resources" are not available for exploitation, but rather, are gifts to be received in gratitude and kept in motion indefinitely. A primary message of the environmental megacrisis is that the illusion of human separateness from the rest of creation is becoming increasingly unsustainable, both conceptually and materially. Rather than leading to a dismal sacrificial environmentalism, this realization can engender a celebratory sense of belonging that is also grounded in scientific understanding. In the words of theoretical physicist John Wheeler, "The universe does not exist 'out there' independent of us. We are inescapably involved in bringing about that which appears to be happening. We are not only observers. We are participators. In some strange sense this is a participatory universe."[28] A holistic ontology of interdependence and reciprocity depicts a fundamentally participatory universe. As human beings, we can uniquely participate by consciously receiving the innumerable gifts that we could not possibly have earned and, by responding with a spontaneous gratitude, offering our own gifts in return. In receiving the gifts of human relationships as well as earth's gifts of water, air, food, and warmth, we participate in a "continuum of personal to cosmic kindness"[29] to which gratitude and self-giving are the natural upwelling response.

Premised on a holistic ontology, an ecological politics of sacrifice would not be about compulsion, guilt, or burdened self-sacrifice; rather, it would grow out of a sense of self as interwoven with earth, cosmos, species, and society. Sacrifice, then, would facilitate engagement with a participatory universe and would therefore regain its original meaning of "to make sacred by giving." Our politics would follow from our sense of who we are in relation to others—other people (perhaps in distant places and perhaps not yet living) and other species. If human development proceeds by the widening of our circles of identification, then an ecological identity rooted in a holistic ontology represents an important developmental achievement and need not entail any loss of individuality. This, in essence, is what Mitchell Thomashow means in saying that "ecological identity is a way of saying grace."[30]

Making Sacrifice Visible

In the previous section, I intentionally painted a fairly rosy picture of sacrifice for two reasons: to show that it can be grounded in a celebratory ontology of interdependence and to counterbalance its contemporary association with loss and self-denial. I also painted a rather stark contrast between a sacrificial cosmology of mutuality and the perpetual flow of gifts, and a market economy based on acquisition and the perpetual drive for increased production and consumption. In this section, I will paint a more complex picture. If we live in an interdependent universe, rather than an atomistic one, then existence without self-offering and mutuality is a chimera. The implications for consumerist culture are twofold: first, sacrifice and self-giving cannot disappear altogether, but rather, must somehow exist alongside individualism and consumption. If this is so, then some of the groundwork for a celebratory politics of sacrifice has been laid because sacrifice is not completely foreign to the status quo, even if it is undervalued. Second, and of vital significance to an ecological politics of sacrifice, to the extent that the *belief* in the primacy of consumption creates the *illusion* of getting without giving, *sacrifice goes underground.* Thus, when interdependence is denied or occluded, people tend to be unaware of what actually *is* being sacrificed, to what "gods," and to what ends. This is precisely why environmental education can be such a painful process, for it entails becoming "disillusioned."

In this section, I show first that sacrifice and the modalities of self-giving associated with an ontology of interdependence are not altogether foreign, but are surprisingly widespread, even in secular society. As a consequence, the task for an affirmative ecological politics of sacrifice is more to tap into what already exists as a strong undercurrent than to generate it ex nihilo. Establishing a positive grounding in what already exists is important for this section's second task: to uncover some of the ways in which consumptive individualism conceals sacrifice. The concepts of shadow ecology and ecological debt are particularly helpful in this task of disillusionment. Finally, I explore the possibility that the ontology of individualism has, paradoxically, made a significant contribution to the unfolding of a holistic ontology. The free, rational, and autonomous individual, even if illusory from a holistic perspective, is now a social construction with real effects in political, economic, and psychological life. An affirmative ecological politics offers the opportunity for that individual to enter into a larger sense of self, sacrificing the more destructive expressions of his separative identity on the altar of ecological vitality and global justice. Such a sacrifice need not entail the death of the individual; instead, it represents his entry into ecological adulthood through a sense of deep engagement with a participatory universe.

If there is anything resembling Sri Aurobindo's perception of a universal law of solidarity pervading the entire universe, then sacrifice cannot disappear even in social conditions that deny its existence or its relevance. Indeed, we find sacrificial practices cropping up both at the margins and even sometimes at the center of modern societies. Similarly, gift economies exist alongside the market economy, both repairing and propping it up. In his comparison of archaic and modern cultures, Mircea Eliade, the pioneering scholar of religions, observed that the sacred persists even in cultural contexts that privilege the profane. Following the logic of the return of the repressed, however, it typically emerges in distorted forms.[31] Likewise, sacrifice persists in secular societies, though it is often misplaced, misshapen, or unacknowledged.

We are all familiar with the notion of sacrificing a lesser good for a greater good. Though they may be rooted in a rational choice approach, which follows from individualism, such forms of sacrifice are still worth noting because they suggest that sacrifice persists even in a context that neglects or devalues it. Such common expressions of this sort of sacrifice include the readiness of families to pay the astronomical costs associated with a college education and the willingness of dieters to forego the pleasures of certain foods in the interest of losing weight. Equally common, perhaps, are the more negative forms of sacrifice, in which the greater good is sacrificed for the sake of the lesser. Some examples that come to mind are so-called workaholics, who sacrifice their emotional ties and physical well-being for the sake of productivity, or those with any other form of addiction. Finally, given that most Americans express some sort of religious or spiritual identity, we should not be surprised to find that a wide range of religiously motivated forms of sacrifice continues to coexist alongside secularism. For instance, the *politics of sacrifice* has been used to describe a social movement among conservative Christians to promote sexual abstinence among teenagers. While the circles of identification entailed in these examples are fairly small and none are solidly grounded in an ontology of interdependence, they do help to demonstrate the enduring nature of sacrifice even within secular societies.

Likewise, as Hyde persuasively demonstrates, gift and market systems are not incompatible but often exist alongside one another. The primary concern of his book is the plight of the artist, who "labors with his gift" in a market society. Exploring gifts as a form of property that forges social bonds, he shows how gifts remain central within certain enclaves of a market system. Within the scientific community, for instance, knowledge circulates as a gift. Even if we academics are painfully aware of the degree of egoism entailed in our enterprise, we can still recognize that papers are "given" at conferences and that scientists gain status on the basis of their "contributions" to the field.[32] Other examples of gift economies within the larger market economy are blood and organ donation, volunteerism, and philanthropy.[33] The recent freeware movement that offers free software through the Internet offers a window into the coevolution of gift and commercial relations. Depending on how they are interpreted, each of these examples may be plausibly read as a minority representation of an ontology of interdependence persisting within a larger social context that emphasizes individualism and autonomy. Gift systems and market systems foster two distinct yet necessary social values. Without gifts, community is lost; without the individuality and anonymity of the market, freedom can be lost.[34] Hyde emphasizes the importance of gift systems because they have been undervalued, yet he also recognizes that the social bonds entailed in gift systems can have negative consequences. For instance, women and girls in many cultures have been treated as gifts, and even in market societies, gift exchange and the care economy are largely the province of women. The converse is that "generosity makes no one manly."[35]

Another common form of sacrifice that persists within secular societies is individual self-giving for one's country. One of the references to a contemporary "politics of sacrifice" that I have found is an analysis of patriotism and "the generational thesis," which holds that each generation's civic engagement is shaped by the degree to which its members encounter events that call them to self-giving.[36] A popular version of the generational thesis is Robert Putnam's *Bowling Alone*, which celebrates "the mobilizing power of shared adversity" and highlights the sacrifices made by Americans in World War II in the name of freedom and equality.[37]

In the aftermath of the 9/11 attacks and with the growing concern over U.S. dependence on foreign oil, some environmentalists have called on Americans to make sacrifices by reducing their energy consumption. For decades, Europeans have made personal sacrifices in the form of higher taxes to reduce their petroleum dependency, and those taxes have spurred the development of more fuel-efficient vehicles. Polls indicate that Americans are "cautiously open" to increased gasoline taxes, but only if those taxes actually help to reduce dependence on foreign oil.[38] Reluctant acquiescence to reduced consumption, however, is a far cry from deeply internalizing a sacrificial cosmology. A crucial conceptual bridge from consumerism to an ontology of interdependence is constructed when people willingly sacrifice the lesser good of egoistic consumption for the greater good of ecological responsibility.

One key element in this ontological shift involves waking up to the myriad levels of sacrifice occluded by the phenomenon of distancing in the global economy.[39] Because consumers live at a comfortable distance from the effects of their consumption, they are largely blind to what and whom are being sacrificed. Moreover, their cultural milieu reinforces a negative understanding of sacrifice, providing a further incentive to turn a blind eye to very real sacrifices. A central theme running through the anthropological literature on sacrifice is that, while it plays a pivotal role in ancient and traditional cultures, it is generally held in disregard in modern societies.[40] Yet, seen through the lens of an ontology of interdependence, modern consumerism is based on the fantastic idea that there can be life without sacrifice. The innumerable gifts of nature are simply discounted, obfuscated, or appropriated by the global economy. From this perspective, it also becomes apparent that economic prosperity is built on the massive conversion of gift wealth to market wealth.[41] A primary contribution of environmental education is to uncover the dynamics of that conversion.

The notion of *shadow ecologies*, whereby the environmental effects of goods are felt across global lines of production, transportation, and waste disposal, rather than where they are consumed, is a particularly useful concept for uncovering the reality of ecological sacrifice.[42] Today's affluent consumers have easy access to a panoply of goods with enormous shadow ecologies: tropical hardwoods, electronic gadgets, petroleum and its countless derivatives, chocolate, coffee, and even green technologies like compact fluorescent lightbulbs. A key (and often disconcerting) facet of environmental education entails learning about the far-flung material and social consequences of our lifestyles. We find ourselves asking, "What is the impact of my lifestyle—the resource extraction, the production, and the waste disposal associated with my consumption habits—on distant peoples and ecosystems?" Likewise, students are increasingly familiar with *ecological footprint* measurements, which consider the amount of land required to sustain a person's lifestyle.[43] Because for affluent consumers, that land is mostly in remote places, the inevitable question arises, whom and what are being sacrificed?

Besides the geographical dimension of ecological sacrifice, there is the generally unrecognized chronological dimension. If there can be no getting without giving, then the vast disparity of wealth between the global North and the global South sparks curiosity about the historical origins of that disparity. If the global economy is premised on an unprecedented conversion of gift wealth to market wealth, then we might ask, from where and whom did the gift wealth of the global overconsumers come, and under what historical conditions? Here, the concept of *ecological debt* adds a temporal dimension to our understanding of the politics of sacrifice. As Andrew Simms demonstrates, the wealth of the industrialized countries came substantially from the third world, beginning with the vast mineral wealth in gold and silver brought from the Americas to Europe from the sixteenth century onward.[44] The flow of wealth from the periphery to the core continued with the slave trade; through a vast array of rubber, sugar, coffee, tea, chocolate, and banana plantations; right up to today's extractive economies for oil, minerals, and timber in the developing world. In this sense, there is some moral justification for claims by representatives of developing countries that not only should their own developmental trajectory not be threatened by international environmental regimes, but the North actually owes them compensation for the current distribution of global wealth. The fact that 20 percent of the world's population controls 80 percent of the world's wealth, and vice versa, is rooted in a long history of wealth being transferred from South to North. Given that most of that wealth transfer occurred as a consequence of colonialism and military conquest, it is more aptly described as plunder than gift.

The notion of ecological debt is particularly salient with respect to global climate change. Here the question is not so much resources—although the question of peak oil does bring that question to bear—but rather, sinks. The atmosphere is a giant global sink for anthropogenic sources of greenhouse gas emissions, and the fairest way of allocating emission rights is on a per capita basis.[45] Because increased wealth has been strongly correlated with fossil fuel consumption, and therefore carbon dioxide emissions, developing countries can make a persuasive case that they are owed a *carbon debt* by the affluent countries. Because developing countries will be most vulnerable to the effects of climate change, that debt casts a shadow into the future. Already, the annual number of deaths caused by climate change is estimated at 150,000–300,000—with as many as 99 percent of those deaths occurring in developing countries.[46] From this perspective, a fair distribution of the world's atmospheric commons would not use a per capita emissions approach, but rather, would issue developing countries a larger per capita share of atmospheric space. This need not mean a literal per capita reduction of industrialized countries' emissions to a level below that of developing countries, but it could mean the North paying its debt by transferring wealth and technology to the South. Of course, to anticipate such responsible behavior in the current political context is unrealistic, but that is only because the global overconsumers of the world are largely blind to what is being, has been, and will be sacrificed as a consequence of their actions. At a minimum, recognizing that its current wealth is based on past and present sacrifices in the South, the North would owe the South an enormous debt of gratitude.

When we project the consequences of today's consumption into the future, we uncover the unconscious and involuntary sacrifice of the unborn, both human and nonhuman. Carbon dioxide, for instance, lasts for over one hundred years in the atmosphere, which means that our children and their children will be the ones to feel the full impact of today's car culture. Similarly, a host of toxic and radioactive pollutants will persist in our air, water, and soil for generations to come. Two ecological legacies of the cold war, the Nevada Test Site and the Hanford Nuclear Reservation in eastern Washington, have been proposed as National Sacrifice Zones.[47] The mass extinction of species is a monumental sacrifice, one that is largely ignored by societies wedded to a notion of progress as perpetual material betterment. Though it might sound odd to speak of a debt to posterity, consumer society is utterly dependent on a transfer of wealth from the future; the involuntary character of that transfer, however, makes it more a theft than a gift.

Thus sacrifice does not disappear in secular modernity; it merely goes underground. The distancing that occurs as a consequence of global commodity chains only serves to obscure the sacrifices made by a global underclass, past and future generations, and nonhuman nature. Just as ancient and traditional forms of sacrifice often required a scapegoat, so do contemporary forms of ecological sacrifice. According to many scholars of sacrifice, especially those following the work of René Girard, such violent sacrificial rites virtually disappeared with the rise of rationality, juridical process, and philosophy of human rights.[48] I would argue that sacrifice did not vanish under secular modernity, but was only rendered unconscious, invisible, and involuntary because it disappeared from view in high-consumption societies. A deeper social and ecological analysis of the contours of global commodity and waste chains reveals how the global economy is actually grounded in the persistence of unacknowledged sacrifice.

You may find that all this talk of debt arouses exactly the kinds of morally burdened and despairing attitudes that I promised to circumvent in articulating an affirmative politics of sacrifice. I would, however, respond by saying that these attitudes are only a necessary and painful first step, and that a fuller inquiry will lead us to an affirmative and celebratory politics of sacrifice. If we have been living in blissful ignorance with respect to what is actually being sacrificed as a consequence of our consumption, then the dawning awareness that comes with uncovering ecological debt and shadow ecologies is bound to cause initial discomfort. To the extent that this is so, then perhaps an initial guilt-ridden ecological politics of sacrifice can serve some of the same expiatory functions as ancient sacrificial rituals. But we need not stop there. For when blissful ignorance[49] is sacrificed on the altar of awareness and integrity, the ensuing sense of wholeness and connection may offer unanticipated gifts.

A deeper inquiry into an affirmative politics of sacrifice raises the further question: to what "gods" are the sacrifices entailed in shadow ecologies and ecological debt being made? In other words, what are the overarching values and purposes that appear to render the wholesale sacrifice of peoples, ecosystems, other species, and future generations acceptable? To the degree that we are not conscious of those values and purposes, then sacrifice is again occluded. While my anecdotal evidence from the classroom hardly constitutes a scientifically valid survey, it is suggestive. When asked what they believe is the purpose of the global economy, my students almost universally respond by saying "progress," "growth," or "development." When pressed to define their terms, most understand these values to be fundamentally about enhancing human material well-being. Among the few who stress more psychological purposes, such as "making people happier," there is still a prevailing assumption that the means to happiness is increased consumption, even if they are vaguely aware that social scientists find no convincing correlation between material wealth and happiness or overall satisfaction. A bit more inquiry reveals that the deeper values implicit in consumer culture are comfort, convenience, and security. Of course, there is nothing wrong with these values, but articulating them explicitly enables us to ask a number of intriguing questions that can take us some steps further on the path toward an affirmative politics of sacrifice. Among these are, is it worth it? Are these the values on which we want to ground our lives? And what values are lost or compromised by sacrificing to the "gods" of material progress and convenience?

Inquiry into what is being sacrificed, and to what ends, therefore, makes possible something very important that otherwise could not occur: *conscious choice*. Once we are aware of the sacrifices that are actually entailed by our consumption habits, and once we have articulated the values that inform those habits, we can ask ourselves whether this is truly how we want to live. For some people, the answer will be yes. But faced with a growing awareness of the previously hidden and largely involuntary sacrifices perpetuated by the global economy, the answer for many will be no. This second group will have begun to articulate an affirmative politics of sacrifice by situating themselves within an ontology of interdependence. Indeed, a quiet minority has already stepped in the direction of a low-consumption, low-waste lifestyle, opting for such things as bicycles, local and organic food, and thrift stores. What is crucial about this step is that it is not compelled or coerced; rather, it is rooted in a free choice and an ability to apply ethical and practical reasoning to one's own life situation. Even if disillusionment sometimes feels painful, even if one is not delighted to have one's eyes opened to what is being sacrificed and to what ends, one can embrace the resulting freedom just as a more mature adolescent can move gracefully into the responsibilities that come with adulthood.

This is the sense in which individualism can, paradoxically, contribute meaningfully to the unfolding of a holistic ontology. The free, rational, and autonomous individual, even if illusory from a holistic perspective, became under secular modernity a social construct with real effects across the gamut of political, economic, and psychological life. An affirmative politics of sacrifice offers the opportunity for that individual to enter into a larger sense of self, offering some of the more shadowy expressions of his or her separative identity on the altar of ecological vitality and global justice. Such a sacrifice does not spell the death of the individual; instead, it represents a developmental achievement for the individual who, as a consequence of extending his or her capacities for reason and care, can now choose to enter into a deeper sense of engagement with a participatory universe.

The choice to embrace an affirmative politics of sacrifice, however, is not an option equally available to everyone. Those in the global under-class, those who are unborn, those who are other-than-human—these are the ones who are *being* sacrificed under the prevailing economic order. Here I part ways with Thomas Princen, who (in chapter 7; cf. chapter 4) understands sacrifice as "the willful, informed 'giving up' of something valued for a higher value." When sacrifice goes underground, as it tends to do in a culture of possessive individualism, much of the "giving up" is neither willful nor informed. To be sacrificed is a very different thing than to sacrifice. When those at the top of the global commodity food chain embrace an affirmative politics of sacrifice, they are consciously rejecting the notion that unknown others should be sacrificed for the sake of their own comfort and convenience. Moreover, if the direst peak-oil or climate change scenarios come to pass, then the ability to make this choice is extremely time sensitive: future conditions will require people to rein in their consumption, whether they like it or not.

Toward an Affirmative Politics of Sacrifice

From the perspective of consumer sovereignty, the transition to an eco-logical politics of sacrifice is likely to be awkward and unpleasant. Awakening to what is actually being sacrificed in the global economy as well as to one's complicity in a host of sacrificial rites of consump-tion is usually a painful process of disillusionment. Acting responsibly on the basis of that awakening, whether through collective political engagement or personal lifestyle changes, requires self-giving—in terms of one's time and one's habits. To deny that responsible action requires real sacrifice would be to perpetuate the foundational delusion of con-sumer society: that getting without giving (beyond monetarily) is pos-sible. The cultural history of sacrifice and gift economics, however, as well as my own experience tell me that sacrifice becomes a more joyful experience as it becomes a more conscious expression of an ontology of interdependence.

This, I believe, is because the environmental megacrisis is not pri-marily a material phenomenon; rather, climate change, the collapse of biodiversity, and the litany of "environmental" problems are symptoms of a larger crisis of meaning. That crisis raises a vital ontological and existential question: how do we understand ourselves in relation to the rest of creation? If we see ourselves as separate individuals vying for an ever proliferating number and sophistication of consumer goods, then ecological depletion and social alienation are the inevitable consequences of our instrumental relationship to others. If we see ourselves as integral members of a participatory universe, we gain the courage and integrity to acknowledge what is actually being sacrificed under current conditions. Likewise, our circles of identification progressively widen as we enter into an I–thou, rather than an I–it, relationship with what appears to be outside ourselves.[50] When we recognize ourselves as recipients of innumerable gifts that make possible our earthly habitation, our natural response is one of wonder, gratitude, and self-giving.

Gratitude entails both a cognitive and an affective dimension: an awareness of being gifted by someone or something beyond oneself and a response of appreciation. Because of its central role in creating and deepening social bonds, gratitude has been described as "the moral memory of mankind."[51] Yet gratitude entails a sense of being dependent on people or forces outside oneself, which perhaps partly explains the inverse relationship between gratitude and narcissism.[52] Likewise, gratitude is inversely correlated with envy, an emotion that is actively promoted by advertisement-driven consumer society. While the cultivation of gratitude may not be an explicit aim for most environmental educators, it is often a central but overlooked result of their work. As one learns more about one's utter dependence on an intricate interplay of solar, atmospheric, hydrological, geological, and biospheric forces, a sense of awe and spontaneous gratitude arises. Affect follows closely on cognition. Dennis Rivers offers this expression of "an ecology of devotion":

The Universe has labored mightily that we might breathe, and see the light of morning. The calcium, carbon, and iron that support these processes were made in the hearts of ancient stars. The caloric energy that lets us run is compressed starlight, the light of the sun conveyed to us from leaf to corn and wheat through countless hands. Our seemingly mundane existence, looked at from this angle, is a miracle of mind-boggling proportions. However ordinary or unworthy we may feel, we are nonetheless recipients of this galactic grace.[53]

An ecological politics of sacrifice need not be a dismal process of self-abnegation; rather it can be not only a way of *saying* grace, as Mitchell Thomashow suggests, but also a way of *living* in a state of grace.

Sensing the urgency of the mounting environmental megacrisis, one might ask a valid question: do we have enough time for such a developmental unfolding, or should we perhaps act with greater urgency in the direction of a more coercive politics of sacrifice? This question deserves a more thorough answer than space allows, but my short answer is that it depends on where our deeper commitments lie. To the extent that we embrace an ontology of wholeness and interdependence, a negative and coercive approach may feel contrary to our newfound sensibilities. Likewise, our sense of living in a participatory universe can foster patience and a friendlier relationship with time. To the extent that we value freedom, reason, and care, a coercive approach may also feel violent or disrespectful to those whom we wish to educate. When we find ourselves confronting those whom we might wish to persuade with a vehement attitude or guilt-inducing tactics, perhaps we have unconsciously reverted to an individualistic worldview. Moreover, from a pragmatic perspective, "environmental police"[54] tactics are unlikely to be persuasive in a culture that values individual freedom. These thoughts are not intended to belittle the very real question of urgency, but rather, to expand the backdrop against which questions of urgency are posed.

One might also wonder, if we focus on ontological and existential questions, don't we risk relegating sustainability to the level of the individual, thereby rendering our responses fairly ineffectual? Here I join Thomas Princen and others in this volume who highlight the sacrificial dimension of citizenship. To sincerely embrace an ontology of interdependence is not to wallow in self-indulgent feelings of oneness with others and nature, but rather, to transform one's whole being into a living expression of that commitment. While changes in one's own thinking and lifestyle may be important elements of that transformation, real solutions will require collective action on every level; indeed, this follows inexorably from the premise of interdependence.[55] Marcel Mauss's early observations apply equally today: sacrifice is "a total social phenomenon, . . . a paradigmatic engagement of the material, the organic and bodily, the psychological and political in a wider choreography of social form." The venues for this dance of sacrificial ecology range from families and neighborhoods to legislatures and courts, from voting booths to food shops, from newspapers to blogs, and from churches to classrooms.

Because the crisis is both planetary and ontological, the creative possibilities are innumerable.

An affirmative politics of sacrifice in an ecologically full world is about seeing the bigger picture, which simultaneously enlarges us. While sacrifice has always been about creating bonds, one consequence of our global economy is that we have unwittingly extended our bonds spatially across the planet and temporally into future generations. An ecological politics of sacrifice is therefore about embedding ourselves in the larger community of life that extends to other people and creatures living now and in the future. And because the structure of sacrifice entails that the lesser is offered up for the sake of the greater, sacrifice also contains an evolutionary impetus. While the politics of sacrifice in an ecologically full world may spell the end of progress as it was defined by consumer society, the evolutionary task before us is to recontextualize progress with a deep appreciation for our lives as threads within a vast tapestry of earthly existence.

Acknowledgments

I am deeply grateful to David Wilkerson for his research assistance. I am also grateful to Jean-Yves Lung, Michael Maniates, John Meyer, Tom Princen, and Paul Wapner for their comments on earlier drafts of this chapter.

Notes

1. Bruce Chilton, *The Temple of Jesus: His Sacrificial Program within a Cultural History of Sacrifice* (State College: Pennsylvania State University Press, 1992), 41.

2. In this formula, *I* stands for environmental impact, *P* stands for population, *A* stands for affluence, and *T* stands for technologies.

3. For a more comprehensive treatment of the global problematique as a legitimization crisis, please see my article "Towards an Integral Perspective on World Politics: Secularism, Sovereignty and the Challenge of Global Ecology," *Millennium: Journal of International Studies* 32 (Summer 2003): 29–56.

4. Mitchell Thomashow, *Ecological Identity: Becoming a Reflective Environmentalist* (Cambridge, MA: MIT Press, 1995), 157.

5. Memorandum from Michael Maniates to ISA panelists.

6. Jose Thachil, *The Vedic and the Christian Concept of Sacrifice* (Kerala, India: Pontifical Institute of Theology and Philosophy, 1985), 3.

7. These definitions of *sacrifice* are drawn from *Webster's New Universal Unabridged Dictionary* (Avenel, NJ: Barnes and Noble, 1992), 1259.

8. Sri Aurobindo, *The Synthesis of Yoga* (Pondicherry, India: Sri Aurobindo Ashram Trust, 1976), 98–101.

9. Thachil, *The Vedic*, 10.

10. Chilton, *Temple of Jesus*, 32.

11. M. F. C. Bourdillon, Introduction to *Sacrifice,* ed. M. F. C. Bourdillon and Meyer Fortes (New York: Academic Press, 1980).

12. Ilana Silber, "Modern Philanthropy: Reassessing the Viability of a Maussian Perspective," in *Marcel Mauss: A Centenary Tribute*, ed. Wendy James and N. J. Allen (New York: Berghahn Books, 1998), 134.

13. Wendy James, "One of Us: Marcel Mauss and 'English' Anthropology," in James and Allen, *Marcel Mauss*, 20.

14. Nancy Jay, *Throughout Your Generations Forever: Sacrifice, Religion, and Paternity* (Chicago: University of Chicago Press, 1992), 18.

15. W. S. F. Pickering, "Mauss's Jewish Background," in James and Allen, *Marcel Mauss*, 53.

16. Thachil, *The Vedic*, 233–236.

17. David Nigel, *Human Sacrifice* (New York: Dorset Press, 1981), 280.

18. 1 Peter 2:5.

19. C. B. MacPherson, *The Political Theory of Possessive Individualism: Hobbes to Locke* (Oxford: Clarendon Press, 1962).

20. Erik Erikson, *Youth: Change and Challenge* (New York: Basic Books, 1963), and Erik Erikson, *Adulthood: Essays* (New York: W. W. Norton, 1978).

21. Felix Warneken of the Max Planck Institute also found that while other primates display spontaneous helpfulness, toddlers do so to an even greater extent. See F. Warneken and M. Tomasello, "Altruistic Helping in Human Infants and Young Chimpanzees," *Science* 3 (March 2006): 1301–1303.

22. Lewis Hyde, *The Gift: Imagination and the Erotic Life of Property* (New York: Vintage Books, 1983), 37.

23. Aafke Elisabeth Komter, "Gratitude and Gift Exchange," in *The Psychology of Gratitude*, ed. Robert A. Emmons and Michael E. McCullough (New York: Oxford University Press, 2004), 199–200.

24. Hyde, *The Gift*, 8, 22–23. Ironically, the term *Indian giver* originates from a meeting of these two worldviews. Apparently, the Native American expected some sort of return for their gifts to the European colonizers, a practice that led to the notion of an "Indian gift." Ibid., 3–4.

25. Ibid., 53.

26. I am indebted to Jean-Yves Lung for this insight.

27. Hyde, *The Gift*, 19.

28. John Archibald Wheeler, "The Universe as Home for Man," *American Scientist*, November/December 1974, quoted in Henryk Skolimowski, *Living Philosophy: Eco-Philosophy as a Tree of Life* (London: Penguin, 1992), 19.

29. David Steindl-Rast, "Gratitude as Thankfulness and as Gratefulness," in Emmons and McCullough, *Psychology of Gratitude*, 284.

30. Thomashow, *Ecological Identity*, 203.

31. See Mircea Eliade, *The Sacred and the Profane: The Nature of Religion* (New York: Harcourt Brace, 1987).

32. Hyde, *The Gift*, 77–80; Warren O. Hagstrom, *The Scientific Community* (New York: Basic Books, 1965).

33. Richard Titmuss, *The Gift Relationship: From Human Blood to Social Policy* (New York: Pantheon, 1971), and Ilana Silber, "Modern Philanthropy: Reassessing the Viability of a Maussian Perspective," in James and Allen, *Marcel Mauss*, 134–150.

34. Hyde, *The Gift*, 38.

35. Ibid., 105.

36. Scott L. McLean, "Patriotism, Generational Change, and the Politics of Sacrifice," in *Social Capital*, ed. Scott L. McLean, David A. Schultz, and Manfred B. Steger (New York: New York University, 2002), 147–166.

37. Robert Putnam, *Bowling Alone* (New York: Simon and Schuster, 2001), 267.

38. Louis Uchitelle and Megan Thee, "Americans Are Cautiously Open to Gas Tax Rise, Poll Shows," *The New York Times*, February 28, 2006.

39. Thomas Princen, "The Shading and Distancing of Commerce: When Internalization Is Not Enough," *Ecological Economics* 20, no. 3 (1997): 235–253; Jennifer Clapp, "The Distance of Waste: Overconsumption in a Global Economy," in *Confronting Consumption*, ed. Thomas Princen, Michael Maniates, and Ken Conca (Cambridge, MA: MIT Press, 2002), 155–176.

40. E.g., in his cultural history of sacrifice, Chilton, *Temple of Jesus*, 25, finds that the predominant perception in modern societies is that "sacrifice is at best a waste."

41. Hyde, *The Gift*, 280.

42. Jim MacNeill, Pieter Winsemius, and Taizo Yakushiji, *Beyond Interdependence: The Meshing of the World's Economy and the Earth's Ecology* (New York: Oxford University Press, 1991). A detailed investigation of the shadow ecology of tropical timber is offered by Peter Dauvergne, *Shadows in the Forest: Japan and the Politics of Tropical Timber in Southeast Asia* (Cambridge, MA: MIT Press, 1997).

43. William E. Rees and Mathis Wackernagel, *Our Ecological Footprint: Reducing Human Impact on the Earth* (Philadelphia: New Society, 1995).

44. Andrew Simms, *Ecological Debt: The Health of the Planet and the Wealth of Nations* (London: Pluto Press, 2005).

45. For more detailed discussions of a per capita emissions rights approach to greenhouse gases, see Peter Singer, *One World: The Ethics of Globalization* (New Haven, CT: Yale University Press), and Tom Athanasiou and Paul Baer, *Dead Heat: Global Justice and Global Warming* (New York: Seven Stories Press, 2002).

46. World Health Organization and United Nations Environment Programme, "The Health and Environment Linkages Initiative," http://www.who.int/heli/risks/climate/climatechange/en/index.html, and Megan Rowling, "Climate Change Causes 315,000 Deaths a Year: Report," *Scientific American*, May 29, 2009, http://www.scientificamerican.com/article.cfm?id=climate-change-causes-315.

47. Donovan Webster, *Aftermath: The Remnants of War: From Landmines to Chemical Warfare—The Devastating Effects of Modern Combat* (New York: Vintage Books, 1998).

48. For the most trenchant analysis of sacrifice as societal sublimation of violence, see René Girard, *Violence and the Sacred*, trans. Patrick Gregory (Baltimore: Johns Hopkins University Press, 1972). Among those influenced by Girard's perspective is Nigel Davies, *Human Sacrifice* (New York: Dorset Press, 1981). Girard warned of a "sacrificial crisis," or the danger of societal collapse as a consequence of the end of sacrifice, yet believed that reason could avert modernity's sacrificial crisis. I would counter that the current "sacrificial crisis" is actually a consequence of the degree to which sacrifice has been occluded and responsibility has been evaded. Yet I would concur that a farsighted rationality, complemented by the affective elements of care and devotion, can play an essential role in averting the crisis.

49. Though if ignorance is bliss, we might wonder why so many people don't seem to be particularly happy.

50. See Martin Buber, *I and Thou* (New York: Free Press, 1971). For an application of Buber's theological and sociological ideas to environmental ethics, see Neil Evernden, *The Natural Alien: Humankind and Environment* (Toronto, ON: University of Toronto Press, 1993).

51. George Simmel, "Faithfulness and Gratitude" (1908, 1950), quoted in Komter, "Gratitude and Gift Exchange," 203.

52. Michael E. McCullough and Jo-Ann Tsang, "Parent of the Virtues?" in Emmons and McCullough, *Psychology of Gratitude*, 130. Sommers and Kosmitzki found that Germans were two to three times as likely as Americans to experience gratitude as a pleasant emotion, with American men being the most likely to associate gratitude with unpleasant feelings of vulnerability. See Shula Sommers and Corinne Kosmitzki, "Emotion and Social Context: An American-German Comparison," *British Journal of Social Psychology* 27, no. 1 (1988): 35–49.

53. Dennis Rivers, "Toward an Ecology of Devotion," *Earth Light* 13, no. 4 (2003): 8.

54. Thomashow, *Ecological Identity*, 146.

55. One of my favorite ways of demonstrating this point to my students is to have them first calculate their ecological footprint as an American and then use exactly the same numbers as if they were living in a developing country. They are inevitably puzzled when their footprint as Americans are five to ten times greater, even using the same numbers. As they consider that their individual footprint includes a small portion of the country's entire infrastructure, ranging from highways to military bases, they begin to realize that solutions require political action and not just lifestyle changes.

7

Consumer Sovereignty, Heroic Sacrifice: Two Insidious Concepts in an Endlessly Expansionist Economy

Thomas Princen

The three big drivers of environmental change have long been framed as population, technology, and consumption, each with its own set of drivers. Since consumption has finally begun to get its share of the attention, it might be time to ask what drives consumption and, in particular, *over*-consumption; that is, what underlies the current patterns of excess throughput of material and energy, irreversible biophysical change, and permanent diminution of ecosystem services? As with population and technology, the list can get long very quickly—materialism, commercialism, commodification, and marketing, for instance. Here, though, I focus on the rhetoric of a consumer economy, the often hidden and taken-for-granted language that simultaneously explains, justifies, and absolves. The rhetoric of primary interest is that which is so dominant, so "natural" in its usage that we hardly notice it. Front and center are the concepts of *consumer sovereignty* and *heroic sacrifice*. These are, we'll see, highly useful concepts in a fast-growing, frontier economy. In an ecologically constrained world, however, they are rhetorical drivers of overconsumption.

The argument, in brief, is this. Consumer sovereignty is a core belief in a consumer economy: it's all about the consumer; consumers exercise free choice; the consumer is the decider, indeed, the ruler. Just as a sovereign king is entitled to privileges and perquisites, the sovereign consumer is entitled to satisfy one's desires, to have ever more goods, and to do so all at the lowest price. But the grand entitlement scheme for consumption can persist only as long as its boosters can defer, displace, and obscure true costs and pressing trade-offs. In the end, the idea of consumer sovereignty is a myth convenient for those who would locate responsibility for social and environmental problems on the backs of those very consumers, absolving those who truly have market power and who write the rules of the game and who benefit the most.

The rhetoric of sacrifice complements consumer sovereignty by ignoring current sacrifices. It makes heroic sacrifice overt, restricted to the few, while unpleasant forms of sacrifice are rendered covert and hidden and dispersed among the many. Most insidiously perhaps, the rhetoric of sacrifice discredits a positive notion of sacrifice and depreciates everyday life by denying the pursuit of higher purposes such as citizenship, social justice, and ecological integrity. In a consumer economy, to sacrifice *in* the marketplace is anathema; to sacrifice *for* the marketplace is acceptable, normal, indeed, necessary.

Before proceeding, a word on terms is in order. *Consumer sovereignty* is not an everyday term, yet it underpins the discourse of consumer economies: "personal choice," "demand," and "customers" (as in, the customer is always right) are common expressions. *Sacrifice* is an everyday term, but, as we'll see, it is everyday only in its overtly heroic and negative variants. My purpose is to expose these two rhetorical drivers for what they are: highly useful concepts in a free-wheeling, cost-displacing economy; highly destructive concepts in an ecologically constrained world. So exposed, society can move a step away from an endlessly expansionist, ever consuming, grossly unequal economy and toward a sustainable economy.

Consumer Sovereignty

The desire to be master of time and space without dependence on schedules was not invented in an automobile factory. It accords with the nature of the modern person and comes from the consumer. Everyone should be able to use the means of transit that best suits his or her individual needs.
—J. H. Brunn, President, German Automotive Industry Association, Baden-Baden, September 27, 1974 speech, "The Automobile Is Another Bit of Freedom"[1]

The beverage industry is doing its part to help [with the problem of soft drinks and obesity]. We've made a wider range of beverages available to school students over the past decade, including bottled water, 100 percent juice, sports drinks, diet drinks and low-fat milk products.

Instead of banning or taxing certain products, we should strive to educate children about exercise and balanced choices. Teaching children to eat and drink properly is teaching them to live a long, healthy life.
—Susan Neely, President and Chief Executive, American Beverage Association, Washington, April 14, 2006; letter to editor, *The New York Times*, April 19, 2006

As a 16-year-old high school student, I strongly object to the lobbying by state legislatures to deny students the right to buy certain soft drinks in school.
It is preposterous that by the middle of my senior year, I will have the right to vote, but the state will consider me unable to make proper lifestyle choices. Although some lawmakers believe that they are endowed with the wisdom to make daily choices for others, I would prefer personal freedom.
—Jonathan Panter, Palisades, New York, May 6, 2006; letter to editor, *The New York Times*, May 15, 2006

MacDonald's has reported an astounding 37 consecutive months of positive comparable sales in the United States. . . .
Customers choose McDonald's because we meet their needs by providing quality menu choices, value and convenience. . . .
Our recent success is largely the result of consistently executing the basics to ensure customer satisfaction.
—Bill Lamar, Senior Vice President and Chief Marketing Officer, USA, McDonald's Corporation, Oak Brook, Illinois, May 11, 2006; letter to editor, *The New York Times*, May 15, 2006

A core belief in a consumer economy is that it is all about the consumer. The consumer expresses his or her preferences in the marketplace, and producers respond by producing the goods the consumer wants and at a price the consumer will pay. If the consumer doesn't buy the product, producers can't sell it, and thus they don't make it. Governments do likewise: they intervene in the economy to serve the consumer. The government takes antitrust action against conglomerates because monopolists restrict production and raise prices, hurting the consumer. Conversely, if firms merge to capture efficiencies and offer consumers lower prices, the government supports economic concentration. If trade barriers prevent tropical fruits from reaching temperate shores, or if they allow domestic producers to charge unrealistically high prices, the government lowers the barriers; not to do so is to restrict choice, to harm the consumer.

The emphasis on the consumer began (at least in the United States) in the Progressive Era, also known as the Age of Efficiency. Frederick

Winslow Taylor applied "scientific management" to the factory, increasing worker productivity beyond anything imaginable. But perhaps the most insidious effect of the efficiency craze of that time was not in the production of goods, but in production's apparent polar opposite—consumption. To spend efficiently was to shop well, to scan retailers' offerings, to monitor prices, and to locate the best and cheapest product on the store shelves. Shopping became the perfect complement to worker productivity. After all, the shopper and the worker are one and the same person. Only now the worker, a serf stripped of discretion and judgment in the factory, could be king in the supermarket.

Consumer sovereignty, a notion originally developed as a theoretical nicety in neoclassical economics, became the new mantra of business and government leaders: industrialists only respond to consumers' wants and needs; if consumers don't want a product, they won't pay for it, and producers can't sell it; what does get produced is only what consumers want. And if there are problems—with safety or pollution, say—it's up to the consumers to demand change. So a firm would be happy to produce wood from well-managed forests or automobiles with safety devices, the argument goes, but it can't do so when the demand isn't there. If the public really wants cleaner production or safer products, preferences will shift, and the market will respond. Moreover, say the appropriators of consumer sovereignty, if individual consumer preferences become collectively destructive—if workers are alienated, forests leveled, and rivers fouled—the problem is ethical; it's educational and political, not commercial. Preferences among the mass of consumers can go askew, but the corrections should occur in one's place of worship, in the school, or in the legislature, not in the factory or bank. To suggest that industry should make such corrections is to violate both private choice and public choice, two pillars of an open society and an efficient economy, indeed, of democracy itself.[2]

Proponents of this belief system, bankers, merchandisers, and others, "believed it was not the business of business to judge other people's desires," writes historian William Leach. "Quite the opposite: Business succeeded (and people got jobs) only when business responded to desire, manipulated it, and extended its frontiers." "The function of our economic organization," Leach quotes one prominent banker of the 1920s and 1930s, "is not to determine what the people *ought* to want, but to make the machinery as productive as possible of what they *do* want."[3]

As with any belief system, language matters. *Free trade, enfranchisement,* and *individual choice* were terms that had to be invented and promoted. So, too, was the very term *consumer,* "a term not in regular currency before" World War I, writes Leach, yet one that

began to compete for prominence with "citizen" and "worker" as well as with an earlier meaning of consumer developed by "consumers' leagues," which implied activism and not the passivity of the newer term. Related phrases or terms became popular, among them "consumer desires and wishes," "consumer appeal," "consumer sovereignty," "commodity flow," "the flow of satisfactions," and "sales resistance." This language expressed what had actually happened and, at the same time, ideologically explained it and gave it credence.[4]

Seventy-five years later, two leaders of global finance could write that "in pursuit of higher living standards, we have created a new world of global markets and instant communication delivering gains in efficiency and competition that are beyond the powers of governments." Reacting to charges that globalization concentrates power among the wealthy few, they say that, quite the contrary, "the goal is not to disenfranchise the individual but to give individuals more power to control their destinies by lowering costs, broadening choices, delivering more capital and opening more markets." People are empowered, in other words, when manufacturers, financiers, and traders are allowed to serve their master (the sovereign consumer) by increasing consumer choice with more goods at low prices. What's more, these financiers insist, if "four billion people exist on less than $1,500 a year," producers, those ever-ready servants to the consumers, "can lift them from poverty and turn them into customers."[5] In this belief system, a world of consumers is an ideal world, one served by those with the capital, the expertise, the vision to make it all happen. But *served*; the consumer decides all. Just as a sovereign king is entitled to privileges and perquisites, the sovereign consumer is entitled to satisfy one's desires, to have ever more goods, and to do so all at low, low prices.

Underlying this belief system is a logic integral to the operation of a modern industrial economy, one that is dynamic and organized to expand. The relevant discipline is, of course, economics. A century ago, the discipline departed from its "laissez-faire ideas of scarcity and self-denial," writes Leach, "in favor of the more appealing notions of [abundant] supply and prosperity."[6] No one need be deprived; everyone can be "lifted from poverty." And for those already freed from the bonds of poverty, they, too, need not worry; abundance was for everyone, rich and poor. Frugality was a thing of the past; spending was the thing of the future. Simon Patten, a founding member of the American Economics Association and professor at the then Wharton School of Economics, not to mention father of consumer theory, put it best nearly a century ago, describing, indeed *prescribing*, a new culture: "We think of culture as the final product of civilization and not as one of its elements. Yet if we look at the facts, we find that culture is an index of activity, not of ancestral tradition and opinion. . . . Culture is the result of more satisfying combinations [of] consumption." Consumer choice unifies a diverse nation and elevates the individual to high moral purpose, Patten argued. Thus, "all traditional restraints on consumption, all taboos against luxury" should be "eliminated."[7]

Now economics takes as axiomatic that an economy serves consumers: "Neoclassical economics sees the delivery of individual consumption as the main object of the economic system," writes economist Angus Deaton in *The Palgrave Dictionary of Economics*. In the modern world, "the flow of goods and services consumed by everyone constitutes the ultimate aim and end of economic life," writes Robert Heilbroner in *The Worldly Philosophers*.[8] In principle, that consumption need not always increase any more than production need always increase. Optimal economic activity, economic theory tells us, is generally not maximum activity: the output of a firm with fixed costs produces where marginal costs and revenues equate, not at full plant capacity; the macroeconomy with known interest and employment rates can grow too fast (risking inflation) or too slow (risking unemployment). Enoughness is not an entirely alien concept, *in the discipline*. In *practice*, though, the allures of abundance and the ethics of material plenty have prevailed. If one's place in society and in natural systems once constituted "traditional restraints," they have indeed been cast aside. And new ones are few and far between. The political economy—firms and the institutions that support the economy—is nearly always one of maximum increase, of a never ending "pursuit of higher living standards." It is "market demand for greater efficiencies and new products" that defines modern capitalism, writes political scientist Robert Gilpin in his lucid account of capitalism worldwide, *The Political Economy of International Relations.*[9] In all this, the idea of the sovereign consumer demanding ever more goods to meet an endlessly insatiable appetite is fundamental. The sovereign consumer knows no bounds.

A common rhetorical device within consumer sovereignty is the mantra of low consumer prices. Political and business leaders frequently point out that Americans "demand" cheap gasoline for their cars and low-priced electricity for their homes. Some imply that American consumers *deserve* low prices. Few rationales are as effective in justifying a public expenditure or opposing a regulation. California's energy crisis of 2001, for example, was preceded by partial deregulation, in which wholesale prices would be competitive but end-use prices would be capped. Consumers, so went the argument, could not bear the burden of market reorganization, even if real costs increased. When those costs did increase, the state (i.e., California taxpayers) spent billions of dollars to keep electricity prices low for its citizens (i.e., for California electricity users). When President Bush reneged in early 2001 on his campaign promise to reduce carbon emissions as called for in the Kyoto Protocol, the first reason given was that carbon dioxide was not a pollutant. The second reason, the one that people could take seriously, was that reducing emissions would raise consumer prices. When the software manufacturer Microsoft was accused of monopolistic practices, it took a position with a long history of success in U.S. antitrust cases: the true beneficiaries of Microsoft practices, however predatory and monopolistic they may seem to some, are the consumers—more choice and lower prices. When garbage is shipped from New York, Illinois, and Ontario to Michigan, state officials and waste management companies explain that such transfers keep dumping fees low, meaning that roadside pickup of unlimited quantities of household trash remains cheap.

The list is endless, but the logic is suspect. Certainly everyone wants to spend as little as possible, but only when there are no implications down the line. Low prices only make sense when all else is equal or when trade-offs are clear. I want lower gasoline prices *if* highway congestion doesn't increase; I want cheap electricity *if* brownouts remain unlikely. That boosters of low prices can avoid spelling out such conditions and avoid being held accountable for such trade-offs testifies to the power of the idea of consumer sovereignty, an idea that, although a technical term conjured up by economists, suffuses much of contemporary policy making.

The explanation for such power may lie in the aptly chosen term *sovereign*. Pharaohs, emperors, kings, and queens enjoy luxuries and conveniences that are widely recognized as the appropriate trappings of power. It's their right and their duty. What's more, such entitlements are recognized by everyone, from the exalted ruler to the commoner. It's the proper order of things. Now, it would seem, consumers have theirs: the right to maximize choice and the right to get the lowest possible price. Everyone from political leader to CEO to worker recognizes this essential rightness, however implicit it might be. It's the proper order of things. Political leadership is exercised when consumer entitlements are promoted by increasing energy supplies (e.g., to keep gasoline prices at a so-called acceptable level) or concluding a trade agreement to open markets and, once again, keep prices low. Citizenship is expressed when the sovereign buys according to belief, to values, and not just to price (e.g., a fuel-efficient car, sweatshop-free shoes, or eco-friendly cleansers).

Such sovereignty indeed knows no bounds. Its imperialism is not geographic (although much of globalization relies on the idea), but commercial and extractive: the sovereign must have more and more goods at ever lower prices, and its agents must scour the globe to find the inputs and waste sites to make it all possible. Of course, this grand entitlement scheme for consumption can persist only as long as its boosters can defer, displace, and obscure true costs and pressing trade-offs; individualization and distancing become essential processes in sustaining the scheme.[10]

In the end, however, the idea of consumer sovereignty doesn't add up. It is a myth convenient for those who would locate responsibility for social and environmental problems on the backs of consumers, absolving those who truly have market power and who write the rules of the game and who benefit the most. It makes the idea of unlimited economic growth appear both natural and inevitable. But consumers don't have perfect information, they're not insulated from the influence of marketers, and they don't write the rules. Their consumption choices seem broad, but are in fact tightly constrained (one chooses between nearly identical car models, not between an automobile-based transport system and a mass transit–based one). Their "rule" over the investment and production decisions of major corporations is limited at best. It is a fiction highly convenient for those who do well with endless economic growth on a planet of seemingly endless frontiers. To believe otherwise, to suggest that consumers do not really rule, that they just might be consuming *too much*, that cutting back might be a good thing to do, is to court disaster. It is to suggest, among other antimodern sentiments, that we might have to *sacrifice*.

Sacrifice: The Depreciative Politics of Endless Consumption

I know we're consuming too much. But if we cut back, the economy will take a dive. People will lose their jobs. Public services will decline. Democracy will be put at risk. And besides, people just won't make the sacrifice. Why should they?

Every time I speak about overconsumption, this is the kind of question I get. A newspaper editor once asked me to write a piece on how we can reduce consumption without hurting the economy. I have tried, but it's always a struggle, and I've yet to come up with a convincing reply.[11] Unpacking consumer sovereignty is straightforward compared to this, the charge of sacrifice, the call for moderns to turn off the lights, crawl into the cave, and shiver in the dark. And yet, in the face of ever increasing use of resources and filling of waste sinks, this may be the crucial issue: if consuming less entails sacrifice, including the sacrifice of our very way of life and livelihood, how can a society possibly save the environment? How, if we take "the environment" as our life-support system, at once adaptive and fragile, can we save ourselves?

This is indeed an important question—maybe the essential question in the face of excess throughput and its attendant impacts, environmental and human. It's the right question. And it's the wrong question.

It's the right question in part because it forces all would-be environmental saviors (this author included) to confront their prescriptions. If one has moved from marginal change, "diddling with details," as Donella Meadows called it, to transformative change, that is, to fundamental restructuring, one can hardly avoid concluding that the economy must change. But in a consumption-driven economy, to say we must restructure and reduce consumption is to invite disaster, and in this it is the wrong question. It is wrong because it requires that we accept at face value the prevailing framing of sacrifice.

In this section, then, I wish to both unpack and reframe sacrifice, recognizing that, for practical purposes, the term is so loaded in societies such as the United States that an entirely new term may be needed. In so doing, I expose the rhetorical use of sacrifice for its insidious effect, promoting ever more consumption. I do this by (1) shedding light on current sacrifice, (2) distinguishing overt and covert sacrifice, (3) positing a notion of positive and negative sacrifice, and (4) arguing that the denial of sacrifice depreciates everyday life, including participatory democratic practices.

Current Sacrifice

The fear of sacrifice and its rejection as an approach to righting environmental wrongs presumes that society is not already sacrificing to pursue the status quo. Every day in the United States, we sacrifice about one hundred people on the highways (plus ten to fifteen times that number of people seriously injured). Day after day, year in and year out. A 9/11 tragedy every month. And we hardly blink. All to pursue a particular value expressed with a particular kind of vehicle—personal mobility via an automobile. Society's endorsement of this sacrifice is evidenced by the huge public investment for automobile infrastructure and the reluctance to slow traffic and protect pedestrians (a significant fraction of deaths and injuries are to nonmotorists). If just one person died every day from airline or railroad accidents, let alone from a new disease, there would be a public outcry. In our commitment to market-based, consumer-led health care, we sacrifice eighteen thousand lives annually for lack of health insurance, according to the Institute of Health.[12] Less obvious (perhaps) is the military expense and lives lost to protect oil supplies. And now, with one confirming report after another about the disruptive effects of global warming, we appear to be in the middle of a long-term project to sacrifice vast coastal areas, mangroves, coral reefs, and cropland, even entire nations, all to maintain a carbon-based economy. The list goes on. Modern industrial societies are sacrificing hugely to pursue a particular vision of the good life.

These forms of sacrifice are well documented, but known, it seems, only to the specialist and the well-informed citizen. Nobody is hiding them, yet they are covert, hidden from view or scrutiny by treating them as anomalies, often temporary at that, as problems that just need fixing, not as signs of a sacrificial consumer economy. They are, the reasoning appears to go, aberrations which, with the will, especially political will, and the money, especially public money, can be solved; in fact, if we rev up the economy, do more of what we are already doing, but with, say, better cars (i.e., more efficient) and more renewables in the fuel mix (even if we end up just doing more of what we're currently doing), we can generate the wealth, the surplus revenues, to tackle these problems. Until then, it's just what society (read the aggregation of sovereign consumers) has chosen.

There are, of course, overt forms of sacrifice, even in a society that talks as if sacrifice would be a new, uncalled for burden. Police officers walk into the line of fire, firefighters enter burning buildings, and soldiers go into battle, all to protect us and ensure our way of life. Noble sacrifice, though, is only for these few, today's gladiators and knights. The rest of us not only are absolved from making such sacrifices, but are expected not to make any at all, certainly not in the commercial realm, not in our producing and consuming, not in that all important task of keeping the economic engine primed. The marketplace is about opportunity, about meeting basic needs. And if the consuming slides from basics to indulgences, from mere choice to greed, from renewing to mining, "the economy" can't and shouldn't distinguish; excess is only in the eye of the moralizer, sufficiency is for traditionalists and rejectionists, for people with a "different set of values."[13] What the sovereign consumer chooses is necessary and right; anything less is sacrifice, for the consumer, for the economy, and therefore for society.

Put in game theory terms, sacrifice is the "sucker's payoff" in the Prisoner's Dilemma. Only a fool would choose a course of action that risks maximizing one's payoff. Indeed, sacrifice is where the magic of the marketplace and social Darwinism join: pursuing one's self-interest automatically aggregates into the public interest, and if some are left behind in the process, society is still better off because the winners increase the overall pie, and besides, the winners are the most fit and should survive; the losers bring down the average and should be weeded out—that is, sacrificed. The losers—the powerless, the poor, the backward—are expendable in this utilitarian vision and are hence rendered invisible, their sacrifice covert and thus acceptable.

In short, to sacrifice *in* the marketplace is anathema; to sacrifice *for* the marketplace is acceptable and necessary, especially if covert (i.e., if we don't talk about it or look for it) and with risks incurred by a select few. In a society ruled by sovereign consumers, in which private purchases define the very identity of those consumers, overt sacrifice is relegated to the public realm, to those relatively rare instances in which heroes are made, not the everyday stuff of driving an industrial and postindustrial economy: buying is what consumers do, and the more they buy, the better.

Positive and Negative

I've hinted at the observation that sacrifice has both positive and negative connotations. Both involve giving up something for a higher value. The difference is in whether the expectation of loss is inherent to a given role.

Positive sacrifice is exemplified by the parent who sacrifices time and resources to raise a child. The typical parent will hardly express his or her efforts as sacrifice;[14] it is just what parents do, part and parcel of having children. It is, in short, inherent in the role. To put it more caustically, if one doesn't want to sacrifice for children, one shouldn't be a parent. Similarly, an artist sacrifices income and job security to do the art. It's not negative because "doing the art" is what it means to assume the role of artist. It is sacrifice, though, because one is giving up economic and social benefit for the higher value of doing the art. One willingly "makes a sacrifice."

Negative sacrifice is exemplified by the coal miners and chemical workers who sell their labor for a paycheck but actually give up their future health. It is the volunteer soldier who sacrifices income, education, and possibly his or her life to protect the nation (positive sacrifice), and then, while serving, loses the mortgage, forcing his or her spouse to seek charity. Here, one is "being sacrificed."[15]

The roles of employee and soldier have no inherent "giving up" of health and economic security. These negative sacrifices are not part of the bargain; they are unexpected and perceived as undeserved. They don't fit the role.

And so it is that in the role of consumer, there is no inherent "giving up" beyond trading money for goods and services. As a consumer, I *only* engage in the commercial exchange. I do not run a government, express my devotion to a deity, feed the poor, or save the environment. I just buy. And I buy the best goods and services I can for the money. Nothing more. To put it differently, anything less, any foregoing of "market value" by the consumer, is a sacrifice, a *negative sacrifice*, a stepping out of role, a denial of the inherent nature of *being a consumer*, as contradictory as being a parent and losing no sleep, as being an artist and punching a time clock.

This construction of the nonsacrificial nature of the role of consumer, then, leads to a crucial question for those of us concerned about overconsumption: what is the appropriate role for reversing the trends in environmental degradation? Is there any role for the consumer? Logically, the answer is no: consumers don't save the environment, they just buy. To underscore this critical point, if I want to help the people of Darfur, do I shift my consumption patterns? If so, which? How? To what expected effect? To save refugees, just as to save the environment, one doesn't shift consumption patterns. One *shifts to a different role*: citizen, say. Even if one can imagine some change in consumption that would help Darfur refugees (proceeds from a T-shirt sale go to the refugees, say), to have any effect would require widespread organizing. And that organizing is not buying; it is not what consumers do, it's what citizens do (and, in this case, what others—government officials, journalists, soldiers—do).

At root, then, sacrifice (whether positive or negative) is a value-neutral notion, contingent on role-specific expectations. I suggest the following definition: sacrifice is the willful, informed "giving up" of something valued for a higher value. I value a good night's sleep, but I'll willingly give it up to care for my baby; I value my personal security but will forfeit (or risk) it to defend my country. I do this because this is what it means to be a parent or a soldier. So sacrifice is role-specific: a sleepless night makes sense as a parent, not as a line worker (worrying about tomorrow's line speed, for instance); risking my life makes sense as a soldier, not as a coal miner. And the value—the higher value—varies with the risk taken. The sacrifice a soldier makes in a war zone is not the same as what a soldier makes on a relief mission, even if the goal—protecting lives—is the same.[16]

It may well be that nearly all roles entail sacrifice. Parenting, soldiering, teaching, legislating, adjudicating, and running a business are, after all, "other-interested," about relations (however personal, strategic, or power-driven), about the coherence and legitimacy and meaning of the larger society and one's place in it. Interestingly, the only roles in modern life without an inherent element of sacrifice, it seems, are the commercial: consumer, producer, investor. In these roles, the ideal role is one devoid of friendship and enmity, of power and weakness, even of competition and cooperation. In these roles, it's all about the transaction—anonymous, abstract, disconnected. Price determines all, not relations, obligations, responsibilities, or justice. There's no commitment.[17] It is the ultimate juvenile playground—no responsibilities, no rules, and a free flow of food and goodies; all fun, no constraint; all benefit, no cost; all indulgence, no consequence; all new and improved, no tradition and no looking back.

In highly individualistic, open, market-driven, commercially oriented and democratic societies (such as the United States), the negative side of sacrifice prevails ("people won't sacrifice, why should they?"). In other societies, in fact, in the great preponderance of societies across cultures and across time, the positive prevails. "Outside our own modern cultural context, sacrifice is a nearly universal practice whose effects have been generally understood as positive," writes Karen Litfin in chapter 6. "Though the forms it takes vary greatly from one culture to the next, anthropologists affirm that sacrifice typically promotes both social cohesion and a sense of deep relationship with the cosmos and transcendental forces."[18]

What is important to recognize from the standpoint of overconsumption and the goal of a sustainable economy is that no society employs strictly a positive or negative notion of sacrifice; they have a mix. Getting the right mix for the assigned goal is the challenge. In a frontier economy, in which rapid industrialization is the goal, the negative makes sense: to get people to extract, produce, consume, and dispose, and do so rapidly and thoroughly and at ever greater levels, the requisite norm is some combination of adventure, exploration, and risk taking. The associated norm of sacrifice must be negative: sacrifice is holding back, being reticent, even weak and cowardly: of course, we should push that frontier; what are you afraid of? In a nationalistic and militaristic society bent on subjugating neighboring populations, a norm of sacrifice as defending the motherland and advancing civilization makes sense, hence, positive sacrifice.

The real issue in understanding and prescribing a politics of sacrifice in an advanced industrial economy is the *distribution of positive and negative* sacrifice. In communal societies (and communal segments of individualistic societies—cohousing and religious groups, for example), members are expected to sacrifice for their families, their communities, and their nation. When they do, and do it well, they are admired. They move up a notch in the social order. When they do it poorly, they lose respect and are shunned, ostracized, or banished. In individualistic societies, people who sacrifice often slip back in the social hierarchy. Soldiers come home injured and find little place in a society that values mobility and youthful health. A corporate manager takes time off to care for her ailing father, and she misses a promotion. A committed environmentalist makes do with one car and a modest house, and friends rib him for his eccentricities and naivete.

So as much as sacrifice—that is, that sacrifice presumed to be negative—may seem anathema in modern commercial societies, it has only been distributed so, pushed "underground," says Litfin. "Far from being an invalid or nonexistent form of human activity, [positive] sacrifice in modernity is ubiquitous but largely unconscious."[19] A careful historical examination of the origins of consumerism might reveal the sources and rationales for such a redistribution. If, for instance, in the United States, thrift and frugality were systematically suppressed to spur domestic consumption and absorb industrial output, all to expand the economy and create a great power,[20] then relegating sacrifice to acts of great heroism and (probably later) parenting (raising the next generation's workforce and consumers) and volunteering (e.g., Kiwanis, women's clubs, Peace Corps), and finally, ignoring the economic losers, would follow. If positive sacrifice was deliberately suppressed, along with thrift and frugality, to create sovereign, free-spending consumers, then we have good reason to treat as suspect statements, ubiquitous in American life, that take for granted that consumers will not, cannot, and should not sacrifice (even in the positive sense): Americans will never get out of their cars; to stop consuming is to ruin the economy; the American way of life is not up for negotiation. These are rhetorical claims that justify the status quo (or, at the last turn of the century, the need to spur a great industrial power). They say that it is normal, even patriotic, to demand more and more and at low, low prices. They put defenders of noncommercial values (e.g., ecological integrity, stable climate, social justice) on the defensive, shifting the burden of proof and the burden of creating an economic alternative to those who see the impossibility of endless material growth and the dismissal of huge externalities, environmental and human.

The Everyday

Just as efficiency seeped out of the factory and permeated nearly every facet of modern life, all to justify a mechanistic and expansionist vision of the good life, sacrifice has been squelched, relegated to the brave (overtly heroic) and the weak (covertly worthless) but not to the man and woman on the street, relegated to patriotism and economic growth but not to provisioning and building a community.

To dismiss sacrifice in the material realm of producing and consuming is to depreciate the everyday, the small and little noticed acts that elevate daily life, that give meaning to being someone other than a valiant soldier or a titan of industry, that build community. When my local shoe store owner gives me a deep discount, the negative version of sacrifice affords only a limited, depreciative interpretation: this is an unnecessary forfeit of profit, or he's "buying" customer loyalty. Without an everyday notion of positive sacrifice, it's impossible (or very difficult, for the commercially oriented) to interpret the deep discount as what he and I know it is: one of many acts (such as my volunteering to sand his store floors) that cements our friendship and makes his business a community enterprise. When I walk to work, avoiding the convenience of my car, the negative version of sacrifice again only affords a particular depreciative interpretation: he's a do-gooder, a fool who doesn't know that the gasoline he saves is trivial. What message is he trying to send? Does he really think he'll make the rest of us feel guilty or that we'll imitate him? In other words, a consumerist ideology, by disallowing a noble notion of everyday sacrifice, can only ascribe irrationality to my "consumer choice" of walking to work. It cannot accept that walking for me confers numerous personal and social benefits, not the least of which is fresh air, exercise, uninterrupted mental space (a scarce item even riding the bus, let alone driving), chance encounters with friends and strangers (including my homeless "regulars"), a sense of my community that no amount of driving or reading or discussing can match, and yes, less impact on others and the environment.[21]

So the depreciation of sacrifice in the everyday, the denial of a positive sacrifice for all but the few, is the denial of other-interestedness, of the chance to pursue higher purposes—democratic participation (aside from mere voting) and living within our ecological means, for instance. It is to relegate people to mere consumers and mere workers. It is to hand over the big challenges to the experts, the global managers, to those with the data and the means. It is to deny citizenship. It is to dismiss as foolish the act of an old man planting an oak sapling (knowing he'll never see its majestic state), a toddler helping an adult pick up a piece of chalk, a teenager committed to saving the planet. Framing sacrifice in political and metaphysical terms, Litfin constructs an alternative vision:

An ecological politics of sacrifice would not be about compulsion, guilt, or burdened self-sacrifice; rather, it would grow out of a sense of self as inter-woven with earth, cosmos, species, and society. Sacrifice, then, would facilitate engagement with a participatory universe and would therefore regain its original meaning of "to make sacred by giving." Our politics would follow from our sense of who we are in relation to others—other people (perhaps in distant places and perhaps not yet living) and other species. If human development proceeds by the widening of our circles of identification, then an ecological identity rooted in a holistic ontology represents an important developmental achievement and need not entail any loss of individuality.[22]

Righting the Consumer Economy

To people who take the threat of global warming personally, driving a car that spews heat-trapping greenhouse gasses into the atmosphere can be a guilt trip.

But to help atone for that environmental sin, some drivers are [purchasing carbon offsets to produce clean energy].

Of course, emissions could be reduced the old-fashioned way—by flying less, turning off the air-conditioner or buying a more fuel-efficient car. But that would probably require some sacrifice and perhaps even a change in lifestyle. Instead, carbon-offset programs allow individuals to skip the sacrifice and simply pay for the right to pollute.

—Anthony DePalma, "Gas Guzzlers Find the Price of Forgiveness," *The New York Times*, April 22, 2006

In the American paper of record, and, it seems, throughout mainstream policy debate in the United States and wherever the Washington consensus prevails, saving the environment and the economy and our lifestyle is all about individual purchasing, about having the choice of relieving our guilt while avoiding that dreaded thing called sacrifice. It's about taking personally something that's best left to the experts. And presumably, all this occurs while the guilt-free continue on their merry gas-guzzling way, and while those pesky externalities (like global warming) just correct themselves, all through consumer choice.

A consumer economy requires at least three things to perpetuate itself. One is members' willingness to accept the consumer role as central, even dominant: what I buy is who I am, and what we all buy is what our society is. A second is the belief that because consumer choice is a superior form of decision making, the more realms that come under it, the better—markets, education, health care, environmental protection.

The third requirement for a consumer economy is ever more choices and ever increasing consumption, irrespective of costs that are shaded and distanced, displaced in time and place. In an ecologically empty world (human impact is minor compared to the resource and waste sink capacities of the biosphere), the construction of a person's primary role (buy and buy more) and of a society's purpose (economic growth) may have made sense. In today's full world, it does not.

A consumer economy all too readily becomes a consumer society, giving the appearance of full democratic participation. We're all consumers, after all. It is a society, though, supremely organized to absolve individuals—consumers, producers, investors, and even rule makers—of responsibility. Consequently, the consumer society can, and does, displace costs in time and place. It concentrates benefits among the powerful few and distributes the costs to the many, and often disproportionately to the disempowered. It severs feedback loops that would otherwise put a brake on endless expansion. It constructs a notion of the good life that centers on goods, not on relations, not on service, not on citizenship. And it all seems so rational, so historically inevitable. But it is not the basis of a sustainable society. The answer to overconsumption is not better consuming by better informed consumers.

For a start, the hedonistic, growth-manic, cost-displacing consumer economy must give way to a purposeful economy, an economy premised on principles of positive sacrifice, of giving (along with receiving), of sufficiency and good work and participatory citizenship. The sovereign consumer must be dethroned; sacrifice must be elevated, restored to its proper, "make sacred" pedestal.

Acknowledgments

I would like to thank Allison Alkon, Michael Bell, Raymond De Young, Jack Manno, John Meyer, and Noah Quastel for their helpful comments on earlier drafts. I especially wish to thank Michael Maniates for the original inspiration regarding the politics of sacrifice and for his extensive comments on earlier drafts.

Notes

1. J. H. Brunn, "Das Auto ist ein Stuck mehr Freiheit" (The Auto Is Another Piece of Freedom), speech to the VDA-Mitgliederversammlung, Baden-Baden, September 27, 1974; quoted in Wolfgang Sachs, *For Love of the Automobile: Looking Back into the History of Our Desires* (Berkeley: University of California Press, 1992), 97, translated from the 1984 German original by Don Reneau.

2. For historical and analytic elaboration of the ideas of efficiency and consumer sovereignty, see Thomas Princen, *The Logic of Sufficiency* (Cambridge, MA: MIT Press, 2005), and Thomas Princen, Michael Maniates, and Ken Conca, eds., *Confronting Consumption* (Cambridge, MA: MIT Press, 2002).

3. William Leach, *Land of Desire: Merchants, Power, and the Rise of a New American Culture* (New York: Pantheon Books, 1993), 277.

4. Ibid., 294.

5. Peter Sutherland, chairman of Goldman Sachs International and of the Overseas Development Council, and John W. Sewell, president of the Overseas Development Council, "Gather the Nations to Promote Globalization," *The New York Times*, February 8, 1998.

6. Leach, *Land of Desire*, 229.

7. Simon Patten, "Reconstruction of Economic Theory" (1912); reprinted in *Essays in Economic Theory*, ed. Rexford Tugwell (New York: A. A. Knopf, 1924), 337; Simon Patten, *The Theory of Prosperity* (New York, 1902), 182; quoted in Leach, *Land of Desire*, 239.

8. Angus Deaton in *The Palgrave Dictionary of Economics* (London: Palgrave, 1987), 599; Robert Heilbroner, *The Worldly Philosophers: The Lives, Times, and Ideas of the Great Economic Thinkers* (New York: Simon and Schuster, 1953), 51.

9. Robert Gilpin, *The Political Economy of International Relations* (Princeton, NJ: Princeton University Press, 1987), 17.

10. See Michael Maniates, "Individualization: Plant a Tree, Buy a Bike, Save the World?" and Thomas Princen, "Distancing: Consumption and the Severing of Feedback," in Princen et al., *Confronting Consumption*.

11. See, however, Thomas Princen, *Treading Softly: Paths to Ecological Order* (Cambridge, MA: MIT Press, 2010), in which I argue that the question of reduc-

ing consumption without hurting the economy is the wrong question, presuming, as it does, that present practices will not "hurt the economy," let alone people and communities and the ecosystems on which they depend.

12. Paul Krugman, "Death by Insurance," *The New York Times*, May 1, 2006, A19(L).

13. This phrase, "different set of values," is a nearly verbatim quote of a business school economist reacting to a question about environmental and long-term impacts of current economic activity. Along with "acceptable prices," such phrases were ubiquitous, unexamined, and unquestioned in a "business and policy" discussion of climate change among business leaders, government leaders, and academics (mostly economists and engineers). "Business and Climate Change: Designing Integrated Strategies," conference, University of Michigan, May 4–5, 2006, Ann Arbor.

14. In part, this apparent reluctance to describe parenting as sacrifice derives from the cultural setting—i.e., in an individualistic, consumer-oriented society, we equate sacrifice with the strictly negative; see the following discussion.

15. I thank Michael Bell for making this important distinction. See also chapter 2.

16. I thank Raymond De Young for raising this point.

17. I thank Jack Manno for pointing out the absence of commitment and the depreciation of relations (with others and the natural world) in a commoditized, consumer economy. Personal communication, May 23, 2006. See also Manno's chapter, "Commoditization: Consumption Efficiency and an Economy of Care and Connection," in Princen et al., *Confronting Consumption*.

18. Chapter 6.

19. Ibid.

20. Leach, *Land of Desire*.

21. I have to admit that, at times, walking to work does feel like sacrifice in the negative sense. Close calls with careless drivers throw some doubt on whether all these benefits exceed the risks to life and limb.

22. Chapter 6.

8

Parental Sacrifice as Atonement for Future Climate Change

Sudhir Chella Rajan

During the past year or two, largely because of my involvement with a popular book on climate change,[1] I have had some modest public exposure in the form of reading events and talks at bookstores, radio shows, and community libraries. The book itself stands out from the rest of the crop of recent titles on the subject mainly in that it emphasizes the impossibility of being able to rely on technology alone to reduce greenhouse gas concentrations to avoid what many are terming *runaway warming*. My coauthors, Mayer Hillman and Tina Fawcett, and I argue that only with a combination of government policies and community action that place substantial limits on the personal shares of the available carbon budget do we have any hope of addressing the climate challenge. This will inevitably require heroic technological change as well as substantial shifts in lifestyles, especially among the well-to-do in all parts of the world.

I have also moved recently from the United States to India, where similar work on the topic provided the opportunity to meet nonspecialist audiences in two different cultural settings and respond to queries on climate change and propose potential solutions. I have had comparable reactions to this argument in both countries, but often in the form of skepticism toward the proposal that sufficient numbers of people need be ready to limit their consumption today even if they are unlikely to perceive the benefits of such action in their own lifetimes. Someone invariably points out that while it does seem obvious that people need to change their lifestyles to avert a climate catastrophe, what would be the point of their sacrifice if they may themselves never see the environmental benefits of foregoing certain simple pleasures and conveniences such as taking airplane trips to Europe and the Caribbean, going on solitary drives, or keeping that extra large refrigerator in the garage? My usual response is that one need not think of future generations in the abstract, but instead relate the idea to one's own children and grandchildren and imagine how their lives would be impacted by actions taken today. My reasoning often goes like this: "Wouldn't it be a horrendous legacy to leave to them to solve, given that we can take relatively painless steps now so that our loved ones will have much less to contend with later? So we might consider making a moderate sacrifice by reducing our consumption of carbon-intensive goods and services. That would give our children and grandchildren a head start and also make it easier for them to emulate us in the future."

Although this line of argument generally seems to quell further discussion, I have felt uneasy about having to resort to it for at least two reasons. First, having no children of my own, I do not actually experience the feeling of parental love and concern that I claim is universal and therefore have no real affectivity for my claims. Indeed, I myself do not relate to future generations except in the abstract. Even as I do try to limit my carbon footprint, often not very successfully, making excuses related to professional advancement and the like when I regress, my motives remain fuzzy to me. Perhaps my involvement in this game for more than a decade has gotten me to the point where I can feel self-righteous and angry that others seem oblivious to the dangers. Thus, when I relinquish driving a car and ride a bicycle instead, I may simply be expressing disdain toward my perplexed peers, instead of truly participating in acts of sacrifice in the service of a larger environmentalist principle. And while I share humanist ideals with most liberals and progressives on the question of fairness for present and future generations, I have no special affinity toward any one group of representatives of the future, other than fondness and concern for the welfare of my nephews and nieces and of my students.

In short, it would be bad faith on my part to claim that I spend substantial time worrying about an entire generation of children facing a dire future; yet I suspect that many parents do face similar questions on an almost daily basis, especially with regard to their own children, and perhaps to some extent with regard to the society and environment in which they will live in the future. I also have friends and siblings who seem to engage in what I deem self-sacrifice when, for instance, they give up opportunities to entertain themselves, even when they can afford babysitters, simply because they feel convinced that spending more time with their children will be "good for them." Deeper forms of parental sacrifice are also in evidence, as when immigrant parents take up multiple jobs and remain frugal in their purchases, hoping that their children, if not they, will ultimately experience the American dream. The logic of these decisions may seem to confound the individualist paradigm of self-seeking rational actors, but clearly the reward to the parents is in the pride of seeing their child "become somebody" in an alien setting.[2] I do not know anybody, however, who uses parental love as the sole basis of their decision to limit their carbon footprint, although one might impute from these observations that environmentally conscious parents could potentially extend their selflessness to cover this area, as well. At least I tell myself that if I were a parent, I would feel that way. But the argument needs to be made more compellingly, which is one of my tasks in this chapter.

A second aspect of my uneasiness is more familiar to political theorists: why should we assume that a parent's concern about her child's security in a world with the severe effects of global warming would translate specifically into a coherent set of actions that mitigate climate change? Why wouldn't she wait for government action or lobby for her peers to act first, or buy extra insurance to protect herself and her child? But other potential problems are also apparent in this general family of difficulties relating to social choice and collective action, including such issues as institutional and consumer lock-in, by which old habits are hard to break and people continue to engage in self-destructive or environmentally harmful behavior, in spite of their best motivations to act otherwise. In different ways, these issues raise the possibility that even if parental love were a sufficient motivation for individuals to engage in selfless actions in the service of reducing climate change, there are several reasons why these actions may not be universalizable or cannot be sustained.

In this chapter, I aim to explore both these concerns and make some progress toward resolving them. Mainly, I try to strengthen the postulate that personal actions to avert climate change can potentially be raised to the iconic status that parental sacrifice in general has come to have in our societies, and that this can, in effect, play a significant role in

changing our collective attitudes and behavior to favor future generations as a group. Moreover, because parental sacrifice is so deeply rooted
in our collective psyche as a basic human value across cultures, I argue
that we can indeed all be socialized, even as nonparents, into feeling
generous toward the interests of children and their peers. That is to
say, even those of us who do not have the personal experience of being
engaged with parental affectivity with our own children can potentially
feel sympathetically inclined toward future generations, simply because
of the resilient symbolic power of parental sacrifice in most societies.
I do not have the resources available to defend a strong form of this
thesis, which would be to elaborate a broad social theory of sacrifice,
and parental sacrifice in particular, and explain what cultural transformations are needed for concerns about future generations, and therefore
climate change, to become embedded as representative social practices
in our time. Instead, I try to address some of the sources of discomfort
that I have expressed previously, first by exploring the powerful importance of parental sacrifice as a binding normative principle in virtually
all societies, and second by examining how the socializing power of this
principle may be able to resolve some of the problems relating to social
choice and to transmitting values and behavior across generations.

Parent-Child Sacrifice in Myth

Perhaps because it is so common, the theme of sacrifice, and of self-
sacrifice in particular, is undervalued in the study of families, according
to Howard and Kathleen Bahr: "The naming of love and sacrifice as
essential concepts, even root metaphors, strikes the modern student of
families as quaint, for neither term plays much part in today's family
theory."[3] Yet parental love is clearly of sociological importance, with
resonances in virtually all cultures and appearing to be the decisive social
mechanism through which succeeding generations can have a running
start for coping with the multiple threats to their survival that they
are likely to face from infancy onward. It is indeed hard to imagine a
sustainable social system in which one or both parents do not routinely
forsake personal pleasures so that their children may gain some sort of
skills or assets. "Crack mothers" and alcoholic fathers who abandon
their children at a very young age symbolize broken social institutions

and signal deep troubles ahead for succeeding generations in any society in which such apparently dysfunctional parenting is prevalent.

But if parental love and self-sacrifice are so important in societal terms, what actually causes individuals to fall into line to keep the community's future intact? How can we explain the normalcy of this pattern as a social phenomenon without having to resort to naturalism, that is to say, without asserting that parenting behavior is nothing other than biological instinct? What socializes parents into believing that self-sacrifice is a routine and expected pattern of behavior? And how, indeed, does this become so entrenched in everyday understandings of parenting that its opposite form, namely, parental neglect or, in the extreme instance, filicide, is treated with utmost horror?

There are, of course, multiple disciplinary approaches to answering these questions, but for my purposes in this chapter, structural anthropology, particularly Victor Turner's concept of liminality, seems especially promising. Turner's point of departure is the forms of otherness that a society recognizes within itself, which in fact mark out the character and limits of its internal connectedness as a community. "To look at itself," Turner argues, "a society must cut out a piece of itself for inspection," and this in turn requires that it set up a frame within which it reorganizes the images and symbols of what it considers its normal (and therefore normative) patterns so that they "can be scrutinized, assessed, and, if need be, remodeled and rearranged."[4] But it is not sufficient to examine its mundane practices if the point of this frame is for the society to experience what Turner terms *communitas*, a moment of exuberance when the community senses that it shares a common state of oneness and equality of purpose. It is only when the society tells stories of imagined possibilities about itself, when it enters a subjunctive condition of wonderment, "a moment in and out of time and in and out of secular social structure," that it recognizes the extent and limits of its social bonds.[5] This is the experience of liminality, which is deliberately sought out in rituals and in myth. Liminal "persons [are those who] elude or slip through the network of classifications that normally locate states and positions in cultural space. [They] are neither here nor there; they are betwixt and between the positions assigned and arrayed by law, custom, convention and ceremonial."[6] It is in the telling of stories of liminal characters and in out-of-the-ordinary circumstances that the audience, too, experiences a state betwixt and between two worlds, the world of their own and that of myth.

In the case of parental sacrifice, even if we were to construe the initial attachment that is formed between most parents and their children in biological terms, we still need to account for its social expression and transmission across generations in linguistic and cultural terms. The primary medium for this transmission appears in a liminal form as myth. Myths have an important place in mediating cultural discourse in all societies and therefore reaffirm certain forms of practice as social norms, even if they have sublimated or displaced appearances. It is therefore striking how common the theme of forsaking the body of the child (in the extreme, actual filicide) for some higher cause seems to be in folkloric traditions across cultures. "Parental sacrifice" appears thus as an ambivalent term in virtually all cultures, associated not only with the idea of a parent giving up something so that his or her child may benefit from that act, but also more darkly with the possibility of having to harm or even kill that child for some higher cause. The former is the mundane sense of the term, but the latter is its liminal form, identifying subjects whose traumas provide object lessons of inverted family priorities, usually under tragic circumstances. Filicide takes place in these myths under situations of extreme duress, and it is precisely because it emphasizes something that cannot be taken lightly that it draws attention to the need for the parent to make small self-sacrificing actions to take care of his or her child in ordinary situations. "How could you possibly allow yourself to kill your own child?" is a question that needs to be asked repeatedly in circumstances of high drama before the young mother or father comes to have absolute conviction that she or he has certain obligations toward the vulnerable personhood of the stranger in his or her home.

The paradigmatic case is the *Akedah* myth, Abraham's offering of his son Isaac to God, simply because God ordered him to do so. This is indeed a story common to other traditions, including Greek and Hindu, albeit with some of its elements varied. At the end of the Trojan War, King Agamemnon agrees to sacrifice his daughter to free up the Greek fleet. In the Sanskrit tale of Harischandra, the father makes a promise to the gods to sacrifice his son, but the latter successfully finds a substitute to play the part. In the *Mahabharata*, Arjuna offers his son to the goddess

Kali so that Arjuna and his brothers can use their weapons with greater power and skill to attain victory in their epic war. In a different twist, the god Varuna strangles his son and thereby sends him to hell, but only so he may gain wisdom.

The many variants on this tragic theme of filicide each has a story line of parental love that is disturbed by a need to fulfill a higher calling. As in all forms of sacrifice, an offering is typically made to meet this demand, but the act entails a tragic conflict between parental love and some larger good. A risk is involved, and the parent is given a cruel choice that invariably involves the permanent severing of an idyllic relationship with his or her child, potentially resulting in death, but the outcome also produces some sort of reward or redemption. The uncertainty of the outcome is an important element of the myth, and in the course of making the choice, a deontological ethical judgment is assumed. Indeed, one does not see Abraham assessing the consequences of his action; he sees it rather as a matter of weighing his duty to obey God against his parental duty to protect his son from harm. Similarly, the philosopher-god Krishna tells Arjuna that his actions in war and life are matters of *dharma*, or "duty," but ultimately does not give him guidance on how to weigh conflicting judgments of duty. The central motif of the myth is not only this profound moral dilemma, but also the psychological injury resulting from the parent having ultimately to forego something that is closely and deeply held.

In Abraham's case, it is his (and Sarah's) long-awaited offspring who is put up as the offering. It is open to question as to whether Abraham already knows that God is testing him, and therefore whether it is on the strength of this knowledge, not to mention the omnipotent power of God, that he endures the emotional pain of binding his only son in preparation for the sacrifice. No doubt he is also fearful of God, which provides him with a strong motivation to take the painful steps, including the ultimate one of picking up his knife to slay Isaac. The dramatic tension is resolved in the form of an ample reward, by which not only are Isaac's and Abraham's lives spared, but their entire future progeny is given a covenant: "By Myself I swear, the Lord declares: because you have done this and have not withheld your son, your favored one, I will bestow My blessing upon you and make your descendants as numerous as the stars of heaven and the sands on the seashore; and your descendants shall seize the gates of their foes. All the nations of the earth shall bless themselves by your descendants, because you have obeyed My command."[7]

Akedah may seem like an inverted metaphor for *self*-sacrifice, but the fact that the object of sacrifice for Abraham is his beloved son makes it obvious that the father is also sacrificing part of himself for some greater cause. As Kierkegaard writes, "would the normal human duty not to kill one's own innocent child be suspended or overridden in the presence of a divine command to the contrary? . . . He did it for God's sake because God required this proof of his faith; for his own sake he did it in order that he might furnish proof."[8] The proof is in the pain, one might say, whereby the mere willingness to sacrifice one's beloved son or daughter provides the evidence that the parental bond can be broken for a higher cause.

Nowhere in contemporary literature does this pain appear with more poignancy than in Toni Morrison's *Beloved*, whose protagonist, Sethe, kills her child rather than allowing her to be captured into slavery. Filicide, it turns out, results as much in loss of oneself as it does of the child: "Counting on the stillness of her own soul, she had forgotten the other one: the soul of her baby girl. Who would have thought that a little old baby could harbor so much rage? . . . Those ten minutes she spent pressed up against dawn-colored stone studded with star chips, her knees wide open as the grave, were longer than life, more alive, more pulsating than the baby blood that soaked her fingers like oil."[9] I did it for you, says Sethe to the apparent ghost of her daughter, Beloved, who reappears several years after the event, but that is hardly any consolation to the dead. Yet we can also see a sort of transference in the sacrifice of Beloved, the baby girl, from the tens of millions sacrificed on slave ships to the higher calling of wealth creation. When Beloved, the ghost, reacts furiously to her mother's plea of innocence, it sounds to Stamp Paid, a former slave and agent of the Underground Railroad, like the chorus of the "black and angry dead."[10]

What, then, was the point of the sacrifice? Much of the social theory of literature on sacrifice focuses on its role in structuring relationships, where the reward is the increased likelihood of social stability. In the Durkheimian view, from Mauss to Girard, the function of ritual sacrifice is to bridge society's profane elements of strife and to resolve them through the sacred ones of a bond, if not covenant, with the divine. For Turner, too, sacrifice plays a similar role, reaffirming the intensity of human bonds through the experience of communitas outside the ordinary structured limits of the society. In *Beloved*, one might thus recast Sethe's action (and that of several black women in postantebellum nineteenth-century North America) as a ritual revival of the past of slavery and its psychological impairment on mothers who lost contact with their children. The social bond of the historical memory of slavery's horrible past, one might say, is kept alive through this dark tradition, and the pain and guilt experienced by the individual mother are conveyed as the collective gasp of astonishment and forced remembering.[11]

Filicide's liminal characters appear not only in myth, but also in a ritualized form in most societies among the parents of soldiers when family tradition or state law requires young males, and occasionally females, to go into military service with the intention of being willing to die for their country. The child is sent off to war, but it is the parent who invariably experiences the sacrifice of loss and redemption: loss of a loved child as well as redemption in terms of knowing that one played a role in serving the cause of one's nation. In the ritual of parental sacrifice carried out in the service of war, communitas is experienced as the social order and is restored during a time of crisis when resources are brought together to heal prevailing social rifts. One of modern warfare's most endearing liminal figures is thus the mother or father of the dead or wounded soldier, who is compelled to remain stoic in the public eye. An already fragmented social structure may thus be reconstructed and strengthened, even if, in the process, we are left with individuals who have lost a bit of themselves.

My reasoning, then, is that sacrifice of the young by their parents expresses an exceptional or liminal hardening of filial affectivity to meet some general imperative for the community. The pain is expressed in unspoken guilt at the moment of, and following, Abraham's and Sethe's actions of lifting their respective knives with the readiness to strike their children. It expresses the capacity of the parent to remain mute, knowing the pain could be permanent, yet recognizing that a choice has been made for a cause that is deemed more important than the interests of the family alone. The ability of a parent to sacrifice her favorite child when called on to do so by a legitimate authority is her ultimate expression of fortitude and good citizenship. But it is not just a lesson for the parent to absorb; rather, in Turner's categories, everyone ends up marveling at the ordeals undergone by the liminal entities. The experience of communitas makes it obvious that parental sacrifice for the good of children and their peers requires the figurative opposite of filicide; parents need simply to engage in acts of self-sacrifice by limiting their own consumption so that their children may potentially lead *better* lives and *avoid* the risk of disease or death. Violence and the tragedy of deep loss are superfluous elements in this form of sacrifice, but not parental love and societal imperative. Societal bonding, as it were, takes place among parents and nonparents alike, reminding everyone that the pain of child sacrifice is itself expressed as a form of self-sacrifice, thereby reaffirming the need for the latter in its ordinary form in our everyday lives.

Future Generations

In the filicide myths, there is typically a triangular responsibility relationship of parent-child love, which is conflicted by parent-Other allegiance, where the Other could be God or simply *dharma*, or a sense of duty. The conflicts take place in the present; indeed, they are a consequence of having to make difficult choices in real time. God asked Abraham to sacrifice Isaac while Isaac was still the vulnerable child toward whom Abraham could feel nothing but tenderness and despair. Abraham, in turn, does not (one presumes) take into account the future consequences of his action, but rather, places himself in the heat of the situation to obey the command of the lawgiver. Isaac and Beloved, on the other hand, are silent for the most part when the dreadful acts are committed but the family trauma endures well into the future.[12]

Parental *self*-sacrifice involves no expectation of reciprocity from the child. Yet it is action that keeps its eye firmly on the future. There appears to be considerable evidence that all parents, not just stereotypical Asian or Central American immigrants, engage in some sort of self-sacrifice, and furthermore, that this is directed toward the future well-being of their children. The mother who toils to keep her baby safe and healthy and continues to nurture him well into his difficult teenage years and beyond seems to expect no reward other than the satisfaction of having introduced a new person into the world. Clearly the ideology of flesh and blood plays an important part in persuading the parent to keep this up, that is to say, the conviction that the child carries within his being the legacy of the parent and that of her ancestors in the form of genetic material and whatnot. Yet, while there may be disappointment if the child turns out not to be the overwhelming success that the parent fantasizes about, no parent ever seems to claim her deposit back when the product has achieved maturity without seeming to fulfill his potential.

This characteristic of parental love provides some useful fodder against a familiar concern among environmentalists regarding social discounting of the future. In its starkest utilitarian form, this is usually expressed as follows: people tend to value their own future happiness somewhat less than present enjoyment of the same event; worse, because of the nonreciprocal nature of our relationship with those living after us, people have little or no incentive to ensure that future generations have any enjoyment of resources we take for granted such as clean air, crude oil, fertile soils, and fresh water. Sacrificing a small part of present wants to set some of these goods aside for the future is therefore unlikely, the utilitarians argue. It may in fact be advantageous for the individual maximizer to adopt a scorched-earth policy that leaves nothing for the future, especially if technologies are available today to provide her with the greatest enjoyment at affordable prices, no matter how great the resulting destruction of resources.

Parental self-sacrifice reminds us that the standard utilitarian argument misses other sources of individual happiness than the pleasure obtained from fulfilling personal wants. The unselfishness of the parent highlights the fact that pleasure can be gained by forging bonds with other individuals and groups, which in turn will inevitably cause the individual to transcend her self-interest. Furthermore, the parent may trade her current opportunities for pleasure-seeking behavior for far-off and less certain ones that may involve the happiness of her children. A child's hopes and aspirations for the future could well form the basis for self-sacrifice.

The utilitarian may retort that parental concern is merely a different form of self-interest, in which the self is extended to the notion of one's family. Together, the family may still have a high "discount rate," that is to say, they would collectively value today's goods more than next year's, which in turn would be valued still more than the following year's. The family as a consuming unit may decide to go on a spending spree this year, leaving less for next year, and so on. Indeed, the household savings rate, especially in the United States and in a surprising number of other countries, tends to be dismally low, indicating that families do appear to act with little or no regard for their own future.

Nevertheless, it is also clear that self-sacrificing behavior by parents toward their children, however unwise in its expression, is ubiquitous. And while the burden typically falls unfairly on mothers through the stereotype of nurturing into which women are compelled to fit, it is also fairly clear that most parents value something about their children that exceeds their own present happiness. For instance, much of household spending is internally skewed toward children, in large part to quell the latter's demands, which are shaped by clever marketing, but also because parents feel some pride in contributing to their children's happiness.

Take, for example, a parent who spends significant fractions of her income in fancy stores for her child's clothes. At the very least, the money she spends on her child represents foregone spending on herself, that is to say, by engaging in such behavior, she is placing a special value on the grooming of her son or daughter as someone who will be better prepared to face the world. In other instances, this logic stands out even more clearly, as when parents take out a second mortgage on their house, often at great risk to their own financial security, and use the money to finance their child's college education, rather than spending it on that special car and luxury cruise they may have dreamed about in their youth. Parents in general tend to treat their children as persons whose future lives are at least as valuable as their own present lives. The implicit discount rates they use for their children are often lower than the ones they may use for themselves. That is probably why an Internet travel Web site advertises to its wealthy clients by reminding them to be a bit more generous to themselves before it is too late: "If you can afford to travel first class and you don't, your children certainly will!"

There is also some evidence that focusing on different forms of consumptive behavior as the sole criterion for welfare maximization may be incorrect where parenting is concerned. In a widely cited study by Sharon Hays on motherhood, several of her respondents seemed committed to the notion that "appropriate child rearing involves sacrifice and that the needs of children should and do take priority over any interest they might have in power or material gain."[13] Her analysis suggests that these sentiments persist against all odds, even in present-day societies, in which one would expect a prevalent market ideology to make demands on parents to act as self-seeking rationalists and to limit their self-sacrifice. Indeed, their actions express "not a passive selflessness but an active rejection of market logic," and at times even "horror" toward this paradigm. "The cultural logic operating here offers an alternative account of what might count as status, power, or self-interest. In this sense, the ideology of intensive mothering persists not only in spite of the fact that it runs counter to the logic of impersonality, competition, and personal profit but precisely because it does."[14]

On the surface, parental selflessness appears to be inward looking and focused on the welfare of the family unit as such. For the parent engaging in self-sacrificing behavior on behalf of his child, the sense of duty that motivates him appears to be direct and focused on a specific person, and only on that person. I believe that may be a limited interpretation, given that most parents have to be concerned about their children becoming ready for a world beyond the home. To the extent that they desire their children to enjoy a satisfying relationship of reciprocity with their peers, the efforts in which they engage at present make up the training wheels that will have to come off in the future. By extension of this argument, it seems reasonable to claim that by engaging in forms of nurturance that entail self-sacrifice, parents act in ways that help fulfill the needs of the next generation as a whole, notwithstanding the multiple failures they often encounter along the way. Their intention may be to bring their children to a level of welfare that they would expect for themselves, but they generally end up serving the interests of their children's or grandchildren's cohorts. Parental self-sacrifice in the interests of saving the planet would no doubt also deprive children of some goods, but the pain, or rather, reduced pleasure that ensues may also be accompanied by a shift in sensibility, like the mother's horror at rampant consumerism, which in turn can lead to an altered conception of the good life. If successful, therefore, there need not be net reduction in welfare, as seen from the utilitarian's perspective. It is nevertheless far from clear whether parents would see their actions that provide common benefits to the entire generation of their children's peers as an *obligation*. Indeed, it is even less likely that they may feel that way about more remote generations. Moreover, the extension of parental sacrifice might suffer from discounting: a parent may be willing to be concerned about his child's future, and even that of his peers, but his concern toward his grandchild's generation might be reduced.

In general, there are several considerations that complicate our duty to far-off generations.[15] They are not composed of people whom we know, neither their welfare nor "malfare" will have any impact on us, and we cannot know for sure what they want from us. More intriguingly, as Derek Parfit has pointed out, slight variations in our actions today can have profound consequences on *who* will be born in the future, which confounds our ability to evaluate the moral relevance of our present-day behavior. Yet, as Avner de-Shalit argues, the fact that we cannot "con-verse" with other generations does not preclude us from interacting with them as our cultural peers. De-Shalit speaks of a "transgenerational community" that can share a moral frame of reference, that is to say, one can recognize obligations to future generations.[16] Certainly our capacity to save the earth from ecological catastrophe can form such a frame of reference across generations. But a culture of parental sacrifice relating specifically to actions to prevent such destruction needs to be socially embedded for it to be transmitted successfully across generations.

Parental Sacrifice as Social Structuring

My argument so far has been that certain familiar patterns of parental self-sacrifice have gotten socially embedded across many cultures and over time. Filicide in myth gives our social imagination an object lesson in the scary depths of parental love and sacrifice, especially when it leaves behind a trace of uncertainty and fear as to whether the choice that is presented—saving the child's life versus responding to a higher calling—can ever in fact be justified. The myths and associated rituals found in soldiering, for instance, allow us to experience communitas, which thereby provides the bonding materials to socialize parental unselfishness as a universal sentiment, one that prevails against other historically contingent forces such as market-driven individualism, for instance.

To the extent that filicide in its various forms is already available to us in myth, it is arguable that as parents and nonparents alike, we are ready, in terms of our social psychology, to engage forms of self-sacrifice needed to address the impending crisis generated by climate change. There also appears to be a societal logic at work to justify a certain degree of self-sacrifice toward children and their generation, notwithstanding the expectations of utilitarians, and indeed it is arguable that its value itself is widely shared. Child rearing and the parental self-sacrifice that is involved, with their far less onerous emotional burden, provide relief in the form of an easily shared social obligation for successful breeding of our species. For good measure, we also have available to us ready-made paradigms of unselfish parental behavior in our everyday lives, which show off in good form against the backdrop of capitalism-driven, rational, self-interested individualism. The task of the parent is simply to follow her peers to learn how to structure her sacrificing relationship with her child, and along the way, she develops bonds of love that are made stronger by the possibility of loss.

Among the thornier questions to resolve is whether and how the practice and belief in parental sacrifice can be put to further work in some coherent way to serve the demands of climate action. That is to say, can the ideological elements of parental selflessness be harnessed to mobilize a set of social practices in which families engage in less consumptive lifestyles, use energy more efficiently, and ultimately assume responsibility as global citizens concerned about the future of the planet? Or, to use Turner's framework, what parts of itself should society "cut out for inspection," and in what exceptional circumstances, so that it not only sees the starkness of its choices with respect to climate change, but also recognizes its communitas, its common equality of purpose, which is to reduce emissions through dramatic changes in consumption patterns?

Perhaps a different icon of sacrifice is called for, one that occupies an unconventional position in this new space in which the parent-child bond is transmuted into broader social commitments toward the earth itself. Society needs to be startled in myth or ritual from its normal state by seeing a liminal figure similar to Abraham, Sethe, and the military mom, but whose exceptional experiences can now provide the societal glue to bond shared commitments for personal/parental sacrifice in the service of averting climate change. As far-fetched as this possibility may seem, I sense some indications of hope. I pointed out earlier that parental sacrifice has worked quite well in the service of mobilizing people for nationalist causes such as war. But it is in the very passion of sacrifice that we also see these causes becoming subverted. For instance, the U.S. occupation of Iraq turned sour almost precisely at the moment that Cindy Sheehan asked President Bush the unanswered question: what was the noble cause for which my son Casey died? In the three years or so since Sheehan left Crawford, Texas, where she and fellow protestors camped outside the Bush ranch waiting for a reply, popular support for the war continued to decline, particularly among women.

For Sheehan and others like her, however, it is not sacrifice so much as the legitimacy of the use for which it is demanded by society that is at stake. After the attacks in the United States in 2001, sacrifice was a common refrain in the media. Commentators like Thomas Friedman repeatedly complained that although citizens seemed ready to forego certain conveniences, such as cheap oil, there were no political leaders who had the courage to make use of the opportunity to wean the country off dependence on imported energy. This in turn would have meant a shift in policy that reduced the likelihood of political resentment from people in the Middle East toward the United States. As complicated as the lines of argument were then, they seem now to be having some resonance in public perceptions, at least as reflected in a growing disillusionment with the Bush administration's policies in Iraq and a generalized suspicion of oil companies about global oil price manipulation.[17] Suddenly, it appears that the traditional ritual of parental sacrifice for war has become devoid of meaning in a context in which new considerations relating to the economy, energy, and global conflict are taking precedence.

The social psychological theory of cognitive dissonance provides some explanation for how such a chain of reasoning and associated beliefs can emerge. It proposes that once a person has developed firm beliefs about one set of ideas, it is more likely that he or she will feel attracted to another logically related set of ideas. To the extent that individuals will want to go on preserving a strong and competent sense of self, they will try to maintain internal consistency among their beliefs. As Elliot Aronson puts it, "my having done something which either astonishes me, makes me stupid or makes me feel guilty" will cause me to engage in dissonance-reducing behavior, for instance, by looking for ways to treat my lies as really true.[18] In a more positive sense, my having gone through a great deal of effort or sacrifice to obtain something will make me happy because I see myself as the competent and sensible person who is properly deserving of the fruits of my labor. That is to say, the rampant use of my SUV, even if I consider myself an environmentalist, can be justified if I tell myself that no other type of vehicle is large or safe enough to transport my son and his gear to weekly soccer practice. Or, if I got the SUV after having worked two jobs for several years to pay off my college loans, I can feel happy even if I have no children to transport. Conversely, if the sacrifice seems senseless, then surely someone else must have put me in that terrible situation. My loss of a child in war cannot be in vain, and if it were, then the war was certainly ill conceived. But if the basis for the war is fraudulent, then the logic of the sacrifice must find for itself some other larger societal goal, and it is the lacuna that forms a broader global crisis of legitimacy.

One might imagine how a broadening sensibility about the dangers of climate change and the need to reduce consumption might be catalyzed through cognitive dissonance, beginning with the symbolic power of parental sacrifice. Just as parental loss in war can accentuate a soldier's valor and also place a broader requirement that the war itself be legitimate and meaningful, so, too, can other issues down the logical chain be open to challenge. An important feature of solutions to climate change is that they tend to be broadly aligned with solutions to the energy and national security problem as outlined by Friedman and others. Especially in the area of personal transportation, it is easy to see why government policies as well as individual efforts to reduce oil use can play a substantial role in also reducing one's carbon footprint. Since continued dependence on oil is a national security threat, it is therefore consistent to believe that it is important to reduce one's energy use so as to contribute to the pool of efforts to mitigate climate change.

The theme of parental sacrifice can then stir the social imagination toward a broader agenda; that is to say, it could well turn out that it is the military mom who initiates the double sacrifice of first sending her son to fight a senseless war and then carrying forward the struggle to fight global warming, and at the same time play a role in strengthening national security. Ultimately, Cindy Sheehan and her fellow travelers may well represent the liminal figures who bring parents (and nonparents) to a point of communitas in which they successfully tie these logics together and demonstrate the socially bonding necessity of sacrificial actions to avert climate catastrophe. The icon is certainly a possibility, given the unique historical conditions of our time, in which ritual forms of filicide for the cause of war can no longer contain the social crisis and render the world more orderly. Our hopes then rest at least in part on the emergence of these dangerous and ultimately subversive social dramas of sacrifice, which in turn could change the paradigm of parenthood toward necessary everyday actions for averting climate catastrophe.

These lines of argument are hardly sufficient to convince my peers in India or the United States that we already have, within our prevailing traditions of parental sacrifice, the cultural resources needed to motivate self-sacrifice to address climate change. But to my mind, they at least help raise one important observation: if we are already socialized into taking for granted the notion that a child's vulnerability must be protected for the sake of sustaining societies beyond one generation, even if it means having to engage in routine acts of self-sacrifice, then it is not inconceivable that we make the collective leap into believing in the need for other forms of sacrifice for the longer term. The tragedy, though, is that we may run out of time before we fully develop our mythical and ritual apparatuses to embed the requisite forms of sacrifice to avert global climate catastrophe. Yet, to the extent that contemporary social change seems to take place at an equally fast pace, there may yet be hope, which, to paraphrase Vaclav Havel, is not a prognostication, but a weapon like courage and will.

Notes

1. Mayer Hillman, Tina Fawcett, and Sudhir Chella Rajan, *The Suicidal Planet: How to Prevent Global Climate Catastrophe* (New York: St. Martin's Press), 2007.

2. Carola Suárez-Orozco and Marcelo M. Suárez-Orozco, *Children of Immigration* (Cambridge, MA: Harvard University Press, 2001).

3. Howard M. Bahr and Kathleen S. Bahr, "Families and Self-Sacrifice: Alternative Models and Meanings for Family Theory," *Social Forces* 79 (2000): 1234.

4. Victor Turner, "Frame, Flow and Reflection: Ritual and Drama as Public Liminality," *Japanese Journal of Religious Studies* 6, no. 4 (1979): 468.

5. Victor Turner. *The Ritual Process: Structure and Anti-structure* (Edison, NJ: Aldine Transaction, 1995), 96.

6. Ibid., 95.

7. Genesis 22:16–18.

8. Sören Kierkegaard, *Fear and Trembling* (Cambridge: Cambridge University Press, 2006), 71.

9. Toni Morrison, *Beloved* (New York: Vintage, 1997), 16.

10. Jean Wyatt, "Giving Body to the Word: The Maternal Symbolic in Toni Morrison's *Beloved*," *Publications of the Modern Language Association of America*, 108, no. 3 (1993): 479.

11. See, e.g., Homi Bhabha, *The Location of Culture* (New York: Routledge, 1994).

12. Sarah dies shortly after the binding, and Isaac is somewhat estranged from his father. Beloved haunts her mother for years afterward, and her sister Denver is also scarred by the original event.

13. Sharon Hays, *The Cultural Contradictions of Motherhood* (New Haven, CT: Yale University Press, 1996), 157.

14. Ibid., 171.

15. Ernest Partridge, "Future Generations," in *Blackwell Companion to Environmental Philosophy*, ed. Dale Jamieson (Malden, MA: Blackwell, 2001), 377–389.

16. Avner de-Shalit, *Why Posterity Matters: Environmental Policies and Future Generations* (New York: Routledge, 1995).

17. According to several public opinion polls in the United States over the last few years, multinational oil companies are mostly to blame for wildly fluctuating oil prices and need more regulations, not less. See, e.g., the Harris Poll 107, November 1, 2007, http://www.harrisinteractive.com.

18. Elliott Aronson, "Back to the Future: Retrospective Review of Leon Festinger's 'A Theory of Cognitive Dissonance,'" *American Journal of Psychology* 110, no. 1 (1997): 127–137.

III

Obstacles and Opportunities

Where might opportunities lie for applying a more creative perspective on sacrifice to environmental affairs? How might these opportunities best be developed? What obstacles or lessons do efforts to highlight or hide sacrifice reveal? And what does all this say about how scholars, activists, students, and citizens might best proceed?

Questions like these are best addressed by teasing apart a distinct set of environmental practices or policies, all the while watchful for dynamics of sacrifice. This is the task that the authors of part III have set for themselves. Not merely case studies, these chapters show how sacrifice becomes structured in everyday life, how language and hidden assumptions undermine careful thinking and insightful policy, and how these structures and frames might best be challenged.

Together, these chapters demonstrate two distinct but related ways of dissecting sacrifice. One is to analyze how political struggle around specific environmental issues is framed to highlight or hide sacrifice, at what cost, and why. Shane Gunster's opening ("Self-Interest, Sacrifice, and Climate Change") and Michael Maniates's closing chapter ("Struggling with Sacrifice") emphasize this first approach. The second is to examine how our built environment—homes, businesses, roads, and transportation networks—shapes the experience of sacrifice and the political possibilities for change. The chapters by Peter F. Cannavò ("Civic Virtue and Sacrifice in a Suburban Nation") and Justin Williams ("Bikes, Sticks, Carrots") are compelling examples of this approach. Simon Nicholson integrates these approaches in his chapter ("Intelligent Design? Unpacking Geoengineering's Hidden Sacrifices"). On one hand, he takes special care to show how conventional treatments of sacrifice can twist environmental politics in peculiar ways. He also describes how large-scale geoengineering approaches to sustainability could structure our lives and politics. The impact will be far-reaching, and Nicholson helps us to anticipate some of the insidious possibilities that might result.

These five chapters raise a new set of challenges for those engaged in environmental politics. We consider these challenges, and more, in our concluding chapter ("Sacrifice and a New Environmental Politics"), which follows part III.

9

Self-Interest, Sacrifice, and Climate Change: (Re-)Framing the British Columbia Carbon Tax

Shane Gunster

On May 12, 2009, Liberal Party leader Gordon Campbell was reelected for an impressive third consecutive term as premier of British Columbia (BC). Environmentalists from Canada and elsewhere were quick to celebrate his victory as evidence of popular support for Campbell's controversial introduction of a broad-based, "revenue-neutral" carbon tax, the first of its kind in North America. Less than six months earlier, the federal Liberal Party under Stephane Dion (which is distinct in philosophy, organization, and party membership from the provincial Liberals) had a disastrous experience in the national election after running a campaign based on an ambitious proposal to shift taxation from income to carbon, leading observers of all political stripes to speculate that carbon taxes had become the new third rail of Canadian (and North American) politics. Campbell's win was celebrated as challenging this perspective, breathing new life into the electoral viability of a policy—the pricing of carbon emissions—that has been consistently championed by environmentalists and economists as the single most effective instrument in reducing greenhouse gas emissions.

A carbon tax consists of a surcharge levied on the purchase of energy (e.g., gasoline, heating oil, electricity derived from coal or natural gas, etc.) that is based on the amount of carbon dioxide discharged on consumption. Such taxes create a strong financial incentive for both businesses and individuals to reduce their reliance on carbon-intensive fuels and thus demand energy-efficient technologies and alternative sources of energy. Revenue neutrality refers to the principle that government will not keep any of the tax revenues for itself, but will instead return all monies raised to the public, usually in the form of offsetting cuts to other taxes. Thus carbon taxes begin to shift the source of government revenues from things that society values, such as income, employment, and profit, to those it wants to reduce, such as pollution. The net effect of this shift means that those who reduce their consumption of carbon pay less tax, while those who are unable or unwilling to do so pay more. The discipline of the market compels all consumers to adopt more sustainable forms of behavior irrespective of their personal levels of environmental awareness or commitment.

Many environmentalists were thrilled with Campbell's victory, especially given the fact that the New Democratic Party (NDP), the left-of-center opposition, had mounted a strong "axe-the-tax" campaign against the Liberal policy. Their defeat at the hands of the Liberals was read by some as a powerful rebuke to the NDP's attempt to exploit (and incite) a populist backlash against such an important environmental initiative. Writing in DeSmogBlog, a Vancouver-based climate change site with a significant international presence, Richard Littlemore enthused that "the only government in North America to implement a carbon tax to fight climate change has been re-elected handily in British Columbia. . . . The carbon tax stands; [NDP leader] Carole James falls."[1] Likewise, Ian Bruce, a climate change analyst with the David Suzuki Foundation, noted that "this is certainly a watershed moment for action on climate change in North America," and Matt Horne of the Pembina Institute, a prominent Canadian environmental think tank, described the election as "an encouraging result for any government that's considering putting a price on carbon across the economy."[2] Charles Komanoff, blogging about the election on the Carbon Tax Center Web site, gushed, "We owe a big debt of gratitude to B.C. Premier Gordon Campbell and his Liberal Party for political courage, and likewise to the voters of British Columbia for rewarding that bravery in the voting booth."[3] In a single night, carbon taxes were rehabilitated from political liability to political asset, proving that the electorate not only wanted action on global warming, but had finally crossed the Rubicon (in North America) of accepting the use of taxation to motivate environmentally sustainable behavior.

For those seeking substantive political action on climate change after decades of denial and delay, it is an encouraging, even inspirational, story. If only it were true. Digging a little deeper into the political fortunes of the carbon tax in British Columbia, one finds that it is less a symbol of an emerging ecological consciousness and more an example of the imposition of an unwanted policy on an unsympathetic public.

Simply put, the tax was (and remains) unpopular with BC residents: in a recent national survey, for example, British Columbians expressed the *lowest* levels of support for a carbon tax of all Canadians.[4] Support for the tax steadily *declined* among BC residents throughout 2008, between February, when it was announced, and its implementation in July, when those opposed to the tax outnumbered its supporters by a two to one margin.[5] Outrage over the tax, however, was rapidly displaced by fear of the economic recession as well as being tempered by falling fuel prices. By the time of the 2009 election, the economy had displaced environmental concerns as the top priority of British Columbians,[6] which proved fortunate for the fiscally conservative Liberals, who were perceived as being more prudent financial managers than their social-democratic opponents. Indeed, Premier Campbell was lucky that the carbon tax did *not* play a significant role in the campaign as polling suggested that it has had a far more *negative* than positive impact on his support among the electorate.[7] As such, it is more than a little disingenuous to trumpet the Liberal electoral victory as a transparent sign of the mass appeal of the BC carbon tax.

Must we, then, resign ourselves to a depressingly cynical realpolitik in which popular support for environmental policies necessarily collapses once the impact of those policies on our pocketbooks or lifestyles becomes evident? Does the BC experience affirm the impossibility of a democratic environmental politics that calls for some measure of sacrifice on the part of taxpayers and consumers? Not at all.

Instead, I argue that it was actually the *failure* (or refusal) to invoke the language of personal sacrifice in the framing of the carbon tax that was largely responsible for its hostile reception. No doubt worried about trying to justify the tax as a means of forcing people and businesses to reduce their use of fossil fuels, the Liberal government instead opted to portray the tax as a painless exercise of tax shifting, by which most British Columbians would be left with more money in their pockets at the end of the day. Accordingly, the environmental rationale (and necessity) of the policy was almost entirely displaced by a campaign that focused on its net positive effects on individuals as taxpayers. The news media echoed this emphasis and spent little time considering the environmental impact of the tax or the problem of climate change that the tax was designed to address. Even the broader economic logic of using carbon taxes to provide market incentives for low-carbon technological innovation and lifestyle change was displaced in favor of a focus on the individual. In the end, however, this attempt to promote the benefits of the tax in terms of associated tax cuts and rebates backfired, cultivating an extremely narrow frame of personal self-interest that led people to reject the tax based purely on the inconvenience and hardship associated with changing their lifestyles and paying more for fuel. Conversely, a more direct and honest reckoning with the logic of making (relatively minor) individual sacrifices to achieve the (immense) environmental and social benefits of tackling climate change would have offered a far more hospitable frame to mobilize public support for the policy.

The British Columbia Carbon Tax: A Brief Introduction

First, a bit of background. Notwithstanding its name, the Liberal party of British Columbia is not at all "liberal" in the progressive sense of the term, especially with respect to fiscal matters. They were first elected in a landslide victory in 2001 on a neoliberal ideological platform that emphasized tax cuts, smaller government, reductions in social spending, and curtailment of the power of special interests such as public sector unions and First Nations. Environmental issues were a very low priority during their first term, and the Liberals attracted a great deal of criticism for prioritizing economic growth over ecological sustainability in a wide variety of sectors, including oil and gas, forestry, and aquaculture. In 2002, Premier Campbell joined with Ralph Klein, then premier of Alberta and outspoken champion of the economically lucrative but environmentally disastrous development of the tar sands, in mounting a strong campaign against Canadian ratification of the Kyoto Accord.

Reelected with a much smaller majority in 2005, Premier Campbell rather abruptly changed course and started to pursue a far more progressive agenda in two particular areas: aboriginal issues and the environment, specifically climate change. While the cause of his conversion is the subject of much speculation, the effects at the level of policy have been remarkable. In February 2007, he announced a set of ambitious targets for reducing greenhouse gas emissions in the province, mandating a cut of 33 percent below 2007 levels by 2020 (roughly 10 percent below 1990 level emissions). In November 2007, the province passed the Greenhouse Gas Reductions Target Act that legislated these cuts as well as adding a target of 80 percent reductions by 2050. A Climate Action Secretariat, run directly out of the Premier's Office, was subsequently tasked with developing policies to reach these targets, which were (and remain) among the most ambitious of any North American jurisdiction.

In February 2008, the Liberal government became the first in North America to announce a broad, consumer-based carbon tax (implemented on July 1). The mechanics of the tax are quite simple. First, the tax is comprehensive, applying to all fossil fuels in the province and thus capturing roughly 70 percent of greenhouse gas emissions in BC.[8] Second, it begins at a relatively low level—$10 per ton—and then rises by a further $10 per ton in each of the next two years. To put this in a more familiar metric, it translates into an additional 2.4¢ CDN per liter of gas (9.1¢ CDN per gallon) in the first year and rises to 7.2¢ CDN per liter (27.3¢ CDN per gallon) by the summer of 2010. At gas prices that fluctuated between roughly $1.00 and $1.50 per liter during 2008, this is a very modest increase. Third, the tax is revenue-neutral, which requires the government to return all of the revenues collected under the tax—estimated to be $1.85 billion over the first three years—to the public in the form of personal income tax cuts, business tax cuts, and a low-income refundable tax credit designed to cushion the impact of the tax on the poor. The government also distributed a one-time climate action dividend of $100 to every person in the province one week before the tax was implemented. Finally, the government's own projections admit that the relatively low level of the carbon tax means that it will likely have quite modest effects in terms of cutting emissions, accounting for less than 10 percent of the reductions required to meet the 2020 targets.[9]

Selling the Tax: Revenue Neutrality, Tax Cuts, and Consumer Choice

The prevailing wisdom among most carbon tax advocates, from Al Gore to James Hansen to Thomas Friedman, is that the only way to make it palatable to the general public (especially in North America, where three decades of neoliberal ideology has cultivated a ferocious antitax sentiment) is to make it revenue-neutral. Such an approach, according to the Carbon Tax Center, is "politically savvy since it blunts the 'No New Taxes' demand that has held sway in American politics for over a generation."[10] Furthermore, revenue-neutrality is especially beloved by many economists who believe that solutions to the climate crisis are best provided by markets and the private sector, not governments. Overall taxation levels are not increased, and the role of government in allocating resources and thereby interfering with market discipline is minimized. Securing the endorsement of economists can defuse the arguments of critics that carbon taxes kill jobs and hurt economic growth. Instead, revenue neutrality allows advocates to mobilize public support for a carbon tax based on *both* its environmental and economic virtues. This is an attractive prospect, given the stubborn persistence of the jobs versus the environment frame that continues to otherwise dominate public conceptions of environmental policy and action.

This perspective informed both the design and the communications strategy around the BC carbon tax. The Liberal promotional strategy had three principal components: revenue neutrality, tax cuts, and consumer choice. Together, these themes encouraged the public to bring a deeply individualistic and self-interested perspective to their assessment of this policy that left very little conceptual or affective room for thinking about the carbon tax in any way other than its impact on one's finances.

For instance, in an interview shortly after the carbon tax was announced, the BC minister of finance, Carole Taylor, was asked how she was going to secure public support for the carbon tax. Her top priority, she replied, was "'to explain the revenue neutrality' aspect of the carbon tax."[11] Second on her list was to reassure the public, and especially those living in rural areas in the province, that the tax cuts and rebates associated with the carbon tax meant that everyone would come out ahead: "The way we are putting dollars back to individuals and families is more than the carbon tax will cost. . . . Whether it's a pickup truck in the north with a lot of mileage—whatever it is, more dollars will go back to those families. For those in the north—and there are many—who can't change their driving patterns because of the weather and the rough terrain, they will still have more dollars in their pockets."[12] Revenue neutrality and tax cuts: in interview after interview and speech after speech, the finance minister and the premier emphasized the net economic benefits of the carbon tax, soothing the general public with assurances that no sacrifices would be required of anyone. Beyond the mass appeal of this promotional strategy, the Liberals also probably believed that accenting tax cuts and revenue neutrality was the only way to maintain the support of their political base, which was otherwise unlikely to accept either new taxes or a more interventionist environmental policy.

Initially, the Liberal government received a great deal of praise from their allies in the business community and largely positive news coverage and commentary from the provincial media. The leading political columnist in the province, Vaughn Palmer, celebrated the revenue neutrality of the carbon tax as its most worthy attribute, while scoffing at the idea that the revenues might also have been used to fund other environmental initiatives:

In the run-up to the budget, Taylor had speculated that the government might hold back some of the revenue for environmental programs. Some of the Liberals were hoping to get their hands on the proceeds for pet projects from investment in technology to funding the transit plan. But the reaction to the implication of a tax grab was so negative—including from some advocates of carbon taxes—that she determined to give back every penny. . . . The commitment to revenue neutrality went a long way toward defusing the most obvious objections to the new tax from the business community. Even the trucking industry . . . found that aspect of the legislation "laudable."[13]

The leading provincial newspaper, *The Vancouver Sun*, likewise marveled that the Liberal government had "brought in the first significant set of carbon taxes in North America and is showing it could be done with remarkably little political resistance. . . . The key was taking the sting out of the new carbon taxes by simultaneously cutting other taxes so the government could not be accused of fattening its coffers with another new tax."[14] Applauding the government's design of a "smart carbon tax" and the consequent reduction of income and business taxes, the Vancouver Board of Trade's chief economist endorsed the tax as "neutral to the pocketbook of the individual consumer and business."[15] While this characterization of the tax as neutral to individuals (as compared to government) was inaccurate, this (mis-)perception was nurtured by the government's relentless revenue-neutral messaging and its insistence that the tax-shifting provisions would be good for everybody.

Consistent with both the government emphasis on personal financial benefits and the dominance of the consumer frame in the media's treatment of all social and political issues,[16] news coverage of the tax was heavily skewed in favor of highlighting how the tax would impact the bottom line of consumers. Accordingly, the principal focus of most initial reporting was on estimates of how much the tax was going to cost individuals and families. Most stories also dutifully included Liberal talking points about how the tax would (at least initially) be more than offset by tax cuts and rebates as well as explaining how simple lifestyle adjustments (e.g., improved vehicle maintenance, reduced use of automotive transport, increasing insulation and energy efficiency, etc.) could reduce the amount of tax paid. Although the public initially offered lukewarm support for the initiative, enthusiasm quickly stalled and then steadily dropped throughout the spring and summer, as gas prices climbed to record levels. Ignoring the tax-shifting provisions of the policy, the public instead seized on the tax's contribution to the rising cost of fuel as reason to disbelieve government claims about the benefits of the tax. By June, for example, an opinion poll found that fewer than 15 percent of British Columbians believed they would receive more in tax cuts and rebates than they would pay in the carbon tax, while more than 70 percent expected to pay more.[17]

Yet rather than shift the public's attention toward a more balanced assessment of the many broader environmental and economic benefits the tax was expected to deliver, the government stubbornly insisted that the best and only way to defend the tax was to maintain the focus on tax cuts and revenue neutrality. Premier Campbell, for example, tried to counter mounting public opposition by arguing that "this is the first tax in the history of the country that I'm aware of where all of the revenue is being used to reduce other taxes. . . . Every family in British Columbia is going to be ahead of the game at the end of this year in terms of tax."[18] In the wake of such explanations, the environmental rationale for the tax receded even further into the background as the justification for the policy came to rest solely on whether taxpayers would gain or lose money. This is *really about growing people's paycheques,* explained Campbell in a subsequent interview. "We're trying to do this in as fair a way as we can. I certainly understand people's concerns [about high fuel prices]. I think this is still fair. They are all going to have more money in their pockets."[19] After replacing Carole Taylor as Minister of Finance in June 2008, Colin Hansen similarly explained that "the government wants to make sure the right message gets out to British Columbians about the combination of tax cuts, dividends, low income relief and other economic incentives. When people actually understand *how the carbon tax fits into their finances* and *how it leaves money in their pockets,* they'll be much more enthusiastic about it."[20] A day before the tax came into effect, Hansen predicted that "once people appreciate that this is a totally revenue-neutral measure, I think people's attitudes will change."[21] But the enthusiasm for tax cuts never did appear, leaving columnists and editorial writers to attribute the seemingly surprising lack of support to the "atrocious job the Liberals have done at explaining that the new tax is being offset by tax cuts in other areas."[22] The problem, in other words, was not too much focus on the financial implications of the tax, but rather, too little: brilliant strategy, weak execution. The possibility that the contradiction of using tax cuts (with their emphasis on personal self-interest) to sell environmental policy (which requires more expansive forms of moral reasoning that take the well-being of *others* into account) might have been a mistake was never considered.

The third plank in the Liberal promotional strategy was consumer choice. At one level, the vocabulary of choice sat rather uneasily with the unconditional guarantees, noted earlier, that the tax shift would bring benefits to all individuals irrespective of their patterns of consumption. Indeed, the reluctance of the government to address (or even admit) the punitive logic of the tax—higher prices will force people to cut back or pay more—likely contributed to the growth of public frustration and anger. Instead of confronting this logic directly, the Liberals tried to put a positive spin on this aspect of the policy. Making the right consumer and lifestyle choices would allow everyone to save even more money, as they minimized their exposure to the tax.

In a March 2008 op-ed piece titled "Carbon Tax Gives People Chance to Choose," the finance minister argued that "we can all make the lifestyle changes available to us" such as purchasing energy-efficient appliances or weather stripping to save on home heating costs. After laying out the benefits that would flow to British Columbians, she explained that "these tax cuts, credits and dividends will more than help the families of B.C. pay for the carbon tax. This model of completely giving the money back to British Columbians does something else. It gives back to the people of B.C. the opportunity to make their own choices."[23] Campbell echoed these sentiments in his own explanation of how the tax would work: "The critical part of this plan is we are putting choices into people's hands."[24] Defending its implementation in the face of widespread opposition, he argued that "the government has tried to put choices in your hands while creating certainty and fairness. . . . We can all fight global warming through choices we make in our daily life that reduce our carbon footprint and save us fuel, energy and money."[25] Just by saving one tank of gas per year, he explained, the average family would recoup all the money paid on the carbon tax and be left with hundreds of extra dollars in their pockets due to the tax cuts and rebates.

For those who believe that a fickle, narcissistic public can only be brought on side in the fight against global warming by appealing to their personal self-interest, the Liberal government did everything right in their design and promotion of the carbon tax. In addition to being set at a modest level, the tax was revenue-neutral, allowing all the money to flow back to the public in the form of tax cuts. Before the tax was even implemented, every man, woman, and child in the province was sent a one-hundred-dollar climate action dividend, demonstrating that the policy was anything but a tax grab. Government communications were relentlessly upbeat, not only foregrounding the economic benefits of the tax shift to consumers, but also portraying climate change as a problem that could be easily solved through smart and virtually painless consumer choices. So-called fear mongering was kept to a minimum, to the point where the negative impacts of climate change did not appear at all in discussions of the tax. Any notion that individual or collective sacrifices would be required was drowned out by pragmatic talk of personal financial gain and economic opportunity.

And yet the carbon tax did not attract the support of a majority of British Columbians. While some attribute this to the public's failure to understand the benefits of tax shifting or people's outrage at the extraordinary rise in fuel prices during the first half of 2008, I believe that it was symptomatic of the individualistic, self-interested frame that dominated debate over the tax. The remainder of this chapter explores this argument by looking at how debate over the tax unfolded in the public sphere. In addition to highlighting what went wrong, this will also allow us to speculate on how the case for the carbon tax could have been made more effectively. In particular, how can the idea of sacrifice be judiciously employed within a broader frame that positions collective, political, and democratic action as a far more meaningful and compelling response to climate change?

What's in It for Me? No Choice, No Vision, No Science, No Thanks

In his exhaustive survey of the literature on motivating sustainable behavior, Tim Jackson notes that "altruistic values are most strongly implicated in the activation of a personal pro-environmental norm [while] self-enhancement (egoistic) values tend to be negatively correlated with pro-environmental norms and actions."[26] Concern for the implications of one's actions on others leads to a greater likelihood that individuals will not only adopt more sustainable forms of behavior, but also a more favorable disposition toward environmental policies and laws. Conversely, when people think first and foremost of their own self-interest, they are much less likely to modify their own behavior or support government intervention designed to achieve environmental objectives. Such value orientations (and the pro- or antienvironmental norms they tend to activate and enforce) are neither static nor all encompassing. Individuals are never always selfish or always selfless in their orientation to the world. Instead, the activation (or suppression) of such values occurs in different ways through a wide range of social relations and practices, communicative and cultural environments, and institutional contexts. Self- and other-regarding value orientations coexist within all of us: their influence on how we think and behave depends a great deal on how they are primed (or repressed) within particular contexts. The range of opinions that the same individual can develop and hold about a specific policy or political initiative, for instance, will vary depending on which values are primed in the presentation, discussion, and/or criticism of that policy or initiative. Context plays a critical role in the salience of particular values. Research in political communication suggests that emotional values-based priming often has a far greater impact on our political judgment than more "rational," fact-based arguments.[27]

From this perspective, framing the BC carbon tax exclusively in terms of its financial benefits to individual taxpayers primed a self-interested value orientation that tends to make people less, rather than more, likely to both support environmental policies and adopt sustainable lifestyles.

Indeed, it is hard to imagine a *less* hospitable conceptual and affective framework for mobilizing public support for this initiative. In this context, three characteristics of the public conversation are especially noteworthy: first, the emphasis on financial benefits and consumer choice was quickly overwhelmed by a hardship frame, in which individuals and businesses railed against the cost of the tax and their *lack* of choice in dealing with it; second, the revenue neutrality of the tax turned into a liability insofar as the government was unable to link the tax with positive, collective action such as expanding public investments in green infrastructure; and third, prioritizing the benefits of tax shifting effectively excluded any sustained consideration of the broader environmental rationale and benefits of the tax.

Taking up the government's invitation to assess the carbon tax in terms of its impact on the daily lives (and finances) of ordinary people, the news media focused much of its attention on how British Columbians felt the tax would affect their lifestyle choices. While early coverage reflected initial public ambivalence about the tax, mounting opposition generated a wave of stories that increasingly depicted the tax as punitive, yet ineffectual. A prominent feature of such coverage were individuals who were frustrated with the fact that they would have no choice but to pay more tax given their inability or refusal to change their consumption patterns. Story after story gradually confirmed the apparent *impossibility* of change for most people, whether it be the difficulty and inconvenience of using mass transit or the unaffordable expense of upgrading the energy efficiency of homes, vehicles, or appliances. Such coverage reflected public skepticism that higher fuel and energy costs would motivate behavioral change. Instead, in a February poll, only 13 percent of those surveyed anticipated driving less as a result of the tax, while more than three-quarters believed the tax would *not* have a significant impact on provincial emissions.[28] Given the complete absence of any attention to the environmental rationale and impact of the tax, these (questionable) beliefs went almost entirely unchallenged. Once people had drawn on their own experience to reject the efficacy of the tax as a means of behavioral change, they could *only* conceptualize the tax as financially punitive and mean-spirited, serving no constructive purpose other than to raise revenues for government by taxing forms of behavior that most felt they could not change.

Resistance was especially fierce from individuals and businesses living in the interior of British Columbia. They mounted a strong campaign against the tax, which was featured prominently in the news media. "Driving vehicles is a reality in the north," explained the mayor of Fort St. John, a small, rural community,

and further taxing residents will not stop it. We don't have the luxury of alternatives such as mass transit, and many renewable energies are not designed to work effectively in sub-zero temperatures. By burdening rural residents and farmers with a levy they can't help but pay, the provincial government would be unfairly punishing residents simply because they chose to live in less populated areas.[29]

"It seems that there are two B.C.'s," agreed the mayor of Williams Lake, another interior community. "There's metro B.C. and there's rural B.C., and I live in the real rural B.C."[30] The apparent plight of northerners and other rural residents quickly became a rallying point for those skeptical of the government's rosy projections about tax shifting or angry about the punitive dimensions of taxing carbon. Statistical data on commuting and energy usage actually disproved the assumption that northern residents would bear a disproportionate burden of the tax,[31] but such "rational interventions" had little effect on blunting popular outrage, which was fueled by the perception of unfairness.

As the hardship frame picked up steam in the media, a populist narrative gradually took shape in which an elitist (and urban) premier was imposing his newfound environmental sensibilities on the hardworking people of the province, essentially punishing them for a lifestyle they did not choose and which they had no ability to change. Expressive of this sentiment, for example, was an angry op-ed from a retired biologist that was published in response to the minister of finance's argument that the carbon tax would empower British Columbians to make their own choices. "I am about to be victimized by a social experiment based on wrong premises that will have extreme consequences for we who are at a stage in our lives where we no longer have the 'choices' prattled about in Taylor's column. . . . None of these changes [to transportation, housing, etc.] are inexpensive and are definitely not choices most of us can make now."[32]

This line of argument raised some valid concerns about the policy's impact on the poor, especially given how the low-income tax credit did not rise in proportion to the doubling and then tripling of the tax into the future.[33] However, it is also fair to say that the vast majority of hardship stories were drawn from the middle class. The carbon tax "may not bother you much if you're driving a few klicks [kilometers] in your Prius," opined a senior *Vancouver Sun* reporter. "But the folks up in Prince George and Fort St. John, who don't much like city slickers fooling with their lifestyles, aren't happy with the premier. They actually need their SUVs and gas-guzzling pickups to drive long distances to work, not simply to look rugged when they're driving to the mall."[34] For those living in urban areas, there was no shortage of news stories in which drivers defended their need for large vehicles and long, daily commutes.

In one typical piece on skyrocketing gas prices (and the contribution of the carbon tax to them), a Vancouver realtor explained that "she doesn't plan to trade in her Highlander for a smaller vehicle because she needs the room to carry people and equipment for her job. 'I need a big car, it's important,' she said. 'Because of my work, I have no choice.'"[35]

I have no choice: this sentiment, more than any other, echoed throughout all the stories and sound bites that appeared on this theme, binding them together into a social norm that was at once descriptive and injunctive in terms of sanctifying the right of consumers to categorically reject the need (or even potential) for behavioral change.[36] If such arguments had been directly measured against the catastrophic impact of climate change on ecosystems and human lives, they undoubtedly would have carried much less weight. More important, they would have certainly invited moral sanction for their callous indifference to the present and future suffering of others who are themselves unable to choose a different ecological fate. At the very least, such a comparative register would have catalyzed more creative and innovative conversations about how best to facilitate the changes that the science of climate change demands that we make. In the absence of such a deliberative context, however, the refusal to consider deeper lifestyle changes appeared as little more than a sensible and pragmatic rejoinder to the government's misleading characterization of such "choices" as not only effortless, but also financially lucrative.

Once the public had categorically rejected the government's claims that tax shifting would leave them with more money in their pockets, the revenue neutrality of the carbon tax became a major political liability, rather than an asset. Much of the harm came from the simple mistake many had made in assuming that revenue neutrality described the impact of the tax on individuals and businesses, rather than government. While this assumption is illogical when one considers the basic objective of a carbon tax, it is not entirely surprising that many held it, given Liberal promises that the revenue-neutral tax would be good for everyone's bottom line. Industry groups quickly capitalized on the confusion, using the broader application of revenue neutrality to foreground the unjustly punitive effect of the tax. "If it's going to be revenue-neutral either it is for everyone or it's not," argued a spokesperson for the Mining Association of British Columbia.[37] The Canadian Trucking Alliance noted that its members would support carbon taxes "if they were actually dollar-for-dollar revenue neutral to our companies and if the funds were used to offset the costs of buying cleaner technology."[38] Defining *revenue-neutral* as a situation in which "everyone comes out even or some people receive more than they pay," the head of the BC Trucking Association noted that an average long-haul owner-operator "will be receiving literally two or three cents back for each dollar in carbon tax paid. Does this sound revenue neutral?"[39] Notwithstanding how opponents of the tax deliberately twisted the meaning of the term to fit their purposes, the fact that such obfuscation could be so easily accomplished speaks to the significant risks (and limitations) of promoting and defending a carbon tax on this basis. Once the realization sinks in that the tax is not at all neutral in its disciplinary effects, public anger and frustration will grow, especially given the (mis-)perception that advocates have been dishonest in their characterization of the tax. As the BC case shows, the term *revenue-neutral* can easily become a potent symbol of government double-talk as well as a perpetual reminder that the tax is not, in fact, neutral for all taxpayers.

The principle of revenue neutrality also deprived the government of the ability to justify the tax as enabling essential public investments in green infrastructure such as expanding mass transit or developing new supplies of renewable energy. Opinion research has found that such investments are far more popular than income tax cuts, suggesting that people are willing to make sacrifices (in the form of taxes) *if* they believe there is a *causal* link between those sacrifices and an environmental public good. In a May 2008 survey, for example, Canadians chose public investment over tax cuts by more than a six to one margin when asked how revenues from a national carbon tax should be spent: 47 percent said renewable energy, 16 percent indicated energy efficiency technologies, and 8 percent selected public transit, whereas only 11 percent picked reduced income taxes.[40] "What Canadians are going to want to see," explained the pollster, "is they're going to want to know that this tax is invested in the environment in some way."[41] Polls on carbon taxes consistently find that support rises significantly when revenues from the tax are *directly* invested in energy efficiency, alternative energy, or other environmental initiatives.[42] On the basis of the comments of resource economist Mark Jaccard, a key adviser to the premier on the design of the tax, the Liberals were aware of such preferences but rejected them, given that tax cuts were a much better ideological fit for their conservative political platform. "Jaccard said he has seen a lot of polls to suggest Canadians support carbon taxes if the money is directed to rapid transit or other transportation improvements. But his own experience on talk shows across the country—and particularly in Alberta—is that both the hosts and the callers indicated a strong preference for lower taxes, instead of transit."[43]

What Jaccard and the Liberals did not appreciate, though, is how the prospect of *collectively* mobilizing the immense social, economic, and political resources of society to tackle environmental issues after decades of neglect and indifference is enormously appealing to large segments of the population, especially in light of the dawning realization of the massive scale and scope of crises such as climate change. Reading recent environmental best sellers such as Chris Turner's *The Geography of Hope: A Tour of the World We Need* or Thomas Friedman's *Hot, Flat, and Crowded: Why We Need Green Revolution, and How It Can Renew America*, one is immediately struck by how the aspirational rhetoric that energizes the expansive environmental imagination at play in such works is invariably *collective* in nature.[44] They celebrate the utopian potential of human beings to work together in making sustainable development something more than just a slogan. Al Gore's February 2008 presentation to the Technology, Entertainment, and Design conference similarly embraced a rousing language of heroic, collective political change.[45] If a carbon tax can be harnessed to these broad ambitions, it becomes *more* than just a tax and *more* than a means of (repressive) behavioral control. Instead, it becomes *the* crucial enabling mechanism, both in terms of generating revenues for public investment and shifting price signals in markets, for catalyzing the enormous technological innovation and institutional capacity building that is required. Compared to such inspirational visions of sustainability revolutions in transportation, energy, and lifestyle, the promise of a few extra dollars can only appear banal, trivial, and insignificant.

Directing tax revenues into infrastructural expansion can also help address and defuse many of the hardship narratives discussed earlier. While carbon taxes are designed to make some choices more expensive (and advocates should be up front about this), the principal objective of environmental public investment is to make other choices much easier, cheaper, and more accessible. Thus a negative discourse of expense and inconvenience can be countered with more optimistic and positive narratives emphasizing the expansion of new, sustainable choices: increasing the affordability, efficiency, and convenience of public transit gives people more choice; subsidizing the retrofitting of homes and businesses to make them more energy efficient gives people more choice; expanding access to alternative forms of renewable energy gives people more choice. Most important, these public investments give individuals a range and type of choice that consumer markets simply cannot offer. This gives carbon tax advocates a tremendous opportunity to promote such taxes—or, more precisely, the investments they make possible—simultaneously empowering some (good) choices, while constraining some other (bad) choices. However, as soon as the principle of revenue neutrality is invoked, the enthusiasm, excitement, and energy that might have otherwise been attached to carbon tax–funded public investment falls to the sidelines. Instead of inspiring visions of sweeping social and technological innovation, the only choices allowed are those that individual consumers (as enabled and encouraged through tax shifting) have within existing markets. But the choice to buy compact florescent bulbs or energy-efficient appliances does little to fire the environmental imagination of the public and probably strikes many as largely irrelevant, given the scale and size of the problem.

Most emblematic of this dynamic in the BC case was the one-hundred-dollar climate action dividend that the government distributed one week before the tax was implemented, as evidence of its revenue-neutral character. In radio, television, and newspaper interviews, Premier Campbell urged British Columbians to invest the money in greening their lifestyles, noting that he planned to put his own dividend toward the cost of a new energy-efficient refrigerator. Few, however, shared this enthusiasm for achieving sustainability through an installment plan. The dividend, which cost the government a total of 440 million dollars, was widely discounted as little more than a political bribe, and many wondered whether it might have been better to spend the money on transit or other environmental initiatives. A television news poll found that only 5 percent of those surveyed intended to use their dividends as prescribed to reduce their greenhouse gas emissions, with most choosing to spend, save, or invest the money as with any other income.[46] Not surprisingly given record fuel prices, many angrily predicted that the money would go straight into their gas tanks. Not only was the dividend utterly unsuccessful in persuading the public of the virtues of the carbon tax; it turned into a public relations disaster, creating yet another opportunity for opponents to rail against the irrelevance and injustice of the tax.

If the Liberals were largely unsuccessful in attracting public support for the tax based on its positive impact on individuals and society, they (and the news media) were spectacularly ineffective in communicating the scientific and environmental rationale of the tax in terms of the mitigation of global warming. *The ecological case for the policy was never made*, either by the government or the media. Occasional reports and features on the science and impact of climate change did continue to appear. However, such stories were invariably positioned in isolation from reporting on the carbon tax, with minimal (if any) linkages made between the state of environmental science and the state of environmental public policy.

While such compartmentalization is an unfortunate characteristic of most environmental journalism, the Liberal emphasis on a consumer/taxpayer frame reinforced the perception that it was better for the public to know about the tax's impact on their bottom line than for them to understand the scientific and economic reasoning driving the policy or its long-term effects on emissions. Gloomy prognostications about the impending climate crisis and the desperate need for action before global warming becomes irreversible would, presumably, have violated the government's preference for the much sunnier (and ideologically neoliberal) story line about how much better off taxpayers would be as result of the rebates and tax shifting. More pragmatically, the Liberals may have also been hoping to avoid focusing on the environmental efficacy of the carbon tax, given how their own projections confirmed that assigning such a low price to carbon was going to have a very modest impact on emissions in the short and medium terms (accounting for less than 10 percent of the government's reduction targets for 2020).

Most telling of the low priority the Liberals assigned to explaining the environmental rationale for the carbon tax was the decision to rely primarily on Premier Campbell and the minister of finance to sell the tax to the public, while the minister of the environment stayed entirely in the background. As debate over the tax heated up in the summer, for instance, the environment minister never once appeared in the pages of the leading newspaper to defend the tax on environmental grounds.[47] In contrast, the premier and finance minister were extensively interviewed and cited; each also authored op-ed pieces that championed the tax as good for taxpayers. Although their comments were sprinkled with occasional statements about environmental imperatives, such sentiments were little more than window dressing and largely peripheral to the central thrust of their arguments about the benefits of tax shifting. Equally significant in this regard was the extensive role played in the media by economists, such as Mark Jaccard, who were primarily called on to comment on the financial aspects of the tax.

Climate scientists, on the other hand, were nowhere to be found, despite the fact that British Columbia boasts an impressive range of scientific expertise in this area, including Dr. Andrew Weaver, a lead author on the second, third, and fourth scientific assessment reports from the Intergovernmental Panel on Climate Change. Scientists such as Weaver are no strangers to the media, being regularly featured in regional (and national) news items that focus on the causes and consequences of climate change; indeed, they are often positioned within such stories as aggressive advocates for climate change policies such as carbon taxes. Yet their voices were conspicuously absent from public debate over the BC carbon tax, their credibility and knowledge in addressing the apocalyptic implications of inaction seemingly irrelevant to the obsessive focus that both media and government narrowly brought to bear on the tax's fiscal consequences. Instead, the scientific case for emissions reductions (and the broader utility of a carbon tax in achieving such reductions) was largely left to environmental activists and organizations. While their defense of the carbon tax on ecological grounds was passionate, thoughtful, and well grounded in contemporary climate science, their status as environmental activists and advocates in the eyes of the public left them ill positioned to serve as objective, impartial representatives of scientific knowledge.

Stripped of any meaningful scientific and environmental context, the carbon tax (as well as other associated climate change initiatives) was easily represented as the personal pet project of Premier Campbell, who had positioned himself as the policy's principal architect and defender. The authority and rationalization for not only the tax, but more important, deep cuts in emissions was thereby portrayed as fundamentally political, rather than scientific, in nature. In an editorial retrospective on the carbon tax, for example, *The Vancouver Sun* dismissed the science behind emissions reductions by noting that "*Premier Gordon Campbell's* ambitious targets for reducing greenhouse gas emissions were in a sense *drawn out of thin air*. Rather than any serious analysis of what it would take to get there, the goal of a 33 per cent reduction from 2007 levels by 2020 was based on *his* determination of what we need to achieve if we want to play an effective role in limiting the potentially harmful effects of climate change."[48] It was the politicians, not the scientists, who were driving the process, making what appeared to be arbitrary and unilateral decisions about setting targets and imposing sweeping lifestyle changes on the public. In this context, the fight against climate change was seen by many as both idiosyncratic and authoritarian insofar as it was driven more by the premier's personal agenda than by the needs of the province. Intensifying such perceptions was the fact that the government never engaged in any broad public consultations or deliberative process with the public in terms of seeking input about how best to achieve the cuts demanded by climate science. Instead, the secretive design of the carbon tax behind closed doors, followed by a one-way flow of government communication about the tax, was a textbook case of what some critics describe as the "decide, announce, defend" model of public consultation.[49]

Writing about the critical importance of framing in communication about climate change, Mathew Nisbet explains that "framing a policy problem or issue endows certain dimensions of the complex issue with greater apparent relevance than they would have under an alternative frame. To make sense of policy debates, audiences use frames provided by the media as interpretive shortcuts but integrate these media presentations with preexisting interpretations forged through personal experience, partisanship, ideology, social identity, or conversations with others."[50] Primed to think first and foremost of their own (financial) self-interest, convinced that others like themselves are both unwilling and unable to change their current lifestyle and consumption habits, uninspired by the promise of a few extra dollars in their pockets, and deprived of any scientific evidence and arguments about the need for urgent action on climate change, most British Columbians rejected the carbon tax. Given how debate about the tax unfolded in the public sphere, this comes as little surprise. Surveying the contours of that debate, though, what emerges with striking clarity is how a different set of conceptual and affective frames, communicative priorities, normative principles, and deliberative practices would have generated much different results.

Future Public: Fear, Sacrifice, Politics, and Climate Change

A consensus appears to be emerging among many who study climate change communication that appeals to the public based on terrifying scenarios of ecological collapse and human suffering are not only ineffective, but ultimately counterproductive, leaving people less, rather than more, motivated to tackle the issue of global warming. As one recent study concluded, "the very images that made participants have the greatest sense of climate change being important were also disempowering at a personal level. These images were said to drive feelings of helplessness, remoteness and lack of control."[51] In a similar vein, Ted Nordhaus and Michael Shellenberger have called for a strategic purging of doom and gloom from environmental discourse in favor of a "politics of possibility" that offers more positive, uplifting, and enabling visions of environmental sustainability *and* economic prosperity.[52]

At one level, I am deeply sympathetic to the utopian injunction to spend less time lamenting how this world is suffering and more time imagining how and why, in the inspirational language of the World Social Forum, another world *is* possible. The sheer ubiquity of consumer culture often blinds us to how deeply dissatisfied so many of us have become with lives filled with hollow pleasures and long working hours and, consequently, how receptive we would be to alternative visions of a life organized around something *other* than consumption. "The crisis," Antonio Gramsci famously wrote, "consists precisely in the fact that the old is dying and the new cannot be born."[53] Utopian dreams of future worlds that inspire us to imagine how things could and should be different are needed more today than ever before. Yet the BC carbon tax case should alert us to the ways in which a more optimistic tone in environmental discourse can decay into a deeply conservative political wisdom that the only way to attract public support for environmental programs and policies, such as carbon taxes, is to avoid all talk of crisis and sacrifice in favor of the more pragmatic (and resolutely *antiutopian*) language of self-interest and the bottom line.

What's in it for me? Forty years of neoliberal hegemony have ravaged and stunted the radical political imaginary such that we twist ourselves into ideological knots trying to always answer this question in the most conservative of terms. The carbon tax is a perfect example of this perverse logic at work. Despite the overwhelming, desperate need for massive public (re-)investment in sustainable infrastructure of all kinds (and the strong levels of public support for such investments among most citizens), the principle of revenue neutrality is widely accepted as an essential component of a carbon tax. As such, we meekly accept and legitimize the conservative axiom that governments are bad and markets are good. In bringing our political ambitions and discourse down to this level, though, we call into being the fictional public that we fear the most: selfish, apathetic, and motivated by nothing other than the utilitarian calculus of financial cost and benefit. This is the political moral to be taken from the experience in British Columbia: framing the carbon tax exclusively in terms of its net benefits to taxpayers ultimately sponsored a "return of the repressed," in which the trope of personal sacrifice that the Liberals had tried so hard to avoid emerged with greater force than ever as the principal reason for the public to reject the tax.

The art of politics, though, teaches us that different publics are possible. And if historical experience is any guide, it may well be that notions of sacrifice help call into being a public that is willing to consider not only the need, but also the many virtues of giving up some measure of personal (consumer) freedom in favor of building a more just and sustainable future for everyone. Most national mythologies, for example, are built around heroic narratives of collective, emancipatory struggles, in which individuals made extraordinary sacrifices in pursuit of something greater than personal self-interest. Civil rights; the fight against fascism in the Second World War; wars and revolutions of national liberation; the women's movement; working-class and indigenous people's struggles for social, economic, and political rights: these are the types of historical experience that inspire and excite our political imagination. Even more important, perhaps, everyday life itself is filled with countless acts of altruism, in which people put the needs of others above their own. The virtues of sacrifice are not foreign to us, but deeply embedded in our culture, social relationships, and daily practices. Human beings have an extraordinary capacity for empathy, cooperation, and self-restraint that manifests itself in countless different ways. This is fertile conceptual, experiential, and affective terrain in which to cultivate new forms of environmental discourse and new environmental publics in which the virtues of personal sacrifice are allied with a visionary politics of possibility, the one inextricably bound up with the other.

Echoing the sentiments of Premier Campbell, I agree that we do have to put choices in the hands of the people: a technocratic model of environmental policy making in which experts determine the best measures to be imposed on a recalcitrant public is neither ethically desirable nor politically sustainable. But where and how should such choices be made? In car lots, shopping malls, and grocery stores? In the dreamworlds of consumerism that seduce us with a never ending flow of fantasies in which we are to think of nothing but how to satisfy our personal needs and desires? In the moral vacuum of a global marketplace that ensures we never have to consider, let alone take responsibility for, the impact of our lifestyles on others? Such spaces are inimical to the simple ethical imperative that animates environmental consciousness and sustainable behavior, namely, ensure that your actions do not (unduly) compromise the health and vitality of other people and ecosystems. The narcissistic currents of consumer culture are especially toxic to any talk of sacrificing convenience and pleasure for the sake of others. They ensure that the emotional framing of sacrifice can only ever be negative, an ascetic, puritan act in which we are denied (or deny ourselves) the things that we really want or need.

There are, however, other spaces in which conversations about the need for institutional and behavioral transformation stand a much better chance of success. At its best, politics nurtures and fortifies collective, democratic forms of reasoning, in which individuals are not only forced, but also inspired, to consider the well-being of others. When we consider the logic of sacrifice in this context, the prospect of giving something up for the public good not only becomes more intellectually compelling, but also emotionally attractive, carrying in its wake the genuine pleasure of working and acting together to make a better world. The affective tonality of sacrifice acquires a complexity and multidimensionality that it lacks in the sphere of consumption: petty feelings of complaint and deprivation give way to loftier sentiments of hope and optimism for the future. Equally significant, environmental crises, such as climate change, that appear utterly intractable at the level of the individual become much less overwhelming when our frame of reference shifts, as Muhammad Ali famously put it to an audience of Harvard graduates, from me to we.[54] Instead of ratcheting down the fear factor to avoid further alienating a disempowered public, we have to expand the scope of collective human agency by invigorating democratic practices of deliberation *and decision making*, in which people can finally begin to make the *political* choices that are necessary to tackle this crisis. We need to start making decisions about our lifestyles and consumer behavior in our town halls, not our shopping malls, in which considerations of the public good and, more important, an appreciation of the power of collective, institutional action determine the choices that we make.

Acknowledgments

This chapter was first presented at "Climate Change Mitigation: Considering Lifestyle Options in Europe and the United States," held by the European Center of Excellence, University of California, Berkeley. My thanks to the conference organizer, Falk Schuetzenmeister, and the participants for a vigorous and productive discussion of the chapter. I would also like to thank Michael Maniates, John Meyer, and Adrienne

Cossom for their thoughtful comments and suggestions on earlier drafts of this chapter.

Notes

1. Richard Littlemore, "Carbon Tax Wins: Cheap Politics Loses in B.C. Election," DeSmogBlog, May 12, 2009, http://www.desmogblog.com/carbon-tax-wins-cheap-politics-loses-bc-election.

2. Cited in Mark Hume, "Will B.C. Premier's Win Bring the Carbon Tax Back to Life?" *The Globe and Mail*, May 14, 2009, A1.

3. Charles Komanoff, "BC Voters Stand by Carbon Tax," Carbon Tax Center, May 13, 2009, http://www.carbontax.org/blogarchives/2009/05/13/bc-voters-stand-by-carbon-tax/. Komanoff praised the government's introduction and framing of the tax in the 2008–2009 budget as "essential reading for any carbon tax advocate seeking to master communication tools for making a carbon tax palatable to the public." As I will argue, the approach of the BC government is exemplary for precisely the opposite reason.

4. Dirk Meissner, "Canadians Like Carbon Tax, but Wary of Cost, Poll Finds," *The Globe and Mail*, May 11, 2009, S2.

5. On February 20, 2008 (one day after the tax was announced), a *Global News Hour* poll found that 46 percent supported the tax, while 52 percent opposed it (though the proportion of those who *strongly* disapproved of the tax was twice the level of those who *strongly* approved of it). By June, opposition had risen to 59 percent; Jonathan Fowlie, "Most Oppose Carbon Tax," *The Vancouver Sun*, June 18, 2008, A1. By mid-July, those against the tax outnumbered its supporters by a two to one margin (64 percent to 32 percent); David Hogben, "Most Don't Like Carbon Tax, Poll Finds," *The Vancouver Sun*, July 30, 2008, B1.

6. An April 2009 survey by Ipsos Reid during the campaign found that 34 percent of voters chose the economy as the most important issue facing BC, while only 10 percent chose the environment. Angus Reid Strategies, "Main Parties Separated by Just Three Points in British Columbia," http://www.angusreidstrategies.com/uploads/pages/pdfs/2009.04.29_BCProv.pdf.

7. In the April 2009 Angus Reid poll, for example, 37 percent of those surveyed said that the carbon tax had made them more likely to vote for the Liberal Party, while 62 percent said that it had made them *less* likely. Exit polling by Ipsos Reid confirmed these sentiments, finding that those who considered environmental issues very important were almost twice as likely to vote for the NDP (53 percent) as for the Liberals (29 percent). Ipsos Reid, "For the Record: Ipsos Reid and the May 12, 2009 BC Election," May 12, 2009, http://www.ipsos-na.com/news/client/act_dsp_pdf.cfm?name=mr090515-1.pdf&id=4391.

8. Ministry of Finance, "Myths and Facts about the Carbon Tax," Government of British Columbia, http://www.fin.gov.bc.ca/scp/tp/climate/A6.htm.

9. Vaughn Palmer, "For the Liberals, the Last Nine Million Tonnes Will Be the Toughest," *The Vancouver Sun*, July 29, 2008, A3. An even more damning

indictment of the efficacy of the tax comes from the NDP leader Carole James's claim that the government's budget estimates actually project the total consumption of fuel to *increase* between 2008 and 2010, suggesting that the government itself does not expect the tax to have any appreciable impact in the short term. Carole James, "Campbell Makes the Wrong Choice," *The Vancouver Sun*, April 16, 2008, A13.

10. Carbon Tax Centre, "No Tax Increase? How?" http://www.carbontax.org/introduction/#no-tax-increase.

11. Cited in Vaughn Palmer, "Even as They Bask in Praise, Liberals Face a Selling Job on Carbon Tax," *The Vancouver Sun*, February 23, 2008, A3.

12. Ibid.

13. Vaughn Palmer, "Taylor's Vaunted Carbon Tax Is Just the First Step," *The Vancouver Sun*, February 20, 2008, A3.

14. "B.C. Liberals Finesse the Politics of Climate Change, but Now Have to Tackle the Economics," *The Vancouver Sun*, February 21, 2008, A16.

15. Derrick Penner, "Businesses Applaud Efforts to Reduce Taxes in Budget," *The Vancouver Sun*, February 20, 2008, A5.

16. On the dominance of the consumer frame in media coverage of economic and labor issues, e.g., see Christopher Martin, *Framed! Labor and the Corporate Media* (Ithaca, NY: Cornell University Press, 2004).

17. Fowlie, "Most Oppose Carbon Tax."

18. Ibid.

19. Cited in Jonathan Fowlie, "Premier Tries to Explain How Carbon Tax Is Good for People," *The Vancouver Sun*, June 27, 2008, A3; emphasis added.

20. Cited in Vaughn Palmer, "The Hard Sell Is Coming in Liberal Bid to Defuse Anger over Carbon Tax," *The Vancouver Sun*, June 25, 2008, A3; emphasis added.

21. Cited in Tim Lai, "Queue Up for Gas Today," *The Vancouver Sun*, June 30, 2008, A1.

22. "Despite Its Opportunism, the NDP Has a Point on Delaying the Carbon Tax," *The Vancouver Sun*, June 19, 2008, A16. Also see, e.g., Vaughn Palmer, "Surprise! Liberals Dole Out More Carbon Tax Cheques," *The Vancouver Sun*, October 10, 2008, A3.

23. Carole Taylor, "Carbon Tax Gives People Chance to Choose," *The Vancouver Sun*, March 4, 2008, A9.

24. Cited in Fowlie, "Premier Tries to Explain."

25. Gordon Campbell, "Climate Change Is Our Problem to Solve," *The Vancouver Sun*, July 5, 2008, C5.

26. Tim Jackson, "Motivating Sustainable Consumption: A Review of Evidence on Consumer Behaviour and Behavioural Change," *Sustainable Development Research Network*, January 2005, 57.

27. Drew Westen, *The Political Brain: The Role of Emotion in Deciding the Fate of the Nation* (New York: Public Affairs, 2007). For a fascinating discussion of the role of values-based priming in the context of talk radio, see David Barker, *Rushed to Judgment: Talk Radio, Persuasion, and American Political Behavior* (New York: Columbia University Press, 2006).

28. "What We Think of the New Carbon Tax," *The Vancouver Sun*, February 22, 2008, B2.

29. Jim Eglinski, "Northerners Carry Unfair Green Load," *The Vancouver Sun*, April 9, 2008, A13.

30. Cited in Catherine Rolfsen, "City Protests, but Mayor to Pay Carbon Tax," *The Vancouver Sun*, May 26, 2008, B8.

31. Economist Nic Rivers notes, e.g., that the average commute in Vancouver is close to three times longer than in Fort St. John. While the colder climate in the interior of the province does translate into higher energy bills, the impact of the carbon tax on the cost of heating a home in the interior as compared to a similarly sized home in Vancouver is less than eight dollars per year. Nic Rivers, "Carbon Tax Coping," *The Vancouver Sun*, April 29, 2008, A13.

32. Maggie Fankboner, "Many of Us Don't Have Taylor's 'Choices,'" *The Vancouver Sun*, March 13, 2008, A19.

33. As noted earlier, a portion of the tax was directed toward low-income individuals and families to insulate those least able to afford the tax from its full impact. According to analysis done by the Canadian Centre for Policy Alternatives (CCPA), the Low Income Climate Action Tax Credit is effective in the first year of the policy but fails to rise in proportion to the increased levels of the tax in years two and three of its implementation. See Marc Lee and Toby Sanger, "Is BC's Carbon Tax Fair? An Impact Analysis for Different Income Levels," Canadian Centre for Policy Alternatives, October 2008. While the CCPA's concerns did attract some media attention, it is fair to say that the regressive impact of the tax on low-income individuals did not play a major role in public debate.

34. Miro Cernetig, "Will Politicians or $200 Oil Save the Planet?" *The Vancouver Sun*, June 7, 2008, B1.

35. Kelly Sinoski, "Gas Price Tops $1.40/Litre, with More to Come," *The Vancouver Sun*, June 6, 2008, A1.

36. See the discussion in Vladas Griskevicius, Robert Cialdini, and Noah J. Goldstein, "Social Norms: An Underestimated and Underemployed Lever for Managing Climate Change," *International Journal for Sustainability Communication* 3 (2008): 5–13.

37. Cited in Nathan Vanderklippe, "Industry Wants Better Return on Carbon Tax," *The Vancouver Sun*, May 28, 2008, D8.

38. David Bradley, "What the Trucking Industry Doesn't Need Is Another Tax," *The Vancouver Sun*, June 4, 2008, A11.

39. Paul Landry, "Revenue-Neutral Carbon Tax? For Whom?" *The Vancouver Sun*, July 3, 2008, A15.

40. The Pembina Institute, "Canadians' Views on a Carbon Tax to Reduce Greenhouse Gas Emissions," May 26, 2008, http://climate.pembina.org/pub/1640. Also see Mike De Souza, "Carbon Tax a Positive Step, Most Say," *The Vancouver Sun*, May 26, 2008, A5.

41. Cited in Mike De Souza, "Carbon Tax a Positive Step."

42. A 2007 BBC poll surveyed twenty-two thousand people in twenty-one countries about their willingness to pay higher energy costs to address climate change. "Support for increased energy taxes is conditional. Asked if they would support higher taxes on types of energy—such as oil and coal—that cause most carbon emissions, only half (50 percent overall) approve. But this rises to three out of four (77 percent overall) if the tax raised was specifically devoted to promoting energy efficiency or developing cleaner fuels. Such a tax receives majority support in all 21 countries polled." See BBC World Service, "Most Would Pay Higher Energy Bills to Address Climate Change Says Global Poll," November 5, 2007, http://www.worldpublicopinion.org/pipa/articles/btenvironmentra/427.php?nid=&id=&pnt=427. Similarly, a November 2007 Field Poll of Californians found that support for a carbon tax on individuals rose from 52 percent to 65 percent if the money from the tax was spent solely on reducing gas emissions. See Field Research Corporation, "Field Poll: Californians See Global Warming as a Serious Threat to State's Overall Quality of Life," November 9, 2007, http://www.yubanet.com/artman/publish/printer_70023.shtml.

43. Scott Simpson, "Come Tax Time, What Will Going Green Really Mean?" *The Vancouver Sun*, February 23, 2008, L2.

44. Chris Turner, *The Geography of Hope: A Tour of the World We Need* (Toronto, QC: Random House Canada, 2007); Thomas Friedman, *Hot, Flat, and Crowded: Why We Need a Green Revolution, and How It Can Renew America* (New York: Farrar, Straus, and Giroux, 2008).

45. Al Gore, "New Thinking on the Climate Crisis," http://www.ted.com/talks/al_gore_s_new_thinking_on_the_climate_crisis.html.

46. Fowlie, "Most Oppose Carbon Tax."

47. A systematic review of *The Vancouver Sun*'s coverage of the carbon tax during 2008 reveals that the minister of the environment did not appear a single time as an advocate for the tax (i.e., cited in a newspaper report or column or as the author of an op-ed piece) until September, when he was briefly quoted offering support for the tax prior to a meeting of provincial municipal leaders (who were upset about the policy).

48. "Global Warming Efforts Will Carry Long-Term Public Cost," *The Vancouver Sun*, August 14, 2008, A12; emphasis added.

49. See the discussion in Robert Cox, "Public Participation in Environmental Decisions," in *Environmental Communication and the Public Sphere* (Thousand Oaks, CA: Sage, 2006), 83–123.

50. Mathew Nisbet, "Communicating Climate Change: Why Frames Matter for Public Engagement," *Environment: Science and Policy for Sustainable Development* 51, no. 2 (2009): 17.

51. Saffron O'Neill and Sophie Nicholson-Cole, "'Fear Won't Do It': Promoting Positive Engagement with Climate Change through Visual and Iconic Representations," *Science Communication* 30, no. 3 (2009): 373. Also see Susanne Moser and Lisa Dilling, "Making Climate Hot," *Environment: Science and Policy for Sustainable Development* 46, no. 10 (2004): 32–46.

52. Ted Nordhaus and Michael Shellenberger, *Break Through: From the Death of Environmentalism to the Politics of Possibility* (New York: Houghton Mifflin Company, 2007).

53. Antonio Gramsci, *Selections from the Prison Notebooks*, ed. and trans. Quintin Hoare and Geoffrey Nowell Smith (New York: International, 1971), 276.

54. As described by George Plimpton in *When We Were Kings*, directed by Leon Gast (1996).

10

Civic Virtue and Sacrifice in a Suburban Nation

Peter F. Cannavò

The United States is now a suburban nation. In 1910, 7.1 percent of the nation's population lived in the suburbs. By 2000, that share had grown to 50 percent. About 62 percent of metropolitan area residents live in the suburbs, up from 25 percent in 1910.[1] Suburban historian Kenneth Jackson defines "suburbanization as a process involving the systematic growth of fringe areas at a pace more rapid than that of core cities, as a lifestyle involving a daily commute to jobs in the center."[2] He dates the beginnings of this process back to roughly 1815.

Suburbanization is not unique to the United States, yet Jackson remarks that "suburbia has become the quintessential physical achievement of the United States; it is perhaps more representative of its culture than big cars, tall buildings, or professional football."[3] Suburbanization is so entrenched in the United States that Jackson's "daily commute to jobs in the center" had, by the 1980s, been significantly replaced by commutes between suburbs themselves, further detaching suburb from city.[4]

Though the suburbs have long housed poor and working-class residents, the detached home surrounded by aesthetic greenery and supposedly safe from urban crime, congestion, pollution, and the noise and smell of industry was, according to Jackson, initially an upper- and middle-class ideal that ultimately diffused throughout American society.[5] Today, the large-lot suburban home is perhaps the preeminent symbol of success in America, the embodiment of the American dream.

At the same time, the American suburban lifestyle has been widely criticized for, first of all, its environmental impact. The criticisms are by now familiar: low-density, far-flung suburban development swallows up farms, fields, and forests and other open space and natural habitat; it contributes to water pollution and water shortages; and it consumes enormous amounts of energy, as residents depend on automobiles, have long commutes, and own excessively large homes. As we confront climate change, habitat loss, and energy shortages, such criticisms become even more timely and urgent. Furthermore, critics see the suburbs as not only ecologically burdensome, but also as devoid of community and culture and marked by self-centered individualism, conspicuous consumption, exclusionary privilege, and a privatistic, parochial disregard of broader social responsibility.[6]

Though some of these criticisms are perhaps motivated by aesthetic or even elitist disdain for suburbia, it is hard to dismiss the argument that suburbia as we know it is ecologically unsustainable. Moreover, the suburban ethos seems fundamentally hostile to environmental sacrifice, virtue, or citizenship, in short, to Bill McKibben's plea that we "think past ourselves" to confront climate change.[7]

Much of this chapter focuses on suburbia's problematic nature in the face of our environmental crisis and calls for a civic spirit of environmental sacrifice. Today's suburban ideal is predicated on elements that militate against sacrifice: consumption, privatization, and exclusion.

Suburban life also involves individualization of risk avoidance as it offers seeming refuge from the social, political, and ecological problems associated with urbanization and overdevelopment. In fact, suburban development in the United States has come to reflect individuals' efforts to escape the consequences of earlier urbanization and suburbanization. As Ulrich Beck notes in discussing the "risk society,"[8] such attempts at escape are ultimately fruitless. Moreover, in promising shelter from risk, suburbia shields its residents from collective sacrifice.

Sacrifice for personal or familial advancement may be part of contemporary suburban life, but sacrifice for the common good, the sort of virtuous sacrifice necessary for transition to an ecologically responsible society, seems antithetical to the suburban ideal. Sacrifice in its most noble, fulfilling sense involves not self-abnegation, but a realization of an expanded self beyond the narrow, impoverished life of privatized consumption. Such a conception of sacrifice entails transcending suburban life as we know it today.

Yet this is not the whole story. The ideological foundations of suburbia are quite complex. America's suburban ideal goes back to a pastoral, republican ethos that stressed civic virtue, material moderation, and connection with nature. The original suburban ideal advanced a combination of independence and civic responsibility that is potentially supportive of the conception of sacrifice noted earlier. These roots now seem forgotten amid contemporary suburban sprawl. However, rather than unrealistically wishing the suburbs away, we can perhaps recover the greener, more civic elements of the suburban ideal in an age of ecological crisis.[9] Such a reconstructive effort also means confronting key contradictions that have emerged in American suburban life.

Defining Sacrifice

The term *sacrifice* is controversial. At its ugliest, it evokes bloody altars or totalitarian demands for absolute allegiance to the collective. On the other hand, sacrifice can have strongly positive connotations. The word's Latin roots—*sacre* (sacred) and *facere* (to make)—point to its larger meaning: *to make sacred by offering*.[10] In its higher expressions, sacrifice is not about ritual brutality, but rather about acting beyond self-interest and realizing an expanded sense of the self that recognizes one's larger social relations and commitments. The sacrificial action affirms communal membership and thus "sanctifies" the self by endowing it with a sense of greater purpose. One who sacrifices does not really lose, but makes an initially difficult, even painful trade of some good for something ultimately more valuable or worthwhile and, importantly, truer to someone's underlying ideals or identity. As Michael Sandel puts it, the person who sacrifices "is likely to experience this less as a case of being used for others' ends and more as a way of contributing to the purposes of a community I regard as my own." He adds, "The justification of my sacrifice . . . is not the abstract assurance that unknown others will gain more than I will lose, but the rather more compelling notion that by my efforts I contribute to the realization of a way of life in which I take pride and with which my identity is bound."[11]

Sacrifice in this sense stands between two extremes. On one hand, there is the atomized, self-contained individual of consumer society, one who rejects any consideration beyond the accumulation of power and material wealth and the pursuit of pleasure. On the other hand, there is the complete negation of the self in a larger, undifferentiated whole. Such a negation is associated with the more brutal forms of sacrifice, wherein the individual is expected to give himself or herself entirely to the collective. This totalitarian notion of sacrifice does not involve an ennobling of the self as there is no true self recognized as distinct from the whole. The self is abnegated, rather than enlarged.

We thus laud and admire the nobility of those who have rejected narrow self-interest and willingly given up comfort, or even lives, for worthwhile causes such as racial or sexual equality, protection of the earth, advocacy for the sick or poor, or struggles against slavery, tyranny, or colonialism. In his 2009 inaugural, President Barack Obama thus remarked, "There is nothing so satisfying to the spirit, so defining of our character than giving our all to a difficult task." By the same token, former president George W. Bush's failure to urge sacrifice after 9/11—discussed later—was so distressing because it made Americans little more than passive, self-interested spectators of the struggle against terrorism. There was a sense that the government had diminished, rather than ennobled, its citizens.

Sacrifice in the sense I am describing can be either an individual or a collective act. In either case, however, it must involve some measure of consent. Otherwise, a person is turned into an unwilling instrument, and the self is abnegated. However, such consent can take more or less direct forms. One can explicitly volunteer to join a cause or a community and make sacrifices on its behalf. Here, consent is perhaps most direct. A more indirect form of consent exists when one is a member of a polity that is democratically governed, ensures basic human rights, and distributes the burdens of social cooperation in a fair manner.[12] In such a case, the government can reasonably ask citizens to make sacrifices, ranging from taxation, to belt-tightening, to military service. In fact, citizens might consent to sacrifice even more directly by using the democratic process to overcome collective action problems and force themselves to do things they would be reluctant to undertake on a voluntary, individual basis. As Mark Sagoff might put it, our *citizen* preferences about what is good for the larger community might override our self-interested *consumer* preferences.[13] As a consumer concerned about my wallet, I might prefer to pay less for gasoline, but as a citizen, I might support a gasoline tax to compel me to consume less. In short, though sacrifice must in some measure be willing, this does not mean that sacrifice is limited to voluntary, individual acts.

It is also arguably the case that one's continued membership in a community, whether social or even ecological, automatically creates obligations to make some sacrifices in time of need. Indeed, communitarians like Michael Sandel and Alasdair MacIntyre have argued that one's basic selfhood is implicated in the good of the communities of which one is a part and that one can have unchosen obligations simply on the basis of that identification.[14] This last case is perhaps the most problematic because it implies sacrifice simply on the basis of membership and identity, whether or not the community is democratically governed. Moreover, individuals may have different conceptions of membership and of what sorts of sacrifice, if any, membership or identity entails. This raises the danger that one person's conception of ennobling sacrifice may be regarded by another person as a brutal, totalitarian imposition. Consequently, while there may be a general, prima facie obligation to sacrifice, the time and nature of the sacrifice ought to be determined through democratic consent, rather than authoritarian coercion. Later in this chapter, I will return to these theoretical issues of sacrifice.

Sacrifice in a Suburban Nation?

Flying over the suburban sprawl of Scottsdale, Arizona, in the wake of 9/11, journalist David Brooks mused, "Is this nation really ready to fight a war?" Brooks fretted, "From up here we seem too affluent and comfortable to be tough-minded, too cosseted by our own peace and prosperity to endure conflict." Brooks calmed his own worries by noting, "Our supposedly complacent suburban nation was able to endure, and win, a forty-year struggle with communism." Moreover, Brooks argued, the rigors of financial uncertainty, job insecurity, competition, meritocratic individualism, and time management meant that "suburban life is more arduous than it appears, and provides more character-building experiences than we imagine."[15]

However, in the wake of 9/11, most Americans, aside from members of the armed forces and their families and friends, were not even asked by their leaders to make any sacrifices to support the war effort. It would have made sense, for example, to reduce gasoline consumption and so lessen our dependence on foreign oil and our entanglement in the Middle East and limit the flow of funds to Islamist extremists. Yet President Bush actually urged Americans to resume business as usual. At one point, he uttered perhaps one of the most absurd statements of American war aims ever: "One of the great goals of this nation's war is to restore public confidence in the airline industry." He added, "It's to tell the traveling public: get on board. Do your business around the country. Fly and enjoy America's great destination spots. Get down to Disney World in Florida. Take your families and enjoy life, the way they want it to be enjoyed."[16]

More consumption would be no less ridiculous as a way to address serious ecological challenges like global warming. Confronting climate change entails a significant shift in our energy consumption habits and a major reduction in our overall demands on the earth as a resource and a waste sink, including cutting back on driving and reducing the size of suburban homes and lots. Inevitably, the prospect of sacrifice arises again, and we are once again faced with the question of whether a suburban nation is up for it.

Americans' expressed willingness to sacrifice consumption to fight global warming is not inspiring, particularly in the face of higher fuel prices or recession.[17] For twenty-five years, Gallup has been polling Americans on whether they would favor environmental protection "even at the risk of curbing economic growth" or the economy "even if the environment suffers to some extent." In 2009, with the economy mired in recession, respondents *for the first time* put the economy first, by 51 to 42 percent. Polls also show a drop-off in support for action on global warming, and even in concern about the problem, between 2008 and 2009. In the face of high gas prices in the summer of 2008, Americans changed their views regarding oil drilling versus energy conservation and environmental protection. Compared with earlier surveys, polls showed marked shifts toward drilling, including in the Arctic National Wildlife Refuge. A 2007 *ABC News–Washington Post*–Stanford University poll showed much greater willingness for the government to address global warming through mandates on, or tax breaks for, industry, rather than through increased gasoline or electricity taxes on consumers. A 2009 *ABC News–Washington Post* poll showed a majority of respondents supporting a cap-and-trade program that would significantly reduce greenhouse gas emissions but mean an extra ten dollars per month in electricity bills but opposing such a program when the monthly surcharge rose to twenty-five dollars.[18]

If sacrifice is so problematic for a suburban nation, how might the suburban ideal have contributed to this state of affairs? Does the suburban ideal offer any way out?

The Pastoral Ideal

In North America, the origins of the suburban ideal go back to the pastoral vision that animated English settlement of the continent.[19] Pastoralism celebrates a cultivated, gardenlike, agrarian "middle landscape"[20] between civilization and wilderness, or "between the extremes of wilderness savagery and metropolitan corruption."[21]

Thomas Jefferson notably advanced a pastoral civic republicanism.[22] He drew on two contrasting influences that anticipated later tensions in the suburban model. First of all, he was greatly impressed by English aristocratic gardens, which he tried to replicate at Monticello. Of Jefferson, James Duncan and David Lambert note, "as the best-known garden designer in the United States, he diffused English landscape tastes to an elite, post-Revolutionary population."[23]

Second, Jefferson also looked to an ideal that was more populist, frugal, and civic in its orientation. He famously extolled the independent, middling yeoman farmer as a paragon of republican virtue.[24] Jefferson's ideal yeoman was self-employed, lived off the land, and practiced frugality and moderation. He depended on nature, rather than on the market, creditors, and public authorities.[25] He had a sense of equality, regular periods of leisure in which to be politically active, and enough material security to be generous and civic-minded.[26] His life was also closer to nature's healthy influences and beauty.[27] Combining pastoralism with notions of republican civic virtue, Jefferson thus saw the yeoman's simple, independent way of life as conducive to self-governing citizenship.[28] Importantly, the yeoman's independence was not a fence against society or a mark of self-centered individualism, but rather, a precondition for good citizenship and pursuit of the common good.

In line with his agrarian values, Jefferson rejected an economy oriented around manufacturing, wage labor, commerce, and consumption.[29] Such an economy promoted various facets of corruption feared by republicans: economic dependence on employers or customers, laziness, inequality, the pursuit of luxury, and attachment to commerce rather than country.[30] Jefferson also feared the urbanization associated with industry and commerce.[31] Cities were centers of dependence and corruption and were crowded and thus physically unhealthy.[32]

Jefferson's opposition to manufacturing and consumption also reflected republican concerns about individuals putting private interest and accumulation ahead of the common good.[33] Michael Sandel remarks, "Consumption, when it figured at all in republican political economy, was a thing to be moderated, disciplined, or restrained for the sake of higher ends."[34]

Adherents of pastoralism hoped that the availability of land through westward expansion could allow an agrarian society to absorb the pursuit of commerce and industry without urbanization and the loss of pastoral virtues.[35] However, nineteenth-century industrialization, urbanization, commerce, and consumerism as well as the rapidity of frontier settlement were fatal to pastoral republicanism. The very settlement of America drained the reservoir of land that could support a virtuous yeomanry and prevent industrialization and commerce from dominating society. This contradiction between the pastoral ideal and its own social and economic basis anticipated aspects of the suburban ideal, whose antiurbanism "has always been predicated on the thoroughly urban reality of phenomenal growth."[36]

Even as the pastoral ideal became more unrealistic, it persisted in what Leo Marx calls a naive "sentimental pastoralism" involving antiurbanism and hollow allegiance to idealized rural images, without recognition of the difficult choices presented by industrialization, material accumulation, and technological progress.[37] Sentimental pastoralism reflected an industrializing of America's belief that it could "have it all," both rural simplicity and the comforts of modern abundance and technology. Our tendency to "neglect our cities and desert them for the suburbs" is one example of this attitude, Marx says.[38] The contradictions of sentimental pastoralism themselves reflected back on the tension in Jefferson's pastoralism between the aristocratic garden, which suggested high consumption and wealth, and the yeoman farm, which suggested material simplicity and a more middling status. This tension has been recapitulated in various forms in the American suburban ideal.

The Pastoral, Republican Suburb

Pastoral republicanism ideals persisted in the suburbs long after America began industrializing. The early- to mid-nineteenth century suburbs were basically country homes for the affluent. However, these suburbs' cultural significance was more complex. A number of writers celebrated the new suburbs, including Andrew Jackson Downing, a horticulturalist, and Catharine Beecher, a writer. In terms that recalled agrarian republicanism, they saw suburban life and country living as conducive to the development of virtuous character and good citizenship. At the same time, they celebrated the suburban home as a status symbol and desirable commodity. Thus the early suburban ideal carried on Jefferson's simultaneous embrace of both the simple yeoman farm and the aristocratic garden. There was also an exclusionary aspect to suburban ideology: as with Jefferson's antiurbanism, the new suburbs were seen as a refuge from the city, its congestion and unhealthy environment, and its poor and other supposedly undesirable residents.[39]

In his 1850 celebration of the suburban home, Downing explicitly evoked republican themes of individual independence, material moderation, equality, and rural virtue. The "republican home" was earned through honest effort, rather than the exploitation of others. It was a "beautiful, rural, unostentatious, moderate home of the country gentleman, large enough to minister to all the wants, necessities, and luxuries of a republican, and not too large or too luxurious to warp the life or manners of his children."[40] In a similar vein, Beecher, who urged women to embrace a life of homemaking in a country or suburban house, connected domestic work with Christian and republican virtues, including a willingness to sacrifice. In 1865, she commented,

It will be found that the democratic principle is no other than the grand law of Christianity, which requires *work and self-sacrifice for the public good*, to which all private interests are to be subordinate. Children are to be trained to live not for themselves but for others; not to be waited on and taken care of, but to wait on take care of others; to *work* for the good of others as the first thing, and amusement and enjoyment as necessary but subordinate to the highest public good. The family is the first commonwealth where this training is to be carried on, and only as a preparation for a more enlarged sphere of action.[41]

So, just as with Jefferson's small farm, the suburban home would be a classroom in moderation, hard work, and civic virtue, not a citadel of rugged individualism. Even as late as the early twentieth century, as Mary Corbin Sies recounts, upper-middle-class residents, designers, and developers of suburban communities were defining the suburban ideal in terms of moderation and civic and communitarian virtues: they saw the home as a manifestation of material success, but also as an environment for cultivating strong familial bonds and associated virtues like temperance, thrift, political and material moderation, law-abidingness, a sense of community, and social responsibility. They also envisioned, in line with the pastoral ideal, the suburb as a middle landscape embracing both urban culture and technology, and rural domesticity and beauty. Despite their class status, such commentators regarded suburban living as an ideal for not only the privileged, but also the working class, whose morals could be improved and politics deradicalized through home-ownership. Though these reformers saw social bonds within individual communities as being fostered through homogeneity and exclusivity, they also expected suburban residents to work for social reform beyond their localities.[42]

However, despite such invocations of civic virtue, tensions were at work. Nicolaides and Wiese point out that the "trend toward domesticity reflected a cultural shift from public to private life."[43] Indeed, Downing's and Beecher's visions were themselves already rife with conflicts between domesticity and public life, between exclusion and social responsibility, and between rural and urban values. Furthermore, the simultaneous embrace of aristocratic elegance, status, and wealth with rural, home-spun simplicity would be difficult to maintain.

Suburban Expansion and Exclusion

With the railroad and electric streetcar or trolley making travel more feasible, the suburbs greatly expanded in the late nineteenth and early twentieth centuries. Given needed pedestrian proximity to transit stops, these suburbs, such as Brookline, Massachusetts (near Boston), were relatively dense by today's sprawling standards.[44] However, such suburban growth "exposed a fundamental paradox in the suburbanization process; the construction of new homes for urban commuters, even affluent ones, inevitably eroded the bucolic atmosphere that had attracted many suburbanites in the first place." This problem was exacerbated by the growth of industry and commerce in the suburbs. Moreover, as middle- and working-class families began moving to the suburbs in greater numbers, more affluent suburbanites felt threatened and feared the arrival of immigrants and nonwhites.[45]

The response was an explicitly defensive exclusivity that set the tone for much suburban development for decades to come.[46] Real estate developers began building subdivisions with various deed restrictions, including minimum lot sizes, setback and side free space requirements, limits or prohibitions on multifamily residences, and most notoriously, explicit exclusion of African Americans and other minority and immigrant groups. The real estate industry also pushed localities, during the first quarter of the twentieth century, to enshrine such development restrictions into law through elaborate zoning requirements designed to maintain property values and exclude undesirables.[47] As part of these efforts, localities mandated single-use districts separating residences, commerce, and industry. Suburbs also began to successfully resist annexation by cities, with the result that political boundaries were erected to keep out urban influences and avoid paying taxes to cities.[48]

The influence of realtors and developers extended to the federal government. Federal mortgage insurance programs, which greatly stimulated suburbanization after World War II, developed preferential guidelines favoring the same sorts of suburban housing enshrined in deed restrictions and local zoning laws as well as mortgages in racially homogeneous communities; indeed, there was outright discrimination against African Americans.[49] Though suburban hostility to white ethnics had considerably faded by the mid-twentieth century,[50] and though racist provisions in housing policy were swept away during the civil rights era, deed restrictions and zoning laws have maintained the model of the detached suburban home and the single-use district and have continued to preserve income and, de facto, racial homogeneity in many areas.

The Sprawling Postwar Suburbs as a Haven for Privatized Consumption

The proliferation of sprawling, low-density suburbs was a phenomenon of the twentieth century, particularly the post–World War II era. In addition to the role of deed restrictions, zoning, and federal mortgage insurance, the far-flung sprawl of postwar suburbia was also facilitated by other key factors, including the popularity of the automobile.[51]

Just as the civic promise of pastoral republicanism gave way to industrialization, development, and commerce, the civic aspects of the suburban ideal faded away as the suburbs evolved and sprawled. The postwar suburbs were far removed from the civic ideology surrounding the early suburbs, though there was still a patina of attachment to nature, which became evident in antigrowth sentiment. At the same time, the consumerist and exclusive aspects of suburbia were considerably heightened; aspirations to elegance, status, and wealth won out over virtuous simplicity.

The suburbs explicitly became havens for consumption. "Middle class status," say Becky Nicolaides and Andrew Wiese, "came to depend less on occupation, more on possessions and way of life. . . . In this milieu, suburban home ownership became an important badge of middle-class status." At the same time, the detached single-family home and the postwar ideal of the nuclear family reinforced the domesticated, privatizing aspect of suburbia.[52]

Today, the centrality of consumption is reflected in the very geography of our sprawling developments. Contemporary suburbia is physically functionalized for more or less pure, unimpeded consumption. Urban planner Peter Calthorpe observes, "Human scale and neighborhood focus have been exchanged for auto access and national distribution. Shopping, even at its most incidental scale, is removed from neighborhood and town, removed from the social dimension it used to play in defining a community."[53] Contemporary suburban life, in fact, directly militates against sacrifice by actually mandating high levels of consumption. By its very layout, sprawl necessitates automobile use even for those who would prefer other options. In fact, as early as 1961, Lewis Mumford called the automobile "a compulsory and inescapable condition of suburban existence."[54] Zoning laws also directly mandate low-density development and, by extension, its associated consumption patterns. Furthermore, the contemporary suburban ideal ties social status to high levels of consumption: large homes, large cars, chemically maintained lawns, and so forth.

Meanwhile, there is an expansion of the private realm as the setting for an increasing number of consumer activities. Single-use zoning and reliance on the automobile mean less walking and reduced availability of pedestrian-friendly public spaces like sidewalks. People are increasingly isolated in their cars and homes.[55] What remains of the public realm becomes unfamiliar and threatening. Richard Moe and Carter Wilkie thus describe a "home-centered" society, in which erosion of the public landscape and associated perceptions of increasing insecurity in the streets lead to a turning inward.[56] In sharp contrast to the model of sacrifice discussed earlier, there is a narrowing of the self, a retreat from engagement with the outside and a focus on the accumulation and protection of material goods. One hallmark of this turning inward is a form of development prominent since the 1970s: the private community.

Suburban Exclusivity and Private Communities

The post–World War II suburb is marked by varying degrees of exclusion, through zoning laws, municipal boundaries, private home owners' associations, and physical barriers like gates, which close off the outside world and externalize risk. Such exclusion maintains unimpeded consumption[57] and also reflects a fixation on maintaining property values and countering security threats from outsiders. Susan Bickford sees in suburbia an overall effort to create geographical boundaries against risk, conceived in terms of threats from others who are different in terms of race, class, or sexual orientation.[58] Such exclusion can be self-reinforcing: "Attempts to satisfy the desire for security and safety can simply intensify the longing; the more homogeneity among those lived with, the more threatening are any indications of difference that manage to creep in (through television, the news, visitors, etc.)."[59] The exclusionary impulse is even couched in environmentalist rhetoric, in the form of antigrowth or slow-growth movements.[60]

Exclusion encourages an increasing proliferation of private communities, which Margaret Kohn describes as "large developments such as condos, gated communities, co-ops, and apartment complexes where residents' units are not accessible to public streets."[61] Such developments often provide their own services and are controlled by what are variously termed home owners' associations or residential community associations (RCAs). Such associations see themselves as private entities, rather than municipal governments. Private communities tend to be homogeneous in population, both in terms of income and race; such homogeneity, as noted earlier, often ties in with a fear of outsiders.[62] Private communities are in many places the dominant form of emerging suburb. Municipalities and suburbs in many metropolitan areas, such as Las Vegas, Chicago, and Dallas, require home owners' associations for new developments so that the local government can save money on providing services. Thus privatization is mandated.[63] It has also become widespread: in 1970, about two million Americans lived in private communities; in 2005, over fifty-four million Americans did.[64] Kohn notes, "Approximately fifty percent of all new homes built in major metropolitan areas nationwide fall under the jurisdiction of RCAs."[65]

Private communities are really communities in name only. There is little more than the illusion of public life. The "defensive suburbanization" associated with exclusionary suburbs professes communitarian ideals, but Duncan and Lambert caution that though it is "predicated on notions of internal identity, sovereignty, and equality, [it] undermines such ideals across the constructed borders."[66] Planner Todd Bressi thus remarks that "current metropolitan settlement patterns have clearly exacerbated social, class, and racial segregation and diminished the importance of common ground on which people of different backgrounds and outlooks might encounter each other."[67] To the degree that true community life is multifaceted and diverse, private communities thus offer little of the real thing.[68] Putnam argues that contemporary sprawling development "is associated with increasing social segregation, and social homogeneity appears to reduce incentives for civic involvement, as well as opportunities for social networks that cut across class and racial lines. Sprawl has been especially toxic for bridging social capital."[69] Sandel sees a retreat to private communities as a kind of secession of the affluent from a sense of shared political community.[70]

Exclusionary or not, private communities could still be internally animated by a democratic, communal life. However, it turns out that these exclusionary communities are themselves undemocratic. The private home owners' associations or RCAs governing these communities are remarkably despotic and intrusive, lacking democratic accountability and prohibiting activities that might lower property values such as hanging laundry outside, parking a boat or RV out front, leaving the garage door open, and even planting a vegetable garden or engaging in acts of political expression like flying the flag, displaying political signs, and distributing leaflets and newspapers.[71] Gerald Frug says that the contemporary legal structures of our suburbanized society "foster a privatized sense of self that structures the consciousness of people when they act as citizens. As a result, they help generate support for withdrawal rather than engagement, sameness rather than diversity, separation rather than openness, avoidance of conflict rather than building the capacity to deal with it."[72] Moreover, the restrictions imposed by private communities further mandate excessive consumption and prohibit individual acts of material sacrifice. For example, one is required to use a clothes dryer even on a warm, sunny day, when the laundry might be hung on a line.

Postwar Suburban Politics

This privatized, individualized, exclusionary, consumption-oriented realm of suburbia is associated with a conservative political culture, most specifically in newer, more affluent suburbs. This conservative perspective is defensively focused on maintaining one's suburb as an exclusive locus for goods like comfortable homes, good schools and infrastructure, high property values, and physical security. There is often intense opposition to redistributive taxes and social programs and to the sharing of wealth, amenities, and undesirable land uses with cities.[73] Such a focus on limiting taxation and protecting property values and resources has made suburbs seem less like governments and more like business enterprises.[74]

In some cases, the desire to preserve open space in rapidly developing suburbs promotes environmental activism.[75] Such activism is not necessarily inconsistent with suburbia's consumer culture. It may reflect a shift from a resource-based economy to one predicated on "aesthetic landscape consumption" by newcomers employed in the professional sectors.[76] It can also involve the protection of local property values.[77] Environmentalists have thus drawn some support from more conservative residents with frankly exclusionary perspectives; antigrowth efforts have sometimes tied in with movements to exclude outsiders, particularly lower-income and minority residents and immigrants.[78] At the same time, the cultural and political overtones of environmentalism may worry conservatives, making such alliances fragile.[79] In fact, antigrowth environmental activism can ultimately challenge privatism and consumption by fostering "increased planning at a landscape scale."[80] I discuss this point later.

Illusory Escape from Risk

What the suburban ideal thus seems to offer, as Bickford suggests, is escape from risk, in the form of crime, pollution, corrupt government, poverty, high taxes, and other ills associated with urbanization as well as risk from exposure to difference, as we saw earlier. Viewed from Albert O. Hirschmann's famous triad of "exit, voice, and loyalty," the suburban ideal favors exit.[81] There is now, in Frug's words, "the common belief that the way to deal with urban problems is to run away from them—to cross city lines and protect oneself from the bad things going on elsewhere."[82] The contemporary suburb is an embodiment of risk avoidance.

Ulrich Beck argues that in the face of modernity's technological and environmental dangers, we have become a risk society: society, suffused with anxiety, is fundamentally concerned with safety from risk.[83] Risks are not borne equally, and the unequal distribution of risk can "follow the inequalities of class and strata positions."[84] Thus Beck says, "Poverty attracts an unfortunate abundance of risks. By contrast, the wealthy . . . can *purchase* safety and freedom from risk."[85] Modern risk society is also individualized; people cannot rely on traditional social networks or classes or place-based communities to manage risk, but rather, must seek out new networks, communities, and solutions on their own.[86] Thus the affluent secede and buy their way into new suburbs with good schools, infrastructure, services, and homes and plenty of green space, even as poorer urban or inner suburban residents are faced with declining tax revenues, environmental conditions, and quality of life.

Like consumption and its privatizing aspects, such risk avoidance involves the erection of boundaries between the self and the outside world. Instead of confronting risks and trying to mitigate them through political action, the individual moving to, say, a private community withdraws behind protective barriers and seeks to protect herself and her possessions and amenities from outside threats. Again, in stark contrast to the expansive, ennobling concept of sacrifice, there is a narrowing or shrinking of the self.

However, the environmental and social problems of modernity are not so easily avoided. Beck warns, "Risks display a social boomerang effect."[87] In other words, the "risks of modernization sooner or later also strike those who produce or profit from them. . . . Even the rich and powerful are not safe from them. These are hazards not only to health, but also to legitimization, property and profit."[88]

Consequently, the suburban escape is ultimately illusory, as the early suburbanites discovered when urbanizing overdevelopment followed them to the countryside. Similarly, contemporary suburban sprawl shows a vicious cycle as overdevelopment ruins places and then the more affluent move on, ultimately bringing the same problems on themselves again and creating an outwardly expanding suburban footprint, with the center subject to disinvestment.[89] The problems of modernity boomerang on those who seek to avoid them.

Complexities, Changes, and Contradictions in Suburbia

It is important, however, not to oversimplify the suburban experience. First of all, throughout the twentieth century, the affluent suburban ideal was belied by the existence of numerous working-class, ethnic, and minority suburbanites and suburban communities.[90] The post–World War II expansion of the middle class to include blue-collar workers also broadened the suburban demographic.[91] The suburbs have become more racially and ethnically diverse since the 1960s, due to an influx of both immigrants and people of color,[92] though within the suburbs, there is still considerable segregation of black residents.[93]

Second, despite the recent trend toward private communities, the American suburb exhibits a variety of forms.[94] For example, as noted earlier, older, higher-density, inner-ring suburbs—some dating back to the nineteenth century—do not conform to the highly dispersed suburban model that emerged after World War II. Meanwhile, many suburbs are moving away from the conservative profile. A shift to a more liberal or progressive politics has been especially pronounced in inner-ring suburbs, which tend to be older, denser, and more demographically diverse and which face issues of aging infrastructure, poverty, and environmental degradation.[95] Such suburbs could make common cause with urban areas and provide support for metropolitan or other regional approaches to social and environmental problems.[96]

American suburbs also face key contradictions that might force change. Contradiction has marked the suburbs from their early roots. There was a contradiction between the maintenance of a pastoral, republican way of life on one hand, and the economic development associated with the expansion of agrarian settlement on the other. Reflecting Jefferson's perspective, there was a contradiction between the suburbs as a place of virtuous, rustic simplicity and as the domain of the aristocratic garden or material affluence. There was a contradiction between the civic virtues prized by Downing and Beecher and the privatized, exclusive aspects of their suburban vision. As the nineteenth century advanced, there also emerged a contradiction between rural suburban charm and the more congested reality of suburban development. Today, there is a contradiction between suburbanites' desire for green acres, high property values, wealth, and risk avoidance and the boomeranging environmental and social costs of suburban growth and excessive resource consumption and pollution.

What seems at issue throughout the suburban story is a basic tension between civic virtue, moderation, and harmony with nature on one hand, and privatism, social exclusivity, material status and accumulation, and unsustainable development on the other. Whether a suburban nation can confront today's environmental, social, and resource challenges and make the sacrifices necessary to move suburbia to a more virtuous, sustainable, and socially responsible footing depends on how this tension or contradiction plays out.

It is certainly possible that the burden of mounting energy prices, which some analysts say reflect long-term shifts,[97] coupled with the threat of climate change and increasing concern about the impacts of suburban sprawl, may doom the post–World War II, highly dispersed, automobile-dependent suburb. The boomerang effect from excessive energy consumption, in terms of high gas prices, may force suburbanites to make sacrifices, even in spite of themselves. The recent rise in fuel prices, coupled with the mortgage foreclosure crisis, seems to have already made living in the outer suburbs less desirable and promoted a population shift back toward cities.[98] The result could be a shift to higher-density communities more integrated into the urban or metropolitan fabric, as advocated by regionalists and New Urbanists.[99]

Suburbs and a Balanced Notion of Sacrifice

Such trends might create more willingness to sacrifice high levels of consumption to address problems like global warming. It is not simply that economic constraints will force people to reluctantly shift their consumption habits and move back to higher-density communities. As people increasingly see alternatives to high-consumption suburban life as practical and within reach and become more critical of norms and regulations demanding such consumption, they will begin to see such sacrifices as realistic and feasible. The consumption associated with suburban sprawl will no longer seem mandatory: one will begin to consider other sorts of places to live and willingly support policies that encourage the restoration or development of higher-density communities and alternative means of transportation.

Would the suburban ideal survive such changes? In sacrificing high levels of consumption for ecological sustainability, would citizens be giving up on the suburbs themselves? It is at this point that we must return to the republican roots of the American suburban ideal. Recall that sacrifice as an admirable act involves an expansion, rather than negation, of the self. One realizes one's self to be bound up with the good of others. The act of sacrifice becomes not a matter of self-denial, but rather involves the satisfaction of participating in a set of ends or principles beyond narrow self-interest.

This positive idea of sacrifice resonates with the civic republican tradition and its communitarian notion of a situated self owing its identity and ends at least in part to its societal ties and commitments.[100] However, as Sandel notes, there are more or less demanding forms of republicanism. More demanding forms of republicanism, such as that articulated by Jean-Jacques Rousseau in *The Social Contract*, involve coercive virtue, in which the good of society is unitary; the individual owes absolute allegiance, indeed his very identity, to the community; and disagreement and contentious deliberation are signs of corruption.[101] Any meaningful distinction between individual self and political community breaks down, and sacrifice is demanded without individual dissent or disagreement. Sacrifice affirms negation of the self.

By contrast, Sandel's republicanism envisions a self that is embedded in a number of communities and networks, rather than in one homogeneous whole,[102] a self that is therefore individually distinct from others. Moreover, such a self does not automatically and unthinkingly make sacrifices for any particular community or set of ends, but rather, engages in a process of self-understanding, sorting out and weighing its various attachments and commitments "by reflecting on itself and inquiring into its constituent nature, discerning its laws and imperatives, and acknowledging its purposes as its own."[103] Such a process of reflection or deliberation affirms a partial distance between a person and his or her attachments or history: "As a self-interpreting being, I am able to reflect on my history and in this sense to distance myself from it, but the distance is always precarious and provisional, the point of reflection never finally secured outside the history itself."[104] In personally making a material sacrifice or in supporting policies such as higher energy taxes, one might be discovering one's fundamental sense of self, finding out that one's identity and interests encompass a set of communal attachments and purposes. Here, sacrifice is thus an expansion of the self after a process of self-reflection. In a democratic society determining environmental policies, such reflection ideally happens collectively, as citizens deliberate and even debate on their identity and ends as a community.

What is evident in this discussion of republicanism, the self, and sacrifice is a delicate balance or dynamic tension between independence and civic responsibility. One cannot simply abandon one's attachments and commitments, and yet one's personhood still stands at a provisional distance from them. Significantly, the original republican ideals of the yeoman farmer and of early suburbia were infused with a similar balance. The yeoman and the early suburbanite lived in a kind of independence from the rest of society, as physically manifested in the small farm or the domicile in the countryside. At the same time, they were expected to engage with the larger community as active, participating, responsible citizens.

But why would suburbanites, in reflecting on their identities and purposes, ever sacrifice the suburban ideal as we now know it? This takes us back to the contradictions of suburbia. With its increasing focus on consumption, the contemporary sprawling suburb has moved further and further away from the original suburban ideal and has become increasingly unsustainable. The home in green, bucolic surroundings, inhabited by democratic citizens, seems more and more a fantasy, as the search for such a suburban haven leads people out to the sprawling exurbs, where they face long commutes, rising energy costs, excessive dependence on the automobile, traffic congestion, pollution, visual blight, intrusive restrictions, mortgage foreclosures, and so forth. However, rather than sweepingly condemn the suburbs and urge everyone into apartment buildings or townhouses, the answer is public deliberation on what makes suburban life meaningful and whether that meaning is consistent with the sustainability of the suburbs themselves and of the planet as a whole. Such deliberation would also concern what must be sacrificed to secure a better suburban future. Arguably, what is unsustainable and ought to be sacrificed would be the far-flung, automobile-dependent exurban development and the private communities favored in recent decades. Fortunately, there is a suburban alternative, and it would simultaneously restore some of the original suburban values and be more sustainable.

Future Suburbs

What might a greener, more moderate, civic, and virtuous suburbia look like? It would no longer be out in the countryside: that option is no longer sustainable. It would probably look more like the earlier, higher-density railroad and streetcar suburbs and be built around mass transit and pedestrian accessibility. Such suburbs would be nurtured through revitalization of older, inner-ring suburbs; through infill of existing sprawl; and through increased investment in mass transit. Their higher density would not rule out single-use housing. As I note elsewhere, "there is a vast difference between a compact, suburban neighborhood of detached homes on relatively small lots—say, six to seven houses per acre—and a low-density development of widely separated homes on larger lots" of, say, one or two houses per acre.[105] Such suburbs could also still have yards and gardens and, if planned properly, green space in the form of parks and even nearby wilderness. At the same time, they would be more pedestrian-friendly, less energy-intensive, more favorable to community, and more aesthetically pleasing than sprawl. This suburban vision has been articulated most notably by New Urbanists.[106]

A move away from highly dispersed, sprawling development would also make the privatized, secessionist exit option less feasible for suburbanites. Geographic proximity among individuals and communities will create more street-level social interaction as well as a need for collective problem solving at a landscape, metropolitan, or regional level, such as now exists in the Portland, Oregon, metropolitan area. Regional government or cooperation would help reverse the problematic municipal fragmentation that took hold over the twentieth century and would turn the suburb from an isolated, privileged haven of consumption and material accumulation into an integrated part of a larger landscape.[107]

A move toward more collective, regional forms of land management and regulation, even at the cost of some measure of freedom of consumption, property rights, and exclusionary localizm, has perhaps been anticipated by suburban environmental activists. Such activism arises as development destroys the open space and wilderness values for which many residents originally left more densely populated areas. Such environmentalism, particularly in newer suburbs or exurbs, where the preservation of open space is still very much at issue, points to a more collective and civic approach to property and suburban life. Ironically, the way to such a civic perspective may initially be through consumption values themselves. Peter Walker and Louise Fortmann, analyzing exurban green activism, maintain that "a 'new' economy based on 'consumption' of rural landscape qualities depends upon a view of the *landscape* as a space of multiple interdependencies and responsibilities to the common good."[108] The desire to protect property values, as Jamison Colburn argues, may also motivate support for environmental regulation and more collectivized, landscape-level land-use planning, through both local and federative, interlocal action.[109] Though such activism has hitherto been concerned with growth and sprawl, the prospect of global warming threatening place-based suburban values may also motivate collective action and responsibility on this issue, as well.

In sum, the challenges of high energy prices, climate change, and sprawl and the inability to escape shared risk may reinvigorate a call for shared sacrifice and the creation of a more sustainable suburb. This would mean a resolution of suburbia's underlying contradictions and a return to suburbia's republican roots and a much greater appreciation on the part of suburbanites of their connections to their own natural habitats, to other human communities and ecosystems, and to the biosphere itself. Today, we face a crisis and a juncture, a juncture at which suburbanites might ask themselves whether it is unrestrained consumption, privatism, and exclusivity, or something less self-destructive and more civic and sustainable, that gives suburbia and their own lives their true value. It is hoped that they will sacrifice the former and affirm the latter.

Acknowledgments

Thanks to Michael Maniates, John Meyer, and the other authors in this volume for their helpful comments and intellectual input. Thanks also to William Wimsatt and other participants at the conference "Does the Environment Have a Right?: Critical Perspectives on Environmentalism and the Left," University of Chicago, Chicago, IL, May 9, 2009, at which portions of this chapter were presented.

Notes

1. Frank Hobbs and Nicole Stoops, *Demographic Trends in the Twentieth Century* (Washington, DC: U.S. Census Bureau, 2002), 33.

2. Kenneth T. Jackson, *Crabgrass Frontier: The Suburbanization of the United States* (New York: Oxford University Press, 1987), 13.

3. Ibid., 4.

4. See, e.g., Joel Garreau, *Edge City* (New York: Doubleday, 1991), 5; Sarah Lyall, "Employers in the Suburbs Try Commuter Management," *The New York Times*, November 4, 1989, 24.

5. Jackson, *Crabgrass Frontier*, 11.

6. There is an enormous literature articulating critiques of suburbia. This includes classic works by urban planners and sociologists, including Jane Jacobs, *The Death and Life of Great American Cities* (New York: Random House, 1992 [1961]); Lewis Mumford, *The City in History: Its Origins, Its Transformations, and Its Prospects* (San Diego: Harcourt Brace, 1961); and William H. Whyte Jr., *The Organization Man* (New York: Simon and Schuster, 1956). For a critical discussion of Jacobs, Mumford, and Whyte, see Becky Nicolaides, "How Hell Moved from the City to the Suburbs: Urban Scholars and Changing Perceptions of Authentic Community," in *The New Suburban History*, ed. Kevin M. Kruse and Thomas J. Sugrue (Chicago: University of Chicago

Press, 2006). More recent critiques of suburbia and suburban sprawl include Peter Calthorpe, *The Next American Metropolis: Ecology, Community, and the American Dream* (Princeton, NJ: Princeton Architectural Press, 1993); Peter F. Cannavò, *The Working Landscape: Founding, Preservation, and the Politics of Place* (Cambridge: MIT Press, 2007); Reid Ewing, "Is Los Angeles–Style Sprawl Desirable?" *Journal of the American Planning Association* 63, no. 1 (1997): 107–126; Peter Katz, ed., *The New Urbanism: Toward an Architecture of Community* (New York: McGraw-Hill, 1994); Matthew J. Lindstrom and Hugh Bartling, eds., *Suburban Sprawl: Culture, Theory, and Politics* (Lanham, MD: Rowman and Littlefield, 2003); Douglas S. Kelbaugh, *Repairing the American Metropolis: Common Place Revisited* (Seattle: University of Washington Press, 2002); Margaret Kohn, *Brave New Neighborhoods: The Privatization of Public Space* (New York: Routledge, 2004); James Howard Kunstler, *The Geography of Nowhere: The Rise and Decline of America's Man-Made Landscape* (New York: Simon and Schuster, 1993); Richard Moe and Carter Wilkie, *Changing Places: Rebuilding Community in the Age of Sprawl* (New York: Henry Holt, 1997); Robert Paehlke, "Environmental Sustainability and Urban Life in America," in *Environmental Policy: New Directions for the Twenty-first Century*, ed. Norman Vig and Michael E. Kraft (Washington, DC: CQ Press, 2002), 57–77; Thomas B. Stoel, "Reining in Urban Sprawl: What Can Be Done to Tackle This Growing Problem?" *Environment* 41, no. 4 (1999): 6–11, 29–33. Jackson, *Crabgrass Frontier*, while mainly a history of suburbanization, ultimately takes a highly critical stance on suburban life, especially its supposed lack of community. Political scientist Robert Putnam has also famously criticized the lack of social capital in contemporary suburbs. See Robert Putnam, *Bowling Alone: The Collapse and Revival of American Community* (New York: Simon and Schuster, 2001). For more favorable views of suburbia, see David Brooks, "Our Sprawling, Supersize Utopia," *The New York Times Magazine*, April 4, 2004, 46–51; Robert Bruegmann, *Sprawl: A Compact History* (Chicago: University of Chicago Press, 2005); Peter Gordon and Harry W. Richardson, "Are Compact Cities a Desirable Planning Goal?" *Journal of the American Planning Association* 63, no. 1 (1997): 95–106; Stephen Hayward, "Legends of the Sprawl," *Policy Review* 91 (September–October 1998): 26–32; and Joel Kotkin, "Get Used to It: Suburbia's Not Going Away, No Matter What Critics Say or Do," *The American Enterprise* 16 (January–February 2005): 32–37.

7. Bill McKibben, "Thinking Past Ourselves," *Bulletin of the Atomic Scientists* 63, no. 6 (2007): 28–31.

8. See Ulrich Beck, *Risk Society: Toward a New Modernity* (1986), trans. Mark Ritter (London: Sage, 1992).

9. For an alternate view, that suburbia faces demise in the face of resource and environmental constraints, see Kunstler, *Geography of Nowhere*, and similar calls for a seismic "paradigm shift."

10. Peter F. Cannavò and Karen Litfin, "Some Ideas for President Obama's Call to Sacrifice," *Seattle Times*, January 23, 2009, http://seattletimes.nwsource.com/html/opinion/2008664375_opinc25litfin.html.

11. Michael J. Sandel, *Liberalism and the Limits of Justice* (Cambridge: Cambridge University Press, 1982), 143.

12. This builds on the notion of implied consent advanced by John Locke, *Second Treatise of Government* (1690).

13. Mark Sagoff, *The Economy of the Earth: Philosophy, Law, and the Natural Environment* (Cambridge: Cambridge University Press, 1990).

14. See Sandel, *Liberalism*, and Alasdair MacIntyre, *After Virtue* (Notre Dame, IN: University of Notre Dame Press, 1984).

15. David Brooks, "On the Playing Fields of Suburbia," *The Atlantic Monthly* 289, no. 1 (2002), http://www.theatlantic.com/doc/200201/brooks.

16. Elisabeth Bumiller, "Bush to Increase Federal Role in Security at Airports," *The New York Times*, September 28, 2001, http://query.nytimes.com/gst/fullpage.html?res=9C07E4D91F3AF93BA1575AC0A9679C8B63.

17. See Michael R. Greenberg, "Is Public Support for Environmental Protection Decreasing? An Analysis of U.S. and New Jersey Data," *Environmental Health Perspectives* 112, no. 2 (2004): 121–125.

18. See http://www.pollingreport.com/enviro.htm; http://www.pollingreport.com/energy.htm.

19. James S. Duncan and David R. Lambert, "Landscape, Aesthetics, and Power," in *American Space/American Place: Geographies of the Contemporary United States*, ed. John A. Agnew and Jonathan M. Smith (New York: Routledge, 2002), 266.

20. Leo Marx, *The Machine in the Garden: Technology and the Pastoral Ideal in America* (New York: Oxford University Press, 1964), 71.

21. J. G. A. Pocock, *The Machiavellian Moment: Florentine Political Thought and the Atlantic Republican Tradition* (Princeton, NJ: Princeton University Press, 1975), 539–540.

22. On Jefferson's importance as a spokesperson for the pastoral ideal, see Marx, *Machine in the Garden*, 118.

23. Duncan and Lambert, "Landscape, Aesthetics, and Power," 266.

24. See Thomas Jefferson, *Notes on the State of Virginia* (1787), in *The Portable Thomas Jefferson*, ed. Merrill D. Peterson (New York: Penguin, 1975), Query XIX and Query XXII.

25. Pocock, *Machiavellian Moment*, 464; J. G. A. Pocock, *Politics, Language, and Time: Essays on Political Thought and History* (Chicago: University of Chicago Press, 1989), 91–92.

26. On the virtues of Jefferson's yeomanry, see Jean M. Yarbrough, *American Virtues: Thomas Jefferson on the Character of a Free People* (Lawrence: University of Kansas Press, 1998), 64–70. For a related discussion on the American Founders' conception of republican virtue, see Gordon S. Wood, *The Creation of the American Republic, 1776–1787* (New York: W. W. Norton, 1969), 46–90.

242   Peter F. Cannavò

27. Charles A. Miller, *Jefferson and Nature: An Interpretation* (Baltimore: Johns Hopkins University Press, 1988), 215.

28. On the Jeffersonians' agrarian republican political economy, see also Michael J. Sandel, *Democracy's Discontent: America in Search of a Public Philosophy* (Cambridge, MA: Harvard University Press, 1996), 137–150.

29. Jefferson, *Notes*, Query XIX, 217.

30. Miller, *Jefferson and Nature*, 210.

31. Jefferson, *Notes*, Query XIX, 217.

32. Miller, *Jefferson and Nature*, 210.

33. Pocock, *Politics, Language, and Time*, 88.

34. Sandel, *Democracy's Discontent*, 224.

35. Pocock, *Machiavellian Moment*, 527, 533–534.

36. Duncan and Lambert, "Landscape, Aesthetics, and Power," 278.

37. Marx, *Machine in the Garden*, 5.

38. Ibid., 5.

39. Susan Bickford, "Constructing Inequality: City Spaces and the Architecture of Citizenship," *Political Theory* 28, no. 3 (2000): 365.

40. Andrew Jackson Downing, excerpt from *The Architecture of Country Houses* (1850), in *The Suburb Reader*, ed. Becky M. Nicolaides and Andrew Wiese (New York: Routledge, 2006), 21; emphasis added.

41. Catharine Beecher, excerpt from "How to Redeem Woman's Profession from Dishonor" (1865), in Nicolaides and Wiese, *Suburb Reader*, 48; emphasis in original.

42. See Mary Corbin Sies, "'God's Very Kingdom on Earth': The Design Program for the American Suburban Home, 1877–1917," in *Modern Architecture in America: Visions and Revisions*, ed. Sidney K. Robinson and Richard Guy Wilson (Ames: Iowa State University Press, 1991).

43. Becky M. Nicolaides and Andrew Wiese, "Family and Gender in the Making of Suburbia," in Nicolaides and Wiese, *Suburb Reader*, 45.

44. Jackson, *Crabgrass Frontier*, 101, 119, 136.

45. Becky M. Nicolaides and Andrew Wiese, "The Tools of Exclusion: From Local Initiatives to Federal Policy," in Nicolaides and Wiese, *Suburb Reader*, 225.

46. For the following points, see Nicolaides and Wiese, *Suburb Reader*, 225–253.

47. Gerald R. Frug, "The Legal Technology of Exclusion in Metropolitan America," in Kruse and Sugrue, *New Suburban History*, 206.

48. See Jackson, *Crabgrass Frontier*, 138–156; Ronald Hayduk, "Race and Suburban Sprawl: Regionalism and Structural Racism," in Lindstrom and Bartling, *Suburban Sprawl*, 157; Henry R. Richmond, "Metropolitan Land-Use Reform: The Promise and Challenge of Majority Consensus," in *Reflections*

on Regionalism, ed. Bruce Katz (Washington, DC: Brookings Institution Press, 2000).

49. Jackson, *Crabgrass Frontier*, 190–218.

50. Becky M. Nicolaides and Andrew Wiese, "Postwar America: Suburban Apotheosis," in Nicolaides and Wiese, *Suburb Reader*, 258.

51. For a more detailed discussion of these factors as well as references to relevant historical accounts, see Jackson, *Crabgrass Frontier*, and Cannavò, *Working Landscape*, 98–103.

52. Nicolaides and Wiese, "Postwar America," 258. See also Barbara M. Kelly, *Expanding the American Dream* (Albany: State University of New York Press, 1993).

53. Calthorpe, *Next American Metropolis*, 24.

54. Lewis Mumford, *The City in History: Its Origins, Its Transformations, and Its Prospects* (San Diego, CA: Harcourt Brace, 1961), 492–493.

55. Calthorpe, *Next American Metropolis*, 23.

56. Moe and Wilkie, *Changing Places*, 72–73. See also Kohn, *Brave New Neighborhoods*.

57. Duncan and Lambert, "Landscape, Aesthetics, and Power," 269.

58. Bickford, "Constructing Inequality," 366.

59. Ibid., 364.

60. Duncan and Lambert, "Landscape, Aesthetics, and Power," 279.

61. Kohn, *Brave New Neighborhoods*, 116.

62. See ibid., 118; Michele Byers, "Waiting at the Gate: The New, Postmodern Promised Lands," in Lindstrom and Bartling, *Suburban Sprawl*, 27. See also Setha Low, *Behind the Gates: Life, Security, and the Pursuit of Happiness in Fortress America* (New York: Routledge, 2003).

63. Frug, "Legal Technology of Exclusion," 208.

64. Becky Nicolaides and Andrew Wiese, "Our Town: Inclusion and Exclusion in Recent Suburbia," in Nicolaides and Wiese, *Suburb Reader*.

65. Kohn, *Brave New Neighborhoods*, 116.

66. Duncan and Lambert, "Landscape, Aesthetics, and Power," 279.

67. Todd W. Bressi, "Planning the American Dream," in Katz, *New Urbanism*, xxix–xxx. See also Kohn, *Brave New Neighborhoods*, 115–166.

68. Byers, "Waiting at the Gate," 33–35.

69. Putnam, *Bowling Alone*, 214.

70. Sandel, *Democracy's Discontent*, 331–333. See also Robert B. Reich, *The Work of Nations: Preparing Ourselves for 21st Century Capitalism* (New York: Random House, 1992).

71. Kohn, *Brave New Neighborhoods*, 115–123; Bickford, "Constructing Inequality"; Evan McKenzie, *Privatopia: Homeowner Associations and the Rise of Residential Private Government* (New Haven, CT: Yale University Press,

1994); Brian Jason Fleming, "Regulation of Political Signs in Private Homeowner Associations: A New Approach," *Vanderbilt Law Review* 59, no. 2 (2006): 571–607.

72. Frug, "Legal Technology of Exclusion," 211.

73. Becky M. Nicolaides and Andrew Wiese, "The Political Culture of Suburbia," in Nicolaides and Wiese, *Suburb Reader*, 379; Robert Bullard, ed., *Growing Smarter: Achieving Livable Communities, Environmental Justice, and Regional Equity* (Cambridge, MA: MIT Press, 2007); Hayduk, "Race and Suburban Sprawl," 157.

74. Jamison E. Colburn, "Localism's Ecology: Protecting and Restoring Wildlife Habitat in the Suburban Nation," *Ecology Law Quarterly* 33 (2006): 981–982.

75. See ibid.; Peter Walker and Louise Fortmann, "Whose Landscape? A Political Ecology of the 'Exurban' Sierra," *Cultural Geographies* 10, no. 4 (2003): 469–491; Gayla Smutny, "Legislative Support for Growth Management in the Rocky Mountains," *Journal of the American Planning Association* 64, no. 3 (1998): 311–323.

76. See Walker and Fortmann, "Whose Landscape?"

77. Colburn, "Localism's Ecology," 990, 993.

78. See Walker and Fortmann, "Whose Landscape?" 481; Colburn, "Localism's Ecology," 998; and Michael Jones-Correa, "Reshaping the American Dream: Immigrants, Ethnic Minorities, and the Politics of the New Suburbs," in Kruse and Sugrue, *New Suburban History*, 183–204.

79. Walker and Fortmann, "Whose Landscape?" 481.

80. Ibid., 479–480.

81. Albert O. Hirschmann, *Exit, Voice, and Loyalty: Responses to Decline in Firms, Organizations, and States* (Cambridge, MA: Harvard University Press, 1970).

82. Frug, "Legal Technology of Exclusion," 219; also Bickford, "Constructing Inequality," 367; Colburn, "Localism's Ecology," 970.

83. See Beck, *Risk Society*.

84. Ibid., 23; emphasis in original.

85. Ibid., 35.

86. Ibid., 87–102, 127–138.

87. Ibid., 37.

88. Ibid., 23.

89. Moe and Wilkie, *Changing Places*, xi.

90. Becky M. Nicolaides and Andrew Wiese, "The Other Suburbanites: Class, Racial, and Ethnic Diversity in Early Suburbs," in Nicolaides and Wiese, *Suburb Reader*, 193–194.

91. Nicolaides and Wiese, "Postwar America," 258.

92. See Jones-Correa, "Reshaping the American Dream."

93. Becky Nicolaides and Andrew Wiese, "Recent Suburban Transformations, 1970–2000," in Nicolaides and Wiese, *Suburb Reader*, 409–411.

94. See Myron Orfield, *American Metropolitics: The New Suburban Reality* (Washington, DC: Brookings Institution Press, 2002).

95. On the foregoing points, see Robert E. Lang and Thomas W. Sanchez, *Suburban Blues: The 2006 Democratic Sweep to the Metropolitan Edge* (Alexandria, VA: Metropolitan Institute at Virginia Tech, 2006); Charles Mahtesian, "Suburban Blind Spot," *National Journal* 38, no. 17 (2006): 30–33; Timothy Egan, "'06 Race Focuses on Suburbs, Inner and Outer," *The New York Times*, June 16, 2006, http://www.nytimes.com/2006/06/16/us/16suburbs. html?_r=1&scp=1&sq=%E2%80%9906%20Race%20Focuses%20on%20Su burbs,%20Inner%20and%20Outer&st=cse&oref=slogin#; Ronald Brownstein and Richard Rainey, "GOP Plants Flag on New Voting Frontier," *The Los Angeles Times*, November 22, 2004, A1; Robert David Sullivan, "GOP's Suburban Advantage Fading with Time?" *The Boston Globe*, July 7, 2008, http://www .boston.com/bostonglobe/editorial_opinion/oped/articles/2008/07/07/gops _suburban_advantage_fading_with_time/.

96. See Myron Orfield, *Metropolitics: A Regional Agenda for Community and Stability* (Washington, DC: Brookings Institution, 1997); Margaret Weir, "Coalition Building for Regionalism," in Katz, *Reflections on Regionalism*, 127–153.

97. See, e.g., Moin Siddiqi, "How High Can Prices Go?" *Middle East*, no. 390 (2008): 43–47. The recent downturn in the global economy has, however, depressed energy prices, at least for a while.

98. See Peter S. Goodman, "Fuel Prices Shift Math for Life in Far Suburbs," *The New York Times*, June 25, 2008, http://www.nytimes.com/2008/06/25/ business/25exurbs.html?_r=1&scp=1&sq=fuel%20prices%20shift%20math &st=cse&oref=slogin; Conor Dougherty, "Cities Grow at Suburbs' Expense during Recession," *The Wall Street Journal*, July 1, 2009, http://online.wsj.com/ article/SB124641839713978195.html?mod=googlenews_wsj; Joe Cortright, *Driven to the Brink: How the Gas Price Spike Popped the Housing Bubble and Devalued the Suburbs* (Chicago: CEOs for Cities, 2008); see also Helen Chernikoff, "Suburbs Feeling the Pinch as Fuel Prices Soar," Reuters, July 10, 2008, http://www.reuters.com/article/newsOne/idUSN3047989020080710. For a contrary view, see Joel Kotkin, "Suburbia's Not Dead Yet," *The Los Angeles Times*, July 6, 2008, http://www.latimes.com/news/printedition/opinion/la-op -kotkin6-2008jul06,0,1038461.story.

99. See, especially, Peter Calthorpe and William Fulton, *The Regional City: Planning for the End of Sprawl* (Washington, DC: Island Press, 2001).

100. See Sandel, *Liberalism.*

101. Sandel, *Democracy's Discontent*, 319–320. See also Jean-Jacques Rousseau, *On the Social Contract* (1762).

102. Sandel, *Democracy's Discontent*, 320–321.

103. Sandel, *Liberalism*, 58.

104. Ibid., 179.

105. Cannavò, *Working Landscape*, 104; Ewing, "Los Angeles–Style Sprawl."

106. See Calthorpe, *Next American Metropolis*; Calthorpe and Fulton, *Regional City*; and Bressi, "Planning the American Dream."

107. On arguments and prospects for regional and metropolitan government, see Cannavò, *Working Landscape*; Calthorpe and Fulton, *Regional City*; Orfield, *Metropolitics*; Orfield, *American Metropolitics*; Bullard, *Growing Smarter*; Katz, *Reflections on Regionalism*; Kelbaugh, *Repairing the American Metropolis*; and Gerald E. Frug, *City Making: Building Communities without Walls* (Princeton, NJ: Princeton University Press, 1999).

108. Walker and Fortmann, "Whose Landscape?" 480; emphasis in original.

109. See Colburn, "Localism's Ecology," 990–997.

11

Bikes, Sticks, Carrots

Justin Williams

Frequently, the idea of mass bicycling is met with a skepticism that approaches ridicule: "People aren't going to give up their cars. They are just too lazy and too attached to them." Although many people undoubtedly herald the bicycle as a solution to environmental problems, enthusiasm for a transportation revolution is tempered by a cynicism rooted in the belief that people prefer to drive: "That's nice; everyone should ride bikes. But nobody will ride their bikes as long as they can drive." If one subscribes to this belief, voluntary sacrifice appears impossible; Draconian policies or "the end of oil" remain to force people out of cars. So bicycling captures what the editors of this book call "the political stickiness of sacrifice," the widespread conviction that although social change might be desirable, it is also impossible if people are left to their own devices. The methods for bringing about social change seem tethered to lifestyles only forcefully abandoned: people want the world they have and will not give it up.

Thus claims about the impossibility of sacrifice focus on personal preference and fail to examine constraints on those very preferences. Regarding bicycles, calls to sacrifice assume the preference to drive. In this chapter, I explore the interaction of bicycles, preference, and sacrifice. First, I argue that cycling has been made difficult and unlikely through a series of structural decisions that place cars at the center, thereby pushing most people toward automobiles. Applying Herbert Marcuse and Matthew Paterson, I challenge that assumed preference for driving. To demonstrate how cycling might overcome driving, I briefly examine cycling's recent, albeit marginal, resurgence. This resurgence was caused partially by carrots that entice cyclists and sticks that deter cars, carrots and sticks that alleviate some of cycling's highest costs and open the substantive possibility for widespread cycling. This discussion suggests a serious limitation to calling for sacrifices: regardless of the normative value of sacrifice—whether sacrifice ought to be celebrated as a democratic impulse or condemned as impractical and shortsighted—the concept of sacrifice can unnecessarily burden our choices and obscure our ability to implement solutions to social and environmental problems. Because calls to sacrifice focus attention on preference, and the legitimacy of preference is approached only cautiously in democratic societies, sacrifice can limit political possibilities. Before sacrifice enters the rhetorical field, people must have meaningful freedoms. I challenge appeals to sacrifice, suggesting that sacrifice, whether coerced or voluntary, is a misguided default position.

Obstacles to Cycling

The U.S. Department of Transporation's (USDOT) National Bicycling and Walking Study describes the stakes involved in riding a bike; in other words, it demonstrates what one sacrifices to ride a bike. This study compiled survey data from twenty cities in the United States[1] and found that respondents reported a consistent list of obstacles to cycling: distance, traffic safety, convenience, time, physical exertion, family circumstances, habit, and social stigma.[2] These are obstacles to cycling, those impediments which, if removed, could promote bicycle usage. The consistent chart toppers—trip distance, lack of facilities, and safety—are worth exploring in more detail.

First, trip distance hampers utilitarian cycling. Researchers, reviewing bicycle commuter statistics, have arrived at various ideal cycle-commuting distances, ranging from two to six miles.[3] Available research describes the work commute, and similar factors probably inform the decision to run errands by bicycle. Assuming that most people are pressed for time in grocery shopping, visiting the doctor, and picking up the kids from school, greater distances between these destinations will diminish the probability of cycling.

Although trip distance might prevent bicycle *commuting*, it does not typically deter *recreational* cycling.[4] We should expect this discrepancy regarding perception of trip distance. The recreational cyclist, traveling a self-determined distance for fun, values equally the journey and the destination. On the other hand, the destination is the primary aim for commuters, who cycle a set distance to arrive at work. The commute rarely achieves recreational status. Thus, as the commute distance increases, the likelihood of cycle commuting decreases.[5]

Second, a lack of cycling facilities deters cycling. These facilities include lockers, parking, showers, and adequate routes.[6] Both cyclists and noncyclists cite these facilities' improvement as a way to encourage cycling.[7] Especially in urban areas with bicycle theft problems, the absence of secure parking prevents cycle use. The social stigma attached to sweaty unkemptness may also prevent people from biking to work. If commuters must travel more than five or six miles, they will likely arrive to work sweaty and dirty. Absent a shower and change of clothes, these commuters may worry about their coworkers' judgments.[8] Also, during their travel to work, the lack of on-street facilities complicates powerful fears of traffic (described later).

While managing sweat and weather may be a problem unique to cycling, motorists must also store their vehicles. The frequent difference between car storage and bicycle storage is subsidy: employers, businesses, and municipalities plan for car parking and thereby ensure plentiful, easy storage for cars. In suburban commercial parks, enormous parking lots provide ample and free storage for motorists. In these same settings, bicyclists may have to scout for a telephone pole, street sign, or other secure parking.

Third, fear of traffic deters cycling.[9] Cyclists encounter angry motorists, oblivious motorists, confused motorists, merging motorists, car doors, potholes, and other traffic-related hazards during their trips. Because motorist training in the United States largely ignores car-bike interactions, motorists are often ill prepared to share the road with cyclists. Similarly, cyclists may lack sufficient training in these interactions.[10] Even in states where bicyclists are legally entitled to full use of the road, traffic dangers can intimidate noncyclists away from riding in the road.

Statistics support noncyclists' fear of traffic. By all measurements, cyclists in the United States are exposed to a substantially higher accident risk than motorists.[11] More often than not, automobiles are the most serious threat to bicyclists' safety as car-bike collisions tend to levy grave physical consequences on the cyclist: car-bike crashes create over 90 percent of bicyclist fatalities, and when bike crashes involve cars, cyclists quadruple their probability of hospitalization.[12] These sobering statistics hint at cycling's high risk compared to driving.

The USDOT report thus reveals what people will relinquish if they ride bikes instead of driving: precious time wrapped up in the commute, vehicle and image security, and physical safety. The report demonstrates, in essence, what people will sacrifice if they choose to ride a bicycle. The particular obstacles outlined previously gesture at the many ways in which would-be bicyclists must navigate a motorists' world. Cyclists are uniquely plagued by the problems of distance, lack of facilities, and traffic safety. The association of these problems with cycling brands cycling as ill equipped to serve the modern commuter. Bicyclists skittishly navigate the dangerous, long commute to work. When they arrive, they must scout for secure parking and accept scowls aimed at their crumpled clothes. Automobiles, by contrast, glide gracefully down highways and parkways, self-contained storage units that safely deliver the neatly groomed driver to work. In this logic, automobiles are convenient and safe; bicycles are uncomfortable and dangerous. Little wonder that bicycling remains a marginal commuting mode in the United States. The automobile is crowned the superior commuting technology.

Challenging Preference

Powerful structural obstacles—trip distance, a dearth of facilities, and fears about personal security paramount among them—therefore deter bicycling. But even if cycling is obstructed, such obstacles might reflect a preference for driving. In other words, if cycling is difficult merely because most people prefer cars, and cyclists cannot muster the political voice to reorient the built environment, then most people will not cycle because most people prefer cars: car-friendly structure appears freely chosen. In this view, a democratic demand for car-oriented streets and policy transcends the need for cyclist infrastructure; people have chosen their constraints. Two theoretical orientations—the first grounded in Herbert Marcuse's analysis of projects of realization, the second informed by Matthew Paterson's analysis of car culture—offer tools for navigating this terrain.

Automobility as a Project of Realization

In *One Dimensional Man*, Marcuse explained the political, intentional nature of technology:

The way in which a society organizes the life of its members involves an initial *choice* between historical alternatives which are determined by the inherited level of the material and intellectual culture. The choice itself results from the play of dominant interests. It *anticipates* specific modes of transforming and utilizing man and nature and rejects other modes. It is one "project" of realization among others. But once the project has become operative in the basic institutions and relations, it tends to become exclusive, and to determine the development of the society as a whole.[13]

Marcuse claims that any technology emerges as one possibility along a path of development. Dominant interests, namely, the state and business, choose one possibility and implement that particular "project of realization." Following initial implementation, alternatives to any project of realization are squeezed out. Technological systems justify themselves: they create the very conditions by which they become necessary. Society organizes itself around a technology, thereby enslaving itself to that technology.

In *The Working Landscape*, Peter Cannavò details many of the factors influencing post–World War II suburban sprawl. Although some of these factors may reflect individual desires for open space, many of these factors "were supply side rather than demand side."[14] These supply-side factors reflect Marcuse's insight into projects of realization. First, a federally funded interstate highway system provided travel routes between distant suburbs and urban centers. The highway system therefore provided the physical means for sprawl, at no small expense.[15] Second, single-use zoning laws restricted compact, mixed-use development. Zoning laws ensured minimum lot sizes that guaranteed that any development would spread outward at a minimum rate.[16] Additionally, suburbs' single-use nature precluded the integration of home and work, ensuring minimum travel between home and work. Third, misguided urban renewal projects transformed thriving neighborhoods into urban blights, thereby making the city less desirable.[17] Thus the current manifestation of suburban sprawl would scarcely have been possible in the absence of government policy that actively promoted sprawl and made cities less desirable.

Supply-side provisions likewise transformed many city centers. Urban environments in the United States have been transformed in no small part because of a process of suburbanization that began in the 1860s, which both required and fueled a reconceptualization of street use. Before the 1860s, urban residents used streets as social gathering places. As suburbanization took hold in the mid-1880s, new suburbanites, who resided outside urban centers, needed streets for transport between two distant points: home and work. New suburbanites needed thoroughfares.[18] For them, the streets' social function disappeared. The old and new conceptualizations of the street coexisted only with difficulty: so long as streets were needed to move people rapidly, socialization had to be excluded. City engineers, under the influence of urban planners like Frederick Law Olmstead, sought to open city streets so suburban residents could gain easy access to downtown. Thus new criteria for pavements emerged: "little resistance to traffic" and "favorableness to travel."[19] Suburban traffic fundamentally changed the use of urban streets. Cities began to legislate in favor of suburbanites, opening city streets to traffic.[20] Some urban dwellers, sensing the danger of high-speed traffic, actively opposed street paving, suggesting a democratic impulse that resisted the coming transportation wave.[21] To transform the built world in both the cities and the suburbs, suburbanization required a political and ideological will that overcame this resistance.

As the twentieth century progressed, such a reconceptualization of streets could have led to public transportation, or else bicycle- and pedestrian-friendly streets. In practice, however, this project obviously favored automobiles. Especially after World War II, transport policy was obsessed with the car. Hugh McClintock, in describing traffic planning after World War II, claims, "It seems that those who made the key decisions on transport experienced the world of traffic very largely from the perspective of drivers, rarely using public transport, seldom riding a bike and infrequently going on foot."[22] Cities generally failed to engage in urban planning that might have contained sprawl. By in-filling instead of promoting outward growth, cities could have kept trip distances to a minimum. Municipalities also promoted car-dependent suburbanization through other means such as assuming the cost of building new roads and widening existing roads to accommodate cars. Likewise, municipalities provided suburbs with schools and connections to utilities, all at the taxpayers' expense.[23] The freeway exemplifies the subsidies levied to motoring and suburbanization. Southern California, with its massive complex of suburbs, is scarcely imaginable in the absence of a web of interconnecting highways. These highways are built at massive public expense, and continued road construction ensures their outward expansion.

City planners devoted roads to cars and thereby chose to promote cars. A political will exists behind the automobile's dominance: the abandon with which planners gave themselves to automobiles ensured cars' structural necessity. Again, the freeway illustrates this point. In both law and spirit, freeways are designed exclusively for cars. In California, for instance, bicyclists can be legally excluded from these spaces.[24] Even if the law remained silent about cyclists on the freeway, highway designers clearly ignored these users' needs: biking along a freeway on-ramp, where traffic whizzes by at sixty miles per hour, evinces this point. While freeways may dramatically illustrate the exclusion of bicycles, urban streets in the United States also demonstrate the bicycle's marginality. Many features of urban streets are designed exclusively for motorists. Speed limits rarely dip below twenty-five miles per hour, a speed that only cars and motorcycles can sustain. Traffic signals cannot sense the presence of anything smaller and lighter than a motorcycle, forcing cyclists to wait for a car, use the crosswalk, or break traffic law by riding through a red light. Lane striping, unnoticeable to drivers, can cause cyclists to lose traction in the rain. Roadway reflectors can wrest control from the unwitting cyclist. Cities exist with motorists in mind, often at the expense of other roadway users.

With the preceding discussion of supply-side factors in mind, we can return to Herbert Marcuse. His analysis of "projects of realization" sheds light on automobiles' rise and points toward the literature of automobility. Automobility is "the overall 'system' which makes the act of driving a car—and more specifically the act of driving a car appear as an act of 'autonomous mobility'—possible."[25] Automobility involves the tangible and intangible components of driving: a system of roads, rules, regulations, economic activity, and ideologies. Automobility rivals all other technological projects in its totality. City planners, valuing suburbanization and promoting the automobile, designed environments to accommodate the internal combustion automobile. They selected and actively promoted one historical project, initiating the exclusion of alternatives like bicycling, public transit, and walking. This process continued and accelerated throughout the twentieth century. Automobiles' dominance was created at least as much as it was expressed. Far from the random, aggregated preferences of the multitudes, automobility was imagined and supported throughout its lifetime.

Because automobility has gained so much power, it is now the logic by which it justifies itself. Because streets are so wholly committed to the automobile, the automobile becomes a seemingly necessary component of modern living. The obstacles to cycling outlined earlier—which remain obstacles because of a sustained, expensive devotion to automobiles—demonstrate automobility's particular power. Commute distances increased as cities developed highway infrastructure that allowed inexpensive travel between home and work. Fear of car traffic—car traffic supported through wide streets, high speed limits, and ample parking—ensures that alternatives like bicycling remain dangerous and impractical. Given the intense structural benefits conferred on driving and the correlative constraints placed on alternatives, bicycling appears materially impossible. Automobility ensures that most people apparently need cars; its impressive totality is the strongest argument for its reproduction. Driving is preferred because it is the only structurally viable means of mobility.

Car Culture

In *Automobile Politics*, Matthew Paterson suggests that car devotion transcends a mere structural attachment and embeds itself within culture.[26] For Paterson, people in car-dependent countries like the United States internalize a commitment to the car, associating it with the ability to move. Such movement is associated with freedom; therefore the car is seen as a natural manifestation of our human desire for movement.[27] Paterson rejects this simplified conception of freedom and illustrates automobility's many paradoxical restrictions on freedom.[28] Rules, regulations, and enforcements were invented to allow the smooth operation of automobility; streets were redesigned to serve the singular goal of traffic movement, restricting freedom to play in the streets; commutes to work become increasingly long, slow, onerous, and soul depleting. To articulate the car as "freedom-enhancing" is to ignore these restrictions on freedom. This, for Paterson, is one of automobility's grand tricks: the culture of automobility reimagines the car's domination as freedom.

For Paterson, car culture accomplishes this trick partly because of its history. When automobiles emerged as a feasible technology, trains dominated popular transportation. But trains began to appear as an oppressive, rather than liberating, force: commuters depended on the abusive, price-gouging rail monopolies that ran the train timetables, which limited available travel times. Automobiles liberated commuters from the trains while erecting new forms of domination: traffic laws, increased distances, increased reliance on fuels, physical confinement to the automobile, and so on.[29]

The move away from trains marked a new relationship between person and technology: object of transport (the person moved by trains) became subject of transport (the person who moves between destinations, the driver).[30] Transport *objects* were enslaved to the oppressive timetable and train monopolies; transport *subjects* actively participate in their own domination, regulating themselves in an orderly fashion. The driver, as negotiator of streets, rules, regulations, and systems, is produced. The automobile subject, free but paradoxically enslaved to the car and its regulatory apparatuses, is born: "People thus participate intimately in the production of their subjection to this order, conceiving it precisely as the realisation of their freedom."[31] The automobile identity is then reflected and reproduced in various cultural forms: music (The Beach Boys' "I Get Around"), film (*The Fast and the Furious*), and advertising (too ubiquitous and obvious to list).[32]

With Paterson's analysis in mind, we can begin to understand the contradictory celebration of automobility as freedom. Automobility produces the subject who demands domination, rearticulating such domination as freedom. Modern individuals enmesh themselves with automobiles: "The individual . . . in the late twentieth- or early twenty-first-century world is comprehensible only as a product of the development of automobility."[33]

Taken together, Marcuse and Paterson show us two forces that constrain freedom to choose transport mode. On one hand, material conditions drastically inflate the costs of automobility's alternatives: cities' outward expansion and car-centric roads push alternatives further out to the margins. On the other hand, cultural conditions produce the *desire* for automobility. The built environment diminishes the practicality of automobility's alternatives (bicycles among them), and culture reinforces those constraints as car enhancing, and thus "freedom enhancing," and thus desirable. Although the choice for automobility appears natural, on closer inspection automobility is a decision coerced by structure and reinforced by culture. The decision to ride a bicycle must oppose this coercion.

If we throw up our hands at the juggernaut formed by technology and culture, if we allow ourselves to be awed by the immutable power of the status quo, then automobility appears inevitable. Little wonder that aspirations of mass cycling provoke cynicism: although zany bicycle messengers and carbon footprint–reducing environmentalists may sacrifice their free time, safety, and image, most people will not make those sacrifices. And even if the built environment allowed room for the bicycle, a sense of cultural attachment would keep many people from giving up their cars.

But Marcuse and Paterson provide a hopeful path through this challenge: they expose automobility as a power structure rather than a genuine preference for driving. Driving is not freely chosen, and bicycling is not freely ignored; instead, structure and culture strongly suggest driving. If this analysis is right, then we should expect deep structural changes to allow different preferences to flourish. If Marcuse is right, that "forces and tendencies exist which may break . . . containment and explode the society,"[34] then transportation alternatives remain possible. Cycling's marginal comeback in recent years, to which I now turn, demonstrates the expression of alternative preferences.

Carrots

Cities with active pro-bike policies have witnessed a cycling resurgence in recent years. In the United States, cities like Portland, Oregon, and Chicago have earned recognition for their commitment to cycling.[35] While not "biketopias," where bikes rule the streets, these cities improved cyclists' ability to coexist with motorists. They have tempted cyclists with carrots: bike-friendly measures that remove some of cycling's obstacles. Portland, for instance, has constructed "bike boxes": safety features that reduce spatial competition between cars and bikes at intersections.[36] Similarly, Portland has painted many of its bike lanes bright green to draw motorists' attention to cyclists.[37] Over the past two decades,

Chicago has likewise devoted itself to cycling, engineering a massive bikeway and bike parking network and implementing policies to ensure cyclists' roadway rights. Both Portland and Chicago have seen vast increases in bicycle ridership. Over the period that Portland expanded its bikeway network by 240 percent, ridership increased 410 percent.[38] In Chicago, ridership has almost doubled since 1990, the period during which Chicago's Bike Plan was implemented.[39] By reengineering the city to increase cyclist safety and visibility, and thereby removing structural obstacles to cycling, Portland and Chicago have drawn cyclists into the transportation fray.

Even though Portland and Chicago are two of the most bike-friendly cities in the United States, their ridership rates pale in comparison to many European cities. In Amsterdam, perhaps the most celebrated cycling city, bicycling accounts for 27 percent of all trips taken.[40] In Portland, bicycling comprises a comparatively paltry 3.5 percent of all trips taken.[41] The Dutch were not always such avid cyclists; instead, government policy created the Netherlands' cycling rates. From the 1950s through the 1970s, cycling rates in the Netherlands plummeted by 50 percent, a trend repeated in other European countries like the United Kingdom. In the mid-1970s, the Netherlands began actively promoting cycling through engineering measures such as separate bike paths. Additionally, the Netherlands strictly enforced traffic laws and implemented policies to contain suburban sprawl.[42] Correspondingly, the Netherlands' cycling rates grew to their current high levels.[43] The United Kingdom's cycling rates, by contrast, have stagnated since the mid-1970s.[44] The United Kingdom has ignored bicycle infrastructure and actively promoted car use through a "predict and provide" strategy. This strategy supposes that growth in car usage is inevitable and that governments should provide the infrastructure to support that growth.[45] Infrastructure partly explains cycling's popularity in the Netherlands and its infrequency in the United Kingdom. The Netherlands actively made itself a cycling-friendly country.

The Netherlands has contained city limits to prevent lengthy trips, created storage and accessibility features, and improved cyclists' safety. In short, the Netherlands enticed cyclists with carrots, addressing consistently reported obstacles to cycling. The Netherlands offers an especially valuable lesson in improving cyclists' safety, concern over which weighs heavily in the decision to cycle. In the Netherlands, despite the previously mentioned steady rise in cycling, the number of yearly cycling fatalities has decreased dramatically.[46] Likewise, the Netherlands' cyclist injury rates remain substantially lower than the United States' rates.[47] Structural factors should at least partly determine cycling's danger.

The preceding discussion of carrots implies two important points. First, if infrastructure and policy help to create favorable or hostile cycling conditions, where cyclists face less or more danger, then such infrastructure helps to determine how much cyclists sacrifice. Contemporary automobility, so frequently hostile to cyclists, causes cycling to be a sacrificial act. Car infrastructure defines this object of sacrifice: safety. As the USDOT study suggests, this obstacle features prominently in cyclists' and would-be cyclists' minds as an obstacle to cycling. Through bicycle-friendly policy, the Netherlands lowered cyclists' probability of loss by decreasing the probability of death and injury. They mitigated one of the greatest sacrifices currently embedded in cycling.

While risk of death and injury constitutes one weighty obstacle to cycling, removing other obstacles will increase bike ridership and entice new cyclists. Integrating cycling with public transit, and expanding public transit, provide cyclists with a means of travel between distant suburbs and urban centers. Provision of cycling-friendly facilities at the workplace and on public streets increases cyclist visibility and legitimacy. These policies, and others like them,[48] can make cycling safer and more convenient, thereby addressing some of cycling's obstacles and encouraging cycling. In the process, these carrots will remove losses presently embedded in cycling.

Second, to the extent that carrots attract cyclists, they reiterate that driving is a constrained preference. Such policies suggest that people seize available alternatives to driving. When planners anticipate and satisfy cyclists' needs, cycling rates increase. Similarly, when planners anticipate and satisfy drivers' needs, driving rates increase. In this view, automobility is a self-fulfilling prophecy: when planners "predict and provide" for cars, cars fulfill expectations. If provision of facilities can similarly attract cyclists, then such facilities allow the expression of a previously unrealizable preference, or at least create a new preference for bicycling. Cycling's popularity in bike-dedicated cities suggests that widespread automobility is not the most desirable choice for all people, but merely the most structurally obvious.

Sticks

Carrots are only one method for encouraging cycling. Although carrots can transform mobility to an extent, sticks—deterrents to cars—further encourage cycling. Deterrents to cars include the reduction of available car parking, reduced speed limits, "car-free zones" that restrict automobiles from urban centers, increased gas taxes, and taxation of automobile ownership. Denmark, Germany, and the Netherlands wield all these sticks.[49] Other examples come by way of New York's Summer Streets program,[50] Los Angeles's ArroyoFest,[51] and San Francisco's Sunday Streets,[52] all of which temporarily ban automobiles from portions of these cities. During these closures, cyclists and pedestrians emerge in droves to explore typically intimidating and inaccessible streets. These policies make car use less easy, less normal, and less natural, if only temporarily, and provide room to walk and bike.

The liberal democratic devotee may protest, "It's one thing to promote cycling; it's another thing to deter car usage. That's a restriction on drivers' freedom." As I have noted earlier, this claim is deeply problematic for several reasons. First, Marcuse's technological analysis suggests that cars are not freely chosen in any meaningful way. In considering both a car-centric built environment and the elimination of cars' alternatives, cars appear as a heavily financed decision made for us by city planners. Cars are a free choice only in the sense that (1) their benefits were systematically enhanced through massive public expense and (2) automobility's heaving momentum legitimates its dominance. Second, as Matthew Paterson suggests, this claim forgets the many constraints placed on freedom under a system of automobility. Even if automobility were a free choice initially, its present manifestation eliminates freedoms at least as much as it enhances them. In considering the time, money, fuel, laws, agencies, health effects, and social constraints inherent in cars, freedoms are lost in the process of adopting cars. This realization mitigates the claim that "cars are freedom."

The preceding two arguments suggest a third—and for my purposes, most important—reason for raising a skeptical eyebrow at the claim that deterring automobiles constrains freedom. At present, the freedom to cycle, a freedom that ought to receive at least some consideration, is heavily constrained by structural and legal obstacles. Even if deterring car usage does, in the end, constrain freedom, such deterrence constitutes only one expression of freedom: the freedom to drive. With the deterrence of cars, people would gain an enhanced freedom to cycle (and additionally, the freedom to walk, socialize in the street, and use public streets). Street closure experiments like those in New York, Los Angeles, and San Francisco demonstrate the potential expression of that freedom. Under present circumstances in the United States, the freedom to cycle is seriously impaired by trip distance, a deficit in facilities, and concern for safety. Policies may not intentionally legislate bicycling's relative difficulty; nevertheless, car-friendly policies cater to motorists at cyclists' expense. Such policies and norms tempt motorists with carrots and brandish sticks at cyclists.

The influence of the carrot-stick relationship exposes itself most clearly in a hypothetical inversion of the car-bike relationship. If 80 percent of parking lots in the United States were ripped up and bicycle facilities were built in their place, then car parking would become scarce and difficult, while bicycle parking became easy and natural. Moreover, new space would be opened for dense urban development, thereby decreasing trip distances and removing a further obstacle to cycling. If cities and suburbs contained only narrow streets absent car parking; if gas stations were replaced with bicycle repair shops; if traffic regulations were designed for cyclists' needs and stop signs replaced with yield signs; if motorists were relegated to one littered, pothole-ridden lane and excluded altogether from certain streets, deviation from which elicited jeers, threats, and heckles; if speed limits were set at fifteen miles per hour; in short, if cycling became the dominant mode of transport with the side effect of deterring driving, and car drivers were exposed to the same level and degree of challenges that cyclists presently face, then driving would appear undeniably burdensome, and few would tout its benefits. The automobile, under such circumstances, might maintain its cultural importance. More likely, however, the car would lose its appeal as "freedom enhancer"; the supposed freedoms attached to cars would cease to exist. Cars' many constraints would be laid bare, and cycling would become the norm from which automobility deviated. Would one "give up" one's car in this world? One might relinquish the automobile because it was impractical, dangerous, and culturally despised; one would likely *lose* nothing in the process. By deterring automobile usage and promoting bicycle usage, the "freedom" to cycle would quite naturally supplant the "freedom" to drive. Thus any freedom lost through the deterrence of cars would be regained in a new freedom to cycle. Presently, the constraint of one implies the flourishing of the other. While the freedom to drive would certainly suffer under a scheme of sticks, the set of all available freedoms would remain at least as broad.

Sticks thus appear as the radical implementation of carrots: "sticks against cars" can be readily rearticulated as "carrots for bikes." If the carrot-stick relationship changes in favor of bicycling, preference in transport mode would undoubtedly also change in favor of bicycles. This reinforces the point that driving must always reference the power structures on which it depends. A preference for driving depends on planning that excludes bicycles, much as the radical inversion of transportation infrastructures would imply the flourishing of bicycling.

Means and Ends

The manipulation of carrots and sticks suggests that a preference for driving does not exist on the scale seemingly implied by current driving rates. A shift in transportation infrastructures would allow the expression of a preference for bicycling. This preference becomes central in discussing sacrifice. Sacrifice presumes that behind the giving up, a valued object or idea exists. Sacrifice must necessarily involve more than a self-interested giving up; otherwise, every time slaves run away from the slave owner and thereby give up slavery, they will have sacrificed their shackles. Only when we give up a valued object will an act qualify as a sacrifice (and even then, we might want to narrow down the category). Therefore calls to "give up your car" presume an a priori valuing of cars, that people prefer their cars.

I may appear to reject the possibility of cycling's inferiority. On this view, bike-friendly policy would allow the expression of an inborn desire to cycle: bicycling will become natural, desirable, and irresistible. Drivers need to be delivered from their own "false consciousness," under the sway of which they trick themselves into loving automobility. Constructing bike-friendly streets can startle everyone into consciousness.

Although most regular cyclists will gush about their fondness for bicycling, although books have been written on the joy of bicycling[53] and the blogosphere brims over with velobration,[54] although many people could and would discover cycling's inherent merits, some will not share this exhilaration. Bicycling will be inconvenient, uncomfortable, and even impossible for some. Nonetheless, many others have been intimidated away from exploring cycling's comfort, convenience, fun, and safety. Cycling might become irresistible for many, but I reach for a different possibility. I advocate the freedom to make a choice previously denied to most people: the freedom to make a true accounting of desired transport mode.

When I say "true accounting," a familiar conceptual distinction comes to mind: the *means* and the *ends*.[55] Some drivers may value the car's inherent virtues (whatever those might be), but I would venture that most drivers do not value automobiles as ends in themselves. Instead, they value what they *attain* with automobiles: safe, quick, easy travel. They do not value the vehicle that lets them pursue that travel. Because most cities are organized exclusively around the car, only the car can provide that safe, quick, easy travel. The *ends,* transport, and the *means,* the car, apparently melt into one: the car is easy, safe transport; easy, safe transport is the car. Although the car has only recently become the ruling mode of transport, its domination is impressive. Many people may perceive that when they give up automobiles, they give up mobility altogether. This hard choice might seem intuitive in light of the car's near-total domination.

Automobility has neatly crammed together mobility's means and ends, eliminating the possibility for a true comparison of means. Any genuine comparison would require the equalization of transportation infrastructures so that opportunities and constraints are equally shared among transport modes. Presently, the seemingly impossible separation of means and ends deceptively suggests that most people really prefer automobiles to bicycling. But the preconditions for that preference—the carrots for cars and sticks for bicycles—ensure that most people never get to evaluate the merits of bicycling. Perhaps all drivers value their cars. But how much do they value their cars, and compared with what?

They must reference the manufactured norm of automobility whenever they think of transport: biking is dangerous, difficult, and time consuming. These evaluations contain truth only as long as biking is compared to automobility, an automobility made safe, easy, and speedy only through massive effort. Presently, mobility must always reference cars. The opportunity to separately evaluate bicycles and cars, to decide whether biking is as safe and easy as driving, whether driving is as fun and fulfilling as biking, should precede any need to sacrifice. After an honest evaluation of means becomes possible, then sacrifice—giving up a *valued* object for some greater good—becomes possible. Carrots and sticks, appropriately applied, can make such an evaluation possible.

Challenging Sacrifice

This conflation of means and ends highlights some of the greatest tensions surrounding the idea of sacrifice in liberal democratic societies. Appeals to "give up one's car" in favor of a bicycle may appear to disrupt automobility, but such claims actually reinforce its dominance by taking for granted cars' structural power. Furthermore, these claims express a faith in the preference to drive. Calls to "give up your car; ride a bike" presuppose the bicycle's inferiority and demand the satisfaction of a greater good. Such claims can be summed up: "It might be hard to give up your car and ride a bike, but it will be worth it in the end because you're saving the planet." Bicycling becomes transportation's booby prize: ride a bike because you still need to get around in a globally warmed world. Take pride in the great thing you've done for the planet and humanity, but know that you let go of something better: fast, furious, violent, beautiful cars. Pick up your bike and ride it in a car's world, but never forget automobility's dominance and normality. And never suppose that an alternative world, built around the bicycle, could exist. Such a call begins with the assumption of a preference for driving. As I have argued, to the extent this preference exists, it was manufactured by the constraint of other means of mobility.

This same a priori assumption ties the hands of policy makers concerned with maintaining a neutral vision of the good life. Can policy makers enlist policy to change behaviors, in other words, to "get people to sacrifice," while preserving a commitment to liberal democratic principles? If we take for granted the assumption that car usage on its present scale represents the expression of deep desires, then deterring car usage or promoting cycling is a distinctly undemocratic course of action: the state actively shapes public roads against the will of the majority driving public and devotes needed funds to a marginal impulse to cycle. Planners and policy makers should make bike-friendly policy only after many people spontaneously give up their cars or demand bicycle infrastructure. Before it acts, the state should wait for a voluntary sacrifice of the car; the burden of change falls on individuals.

On this view, it seems that the market is the only democratic mechanism for a shift away from automobility. A collective, spontaneous giving up would not involve a sacrifice; it would more closely resemble the invisible hand's guidance. Driving would not be valued any longer and therefore not sacrificed for a greater good. Alternatively, the abandonment of the car might signal a sacrifice because people stepped back from their car devotion to save the planet. In either case, the state can omit itself from the process. Presumably, people can ride bikes on existing roads and independently express their new bike devotion. Therefore any state involvement in bicycle infrastructure seems undemocratic, or at least unnecessary. The a priori assumption—that automobility, on its present scale, was brought about through personal preference—carries heavy implications for policy makers trying to transform car-centered cities. Policy makers are left with the unattractive proposition of legislating people out of their cars. This assumption then forces popular cynicism about sacrifice: given the present sacrifices thrust on bicycling, a mass movement toward bicycling appears unlikely without paternalistic manipulation or coercion. In the context of the bicycle, to begin at sacrifice is to end in despair: sacrifice's animating assumption, that people prefer to drive, produces the conclusion that automobility will be abandoned only with force.

If driving is not an expression of freedom, but instead an issue of too many deterrents to alternatives, then an entirely different plan of action is legitimated. Promoting cycling at automobility's expense remains a democratic course of action because (1) automobility is not an expression of freedom, but merely the structurally obvious "choice," given the constraints placed on alternatives, and (2) the freedom to cycle is impinged on by current automobile infrastructure. Promoting cycling would allow the expression of a presently squashed freedom that might reasonably compete with the taken-for-granted freedom to drive. In other words, dormant desires to cycle, presently constrained by automobility, can find expression. If automobility depends on state intervention, perpetuates itself through sheer momentum, and in fact restricts other forms of freedom, then policy makers should promote bicycling at the expense of driving to maintain their commitment to state neutrality. To question the a priori assumption that driving is valued—that because people drive, they have made an informed choice; that the status quo expresses that rational choice—is to question the need to sacrifice. The question of sacrifice becomes moot in favor of creating viable alternatives. The imperative to sacrifice is unnecessary. Figuring out "how to get people to sacrifice their cars," or even presuming that cars are so highly valued, needlessly ignores the powerful forces that actually inhibit the ability to choose, the ability to form uncoerced preferences.

In this context, the need to sacrifice is unnecessary because the status quo is constrained. People may or may not give up their convenient cars; people may or may not sacrifice their car-centered lifestyles to serve their country and planet; however, this sacrifice is a needless first step. Structural decisions have ensured that cars are the only means for pursuing mobility. Before calling for sacrifice emerges as a political and rhetorical strategy, substantive options should exist. Only when we have substantive options can we discover, or affirm, what we value.

Conclusion

So will people give up their cars and ride bikes, or are they hopelessly devoted to their car-based lifestyles? Countries like the Netherlands begin to answer this question with their flourishing cycling rates, rates prodded upward by a state commitment to cycling. In the United States, cities like Portland have similarly kick-started cycling as a viable alternative to automobility. These places suggest that people are wed to their cars to the extent that they see no alternative. People may not value their cars in themselves, but instead see their cars as the only viable means for transportation. Because means and ends are so tightly woven together, people have to sacrifice too much when they give up their cars. Before calling for sacrifice, those serious about the transformation of automobility should ensure that ends (safe, easy mobility) and means (bicycles, cars, walking, public transportation) are separable. If infrastructures were equal, and real decisions about mode of transport were possible, then calls to sacrifice would appear reasonable. Until then, calls to sacrifice suggest that automobiles are valued as ends in themselves. Such a statement reaffirms automobility's dominance, instead of creating badly needed opportunities to choose. Before calling for sacrifice, environmentalists should seek to minimize or eliminate the impact of that sacrifice.

Bicycling shows us a serious limit to sacrifice as a rhetorical and conceptual framework. Appeals to sacrifice, without an examination of the forces that constrain meaningful choices, can limit our ability to address social and environmental problems. These appeals direct our attention away from specific problems and their solutions, instead directing us toward personal preference. Personal preference, the expression of private will, is contested only cautiously in liberal societies. In this context, calls to sacrifice embed status quo arrangements as inevitable and desirable. As long as the status quo is considered an expression of free choice, any policy to deter socially undesirable behavior will necessarily dictate from on high. Especially in an environmental context, this focus on preference often recommends the paternalist posture that "we're going to have to force people to change."

This inappropriate focus on preference undermines the possibility of democratic politics. In essence, the focus on preference shifts all social change to the market and eliminates—or at least critically wounds—the possibility of a political will. On one hand, if most people actually prefer socially and environmentally destructive behavior—if they want to drive everywhere, to buy cheap plastic packaging, to use dangerous pesticides—then we face a crisis of democracy. If the people can be trusted only to pursue awful destruction, then benevolent dictators may offer the only hope for social and environmental change. On the other hand, if forces beyond popular control strongly encourage destructive behaviors, then democracy might guide us through social challenges. If powerful forces coerce us in certain unsustainable directions, then we need to destroy or transform that coercion. We need opportunities to make socially and environmentally desirable choices; we need more democratic institutions and infrastructures.

Acknowledgments

Thank you to Jill Leuchner, Maxwell Schnurer, Michael Bruner, Michael Maniates, and Jim Dodge. Special thanks to John Meyer, who always offers encouragement and pointed guidance. I dedicate this chapter to Humboldt State University's Bicycle Learning Center, where I first found bicycle politics.

Notes

1. Federal Highway Administration, *National Bicycling and Walking Study. Case Study No. 1: Reasons Why Bicycling and Walking Are and Are Not Being Used More Extensively as Travel Modes* (Washington, DC: Department of Transportation, 1993), 1.

2. Ibid. See also D. Davies, M. E. Halliday, M. Mayes, and R. L. Pockock, *Attitudes to Cycling: A Qualitative Study and Conceptual Framework* (London: U.K. Department for Transport, 1997).

3. Federal Highway Administration, *Case Study No. 1*, 7.

4. Ibid., 20.

5. Ibid.

6. Ibid., 21.

7. Davies et al., *Attitudes to Cycling*, 18.

8. Ibid.

9. Ibid., 11. Federal Highway Administration, *Case Study No. 1*, 7.

10. Federal Highway Administration, *Case Study No. 1*, 7.

11. John Pucher, Charles Komanoff, and Paul Schimek, "Bicycling Renaissance in North America? Recent Trends and Alternative Policies to Promote Bicycling," *Transportation Research Part A* 33 (September/November 1999): 647.

12. Ibid., 650.

13. Herbert Marcuse, *One Dimensional Man* (Boston: Beacon Press, 1964), xvi.

14. Peter Cannavò, *The Working Landscape: Founding, Preservation, and the Politics of Place* (Cambridge, MA: MIT Press, 2007), 103.

15. Ibid., 102.

16. Ibid., 99.

17. Ibid., 102–103.

18. Clay McShane, *Down the Asphalt Path: The Car and the American City* (New York: Columbia University Press, 1992), 80.

19. Ibid., 78.

20. Ibid., 67.

21. Ibid., 80.

22. Hugh McClintock, "Post-war Traffic Planning and Special Provision for the Bicycle," in *The Bicycle and City Traffic,* ed. Hugh McClintock (London: Bellhaven, 1992), 20. Although McClintock here describes the Western European experience, he notes explicitly that European traffic planning self-consciously mimicked American traffic policy: "This emphasis in transport planning reflected a common attitude at that time that, in terms of transport, as in other spheres, the American way of life pointed to the future and that Europeans only had to examine current American trends to learn how things would and should on in their societies too" (20).

23. Jane Holtz Kay, *Asphalt Nation: How the Automobile Took Over America and How We Can Take It Back* (Berkeley: University of California Press, 1997), 180.

24. California Department of Motor Vehicles, "Freeways and Expressways: Use Restrictions," 2008 California Vehicle Code, Division 11, chap. 5, Section 21960(a).

25. Matthew Paterson, *Automobile Politics: Ecology and Cultural Political Economy* (New York: Cambridge University Press, 2007), 25.

26. Ibid., 19.

27. Ibid., 65–90.

28. Ibid., 132–142.

29. Ibid.

30. Ibid., 134.

31. Ibid., 142.

32. Ibid., 142–165.

33. Ibid., 221.

34. Marcuse, *One Dimensional Man,* xv.

35. Portland's devotion to cyclists earned it the League of American Bicyclists Platinum Award for bike-friendly communities. See Michael Rollins and Wade Nkrumah, "Portland Pedals to Platinum," *The Oregonian,* April 30, 2008, http://www.oregonlive.com/news/oregonian/index.ssf?/base/news/1209525929199200.xml&coll=7. Chicago's efforts earned it a place among *Bicycling* magazine's top cycling cities. See Brian Fiske and Loren Mooney, "Urban Treasures," *Bicycling Magazine,* March 2006: 62.

36. City of Portland Office of Transportation, "Bike Boxes," Portland Online, http://www.portlandonline.com/transportation/index.cfm?c=eghbh. An illustration of bike boxes can be found on the same Web site.

37. City of Portland Office of Transportation, "Improving Bicycle Safety in Portland," Portland Online, http://www.portlandonline.com/shared/cfm/image.cfm?id=185776.

38. City of Portland Office of Transportation, "Improving Bicycle Safety," 3.

39. Chicago Area Transportation Study Plan Development Division, *Soles and Spokes: The Pedestrian and Bicycle Plan for Chicago Area Transportation. TASK 2 Report: Existing Conditions and Regional Trends* (Chicago: Chicago Area Transportation Study, 2004), 25.

40. John Pucher and Ralph Buehler, "Making Cycling Irresistible: Lessons from the Netherlands, Denmark, and Germany," *Transportation Reviews* 28, no. 4 (2008): 500.

41. Ibid.

42. Ibid., 511–523.

43. Ibid., 503.

44. Ibid., 502.

45. Phil Goodwin, "Transformation of Transport Policy in Great Britain," *Transportation Research Part A* 33 (1999): 657–658. Notably, the United Kingdom has abandoned "predict and provide" in recent years, perhaps most symbolically with London's congestion tax. See "Congestion Charging," Transport for London, http://www.tfl.gov.uk/roadusers/congestioncharging/.

46. Pucher and Buehler, "Making Cycling Irresistible," 505–506.

47. Ibid., 506–507.

48. See ibid., 510–520, for a list of carrot policies.

49. Ibid., 522.

50. Javier C. Hernandez, "No Traffic on a Saturday? Well, No Cars, Anyway," *The New York Times*, August 10, 2008, A-31.

51. Robert Gottlieb, "Just Plain Spokes," *The Los Angeles Times*, June 15, 2008, M-8.

52. Janna Brancolini, "Reclaiming San Francisco, from Cars," *San Francisco Bay Guardian Online*, August 27, 2008, http://www.sfbg.com/entry.php?entry _id=6989&catid=&volume_id=317&issue_id=393&volume_num=42&issue _num=48.

53. See, e.g., Jim Joyce, ed., *The Bicycle Book: Wit, Wisdom, and Wanderings* (Hardwick, MA: Satya House, 2007).

54. See, e.g., BikeBlog, http://bikeblog.blogspot.com/.

55. Thank you to John Meyer for proposing these labels.

12

Intelligent Design?: Unpacking Geoengineering's Hidden Sacrifices

Simon Nicholson

I have been reading predictions of the future by those who believe they can predict what the world of tomorrow is going to be like. In all cases, the future of which they speak is merely a grotesque extension of the present—simply more and more loading of our environment with the waste production of an industrial civilization. In my opinion, there is no chance of solving the problem of pollution—or the other threats to human life—if we accept the idea that technology is to rule our future.

—René Dubos[1]

In early 2006, Paul Crutzen, a Nobel Prize winner for his work on the chemistry of stratospheric ozone depletion, made a provocative foray into another arena of atmospheric science with a widely read lead article in the journal *Climatic Change*.[2] Crutzen began his article not in the detached voice one might expect of a venerated scientist; rather, he opened with a strong, impassioned dig at mainstream environmental action. The political processes and calls for social change that are at the heart of the global response to climate change have, he suggested, been "grossly unsuccessful."[3] While policy makers and the public dither, continuing to place hope in protracted international negotiations or the "pious wish"[4] that individuals will voluntarily reduce greenhouse gas production, the climatic condition is rapidly worsening such that the need for large-scale action grows more pressing with each passing day. For these reasons, Crutzen argued that slow-moving political options may soon have to give way to fast-acting technological ones, beginning with the development and deployment of some dramatic, technology-based climate stabilization measures.

Such contentions from such a well-regarded source have given a great boost to proponents of climate geoengineering. As a field of study, climate geoengineering is concerned with the development of far-reaching technology-based means to alter and control aspects of the climate system.[5] Dreams of climate control have long been with us. Climate geoengineering has, however, been largely seen as hubristic, expensive, and shortsighted and has been confined to the fringes of climate change discussions. Things, though, have changed since Crutzen's article. Geoengineering proposals are now showing up on the pages of the world's best science journals;[6] are providing the basis for important conferences;[7] and are receiving consideration by serious media outlets, commentators, and policy makers.[8]

Some of the high-tech options that have been receiving recent attention include the following:

• Sulfate aerosols introduced into the stratosphere via ballistics or giant hoses, to reflect solar radiation;

• Construction of giant mirrors or reflective sunshades that could be launched into planetary orbit;

• Seeding the oceans with iron to encourage an explosion of carbon dioxide-hungry plankton;

• Chemically altering the composition of the cloud layer to boost its reflectivity;

• Genetically engineering shinier, more reflective crops;

• Large-scale carbon capture and storage programs that aim to stow carbon indefinitely under the earth's surface;

• Filling unused reservoirs and crater lakes with genetically engineered, greenhouse gas–absorbing algae.

There is no serious question now that human-induced climatic change demands action. Do the types of proposals set out in the preceding list represent the way forward? They are certainly garnering a passionate set of backers. One of the reasons that geoengineering seems, to many, so tantalizing a prospect is because it appears to be a *sacrifice-free* form of action. The thinking goes that if the development of new technologies can allow the earth's living and life-supporting systems to be manipulated at will, then climate change, along with all other environmental concerns, can be readily managed as discrete, solely technical problems. The effects of greenhouse gas emissions, for instance, are nothing to worry about if the planetary thermostat can be controlled via sulfur, satellites, or sun-shades. In such a world, there is no need for political or social reform.

Geoengineering, in fact, appears to offer a way around the messy realm of politics for the sanitized world of technocracy, in which a ready prescription for action awaits: (1) identify a problem, (2) deploy a technofix, (3) avert the crisis, (4) repeat as needed. Even better, effective geoengineering would mean that no individual needs to give anything up in the service of environmental well-being. Industrial life can carry on along its present path, with all of its harmful side effects scrubbed away.

There are good reasons, though, to be cautious about rushing to embrace a geoengineered future. Here, the lens of sacrifice is used to interrogate the climate geoengineering project. This chapter shows that far from being sacrifice-free, geoengineering, and by extension, other technological approaches to environmental problem solving, actually produce significant costs and hardships. These "technological sacrifices" are part and parcel of any large-scale technological development. However, they are largely hidden from view by the functioning of contemporary technopolitics, falling principally on those who are most fully excluded from the processes of technological decision making. Another way to say this is that technological development is political to its core. Some would win and some would lose in a geoengineered world. The winners claim that geoengineering is sacrifice-free. For the losers, by contrast, the sacrifices demanded of such large-scale technological projects would be real, if neatly ignored by those with most to gain.

The perspective afforded by a focus on sacrifice illuminates the downsides of geoengineering. The key message here is that technological sacrifices are too often glossed over in the heady rush toward technological deployment. They are present, though, and must be revealed and shouldered if technologies are to be advanced in ways that are democratically and ecologically sustainable. By looking at the current calls for geoengineering in the light of other, older efforts to control the weather, these hidden sacrifices are unpacked here, and their major implications are explored.

All of that said, although this is a critical piece, it should not be read as an argument against all the options that geoengineers are considering, much less against all technology. It is meant, instead, to suggest that often neglected costs and risks must be given adequate attention in any discussion about technological deployment. If there is one thing that the long history of technology teaches, it is that sacrifices readily ignored in the short-term rush for easy solutions often rebound to the long-term detriment of our species and the planet. Ultimately, what appear to be cost-free technological solutions to environmental problems do, in fact, demand significant sacrifices. Though these sacrifices are hidden, they are present and demand our close scrutiny, lest particular technological developments be allowed to draw us in unexpected, gnarly directions.

Sacrifice and the Politics of Technology

Geoengineering, with its sacrifice-free veneer, feeds into a widespread, depoliticized understanding of technological life. However, this is a specious view. Far from being apolitical, technological artifacts and systems are, in fact, political through and through. A staple insight from recent work on the history and sociology of science and technology is that technological artifacts and systems do not just emerge from the ether or fully formed from the minds of individual inventors. Nor is any given technology solely the product of technical decisions; rather, the techniques and technologies of geoengineering, in common with all technologies, are produced as much by social as by scientific forces. Pushing this further, the social world and technologies can be considered mutually constitutive, in the sense that through their interaction, technologies and societies shape and give rise to one another. Technologies are part of the basic fabric of social life. "We live our lives," as Donald MacKenzie and Judy Wajcman have put it, "in a world of things that people have made."[9] Particular technologies, in turn, are ultimately products not of apolitical and asocial "technological breakthroughs," but of deeply political contestation.[10]

Technology, then, beats at the heart of the modern industrial world, giving it form and life, structure and character. All the while, technologies operate to produce some of the present age's most thorny contradictions. The world's present, unprecedented levels of material affluence flow directly from technological development such that many in the rich world have now escaped "the callous brutality, the unbelievable pain, the ever present threat of untimely death for oneself (and worse one's children) which were the 'natural' realities with which our ancestors lived."[11] At the same time, though, technologies are implicated deeply in the age's most pressing problems, from the production of widespread social inequality to ecological distress on a global scale. In this sense, it is a characteristic of industrial-age technological systems that they are both purveyors of extraordinary gifts and creators of dreadful harms.

Yet, for all this, technology's effects and the prevailing direction of its advance tend to go largely unquestioned. Most of us are guilty of what Langdon Winner once termed "technological somnambulism."[12] We are content, that is, to sleepwalk our way through technological life. By this, Winner is pointing out that while we often pay close attention to the operations of particular devices, forging intense relationships with our vehicles or our iPods, for instance, we too often treat the overall direction of technological development as autonomous, as something entirely beyond human control. Autonomous technology drives social development, rather than the other way around. This is the view of technology captured by Ralph Waldo Emerson in his *Ode Inscribed to W. H. Channing*: "Things are in the saddle, / and ride mankind."[13] The same sentiment was expressed in an even more memorable fashion by Marshall McLuhan. We have become, he suggested in 1964, "the sex organs of the machine world."[14] Yet such a view of technology is inherently fatalistic. This somnambulistic orientation leads to a blanket acceptance of the political and other impacts of technological developments. It is to see the sacrifices that technological developments demand as the inevitable consequences of "objective" technologies that cannot be opposed or refashioned.

The hold of technological somnambulism is deeply rooted. It has emerged in part because technology is so ubiquitous, and we are by now so used to even sweeping technological change and upheaval that only rarely are technologies able to hold our collective attention for any length of time. More often, though, and more important for the purposes of this volume, this lack of critical engagement reflects the immense hold of the idea of progress on contemporary social thought. Technology is at the forefront of the modernist enterprise and its quest for steady improvement of the human condition. As such, it is largely taken on faith that technology has a positive or, at the very least, a benign influence (often despite mounting environmental and other evidence to the contrary).

Yet Winner's work and the contributions of many other scholars from the field of science and technology studies suggest that far from being invariably positive, technological development always demands sacrifices of one sort or another. These technological sacrifices come in three main forms. First, complex technological systems inevitably require *material sacrifices*. There are always costs and risks associated with complex technologies, and these costs and risks are seldom borne equitably. As a result, benefits to some are often offset or overwhelmed by costs to others. At the same time, complex technological systems tend to "bite back," as Edward Tenner has put it, in unexpected ways so that their deployment in the service of some particular end often results in new, more troubling problems.[15]

Second, technologies produce *political sacrifices*. Investing faith in complex technical systems ultimately means vesting significant power in those who develop and maintain those systems, threatening democratic governance by giving more and more control to technological elites. Technofixes also have a habit of papering over the complex social and political drivers of environmental harm and social injustice, with the result that they can serve to entrench and re-create situations of gross economic and political disparity. Third, and finally, complex technologies can induce *existential sacrifices*, particularly when those technologies are concerned with control of some aspect of the nonhuman world. This is to say that there are spiritual, psychological, and aesthetic costs to a technology-induced decoupling from nature that are often difficult to quantify but that embody real sacrifices nonetheless.

These sacrifices tend to be obscured by the very processes that produce technological somnambulism and downplayed by proponents and those who are liable to gain directly from particular technological developments. For these reasons, it is only with moments of heightened and overt political drama that the curtain is pulled back on technology's political constitution and the hidden sacrifices at the machine's heart are exposed.[16]

While geoengineering currently rides atop a heady wave of interest, such moments of political drama have occurred previously in the history of weather control efforts. For much of the twentieth century, attempts to control the planet's atmospheric system were viewed as a rational and reasonable extension of other forms of human intervention in nature. In the last few decades of the century, however, grand weather control schemes largely fell out of favor. From a boon for humankind, intentional atmospheric modification came to be seen as dangerous and politically suspect. This rise to favor and subsequent fall from grace of weather control programs in the last century has much to teach us about the sacrifices that geoengineering implicitly demands, as set out in the remainder of this chapter.

Unpacking Three Forms of Technological Sacrifice

The current spate of interest in geoengineering is hardly, then, the first time that attention has been turned to control of the earth's climate. Geoengineering can be thought of, in fact, as the third wave of science-age attempts at climate engineering.[17] A first wave of science-age attempts to control the weather was evident in the United States as far back as the early 1800s. These early rain-making aficionados, or "pluviculturalists," as they were known, theorized and tried to prove that rain could be induced via convective updrafts from the lighting of vast forest fires or from battlefield explosions designed to unsettle weather systems.[18] Such efforts at weather control ultimately proved fruitless, as might be expected, though not for want of effort. At various times, this first wave of would-be climate engineers attracted serious minds and significant government funding. Perhaps more important, these early experiments paved the way for more systematic weather modification experiments, which began in the years immediately following World War II.

The early base for the second and marginally more successful wave of weather modification experiments in the United States was the General Electric (GE) Research Laboratory in Schenectady, New York. There, beginning in 1946, attempts at "cloud seeding"—the introduction of chemicals into cloud cover to promote rainfall—convinced researchers that large-scale weather control was not just possible, but almost within their grasp.[19] That year, Vincent Schaefer, a research chemist for GE, overflew Mount Greylock in Massachusetts and tossed a few handfuls of crushed dry ice out of his plane. This action is attributed with setting off a small snow flurry and is widely considered the world's first successful cloud-seeding experiment. Later in 1946, Bernard Vonnegut (brother of the famed novelist) achieved a similar result with silver iodide smoke. The age of science-age weather modification had truly begun.[20]

Following these experiments, interest in the possibility of weather control was high, and the promises made by proponents were even higher. Reports from GE researchers around that time forecast "*inestimable* benefits for mankind."[21] Nobel Prize winner Irving Langmuir, then working with GE, was a particularly fervent advocate. Extrapolating from laboratory experiments and the early outdoor tests, Langmuir anticipated a near-future day when the arid regions of the American Southwest would be induced to bloom and when cloud-seeding techniques could be used to prevent "all ice storms, all storms of freezing rain, and icing conditions in clouds."[22] GE seized on this early promise, devoting extensive resources to the atmospheric modification cause. The hope, of course, was that the company could make a handsome profit from the development of weather control technologies. And in fact, it wasn't long before a commercial payback from GE's efforts was apparent. By 1951, for-profit cloud-seeding operations were working across as much as 10 percent of the United States.[23] The activities were widely seen as beneficial, even though evidence of increased rainfall from the seeding activities was patchy at best. Yet for most of the nineteenth and twentieth centuries, these failures were cast in a positive light. The results were time and again seen as "inconclusive but promising,"[24] justifying further, more far-reaching efforts.

Material Sacrifices

Still, despite all the hype and promise, all was not entirely sunny in the world of weather modification. By the 1970s, critics of cloud seeding were beginning to point out two things. First, and most obviously, there was very little evidence that all the money and effort being devoted to rainmaking was actually having any effect. And second, critics were noting that even should cloud-seeding techniques work as promised, benefits to some would almost certainly be offset by costs to others. This is because a working cloud-seeding operation is only likely to change the location, not the amount, of overall rainfall. The implication was that to use this technique to cause rain to fall on one patch of farmland, for instance, would in turn prevent it from falling on another patch that lay downwind.

There were also growing concerns that if weather control technologies could actually be made to work, accidents could occur, with the result that the very people who were supposed to benefit from the weather control system could be harmed by it. This was a concern that came to a head in 1972. That year, a U.S. government–sponsored rainmaking effort in South Dakota was followed almost immediately by a swift deluge of twelve to fourteen inches of rain. The result was a massive, devastating flood. Two hundred and thirty-five lives were lost, and property damage was estimated at 155 million dollars. The whole government-sponsored rainmaking enterprise then became the focus of a class-action lawsuit—a lawsuit that ultimately failed because it could never be proved to the satisfaction of the courts that cloud-seeding efforts ever produced any significant rainfall, let alone that they could have been responsible for the dramatic flooding witnessed in South Dakota.[25]

The creation of winners and losers, along with the potential for accidents that accompany most geoengineering options, would be an order of magnitude greater than those experienced with earlier weather modification efforts. Crutzen's geoengineering article, for instance, went on to look at the possibility of harnessing the cooling power of sulfate aerosols. It has long been known that heightened concentrations of sulfates in the upper atmosphere have a cooling effect. This effect occurs naturally for a short time following a volcanic eruption, for instance, or can be brought on by human actions with the burning of sulfur-rich fuels. Crutzen considered whether this cooling effect might be replicated in a purposeful way, using giant hoses to deliver sulfate aerosols directly into the stratosphere. He concluded that not only could this method almost certainly be used to effectively tweak the earth's climatic condition, but that its implementation could likely counter the effects of anthropogenic heating at the bargain price (when compared to the expected global costs associated with climate change) of around twenty-five to fifty billion dollars each year.[26]

However, while the sulfate aerosol option may indeed reduce average global temperatures, a likely side effect is increased levels of acid rain and further acidification of the oceans. These problems would then require their own technical responses.[27] The aerosol option is also what Langdon

Winner would call an "inherently political" technology.[28] Building on his notion of technological somnambulism, Winner has noted that some technologies require and produce particular forms of social organization. Nuclear power stations, for instance, demand a vast centralized industrial complex for their development and operation. An energy system based on solar collection is, by contrast, intrinsically less centralized and more egalitarian. In this sense, the spraying of sulfate aerosols is more like nuclear energy, given that the aerosols would have to be sprayed into the stratosphere indefinitely, necessitating strong institutional control to ensure proper operation. In this way, technological solutions come to be layered atop one another, like sandbags arranged to hold back an encroaching tide. This layering is itself premised on the belief that the effects of geoengineering are known and predictable.[29] A sixty-plus year history of failed scientific-age weather modification efforts, though, gives lie to this notion.

Yet this does not stop hype and hope from routinely overwhelming good sense. James R. Fleming, a professor of science, technology, and society at Colby College, has written of a particularly revealing exchange at a geoengineering conference organized in 2007 by NASA. "Even as [participants at the conference] joked about a NASA staffer's apology for her inability to control the temperature in the meeting room," he reports, in deadpan prose, "others detailed their own schemes for manipulating the earth's climate."[30] The irony is obvious. Anyone who has struggled with a broken thermostat in his or her home or office must question the wisdom of trying to affix the equivalent of a gigantic thermostat to the planet's climatic system. More to the point, there is no guarantee that human understanding of the earth's complex systemic interactions will ever reach a level to allow for radical geoengineering. Interfering with the earth's living systems to such an extraordinary extent must be considered a drastic, last-resort undertaking, particularly given that indiscriminate alteration of the earth's natural systems is precisely what gave rise to our present environmental predicament.

A final material sacrifice concerns the basic question of who will pay for geoengineering. All technological systems have costs and benefits that must be shared. The U.S. federally funded weather experiments were conducted largely with taxpayer money, often with great secrecy and limited oversight, and with ultimately little tangible benefit. Private companies in pursuit of profit covered the rest. Considering Crutzen's sulfate option again, a price tag of twenty-five to fifty billion U.S. dollars is hardly a negligible figure. To launch such an effort on a global scale would still require overcoming the usual set of political coordination problems. It is hard to believe that in such a world, the results would benefit all equally. British climate expert Hubert Lamb once suggested that before taking any geoengineering action, it seemed like "an essential precaution to wait until a scientific system for forecasting the behavior of the natural climate . . . has been devised and operated successfully for, perhaps, a hundred years."[31] This seems, given all of the material sacrifices that such an enterprise embodies, a sound recommendation.

Political Sacrifices

Sacrifices are not just present when things go wrong with new technologies. There are also sacrifices associated with everything going *right*. One of these "positive" sacrifices concerns control—who has it and how it is used. Powerful technologies always invite competition for control. Even in the early days of the second wave of climate engineering research, the corporate sector was not able to hold its monopoly on research into atmospheric manipulation for long. The possibilities offered by harnessing the power of the weather also quickly caught the attention of the U.S. military. Indeed, by the late 1940s, the U.S. government and GE had joined forces to work on a classified project, Project Cirrus, concerned with possible military applications of climate modification. A *Harvard Law School Record* article on the project put the justification for the project in even plainer language: "[Weather modification has attracted] military and naval funds because of its war implications—bogging down enemy troops in snow and rain, clearing airfields of fog at lowest cost, and infecting induced storms with bacteriological and radiological materials. The Battle of the Bulge, in which the Nazis mobilized and attacked under supercooled fog, could have been much altered by a few pounds of dry ice."[32] Project Cirrus produced a paucity of results from these efforts, and government funding for the work was pulled around 1954.[33] Yet still, dreams of weather control never really faded. In fact, the promise that weather control seemed to hold for military and commercial applications drove the U.S. government to even higher levels of investment.

A government Advisory Committee on Weather Control, established as Project Cirrus came to an end, maintained a characteristically upbeat attitude. During preparation of the committee's final report in 1955, famed economist and computer pioneer John von Neumann spoke on a panel devoted to the "possible effects of atomic and thermonuclear explosions in modifying weather." Taking the floor during a discussion period, von Neumann foreshadowed the current conversation about climate geoengineering by raising the possibility of changing the albedo of the earth via the deployment of strategically positioned reflective materials. He went on to say, "Our knowledge of the dynamics in the atmosphere is rapidly approaching a level that will make possible, in a few decades, intervention in atmospheric and climatic matters . . . . There is little doubt that one could intervene on any desired scale, and ultimately achieve rather fantastic results."[34]

Weather modification efforts reached new efforts during the Vietnam War. Between 1967 and 1972, the U.S. Department of Defense ordered significant cloud-seeding operations in Vietnam, Laos, and Cambodia, with the aim of inducing rainfall to interrupt the supply line of the North Vietnamese Army along the Ho Chi Minh Trail. "Operation POPEYE," as it was known, resulted in the flying of twenty-six hundred cloud-seeding sorties by U.S. pilots and the deployment of an estimated forty-seven thousand silver iodide flares. The program required an annual budget of 3.6 million dollars yet was conducted almost entirely in secret. Hopes were clearly high in the Johnson and subsequent Nixon administration that weather modification would turn the tide of the war. Ultimately, though, cloud seeding appears to have had a negligible impact at best on rainfall patterns or the war effort.[35]

The secret operations in Vietnam did, though, ultimately have a significant impact on general opinion about weather modification attempts. The story of Operation POPEYE was originally broken in *The Washington Post* in 1971 and was picked up by Seymour Hersh of *The New York Times* in 1972, following the leaking of the Pentagon Papers. The Nixon administration, though, adopted a firm stance of denial in the face of these exposés, pushing aside any efforts to discover the full extent of the U.S. weather modification program. It took another two years for details of the failed cloud-seeding operations in Vietnam to become public, with the release, by Senator Claiborne Pell of Rhode

Island, of a one-time classified briefing on weather warfare that had been given at the Department of Defense. With publication of this document, it emerged that the Central Intelligence Agency had been trying to alter rainfall in South Vietnam as early as 1963, in an effort to break up protests by Buddhist monks. Furthermore, it was reported that cloud seeding had probably been attempted to disrupt sugarcane production in Cuba and that the technique had been used for some time, ineffectively, in U.S. drought relief efforts in a range of countries. All these programs were linked to the U.S. military and were undertaken with the blessing of the White House.[36]

This news created a domestic and international outcry. Already, by 1973, the U.S. Senate had reacted to early news of Operation POPEYE by adopting a resolution that called for an international treaty prohibiting the use of "environmental or geophysical modification" for military purposes. The Soviet Union used international concern about seemingly nefarious U.S. actions to push a similar proposal at the United Nations. This political maneuver, coupled with rising global public concern about the vast potential consequences of the unchecked use of atmospheric manipulation, led, ultimately, to a 1976 international convention, the United Nations Convention on the Prohibition of Military or Any Other Hostile Use of Environmental Modification Techniques, which prohibits the use in wartime of any and all "environmental modification techniques." With these actions, the curtains came crashing down on the second wave of climate modification research.

Following the fallout from Operation POPEYE, federal funding in the United States for weather modification research largely dried up. There are still some state and local funds that support cloud-seeding operations in the American West, though these outfits now operate on a much reduced scale, as what was once seen as an entirely beneficial scientific enterprise came to be seen as something on which to place dramatic limits. Yet if all the technical challenges associated with geoengineering could be ironed out, and if such options could be deployed with no unforeseen accidents, then the bulk of the material sacrifices discussed previously, bar the astronomically high costs of development and upkeep, could be avoided. There must be reasons other than recognition of material sacrifices that explain the sudden change in thinking about weather modification.

Ultimately, the strongest critics of Project POPEYE were from within the antiwar movement. Many of these protestors were not concerned by the actual or potential environmental or humanitarian implications of weather control activities so much as they were concerned that this new technology had been deployed without the knowledge of most of the people on whose behalf the government was supposed to be acting. Now, again, calls for geoengineering are forcing us to confront the urge for control that such far-reaching technologies entail. The U.S. Air Force has recently claimed that "in 2025, U.S. aerospace forces can 'own the weather' by capitalizing on emerging technologies and focusing development of those technologies to war-fighting applications."[37] This above all else should give pause. The geoengineering strategies that are being proposed by Crutzen and others represent an extraordinary consolidation of power—power that promises ultimately to be vested in the military arms of the world's richest governments or in largely unregulated transnational corporations.

Tasking the world's militaries or its most powerful corporations with controlling the climate system sounds like a very risky proposition indeed, especially when we consider that some of the choices that would present themselves in a geoengineered world verge, in the words of a reporter for *The Boston Globe*, "on the Solomonic."[38] Daniel Schrag, of Harvard's Laboratory for Geochemical Oceanography, suggests a thought experiment: imagine that the U.S. government possesses the ability to control hurricanes but that preventing a particular storm would result in scorching temperatures in Africa, destroying the continent's crops. How would this decision be made? Or imagine a mirror in space that could be used to redirect a small percentage of solar radiation. If, in a given year, the United States is having a cold, miserable summer and Europe is in the midst of a dramatic heat wave, then "who," asks Schrag, "gets to adjust the mirror?"[39]

Ultimately, the appropriate questions are, who decides? Who benefits? And who, given any deployment of geoengineering technologies, is being asked to sacrifice? These are clearly normative concerns. There is no guarantee that a technological elite is best situated or best equipped to provide the answers. There is also no guarantee that the rich beneficiaries of these technological solutions would act in the interests of the poor, who would likely suffer the bulk of the costs of their use. This is part of the equity question that is built into discussions of climate change and all other environmental "problems." Says J. T. Kiel, "On the issue of ethics, I feel we would be taking on the ultimate state of hubris to believe we can control Earth. We (the industrially developed world) would essentially be telling the (rest of the) world not to worry about our insatiable use of energy. In essence we are treating the symptom, not the cause."[40] This introduces a further sense in which geoengineering demands political sacrifices. Treating the symptoms of climate change via implementation of adaptive strategies has always been a more appealing choice to rich nations than activities aimed at mitigation. Instead of mustering the political resources required to generate large-scale proactive social change, rich countries are, for the most part, happy to try to respond to climate change in an ad hoc, after-the-fact fashion. This luxury comes with economic wealth and power. But in the meantime, the poorest among us are forced to suffer the consequences of a failure to tackle climate change head-on. Said differently, climate change already sacrifices people, livelihoods, and landscapes daily. For the most part, though, these sacrifices are not recognized for what they are: the entirely foreseeable products of an industrial civilization that neglects many people and despoils much of the nonhuman world.

Peter Dauvergne has made a similar point about the people killed each year in car wrecks: "There is . . . a reason," Dauvergne writes, "that we call these consequences 'accidents' rather than 'sacrifices,' as such soft language helps avoid taking a hard look at the guts of global morality in an era of consumptive prosperity."[41] But climate change, like deaths on the road, is a deeply political, as opposed to a solely technical, problem. Seeing climate change as a technical problem is to see geoengineering as perhaps the only logical way forward. And yet via geoengineering proposals, responsibility is neatly avoided by those who have the most power to take other forms of constructive action.

Literary critics use a phrase borrowed from the ancient Greeks, *deus ex machina*, to refer to a plotline that introduces an improbable device to resolve an apparently irresolvable problem. In ancient Greek dramas, a particularly tangled plot element was sometimes resolved by divine intervention. The physical representation of a meddling god was introduced to the stage by a complicated piece of equipment—hence *deus ex machina*, literally, "god from the machine." *Technological fix* must be assigned the same sense in the political realm. To focus on one-shot technological solutions is ultimately a sign of political evasion, rather than a real account of the roots of the climate crisis.

Existential Sacrifices

Chunglin Kwa, a researcher in science and technology studies, has suggested that one of the main reasons Operation POPEYE caused a public backlash was not because it revealed a mismatch between promise and results, or even because of concerns about military control, but because the news was able to be meaningfully deployed by the burgeoning environmental movement.[42] By the early 1970s, an understanding that human actions can upset planetary systems was beginning to take hold. This was a decade after Rachel Carson's *Silent Spring* and coincided in the United States with the first Earth Day, passage of the Clean Air Act, and establishment by the Nixon administration of an increasingly strong federal environmental apparatus. At the same time, concern was rising elsewhere around the world about the dangers of human interventions in natural processes.

Kwa argues that until the 1970s, the evaluation of weather modification schemes was heavily weighted toward their potential economic, political, and military benefits. However, the growing power of the environmental movement meant that the indeterminacy of climatic processes was more widely appreciated. This made it clear that not only could the long-term effects of weather modification schemes never be accurately predicted, but the potential for catastrophic effects could never be adequately dismissed. What was once seen as positive or benign human involvement was now framed as dangerous meddling. This points to the importance of a third, less tangible variety of technological sacrifice. It has to do with the losses that can be experienced when humanity gives up its role as a full member of the biotic community and assumes a position of uncritical control over it.

Along with all his other contributions, Paul Crutzen is also attributed with coining the term *anthropocene* to describe the current epoch.[43] The implication of this term is that humanity's technological prowess has allowed our species to rise to a position of dominance on the planet, casting humanity in the role of a geological force, indelibly shaping all aspects of the living and nonliving planet by our considered and accidental actions. For some, living in the anthropocene entails that humanity should strive to perfect the management of the earth. And so, by this view, the proper goal of technological development, made imperative by the deteriorating state of the planet, should be ever more far-reaching intervention in natural processes—earthwide biosystemic control as a natural extension of the present technological path. Geoengineering fits neatly with this view. On this basis, environmental challenges are coming to be defined increasingly in technical terms, as problems to be resolved by the application of technological fixes. As a result, the dominant vision in the search for a sustainable world has become a sort of global biospheric management. The vision is one in which the unintended environmental consequences of technical actions are met with ever more sophisticated technological solutions and, ultimately, in which the whole of nature is to be brought under a human yoke.[44]

For others, though, the emergence of the anthropocene demands something else: a sense of what Thomas Princen has called "sufficiency" as a way to temper the urge to control, and a striving for connections with the nonhuman world that overcome the layers interposed by increasingly complex technological systems.[45] Technological development, say these critics, is too often seen as an end in itself or is utilized strictly in the service of more complete capital accumulation. In this way, technology acts as a driver of environmental harm, and the resultant environmental harm is then itself used to justify even greater levels of technological intervention in nature. This interplay of environmental harm and the increasing alienation from all things beyond the technological are mutually reinforcing factors. Together, they result in more and more complete domination by the human over the natural world and an entrenchment of the structures of power that thrive via that domination.

Perhaps the technophilic vision of a heavily managed, biospheric nature ruled by the dictates of technology is to be the planet's fate. It certainly seems a fair assessment of the present technological trajectory. Yet something would be lost in such a world—a set of sacrifices that would affect us all. In Peter Huber's conservative manifesto *Hard Green*, he compares the "Malthusian hell" forecast by neo-Malthusians with what he calls a "Faustian hell"—a vision of what the world may look like if the dream of planetary-spanning technological control is made real:

The new ecological hell now in sight is very different from the old. The Malthusian hell is as black as the waters before God's creation; the Faustian hell is merely beige, the color of man's concrete and computers. In the Malthusian hell, the ascent of man causes the collapse of everything else and that, in turn, destroys man, too. The whales and the ocean drown first, followed almost immediately by all the human occupants of the lifeboat. In the Faustian hell, the ascent of man causes the collapse of everything except man. Everything sinks but humanity.[46]

Humanity could, all material sacrifices and accidents aside, survive in such a world. Yet human life would, in some basic ways, be stripped of meaning, color, and worth. This is an observation that was famously foreshadowed by Bill McKibben in declaring the "end of nature" and has long been of interest to environmental philosophers and historians.[47] It is a sacrifice that technologists often ignore, but one that the environmental movement was able to identify and tap into to effectively oppose Operation POPEYE and has been able to bring to bear in opposition to other entirely instrumental technological developments.

An alternative future would not be antitechnological by any means, but would instead be much more reflexive and open about the ends to which technologies are put, and to which they lead. Far from inviting further pursuit of earth-spanning technological dominance, the anthropocene demands, as Simon Dalby has made clear, a shift in focus for regulators and designers alike, from after-the-fact interventions to systematic choices that "minimize ecological throughput."[48] A deteriorating ecological condition demands a radically new technological ethic, one that holds a recognition of the real sacrifices produced by technological life at its core.

Conclusion

Whatever awaits, given that there is substantial risk and potential for surprising outcomes associated with any use of technology, and given that many would mourn the loss of a natural world apart from human will, it seems vital that options apart from the present technological trajectory be explored. There are foreseeable technological futures, for example, in which the needs of all people can be comfortably met, and in which the needs of a self-willed, self-directed natural world are also respected. All complex technological systems demand sacrifices. Some, though, are less costly in material, political, and existential terms than others. These categories of technological sacrifice can help in the important deliberations ahead about what kinds of technological options to pursue and, by extension, what kind of world is being created.

Some technological systems demand great material sacrifices, while ceding control to powerful actors. Stratospheric sulfur schemes, the genetic modification of organisms, and large-scale nuclear power generation fall into this category. Other technological options, by contrast, disperse control widely, foster connection between the human and non-human worlds, and afford much more limited material costs and risks. In this category are technologies like installing white roofs on built structures, the development of dispersed and low-input systems for food provisioning, and distributed solar and wind-based energy systems. Only by paying attention to the implicit sacrifices demanded by technological development can these choices be effectively weighed and compared and truly democratic decisions be made about which to pursue.

Too often, technophiles make it sound as though there are just two options open to us: either we embrace the present technological direction and treat every new innovation as the advance of humankind, or we, as Thomas Princen has put it in chapter 7, "turn off the lights, crawl into the cave, and shiver in the dark."[49] These, though, are not our options at all. A host of technological futures are open, to be brought into being through choices taken today. This means, ultimately, recognizing that technological choices turn on politics, not just technical capacity. In the preface to his recent book *The Bridge at the End of the World*, James Gustave Speth makes the point that it won't take anything dramatic to bring about environmental ruin.[50] All we need do is continue on our present path. Humanity is already pushing some of the planet's key life-supporting functions to their limits. Growing populations and expanding appetites, working in tandem with the technophilic notion of a limitless planet, will be enough to completely overwhelm earth's ability to support large-scale human civilizations. This doomsday scenario is by no means certain. The scientists may be dead wrong, after all, about the abilities of the planet to absorb our abuse. Or perhaps some radical technological solution really does wait just over the horizon. Yet what if the worst were to happen? Pockets of human life could well survive environmental collapse, but humanity—that accumulation of history and social life that sits atop our animal inheritance—is liable to be lost. In that case, our species will have made the ultimate sacrifice—the sacrifice of the long-term thriving of humankind in return for a short-term orgy of material excess. Geoengineering does nothing, unfortunately, to address this most basic of our problems.

Acknowledgments

I would like to thank the editors of this volume and Eve Bratman for valuable suggestions and the volume's reviewers for insightful comments. Thank you, too, to Emily Kennedy for her research assistance.

Notes

1. Kirkpatrick Sale, *Rebels Against the Future: The Luddites and Their War on the Industrial Revolution—Lessons for the Computer Age* (Reading, MA: Addison-Wesley, 1995), vii.

2. Paul J. Crutzen, "Albedo Enhancement by Stratospheric Sulfur Injections: A Contribution to Resolve a Policy Dilemma?" *Climatic Change* 77 (2006): 211–219.

3. Ibid., 212.

4. Ibid., 217.

5. Research on climate geoengineering options tends to break down into two different categories. A first area of focus is the extensive manipulation of the atmosphere or the disruption of solar energy flows to reduce concentrations of solar radiation reaching the earth's surface. A second line of research proposes the widespread transformation of terrestrial or aquatic ecosystems so that they better absorb greenhouse gases or so that they are rendered less susceptible to harm from climatic heating. David Keith has noted that the two factors central to a clear definition of geoengineering are scale and intent. A home garden is an intervention in nature for human ends but does not qualify as geoengineering because its scale is too limited. At the same time, the destruction of the ozone layer by the release of chlorofluorocarbons certainly meets the scale requirement but was an unintentional side effect of industrial and consumptive processes. See David Keith, "Geoengineering the Climate: History and Prospects," *Annual Review of Energy and the Environment* 25 (2000): 245–284.

6. Oliver Morton, "Climate Change: Is This What It Takes to Save the World?" *Nature* 447 (2007): 132–136; Alan Robock, Dan Whaley, Ken Caldeira, Margaret S. Leinen, and Tom M. L. Wigley, "Roundtable: Has the Time Come for Geoengineering?" *Bulletin of the Atomic Scientists*, 2008, http://www.thebulletin.org/web-edition/roundtables/has-the-time-come-geoengineering.

7. American Enterprise Institute, "Geoengineering: A Revolutionary Approach to Climate Change," http://www.aei.org/events/eventID.1728/event_detail.asp;

Cornelia Dean, "Experts Discuss Engineering Feats, Like Space Mirrors, to Slow Climate Change," *The New York Times*, November 10, 2007, A11.

8. William J. Broad, "How to Cool a Planet (Maybe)," *The New York Times*, June 27, 2006, F1; The National Academies, "Joint Science Academies' Statement: Climate Change Adaptation and the Transition to a Low Carbon Society," http://www.nationalacademies.org/includes/climatechangestatement.pdf.

9. Donald MacKenzie and Judy Wajcman, *The Social Shaping of Technology* (Buckingham, UK: Open University Press, 1999), xiv.

10. Andrew Feenberg, *Questioning Technology* (London: Routledge, 1999).

11. Andrew Kimbrell, "Recreating Life in the Image of Technology," *The Ecologist* 29, no. 3 (1999): 169–170.

12. Langdon Winner, *The Whale and the Reactor: A Search for Limits in an Age of High Technology* (Chicago: University of Chicago Press, 1986), 10, 169.

13. Quoted in Val Dusek, *Philosophy of Technology: An Introduction* (Malden, MA: Blackwell, 2006), 176.

14. See Marshall McLuhan, *Understanding Media: The Extensions of Man* (New York: McGraw-Hill, 1964), 46.

15. Edward Tenner, *Why Things Bite Back: Technology and the Revenge of Unintended Consequences* (New York: Vintage Books, 1997).

16. Sheila Jasanoff, *Designs on Nature: Science and Democracy in Europe and the United States* (Princeton, NJ: Princeton University Press, 2005), 205–208.

17. James R. Fleming, "The Pathological History of Weather and Climate Modification: Three Cycles of Promise and Hype," *Historical Studies in the Physical Sciences* 37, no. 1 (2006): 3–25.

18. Ibid., 4–8.

19. Keith, "Geoengineering the Climate," 252–253.

20. Fleming, "Pathological History," 8–9.

21. James R. Fleming, "Fixing the Weather and Climate: Military and Civilian Schemes for Cloud Seeding and Climate Engineering," in *The Technological Fix: How People Use Technology to Create and Solve Problems*, ed. Lisa Rosner (New York: Routledge, 2004), 177.

22. Ibid.

23. Drake Bennett, "Don't Like the Weather? Change It: The Weird Science of Weather Modification Makes a Comeback," *The Boston Globe*, July 3, 2005, K1.

24. Chunglin Kwa, "The Rise and Fall of Weather Modification," in *Changing the Atmosphere: Expert Knowledge and Environmental Governance*, ed. Clark A. Miller and Paul N. Edwards (Cambridge, MA: MIT Press, 2001), 162.

25. *Lunsford v. U.S.*, 418 F.Supp. 1045 (1976).

26. Crutzen, "Albedo Enhancement."

27. See James Lovelock, "Medicine for a Feverish Planet: Kill or Cure?" *The Guardian*, September 1, 2008, http://www.guardian.co.uk/environment/2008/sep/01/climatechange.scienceofclimatechange.

28. Winner, *Whale and the Reactor*, 19–39.

29. J. T. Kiehl, "Geoengineering Climate Change: Treating the Symptom over the Cause?" *Climatic Change* 77 (2006): 227–228.

30. James R. Fleming, "The Climate Engineers: Playing God to Save the Planet," *Wilson Quarterly*, Spring 2007, 46–60.

31. Hubert H. Lamb, "Climate-Engineering Schemes to Meet a Climatic Emergency," *Earth-Science Reviews* 7 (1971): 95.

32. Fleming, "Fixing the Weather and Climate," 168.

33. Ibid., 180–181.

34. Kwa, "Rise and Fall of Weather Modification," 141–142.

35. Fleming, "Pathological History," 13.

36. Fleming, "Climate Engineers."

37. Fleming, "Pathological History," 15.

38. Bennett, "Don't Like the Weather?"

39. Ibid.

40. Kiehl, "Geoengineering Climate Change," 227.

41. Peter Dauvergne, "Dying of Consumption: Accidents or Sacrifices of Global Morality?" *Global Environmental Politics* 5, no. 3 (2005): 36.

42. Kwa, "Rise and Fall of Weather Modification."

43. P. J. Crutzen and E. F. Stoermer, "The 'Anthropocene,'" *Global Change Newsletter* 41 (2000): 17–18.

44. See, generally, Aidan Davison, *Technology and the Contested Meanings of Sustainability* (Albany: State University of New York Press, 2001).

45. Thomas Princen, *The Logic of Sufficiency* (Cambridge, MA: MIT Press, 2005).

46. Peter Huber, *Hard Green: Saving the Environment from the Environmentalists—a Conservative Manifesto* (New York: Basic Books, 1999), 81.

47. Bill McKibben, *The End of Nature* (New York: Random House, 1989).

48. Simon Dalby, "Anthropocene Ethics: Thinking Politically after Environment" (paper presented at the annual meeting of the International Studies Association, Le Centre Sheraton Hotel, Montreal, QC, March 17, 2004), 5.

49. Chapter 7.

50. James Gustave Speth, *The Bridge at the End of the World: Capitalism, the Environment, and Crossing from Crisis to Sustainability* (New Haven, CT: Yale University Press, 2008).

13

Struggling with Sacrifice: Take Back Your Time and Right2Vacation.org

Michael Maniates

Over the past year, I've received at least a dozen emails from friends, colleagues, and students about "The New American Dream Wallet Buddy." "Just the thing to keep us focused on making a difference," says one email correspondent. "If everyone were to download and use this," shares another, "we'd be on our way to real environmental sustainability." "A great way to get regular people energized about environmental issues," offered a third. With endorsements like those, I couldn't resist. Off to the Web I went.

What I found was a colorful, printable guide[1] on "how to make a difference," courtesy of the Center for a New American Dream, a Washington, DC, environmental organization promoting sustainable consumption. Once properly folded and taped, New Dream's Wallet Buddy becomes a protective holder for that frequently used credit or debit card. One side of the sleeve asks the reader to consider five questions before any purchase: do I need it and do I need it now? Was it made sustainably? Were the workers who made it treated well? Does it have too much packaging? Is it worth the money? The flip side offers this inspirational reminder: "Every dollar I spend is a statement about the kind of world I want and the quality of life I value." I haven't printed out a Wallet Buddy for my billfold, but if Google is any indication, I'm the odd man out. The Web is replete with testimonials to the Buddy's centrality to an effective politics of environmental sustainability, and there are several third-party links to the Wallet Buddy's Web site.

Around the same time I began receiving Wallet Buddy endorsements, my daughters' high school sponsored an evening event about "solving environmental problems." I live in northwestern Pennsylvania, but if you've been in high school or have children that are, you know the scene no matter where you live: lots of student displays, plenty of handouts, good cookies and passable coffee, and more than a few people hoping to learn how to translate their environmental concern into meaningful action. There was plenty to see and do, but a clear crowd favorite was a slick, wallet-sized, multifold brochure in the freebie pile at the exit. It had the earth centered on the cover and the words "1° of Change Will Make a World of Difference" wrapped around the planet.[2] At the bottom was the hook, "How Individuals Can Make a Big Impact on the Fight against Global Warming" (with the suggestion that one read on). The message on the flip side was hard to miss:

Consumers Will Dictate the Future

Your purchases and decisions speak for you!

Here are five easy ways you can help the fight against global warming.

The "five easy ways" were predictably consumeristic and already familiar: change lightbulbs, buy locally, recycle, and the like. What engaged people's interest and optimism, though, wasn't the to-do list per se, but rather the theory of individual power and collective change articulated by the Pittsburgh Zoo (the sponsor of "1° of Change") in the brochure's closing paragraphs:

1° of Change may not seem like much at first glance. But remember this: a drop of just four degrees in average temperature constitutes an ice age, so 1° of Change is significant.

Small changes can have big effects. When even a handful of people change their behaviors, the results can cause a ripple effect, until a "tipping point" is reached, when it seems everyone is working towards the solution. We wake up to find the world has changed for the better, seemingly overnight.

The Perils of Green Consumption

The Center for a New American Dream and the Pittsburgh Zoo are but two of thousands of U.S. environmental organizations responding to the desire of many to "do something" about environmental threats to human well-being. They're fundamentally different organizations in terms of culture, scope, history, and goals. That they're promoting similar strategies reflects the breadth of a consumer-centric politics of environmental action—a politics that seems to grow more ubiquitous as public concern about environmental ills and energy vulnerability mounts. This politics embraces and reinforces several beliefs about political change in service of environmental sustainability. One is that most of us are busy and easily distracted, with environmental commitments that are superficial at best. We therefore require a range of easy, straightforward, even fun ways of making a difference from which to choose, like replacing a lightbulb, taking a canvas bag to the market, or reducing the idling time of our car. These "low-hanging fruit" measures[3]—simple to seize, cost-effective, apolitical, noncontroversial—thus become the primary mechanism for drawing people into a more engaged politics of environmental change. This strategy rests on a second assumption: that individuals will experience these simple, consumeristic measures as empowering (and as a welcome respite from a conflictual environmental politics) and will therefore want to do more, which in turn begets a third assumption, namely, that producers will respond to growing consumer demand for green products by providing even more environmentally sustainable and socially just choices. Finally (the last assumption), the accumulated impact of the millions of small, largely uncoordinated green consumer choices will trigger deeper changes in how products are produced and consumed (think back to Thomas Princen's discussion of consumer sovereignty in chapter 7). This impact will grow as consumers, flush with confidence that comes with making a difference by voting with their dollar, engage in ever more determined acts of environmental consumption.

This is the magic of the marketplace, facilitated by a big-tent, every-one-can-help approach to saving the planet. It doesn't matter what specific consumer action you take, the wallet cards (and the larger approach to environmental politics they represent) seem to say, just so long as you spend your money, where and when you can, in support of sustainability and justice. Anything you do is good. One action isn't especially more important or effective than another because the goal is to get everyone on board in sufficient strength to drive society toward those tipping points for change.

If this sort of thinking continues to dominate discussions of environmental action, the prospects for ambitious policies for sustainability are dim. One reason, as I've suggested elsewhere,[4] is the inevitable failure of a politics of uncoordinated consumer action. Everyday shoppers, for instance, find it neither affirming nor empowering to assess continuously the environmental and justice implications of their consumption choices. The Wallet Buddy's five questions may feel good in your wallet, but bringing them to bear on even a small portion of daily consumption decisions generates information overload and compassion fatigue.[5] Do the math, moreover, and you realize that these actions are wildly incommensurate to the problems at hand or that the benefits they generate will quickly be swamped by those less committed to the cause.[6] It's true that the idea of getting everyone on board with the small and easy actions in pursuit of societal tipping points undoubtedly seems promising, even exciting—until, that is, one is confronted by the many who neglect voluntary eco-behaviors, no matter how compelling the economics or enticing the information.

Another, more pernicious reason for worry goes to the heart of this volume. Because a consumer-led politics of environmental sustainability is unable to speak in any meaningful way about sacrifice, its dominance crowds out coherent discussion of three issues: the immense sacrifice of planetary environmental capacity and human well-being currently under way, the sacrifice that must be offered to halt and reverse this destruction, and the sometimes false rhetoric of sacrifice that stifles creativity and deters action in the face of enormous environmental challenges. Voting with our pocketbook only sounds plausible as a primary strategy for arresting ongoing environmental degradation if current patterns of environmental sacrifice are glossed over or understated. And green consumption cannot speak directly to those circumstances in which doing the difficult thing might be necessary to make an environmental difference because it's positioned as the "convenient and easy way" of addressing environmental problems. In addition to the many problems with "saving the world" one conscious-consumption act at a time, add this to the list: doing so desensitizes us to the importance of thinking hard about the place of sacrifice in environmental politics.

For eighteen months between 2007 and 2009, I raised these concerns in conversations around the United States with advocates and practitioners of green consumption. I argued that a consumer-oriented politics, by avoiding any meaningful confrontation with sacrifice, cuts itself off from enticing sources of change and activism. An individual, for example, can be persuaded to purchase an energy-efficient lightbulb as part of a strategy for slowing climate change, and he or she may feel good about the purchase. But important factors known to generate lasting, confident commitment to social change—elements like a deepening sense of community and connection that comes from struggling with others around tough issues—are inherently absent from purchases performed in the privacy of one's home or in the checkout line. In the same vein, offering a broad, accommodating menu of actions on behalf of the planet may seem to be an effective way of drawing people into environmental politics. But because people glean meaning from struggling with others around *specific* outcomes that matter, an anything-goes approach can be counterproductive. Indeed, relying on small *consumer* steps to activate individual *citizen* capacities is a round peg–square hole problem. Small steps (what psychologists call "small wins"[7]) are critical for easing people into more ambitious, complex roles and tasks. But these small wins may need to be in the domain of active citizenship, not enlightened consumption, given the profound ways in which these two spheres differ in their sense of how societies change, and why.[8]

My colleagues and correspondents respectfully replied that, as valid as my concerns may be in theory, any invocation of sacrifice as part of a broader debate over environmental policy would be a political showstopper. Too many already view environmentalists, they insist, as wolves in sheep's clothing, ready at the first opportunity to promote policies inimical to economic growth and material progress. It isn't possible—or, at the very least, it is enormously difficult—to speak of sacrifice in effective ways with concerned publics without later needing to apologize for appearing too Draconian in one's outlook. Academics, they've gently suggested, have the luxury of pursuing exotic possibilities denied those working in the trenches. Better to appeal to the power of new technologies and market forces, while hoping that the green consumers of today become the green activists of tomorrow, than run the risk of a conversation about sacrifice that could generate political backlash.

These have been illuminating conversations. It seems, though, that moving them forward now requires a shift from abstract debate to empirical reflection on the experience of environmental activists who've invoked sacrifice in their public outreach. What do these experiences tell us about a discourse and politics of sacrifice? Do they affirm the commonly held view that sacrifice is too hot to handle politically? Or are there ways, or at least an inkling of ways, in which sacrifice can—and perhaps should—become part of public deliberation about the drivers and best responses to environmental ills?

With these questions in mind, the remainder of this chapter explores the work of one organization that has sought to tackle the sacrifice question, sometimes head-on and sometimes obliquely: Take Back Your Time (TBYT) and its newly emerging initiative Right2Vacation.org. TBYT is one of a few public policy initiatives in the United States that seeks real reductions in individual consumption. Organized around the notion of "time famine," TBYT argues that a significant portion of consumption in the United States is compelled by structure and circumstance, and if offered other choices, especially choices regarding the structure of work, Americans *in the rational pursuit of their own happiness* will sacrifice consumption in exchange for greater leisure time. TBYT's framing of sacrifice as something that American workers now experience *and* as something they would willingly embrace makes the initiative a potentially illuminating case.

Three sections follow. The first describes the evolution of TBYT/Right2Vacation.org's policy agenda and situates it within a broader politics of work, environment, and sacrifice. Like Shane Gunster's tale of the carbon tax (chapter 9), this is a story of the political costs that come from retreating from frank talk about sacrifice. The second section describes TBYT's return to sacrifice in its recently launched Right2Vacation.org initiative—an intriguing program with an uncertain future. A final section returns to two central questions: Can an environmental politics that speaks frankly to sacrifice thrive in today's political environment? Can, moreover, such a politics counter the allure of a green-consumption approach to environmental sustainability that promises large change with minimal effort?

Take Back Your Time: Roots and Branches

Roots

TBYT traces its origins back to 2001, when the Fetzer Institute[9] convened twenty-four U.S. leaders of the so-called voluntary simplicity movement (VSM) for conversation about the future of simplicity in the United States. The timing was right. A tightening middle-class squeeze of flattening salaries and rising expenses, together with an upward creep in the length of the average workweek, meant that Americans were spending more time at work even as the proportion of two-income families was growing.[10] As work drew more time and energy away from home and leisure activities, families increasingly characterized their lives as harried and "out of control."[11] The notion of simplifying one's life—of limiting one's material needs as a way of reducing one's dependency on a disliked job—emerged as one mechanism for regaining control or, at the very least, mounting some small resistance to a way of life that was no longer fully rewarding.

These so-called simplifiers were typically mainstream and more common than imagined. Indeed, during the late 1980s and 1990s, some 15 to 25 percent of U.S. households were intentionally "downshifting" by consciously living below their means, refusing to take higher paid work to avoid job stress and long work hours, or voluntarily reducing work hours at an existing job, even in the face of diminished opportunities for advancement and salary increases. A majority of these simplifiers were more highly educated than the average citizen; college degrees were common, and advanced degrees and special skills weren't rare. Most simplifiers, moreover, were at or near median household income levels before their tilt toward frugality. Few were trading down a Jaguar for a BMW. The intensity of their actions varied, from limited consumption shifts among many to radical lifestyle changes by a few.[12] Yet those acting in the name of "simplicity" typically shared a preoccupation with "taking control" of one's life and escaping, if for just a bit, the demeaning, numbing effects of everyday commercial life.[13]

A vernacular of sacrifice was emerging across the middle-class landscape. It focused on the *sacrifice of* family life, leisure time, and social connectivity to the escalating demands of work. And it imagined a "way out" through *sacrifices in* material consumption and consumer desire. The VSM became the carrier for this reemergent grammar of possibility, but it had no formal leaders, designated spokeswomen and men, central agenda, or real capacity for the kind of focused social action that distinguishes effective social movements. Yet it had millions of members, all active in varying ways. It was a movement in waiting, one pregnant with possibility.

The 2001 Fetzer Institute conference meant to catalyze these possibilities. Two strategy sessions followed this first gathering: one in March

2002 in Kalamazoo, Michigan, and the other in August that same year
at Oberlin College in Ohio. These meetings saw the organizing group
(dubbed "The Simplicity Forum") grow to sixty-eight members, including several academic researchers, this author included.[14] Though far
ranging, the discussions returned to the political mobilization of the
millions of Americans who understood themselves as "simplifiers." The
slowly emerging answer was the Take Back Your Time project. John
de Graaf, a documentary filmmaker and simplicity activist, was named
TBYT's director.

De Graaf and others initially understood TBYT as a mechanism for
tapping middle-class frustration in support of national legislation for
an optional thirty-two-hour, four-day workweek. (Under this scenario,
workers would have the right, with some exceptions, to work four-
fifths time for four-fifths pay, while keeping employer-provided benefits.)
The central political task was to move the national conversation in
new directions, away from the claim that Americans would never willingly sacrifice for broader environmental and social aims and toward a
debate over the kinds of policies that would facilitate such willing
sacrifice.

These debates aren't new to the American landscape, but they've
been underground for decades. As Benjamin Hunnicutt describes in
his book *Kellogg's Six-Hour Day*, the 1930s were a time of vigorous
conversation over the relative virtues of shorter workdays, vacation
time, and greater employee control over work schedules. In 1933, for
example, the U.S. Senate supported legislation to cut the official U.S.
workweek to thirty hours. Hunnicutt notes how the Kellogg Company,
then the world's leading producer of cereal, shifted production from
eight- to six-hour days, with some reduction in pay, in order that it
might employ more workers during a time of economic depression.
It is clear from Hunnicutt's description, though, that Kellogg's intent
went beyond increasing local employment. It saw the six-hour day as
an experiment in liberating American workers from the drudgery of
extended work. Although employees took a pay cut (partially offset by
production bonuses to acknowledge the increased productivity of well-
rested workers), the U.S. Department of Labor, *Forbes*, and *Business
Week* reported broad worker satisfaction with the new arrangement.
Interviews of that day suggest that the belt-tightening required by some-

what lower pay was more than worth the additional leisure time, which workers used to connect with family, garden and can vegetables, or become more deeply engaged in school and civic life.

As a political project, TBYT sought to resurrect forgotten arguments for a competing understanding of prosperity, one that privileges sacrifice in some arenas (namely, the capacity to consume) in exchange for rewards in others. One might think this would make TBYT a major force in today's politics of the environment. Surprisingly, though, the depth of TBYT's roots in the VSM, and in broader debates about U.S. labor policy, is matched only by the shallowness of its connection to contemporary environmentalism. Given compelling assessments of the many links between overwork and environmental degradation,[15] this should be alarming. One reason for the disconnect is the historical foundation of mainstream environmentalism. The Progressives of the early-twentieth-century United States were greatly concerned by environmental despoliation, but their answer was to enhance the efficiency of the production process, while minimizing waste and the irrational depletion of natural resources.[16] At the same time, a preservationist movement was intent on framing "nature" and "the environment" as a place of refuge from the assaults of an industrial life that could not be meaningfully reformed.[17] Neither view was inclined to consider the nature of work and its connection to consumption. Today's environmentalism is understandably hobbled by the blind spots of its parents—a handicap that is amplified by a current politics of the environment that holds overconsumption (and the workplace alienation that feeds it) at arm's length.[18]

The primary impediment, though, to a meaningful connection between critiques of work and concern for the environment is the hegemonic view that *any* decline in individual or household consumption *always* leads to a loss of happiness, or to what is sometimes called "negative sacrifice."[19] That this article of faith is so easily received, even as a growing body of transnational research demonstrates the contrary, frustrates those who'd hope for an environmental politics that could speak powerfully to the trade-offs between work and leisure, and overconsumption and community. From the standpoint of individual human happiness and socially collective well-being, more isn't always better. Less is sometimes best.[20] Yet, if "material restraint" or "reduction in consumption" remains synonymous with "sacrifice and pain," no policy maker or politician will rise to the challenge of forging new avenues for debate and change. And few environmental groups will take the lead. Bold environmental policy making will come only in the face of intractable crisis, long after windows of creative, effective, anticipatory policy have closed.

From the beginning of TBYT, de Graaf has seen this hegemony of negative sacrifice to be the single greatest threat to an ambitious politics of environmental sustainability. By joining a critique of work with a frank assessment of what is being truly sacrificed, and when, TBYT sought to generate a new politics of work that could engage mainstream environmentalism. The interplay of early success and the risks of speaking too frankly about sacrifice served, however, to complicate this plan.

Branches

In the early years of its existence, TBYT generated a level of public attention and debate about work, consumption, and sustainability well out of proportion to its meager resources. Groups ranging from conservative businessmen to college students warmed easily to TBYT's message that overwork, lack of vacation, and few, if any, options for part-time work for part-time pay generate levels of consumption that are unhealthy for people and the environment. Many quickly grasped the message that working less and consuming less, if offered as an option, would be seized on by many Americans, not as a painful sacrifice for some lofty environmental ends, but as a means to a better life.

This early momentum was channeled and amplified by an annual "Take Back Your Time Day" event, which was inspired by the success of the first Earth Day in 1970 and quickly became TBYT's primary vehicle for public outreach. Observed on October 24 since 2003, Take Back Your Time Day commemorates what would be the final day of work for the year if Americans enjoyed, on average, the same vacation, sick leave, and holiday benefits of their European counterparts.

Take Back Your Time Day became a publicist's dream. In those early years, dozens of colleges and universities sponsored teach-ins or activities around time famine and the environment, more than two hundred communities initiated Time Day observances, and over three hundred pieces appeared in major newspapers and other media outlets, especially around October 24—all this in a national political environment generally hostile to worker's rights. From one perspective, the battle to broaden the conversation about sacrifice was successfully joined.

But this success was not without its temptations, which eventually proved impossible to resist. Loathe to prescribe particular actions for the early observances of Take Back Your Time Day, de Graaf and his staff solicited suggestions and testimonials from those organizing events in their communities. The result was the rapid growth, in size and breadth, of the official "what to do for TBYT Day" list, with an accompanying loss of focus on a language of sacrificing consumption for leisure time.[21] As competing ways of observing Take Back Your Time Day expanded, so, too, did the organization's public policy agenda—this in an effort to retain the interest of diverse constituencies initially drawn to the TBYT message. That agenda grew to include demands for more sick leave, better vacation policy, release from mandatory overtime, and even Election Day as a federal holiday. The overall tenor of TBYT's message shifted from questioning fundamental assumptions about sacrifice to calling for additional rights for workers. With multiple activities and messages, TBYT spoke to more constituencies, received more media attention, and generated more community and university inquiries. "We've clearly struck a nerve with Take Back Your Time Day," said Gretchen Burger, then a national staff person for TBYT, in a 2006 phone conversation. "I'm amazed by the number of emails and phone calls that I receive, from people all over the country, wanting to learn more or become part of this initiative."

Despite all this buzz, there was little, if any, actual policy-making bounce. Tens of thousands of people around the country became involved in some way in TBYT's initiatives, but those efforts failed to cohere into a single set of clear, powerful actions. Hindsight reveals this diffusion of message to be unintentional; it arose incrementally as the organization sought new opportunities to broaden its base and cultivate funding, which drew it away from a consistent focus on sacrifice (either the sacrifice workers experience from overwork, or the sacrifice of buying power that would come from shorter workweeks). And while financial support for TBYT has been a persistent worry, activists and funders interviewed for this chapter (some working for sustainable-consumption nongovernmental organizations, others more tightly linked to the foundation community) believe that funding would flow to TBYT if it honed its message, developed a political strategy for mobilizing support around a legislative agenda (a strategy that moves beyond "celebrating" Take Back Your Time Day in often innocuous ways), and focused its attention on a handful of core constituencies willing to take on the sacrifice agenda once again.

On reflection, de Graaf is inclined to agree. "Perhaps we tried to be all things to all people," he said in early 2007, "and as a result, we didn't stick with one or two tough items around which to rally a critical mass of people." But generating a potent strategy and working closely with dedicated constituencies takes staff, and TBYT is a distinctly two, sometimes three-person operation at best. It hasn't had the capacity to capitalize, in politically tangible ways, on the enthusiasm generated by scores of Take Back Your Time Day events that regularly occur around the United States. And yet, other political movements have gotten off the ground with less coordinated support and publicity. The student antisweatshop movement in the United States, which swept university campuses in 2002 with an agenda of ridding bookstores and university clothing shops of products made under substandard working conditions, is but one example. That endeavor had a tight, simple message (no sweatshop products will be sold in college bookstores) and sought to mobilize a relatively few number of people (students at just a few campuses) around very specific activities focused on broader institutional change.

Examples like these weren't lost on de Graaf and those around him. Their answer: take a vacation.

From Politely Taking to Demanding Rights: Moving from Mass Appeal to Targeted Action

Pairing Rights with Sacrifice?
Despite its considerable success in focusing public attention on time famine and overconsumption, TBYT suffered from two problems: one of practical politics, the other of political psychology. Practically speaking, the media-savvy choice to center the initiative on an annual Take Back Your Time Day left participants unsure about how they might best foster meaningful change. TBYT's range of suggested actions were typically polite and symbolic, usually too broad and often too trivial to create a sense of solidarity around the felt possibility of meaningful

change and increasingly distant from a pointed conversation about the nuances of sacrifice and simplicity that spawned the initiative. And they became increasingly out of sync with the original sacrifice frame of the program.

The political psychology of the initiative was equally ambiguous. Should participants be forceful, even angry, about the erosion of leisure time and the loss of worker control and seek ways to ameliorate the situation? Was TBYT essentially a movement of resistance and protest? Had something been taken from us (our time), which we now had the right to reclaim? Or was the program more of a lighthearted affair meant to foster conversational openings about the benefits of better work-life balance?

TBYT's experience underscores the difficulty of mounting an effective political action in the absence of a clear sense of rights—rights enjoyed, revoked, violated, or sacrificed.[22] Yes, TBYT flirted with the sense of rights in its discussion of U.S. labor history, pointing out that a thirty-two-hour workweek was once on the cusp of passing as the law of the land. But de Graaf and others were never comfortable asserting a thirty-two-hour workweek as a right in and of itself. Even the right of having *the option* of working thirty-two hours a week (four-fifths work for four-fifths pay, in other words, as a mechanism for facilitating the choice of earning less and consuming less in exchange for free time) was thought too risky a case to make as the popularity of an increasingly diffuse TBYT message continued to grow.

TBYT was left, then, to float a sacrifice-free policy agenda of guaranteed leave for birth or adoption, guaranteed sick leave, and guaranteed vacation, a day off for national elections, and making it easier to choose quality part-time work. The supporting language was timid ("let's bring the United States up to the standards already in place in all other industrialized countries") and inevitably scattershot. It was a strategy based on the belief that if enough people signed onto TBYT's agenda, and just did *anything*, meaningful change would emerge. Ironically, in its growing aversion to speaking frankly about sacrifice, TBYT assumed many of the same disabling assumptions of those who look to green consumption to drive sustainability. More ironic still is that this aversion sprang from the desire to maintain public support that was initially achieved through an especially clear articulation of sacrifice.

By the spring of 2008, the limitations of a rights-averse, sacrifice-free strategy were fully apparent. Joining forces with Joe Robinson (author and director of a small organization called Work to Live), de Graaf created Right2Vacation.org, a sister initiative of TBYT. The new Web site launched with a national poll showing broad public support for a mandatory, annual, paid three-week vacation in the United States, *even if such vacations might mean some loss of formal compensation*, a marked departure from current conditions.[23] The shift in political tone was palpable. Rather than politely suggest that workers reassert some claim over their time in any number of small ways, TBYT is urging Americans to assert their *right* to vacation time, a right others readily enjoy, and pay for, but which has been denied to U.S. citizens. The tagline "the United States remains the only industrial country without a law guaranteeing paid vacations" permeates their public outreach materials and highlights the current sacrifice borne by Americans. It's supported by a four-pronged argument: loss of vacations (1) raises health care costs, (2) reduces productivity, (3) undermines desirable social outcomes (time with family, connection to neighbors, civic engagement), and (4) costs the travel and vacation industry, with considerable loss of public engagement with nature. Each argument speaks to different constituencies, but the focus rests on a single goal: recover the right of citizens in *all* industrialized countries to claim time for relaxation and renewal.

By underscoring rights, de Graaf can speak more directly to sacrifice in politically efficacious ways. Americans are sacrificing now, Right2Vacation argues. They'll have to sacrifice in the future by working hard as citizens to correct the current situation and accept less formal compensation in exchange for more vacation time. But this sacrifice isn't "negative": it pays rich dividends down the line, not just for employees, but for everyone affected by the erosion of civil society, the increase in worker stress, and the forces of overconsumption unleashed by overwork.

Vacation, Sacrifice, and Strategic Coalitions

The notion of vacation as the springboard for a more aggressive politics of leisure and reduced material consumption may seem odd at first. After all, aren't vacations resource-intensive affairs, marked by long airplane flights and too many trips to the buffet? Aren't they part of the problem, both materially and politically?

Not necessarily. The binge vacationing common to the United States— three- or four-day trips to exotic locales, marked by intense consumption—is as much a reaction to the paucity of vacation time and mounting job stress as anything else. Vacationing needn't be hurried and hedonistic. If workers knew they had an extended paid period of time away from work, they'd be less inclined to concentrate their recreation into short bursts of activity that can leave one feeling less refreshed at the end of it all.

Also, paid vacation doesn't mean more consumption because paid leave doesn't mean being paid more. (The exception: taking another job during your vacation.) Indeed, it might mean less: if the productivity gains of paid vacations fail to offset the costs of these supported leaves, American workers might find themselves paying for their vacation leave through more modest increases in salary. TBYT argues, however, that workers would be willing to absorb the costs associated with this plan, as long as any such costs are fully defrayed by the productivity gains (rested workers produce more per hour) and reduction in health care costs (less job stress means lower health care needs) that come with increased vacation.

TBYT's muscular discussion about rights within the context of sacrifice has already alienated some of its longtime supporters, especially those drawn to the nonconfrontational elements of the Take Back Your Time Day celebrations. It opens the door, though, to three intriguing possibilities. The first is increased collaboration with U.S. businesses that currently provide paid vacation and life-work balance programs (often to enhance productivity, reduce health care costs, and stem worker turnover). Should these programs become mandatory, those businesses that already provide them would face no transition costs and might therefore enjoy a competitive advantage (at least in the short term) over their less enlightened competitors. Wouldn't these businesses find it in their interest to support "the right to vacation"? That's de Graaf's thinking.

Second, forceful conversation about the sacrifices inherent in limited vacation could also be a catalyst for action on college and university campuses. De Graaf has visited scores of campuses over the past several years. He's an engaging speaker who generates considerable enthusiasm. Yet he has little to show for it in terms of sustained student activism. A narrower focus on vacation could be the game-changer, especially in light of reports that today's students value work flexibility and free time far more than their predecessors, even if this means lower levels of remuneration.[24] Engaging students in a concrete struggle for workplace reform could drive change across the range of TBYT's public policy agenda.

Finally, tough talk about vacation invites novel coalitions with the travel industry and major environmental groups. The decline in visits to U.S. national forests, as fewer Americans engage in camping and hiking, offers one example.[25] The sources of this decline are unclear, though many believe that one culprit is the increased fragmentation of vacation time. A day here and there, rather than two or three solid weeks away from work, makes it hard to load the family into the car and head for the wilds. Environmental groups working on public lands and wilderness issues are concerned because reduced visitation could translate into declining public support for protecting natural lands. It's no accident, then, that the Sierra Club Foundation, in mid-2008, chose to support the production of a documentary (by de Graaf) on the centrality of vacations to the national life. (Contrast this support against the general reluctance of environmental groups to engage work and leisure time as core issues.) To the extent that more vacation time would shift existing consumption toward travel—and perhaps more hiking, camping, and lower-cost eco-travel (recall that additional vacation time doesn't come with additional income)—a potent coalition among travel specialists, environmental groups, outdoor equipment businesses, and nature educators is waiting to be born.

Struggling with Sacrifice

The outcomes of these three strategic possibilities remain unclear.[26] What is certain is that they emerged once a rights-based political agenda was joined to a clearer narrative of sacrifice—of the hidden but real sacrifices that accompany current structures of work and spending, and of the sacrifice, real but welcome, that would come with working less and being paid less. TBYT becomes yet another example of how confronting sacrifice, rather than skirting it, may prove to be one of the best springboards for creative strategizing by activists and scholars drawn to environmental politics.

Can an environmental politics that speaks plainly about sacrifice thrive in today's political environment? Can, moreover, such a politics counter the allure of a consumer-led green-consumption approach to environmental sustainability that promises large change with minimal effort? To the first question, John de Graaf and others working closely on TBYT would offer an unequivocal yes—in theory, at least. Especially when it comes to work-leisure balance and the many pressures to consume, many Americans already grasp the broad outlines of the structural forces in play. Speaking forcibly about these dynamics and the sometimes difficult choices they suggest elevates the conversation in ways that call forth the best angels of our citizen nature.

In practice, though, de Graaf is far less certain. As he struggles to overcome earlier organizational miscues, he cannot help but wonder if Right2Vacation.org's timing is right. Most Americans are focused on the economy, but they're complaining about too much "forced vacation" (in the form of layoffs and furloughs), rather than too little. Simplicity and frugality are again back on the national agenda,[27] but in ways that could cut against a vacation-rights agenda. Retooling a political initiative that complicates our political understanding of sacrifice at a moment when the economic sacrifice borne by many is startling uncomplicated and stark could prove to be a failed strategy.

The second question is more complicated. It would seem to wonder if environmental groups, by embracing a more nuanced discussion of sacrifice (rather than simply assuming that "those Americans will never sacrifice"), could blunt consumer fascination with "saving the world" through random acts of green consumption. In hindsight, this is the wrong question. We ought not to ask if an environmental politics more open to conversation about sacrifice can alter public sentiment. Instead, the question should be, can those who would change public sentiment find the courage to harness the creativity and credibility that comes with a more nuanced integration of sacrifice into their political agendas? We shouldn't worry, in other words, about talking straight about sacrifice for the sake of everyday people trying to make a difference environmentally. Even as they engage in green consumption, they frequently know that it's insufficient to the task. We should worry, instead, about the key actors in contemporary environmentalism, who, by dismissing any talk of sacrifice as counterproductive, risk marginalizing themselves in a dynamic politics of progressive change.

Acknowledgments

My thanks to John Meyer, Ben Slote, and David Swerdlow for their insightful review of earlier drafts of this chapter and to Allegheny College, David Orr, and Adam Joseph Lewis for support that facilitated some of the research interviews. Special thanks to John de Graaf for his patient replies to my seemingly endless questions, close reading of the text, and continued sacrifice for the public good.

Notes

1. Center for a New American Dream, "The New American Dream Wallet Buddy," http://www.newdream.org/walletbuddy.pdf.

2. A scanned copy of this wallet card is available at http://webpub.allegheny .edu/employee/m/mmaniate/onedegree.pdf.

3. See, e.g., Michael Vandenbergh, Jack Barkenbus, and Jonathan Gilligan, "Individual Carbon Emissions: The Low-Hanging Fruit," *UCLA Law Review* 55 (2008): 1701–1758.

4. Michael Maniates, "Individualization: Plant a Tree, Ride a Bike, Save the World?" in *Confronting Consumption*, ed. Thomas Princen, Michael Maniates, and Ken Conca (Cambridge, MA: MIT Press, 2002), 43–66; and Michael Maniates, "Going Green: Easy Doesn't Do It," *The Washington Post*, November 22, 2007, A37.

5. For a clever but revealing response to "saving the world" through consumption choices, see Lisa Cullen, "It's Inconvenient Being Green," *Time Magazine*, November 21, 2007, 110. For a competing perspective on this issue, see Margaret Willis and Juliet Schor, "Does Changing a Light Bulb Lead to Changing the World?" (paper presented at the research workshop of the Sustainable Consumption Research and Action Initiative [SCORAI], Clark University, Worcester, MA, October 17, 2009).

6. See, e.g., Thomas Friedman, "205 Easy Ways to Save the Earth," in *Hot, Flat, and Crowded: Why We Need a Green Revolution, and How It Can Renew America* (New York: Farrar, Straus, and Giroux, 2008), 203–216; and Paul Wapner and John Willoughby, "The Irony of Environmentalism: The Ecological Futility but Political Necessity of Lifestyle Change," *Ethics and International Affairs*, 19, no. 3 (2005): 77–89.

7. See Karl Weick, "Small Wins: Redefining the Scale of Social Problems," *American Psychologist*, January 1984, 40–49. A more recent application of the small wins idea is presented in Center for Applied Research, "Briefing Notes:

Small Wins—The Steady Application of a Small Advantage," 1998, http://www .cfar.com/Documents/Smal_win.pdf.

8. See, e.g., Mark Sagoff, *The Economy of the Earth: Philosophy, Law, and the Environment*, 2nd ed. (Cambridge: Cambridge University Press, 2008).

9. "The Fetzer Institute's mission, to foster awareness of the power of love and forgiveness in the emerging global community, rests on its conviction that efforts to address the world's critical issues must go beyond political, social, and economic strategies to their psychological and spiritual roots." From the Fetzer Institute home page, http://www.fetzer.org/.

10. Elizabeth Warren and Amelia Tyagi, *The Two-Income Trap: Why Middle-Class Mothers and Fathers Are Going Broke* (New York: Basic Books, 2003).

11. The Harwood Group, "Yearning for Balance Views of Americans on Consumption, Materialism, and the Environment," 1995, prepared for the Merck Family Fund, http://www.iisd.ca/consume/harwood.html, with figures available at http://www.globallearningnj.org/global_ata/Yearing_for_balance.htm.

12. Amitai Etzioni provides a typology of simplifiers in "Voluntary Simplicity: Characterization, Select Psychological Implications, and Societal Consequences," *Journal of Economic Psychology* 19 (1998): 619–643.

13. Michael Maniates, "In Search of Consumptive Resistance: The Voluntary Simplicity Movement," in Princen et al., *Confronting Consumption*, 200–235.

14. Meeting summaries are available from the Simplicity Forum at http://www .simplicityforum.org/congressreports.html.

15. See, e.g., Anders Hayden, *Sharing the Work, Sparing the Planet: Work Time, Consumption, and Ecology* (London: Zed Books, 1999), or more recently, David Rosnick and Mark Weisbrot, *Are Shorter Work Hours Good for the Environment? A Comparison of U.S. and European Energy Consumption* (Washington, DC: Center for Economic and Policy Research, 2006).

16. Samuel P. Hayes, *Conservation and the Gospel of Efficiency: The Progressive Conservation Movement, 1890–1920* (Pittsburgh: University of Pittsburgh Press, 1999).

17. Roderick Nash, *Wilderness and the American Mind* (New Haven, CT: Yale University Press, 2001).

18. Thomas Princen, Michael Maniates, and Ken Conca, "Confronting Consumption," in Princen et al., *Confronting Consumption*, 1–20.

19. As described in chapter 7.

20. E.g., Tim Kasser, *The High Price of Materialism* (Cambridge, MA: MIT Press, 2003).

21. See "Take Back Your Time," http://www.timeday.org/tbyt_day.asp.

22. James Jasper, *The Art of Moral Protest: Culture, Biography, and Creativity in Social Movements* (Chicago: University of Chicago Press, 1997).

23. Paid (or, indeed, even unpaid) vacations are not mandated in the United States, and only 14 percent of working American take two weeks or more of vacation a year.

24. E.g., P. Trunk, "What Gen Y Really Wants," *Time Magazine*, July 5, 2007, http://www.time.com/time/magazine/article/0,9171,1640395,00.html.

25. See, e.g., MSNBC's report on "Visitors to National Forests on the Decline," November 29, 2008, http://www.msnbc.msn.com/id/27970449/.

26. The political possibilities and core strategies of each are described in more detail in Michael Maniates, "Cultivating Consumer Restraint in an Ecologically Full World: The Case of 'Take Back Your Time,'" in *Sustainable Production Consumption Systems: Knowledge, Engagement and Practice*, ed. Louis Lebel, Sylvia Lorek, and Rajesh Daniel, (London: Springer, 2010), 13–37.

27. See, e.g., Wendy Koch, "For Many, a Simpler Life Is Better," *USA Today*, July 13, 2009, A1.

14

Conclusion: Sacrifice and a New Environmental Politics

Michael Maniates and John M. Meyer

Given the choice, we wouldn't have produced a book about *sacrifice* in environmental politics. The term is a minefield. It's understood in several competing ways and lived in many others: positive for some, negative for others, sometimes affirming and democratic, but often hidden and forced. In part, it is this conceptual slipperiness that makes sacrifice such a charged notion for those who would pursue political change in service of environmental sustainability. As authors, it's easiest to build our arguments and analyses on stable terms and agreed-on concepts. *Sacrifice* is anything but that.

Yet here we are, at the end of a volume about an idea that we felt compelled to confront because of the uncritical insinuation of *sacrifice* into conversation about how best to address escalating environmental degradation. In our political science and environmental studies courses, for example, students continue to speak with confidence about the inherent inability of so-called selfish Americans to entertain *any* acts of sacrifice, for the environment or for one another. But why should this be surprising? Many mainstream environmental groups treat sacrifice as an idea to be avoided at any cost, lest environmentalism become identified as a movement of deprivation and hair shirts, and thus politically marginalized. Likewise, many scholarly communities continue to accept the assumption that humans are wired to reject sacrifice; altruism, in other words, is for suckers. (Maniates, for instance, recently returned from an international conference of consumer researchers at which the notion that people might invite and even prosper from some forms of sacrifice proved startling to many.) Exceptions exist, of course—some of our students resist this caricaturing of Americans, some activists struggle with how to speak about environmental obligations and shared sacrifice, and many scholars labor to illuminate the surprising malleability of human behavior and sense of well-being. But a larger pattern of narrow thinking about sacrifice dominates, in ways that readers will now notice with heightened (and sometimes annoying) acuity, where others do not.

Such shallowness, by funneling contemporary environmental politics into two camps, damages our ability to think imaginatively and boldly about our current environmental predicament. In one camp are proponents of an environmental politics that assert that technological innovation, even geo-engineering, can restore ecological health with little, if any, pain to consumers. In the other are those who advance apocalyptic environmental imagery, which they hope will be sufficiently alarming to coerce sacrifice from otherwise unwilling citizens. Each has its strengths, but both rest on the unexamined notion that sacrifice itself will always be resisted and cannot be openly discussed and explored absent a riveting crisis. Until this notion is tested by intense scrutiny and debate, we do not believe that sufficient progress on resolving environmental ills will be possible.

Noticing how unexamined assumptions about sacrifice assert themselves in conversation about our shared future is a first, critical step in moving beyond a binary politics (technological innovation vs. coercion) of environmental sustainability. In light of the 2008 U.S. elections, one might think that noticing wouldn't be the problem. Both candidates for president, John McCain and Barack Obama, wove images of sacrifice into their speeches more frequently and deeply than in any other presidential election in recent times. On his election, Obama continued this imagery. His inauguration speech began, for instance, by invoking the "sacrifices borne by our ancestors" and then highlighting the need for sacrifice and responsibility "at a time of gathering storms." The speech was well received, as much for its frank talk about coming struggles as for its ability to frame sacrifice as something other than demeaning hardship to be resisted or endured. Such rhetorical elevation of sacrifice as a necessary component of a national politics continues (as of this writing) as a distinctive element of President Obama's public commentary.

Yet, as we make the final changes to this volume, we see little evidence of such rhetoric making its way into environmental politics. Struggle over climate legislation, for instance, continues between those who argue that we have a problem and must act decisively and those who insist that the problem is overblown, with proposed remedies that will cost more than they will help. Each side marshals its scientists and economists to make the case. Yet there is little discussion of the hidden and coerced sacrifice already borne by those most vulnerable to climate disruption, of who will bear the costs of climate legislation (regions with old manufacturing economies, apparently, and those in coal states), and of who will decide. If sacrifice appears at all, it does so only in its most narrow and alarming of forms. Until those who promote climate legislation speak powerfully to the democratic distribution of current and future sacrifice, one debate, that of science and economics, will unproductively substitute for the other, that of the extent, visibility, and distribution of sacrifice. Should this issue be resolved by the time this book goes to press, let it be an object lesson for the need to speak frankly and confidently about sacrifice in other environmental arenas. And if it hasn't (as we suspect), let it stand as an example of the difficulty of raising the *S* word within the arena of environmental politics.

At this moment of possibility, when the ideal of sacrifice is raised rhetorically but doesn't yet hold meaningful potency for environmental policy, five challenges hover on the near horizon. Each asks something urgent of activists, scholars, students, and citizens. Together, they point to a new environmental politics, one in which a strategic appreciation of the possibilities inherent in positive forms of sacrifice (leavened by healthy skepticism of those who call for sacrifice) replaces a reflexive certainty about the impossibility of sacrifice in all its forms.

Five Challenges

Sometimes the simplest of questions can be the most difficult to raise yet prove to be the most revealing. Few have made this point better in recent years than award-winning author and activist Frances Moore Lappé, author of *Diet for a Small Planet* and additional books, articles, and speeches that shape the way a great many think about food, hunger, the environment, and social change. In her 2002 best seller *Hope's Edge*, Lappé attributes her early success and ongoing influence to a simple, often difficult commitment to "keep asking 'why?'" From hunger in Africa to landlessness in Brazil, Lappé credits her greatest insights and most potent policy successes to her insistence on asking why, when others seemed content to accept assumption as truth and assertion as fact.

Creating space for a new environmental politics demands, first and foremost, conscious emulation of Lappé's doggedness. As many of our authors demonstrate, the sacrifices people make—and are prepared to make—are typically dependent on structures (like land-use patterns, tax policy, or workplace rules), processes (such as who makes decisions about how to solve environmental problems, and why), and assumptions (like consumer sovereignty) largely beyond individual control. Change any of these factors, and individual capacity and willingness to sacrifice can shift as well. Seeing these levers for change is difficult, however, in the face of the prevailing story about sacrifice that locates the problem in human nature, rather than in the interaction between human complexity and the structures within which we live. The best weapon for pushing this story aside is asking why—repeatedly, persistently, provocatively, and unyieldingly.

For students, this means asking for explanation and evidence whenever a peer asserts that environmental progress is impossible because of "our unwillingness to sacrifice." Why, one could ask, might this claim be true? And when might it be false? For environmental activists, this could mean asking (of themselves and one another) why any hint of sacrifice is pushed to the margins of mobilization strategies in favor of "easy ways of saving the planet," even as notions of shared sacrifice resonate in some national circles and evidence mounts that the difficult challenges are those that most engage public enthusiasm. The why question for scholars could center on why it is that narrow assumptions about the capacity and willingness of humans to sacrifice appear to prevail over others. And all of us in our citizen role could ask why leaders remain reluctant to call on our ability to sacrifice on behalf of broader, even noble, public aims.

On its face, this focus on asking why may seem trivial. We remain struck, however, by the rich conversation that unfolds—in the classroom, in academic conferences, in working with environmental activists, or while dining with friends—when we stop to ask *why* someone assumes that sacrifice must play out in a particular (and usually negative and constraining) way. Sacrifice as a barrier to engaged environmental action becomes less formidable when we speak of it, interrogate it, and question it. If generating such conversation is the only outcome of this volume, we will consider our effort a success.

Asking why provides the springboard for a second challenge, that of becoming more aware of the many rich ways in which sacrifice infuses daily life. Everyday forms of sacrifice, ranging from the nearly automatic to the most ritualistic, hide in plain sight, as many contributors to this volume note. They range from simple to more complex acts of giving or restraint, at places of worship, in the office and home, and in the community or on the sports field. Together, these patterns of abnegation complicate the argument that humans are inherently selfish and self-centered and incapable of thinking expansively about the environment, or that they take the long view only when it is easy or unavoidable. These patterns suggest the possibility of extending a deeper interpretation of sacrifice to the demands of environmental sustainability, and they raise the question of enabling conditions: what factors and dynamics cultivate and tease out the capacity, even yearning, to sacrifice on behalf of something larger, even when the payoffs are uncertain?

A deeper awareness of everyday forms of sacrifice is necessary, and there is plenty of work to go around. Students, especially those studying environmental politics and social change, might demand of their instructors course work and readings that drill into these questions. Scholars could reorient their research agendas toward these questions. Environmental activists could begin to think differently about sacrifice and contemplate ways of authentically connecting their message to existing patterns of everyday sacrifice. As citizens, finally, we might search for moments of sacrifice in everyday life, highlight it for others and ourselves when we see it, and reflect on how these capacities can be connected more robustly to environmental concerns.

Yet, as important as these activities are, they alone will prove insufficient to align the politics of environment with a future that hinges on the global wealthy consuming less. Therefore a third challenge is to reshape the practice of environment politics so that it cultivates the capacity for sacrifice (or, at the very least, informed conversation about sacrifice). This, for us, is the pivot point for making our collective way to a just, sustainable future. If environmental politics is best understood as struggle driven by environmental threats to human well-being, it is no longer sufficient to evaluate the efficacy of this politics by the policies it ultimately generates. We must also judge it on the extent to which it enhances the capacity of citizens and their leaders to confront sacrifice as an unavoidable component of a shift to long-term, sustainable prosperity. Looking through this volume, we see glimmers of an alternative architecture of political practice that could make it easier for citizens and leaders to take some forms of sacrifice seriously. Enhanced democratic deliberation that would diminish the sense of imposed sacrifice may be one critical component. Political pressure framed to create meaningful choice—in transportation and work, for example—could be another. Decentering economistic frames and arguments that privilege a narrow understanding of interests and motivation may be a third. Drawing connections between sacrifice (hidden and visible, positive and negative) in the environmental realm and sacrifice in other realms of life (e.g., family) might be a fourth. Other, perhaps better, principles surely exist. The challenge, especially for scholars and activists working together, is to develop principles for an engaged environmental politics that enables public conversation about equitable and effective forms of shared sacrifice, as opposed to a politics that denies the need to have this conversation.

In this search for principles of environmental political practice, real-world cases are especially useful. Where have communities in the United States, for example, chosen to sacrifice (perhaps in the form of higher taxes) for distant and uncertain environmental or other social benefits? How did this come about, and why? In addition to U.S. cases, a cross-cultural component would be invaluable. How do ideas about sacrifice enter into environmental politics outside the United States? What salient parallels and differences exist in the European context? In China? India? Elsewhere in the global South? To the extent that sacrifice is less of a roadblock in any of these contexts, what lessons can the United States import? Identifying illustrative cases becomes an important fourth challenge posed by this volume.

A fifth and final challenge centers on a more nuanced engagement with the rhetorical power of sacrifice. Conversations with our colleagues working as activists remind us that *sacrifice* remains a perilous word in public debate. It opens doors to cutting and sometimes acrid attack by political opponents, and it can be heard by important constituencies as a demand for deprivation. But avoiding the term, and the concepts and choices to which it speaks, is not politically wise either. How, then, are public advocates for environmental sustainability to proceed? When is *sacrifice* in its many forms best used, and why? And when are other frames (e.g., enlightened self-interest or stewardship) better choices? These questions are ripe for research by scholars in ways that would prove immediately relevant to activists. Fully addressing the environmental politics of sacrifice means, therefore, new and potentially exciting collaborations between academics and activists.

A New Environmental Politics

What, then, is this new environmental politics, and what are its prospects? By now, its general contours are clear. Centrally, it would be a politics that does not shrink from forthright discussion of the political choices available to us. Such discussion must be open about the sometimes very real sacrifice inherent in policies for environmental sustainability. But it must be equally attentive to the often massive sacrifices entailed by *not* addressing the awesome challenges that we face.

We hope that readers will find this approach to be intellectually inviting. Yet in calling for an open accounting of the environmental choices we face, with a full measure of the cost and benefits of action *and* inaction, some will deride us as naive or utopian. The question no doubt lingers: as a political strategy, could frank talk about sacrifice really be a recipe for success? Critics will surely suggest that though this approach might curry favor in the ivory towers of academia, it would prove to be political suicide in the real world.

Perhaps. But such criticism might be more persuasive if proponents could point to a more promising political strategy for addressing the deep challenges of global environmental sustainability. They cannot. As Shane Gunster illustrates with particular clarity in chapter 9, even that rare bird—the seemingly successful policy—can readily be undermined by the failure to address sacrifice openly and honestly. The charge of naivety, moreover, would be more compelling if, in fact, this new environmental politics was simply a matter of pleading with people to give up what they value. The contributors to this book have gone a long way toward making it clear that this is not what it means to confront sacrifice.

In the end, however, the possibility of a new, more democratic, ultimately more *adult* environmental politics can only be realized when and where we act—in our roles as citizens, activists, students, and scholars—to address the challenges outlined previously. At times, such efforts may be more successful at sharpening disagreements than in promoting accord. So be it. Our future prosperity requires a clear-eyed view of the present, one unclouded by uneasiness or fear to tally the sacrifice involved, to judge what is likely to be gained and lost by any future action. A new environmental politics is only possible if we recognize and engage—rather than paper over and suppress—the values at stake.

Contributors

Peter F. Cannavò is assistant professor of government at Hamilton College in Clinton, New York. He is the author of *The Working Landscape: Founding, Preservation, and the Politics of Place* and is writing a book on the historical and philosophical connections between American environmentalism and civic republicanism.

Shane Gunster teaches communications and media studies in the School of Communication at Simon Fraser University. He is the author of *Capitalizing on Culture: Critical Theory for Cultural Studies*, and his current research interests include media coverage of climate change and conservative political discourse.

Cheryl Hall is associate professor in the Department of Government and International Affairs at the University of South Florida, where she teaches political theory and feminist theory. Before turning to environmental issues, she published *The Trouble with Passion: Political Theory beyond the Reign of Reason* and numerous articles on the role of passion and reason in politics. Her current work explores the ways in which different conceptions of freedom and agency influence our imagination of the possibilities for creating environmentally sustainable societies.

Karen Litfin is associate professor of political science at the University of Washington. Her writings reflect her belief that "the personal is political." She is currently writing a book on the eco-village experiments around the world.

Michael Maniates is professor of political science and environmental science and coordinator of the Energy and Society program at Allegheny College. He is a coeditor of *Confronting Consumption*, the editor of *Encountering Global Environmental Politics*, and the author of several book chapters, academic articles, and public essays on overconsumption, voluntary simplicity, green consumerism, and climate change.

John M. Meyer is professor and chair of the Department of Politics at Humboldt State University. He also teaches in the university's interdisciplinary graduate program on environment and community. He is the author of *Political Nature: Environmentalism and the Interpretation of Western Thought*, as well as journal articles, essays, and book chapters on topics related to political theory and environmental politics. He is at work on a book titled *Environmentalism as Social Criticism*.

Simon Nicholson   is assistant professor in the School of International Service at American University. His recent work focuses on the global politics of food and agriculture and on issues to do with emerging technologies.

Anna Peterson   is professor in the Department of Religion at the University of Florida. Her research and teaching focus on environmental and social ethics. She has published widely, including the books *Martyrdom and the Politics of Religion: Progressive Catholicism in El Salvador's Civil War*; *Being Human: Ethics, Environment, and Our Place in the World*; *Residence on Earth: Utopian Communities in the Americas*; and *Everyday Ethics and Social Change: The Education of Desire*, as well as two collaborative books and numerous journal articles. She is currently cowriting a book on teaching the ethics of sustainability for scientists and technology professionals.

Thomas Princen   teaches at the University of Michigan's School of Natural Resources and Environment, focusing on norms and institutions for sustainable practice. His latest book, *Treading Softly: Paths to Ecological Order,* imagines an economy that fits one planet. Two of his previous books, *The Logic of Sufficiency* and, as lead editor, *Confronting Consumption*, won the International Studies Association's award for "best book in the study of international environmental problems." Princen was named an Aldo Leopold Leadership Fellow, and before that, he was a Pew Faculty Fellow for International Affairs.

Sudhir Chella Rajan   is professor of humanities and social sciences at the Indian Institute of Technology Madras and the author of *The Enigma of Automobility: Democratic Politics and Pollution Control*. He is interested in ideas of environment and political theory and has written mostly on their interface in the context of automobility, cosmopolitanism, climate change, and energy.

Paul Wapner   is associate professor and director of the Global Environmental Politics program in the School of International Service (SIS) at American University. He is the author of the award-winning book *Environmental Activism and World Civic Politics* and coeditor of *Principled World Politics: The Challenge of Normative International Relations*. His latest book, *Living through the End of Nature: The Future of American Environmentalism*, explores the challenges of being an environmentalist in a humanized world.

Justin Williams   an active cyclist and bicycle mechanic, is a doctoral student at the University of Michigan. He studies political theory, especially as it relates to environmental issues.

Index

liminality and, 169–170, 173–174, 179, 181
multiple jobs and, 167
in myth, 168–174
as obligation, 177–178
personal frugality and, 167
religion and, 92, 102–103, 106
self-sacrifice and, 166–179, 182
Sheehan and, 104–105, 180–182
social discounting and, 175
as social structuring, 178–182
societal importance of, 168–169
taking back time and, 301
utilitarianism and, 175
Pastoralism, 223–226, 228, 234
Paterson, Matthew, 247, 250, 254–256, 259
Patten, Simon, 150
Peace Corps, 159
Pell, Claiborne, 282–283
Pembina Institute, 188
Penance, 93, 99, 110
Peterson, Anna, 87–88, 91–115
Petit, Philip, 78
Philanthropy, 129
Pilgrimage, 93
Pittsburgh Zoo, 294
Policy
  asking why and, 315–319
  bicycling and, 263–266
  Clean Air Act and, 286
  geoengineering and, 271–292
  Kyoto Protocol and, 41, 151, 190
  new environmentalism and, 34–55, 313–320
  public schools and, 79
  Take Back Your Time (TBYT) and, 298–309
  trade-offs and, 34
  Washington consensus and, 161–162
Political Economy of International Relations, The (Gilpin), 150–151
Politics
  affirmative politics of sacrifice and, 136–139
  age of comfort and, 48–55

authoritarian control and, 13–14, 61, 80, 206, 221
automobiles and, 254–256
axe-the-tax campaign and, 188
British Columbia carbon tax and, 187–215
Campbell and, 187–190, 194–196, 204–206, 209
Christian military regimes and, 97–98
climate action dividend and, 203–204
consumer-centric, 293–298
consumer sovereignty and, 145–164
five challenges for, 315–319
generational thesis and, 130
Liberal Party and, 187–196, 201–205, 208, 211n7
necessity of sacrifice and, 1–8
New Democratic Party (NDP) and, 188
new environmentalism and, 34–57, 313–320
of possibility, 39
shallowness and, 313–314
stickiness of sacrifice and, 2
suburbs and, 231–232
technology and, 274–277, 281–286
terrorism and, 108
weather control and, 277–286
Pollan, Michael, 55
Positive sacrifice
  age of comfort and, 29
  civic virtue and, 219, 235
  climate change and, 189, 195
  consumer sovereignty and, 146, 154, 156–162
  democratic sacrifice and, 29
  geoengineering and, 281
  new environmental politics and, 313, 315, 318
  parental sacrifice and, 180–181
  religion and, 119
Possessive individualism, 15
Postmaterialists, 44
Potlatch, 125
Poverty, 44, 88, 149–150, 232–233